# Leaders of the Church of England
## 1828–1978

*Books by the same author*

*about Christianity*

GOD'S CROSS IN OUR WORLD
THE LAST THINGS NOW
RELIGION AND CHANGE
WHAT IS REAL IN CHRISTIANITY?
GOOD NEWS IN ACTS
JESUS FOR MODERN MAN
A KEY TO THE OLD TESTAMENT
HERE WE ARE

*about the life of the Church*

NOT ANGELS BUT ANGLICANS
THIS CHURCH OF ENGLAND
A HISTORY OF THE KING'S SCHOOL, CANTERBURY
F. J. SHIRLEY, AN EXTRAORDINARY HEADMASTER
IAN RAMSEY, BISHOP OF DURHAM
ST. MARGARET'S, WESTMINSTER
THE BRITISH CHURCHES TURN TO THE FUTURE

*edited*

THE HONEST TO GOD DEBATE
CHRISTIANS IN A NEW WORLD
TODAY'S STORY OF JESUS
TODAY'S STORY OF GOD

# LEADERS OF THE CHURCH OF ENGLAND
## 1828-1978

David L. Edwards

HODDER AND STOUGHTON
LONDON SYDNEY AUCKLAND TORONTO

# Contents

# Preface (1978)

The Church of England, like most other English institutions to-day, is often criticized; and its own members are foremost in their criticism. But it continues to play a substantial part in the life of the nation and to hold an interest for people in many other countries. It deserves to be understood, and it cannot be understood without some knowledge of its past. I believe there is a special value in studying the history of the last hundred and fifty years, a time of great activity and many controversies. In particular I believe that it is worth while getting to know some of the outstanding Englishmen who have led their National Church through these years.

*Leaders of the Church of England, 1828–1944*, first published in 1971, seems to have been used for the purpose I intended – as an introduction to some interesting personalities and some important ideas. Large books exist about them, but I wrote for readers who do not have the leisure or the opportunity, or even perhaps the inclination, to get hold of those tomes. I greatly enjoyed the writing, and its reception has encouraged me to think that some of my own enjoyment has communicated itself.

I wrote most of the book in Cambridge when I was Dean of King's College. In those years I had the stimulus of having to lecture on modern history in the Faculty of Divinity, and of being able to use the University Library. I still feel very grateful to my colleagues and audiences, and to the late Geoffrey Hunt, who suggested the book and arranged for the Oxford University Press to publish it.

I am also grateful to those who have been willing to embark on a new edition in Hodder Christian Paperbacks. I have revised the text, cutting out all the footnotes, two character-studies (which meant saying good-bye to the relatively minor Stanley and Hort), and the old Epilogue. At the end I have added a new chapter on the trends in the leadership of the Church of England since 1945, together with a short list of books for further reading. I hope that in this new form the book will serve a wider public.

D.L.E.

# Prologue

It is roughly true to say that the revival of English religion in the nineteenth century corresponded with the power of the middle classes. In 1877 Matthew Arnold described the Church of England as 'an institution devoted above all to the landed gentry, but also to the propertied and satisfied classes generally: favouring immobility, preaching submission, and reserving transformation in general for the other side of the grave'. Going to church or chapel was an important part of being respectable. Sociologically speaking, the only other cause of widespread religious observance in Victorian England was going to Mass, which was an important part of being Irish. Since the 1810s a constant theme to be heard in all the English Churches except the Roman Catholics and some Nonconformist quarters such as the Primitive Methodists has been a lament for the absence of working people.

However, it would be a travesty of the historical facts to think of all the Victorian Churches as temples entirely dedicated to a crude middle-class self-interest. While they inevitably reflected many of the social and mental habits of the people who supported them in such numbers, part of their function as teachers of respectability was to raise the attention of the middle classes above money-getting, at least on Sundays. The entirely voluntary efforts of the Nonconformists held up some kind of a vision in ten thousand chapels; this was the age of Robert Browning. The Church of England slowly got to work on the evangelization of the lower middle classes, and even tried to preach to the people; and its message, although not normally a social gospel with the full courage of the Christian Socialists, was also not usually a completely simple manifestation of class snobbery. 'Duty' was a word constantly repeated, and it was a

9

duty that could cut across self-interest. Of course there was a great deal of hypocrisy in all this respectability; hypocrisy must accompany any great effort by human societies in the sphere of religion or in any other enterprise calling for nobility. Such has been the way of all flesh. But that is not the whole truth about Victorian religion.

It is a great pity that so many of our most vivid impressions of Victorian clergymen have been formed by the novels of Anthony Trollope. When Trollope thought about the Church, he thought of his father who amid the ruins of his life had contracted religious mania trying to compile something to be called the *Encyclopaedia Ecclesiastica*. It all seemed comically, or tragically, irrelevant to an age when Trollope had to proclaim that he manufactured words for money; it was natural to ask if the Church would survive the fall of Barchester. Trollope hit off so neatly the various clerical types as the Victorians knew them. But his should not be taken as the last word on the Victorian Church. His first-hand acquaintance with the ecclesiastical scene was small; London was, as he said, the only cathedral city he knew from the inside; and it has been wisely noted (by A. O. J. Cockshut) that 'most of Trollope's characters are incapable of connected thought on religious questions'.

What religion was to millions of Englishmen in the nineteenth century is shown by a story then widely circulated about Bishop Joseph Butler's death in 1752. According to this edifying tale, for which there is no authentic foundation, when the great philosopher-bishop was in his last sickness in Bath he summoned his chaplain to his bed, and said to him: 'Though I have endeavoured to avoid sin, and to please God, to the utmost of my power, yet, from the consciousness of perpetual infirmities, I am still afraid to die.' The anecdote continues that the chaplain replied: 'My lord, you have forgotten that Jesus Christ is a Saviour.' Religion, a feeling for the mystery around human life, and a fear of it, was also a response to the figure of Christ who had dominated the imagination of England and Europe for more than a thousand years. And it is reported that the bishop said to his chaplain: 'True, but how shall I know that he is a Saviour for me?'

Many Englishmen in the nineteenth century thought that they needed 'a Saviour for me'. In a famous outburst against Butler's successors (such as Archdeacon Paley) who had tried to prove the designing power and benevolence of the Creator from the 'evidences' of nature as well as of the Scriptures, Coleridge exclaimed: 'Evidences of Christianity! I am weary of the word. Make a man feel the want of it; rouse him, if you can, to the self-knowledge of his need of it; and you may safely trust to its own Evidence ...' Many Englishmen felt this need with a special intensity because a process of secularization, going deeper than the intellectual enlightenment which had confronted Bishop Butler, was gradually penetrating the foundations of personal confidence and of the social order. If God was not in his heaven (not even the Deists' God to whom Tom Paine and Robert Owen clung), what was right in the world? And what was the point of setting the world right? And what remained for anyone at the end of the road?

Such ultimate questions threatened the young John Stuart Mill with a breakdown, until he turned to the poetry of Wordsworth and to his marriage. But others, who included Wordsworth, turned with a new earnestness to the possibility gaining evidence of 'a Saviour for me' within the community of the Christian faith. To some observers such as J. A. Froude, the new zeal for traditional doctrine made Christians resemble men caught in a thunder-storm, flying for refuge to a tree which only the more certainly would attract the lightning. But many people in the nineteenth century did sincerely believe that when the lightning of modernity struck the Church, not everything would be consumed. At the end of *Marius the Epicurean* (1885), Walter Pater made a typically Victorian assessment (although he was himself far from being a typical Victorian). He wrote that in Christianity 'there had been a permanent protest established in the world, a plea, a perpetual afterthought, which humanity would ever possess in reserve against any wholly mechanical and disheartening theory of itself and its conditions'.

All over Europe the nineteenth century saw a rally in the Christian forces, while the Christian advance in North

America, Africa, Asia, and Australasia made the century the greatest era ever known in missionary expansion. In many places the energy of the rival churches produced both conversions and controversies. In Scotland, for example, the Established (Presbyterian) Church was torn asunder by questions which were basically similar to those which agitated England under Victoria: questions about the presentation of the Gospel in an age of new knowledge (in Scotland the Evangelical and Moderate parties were well organized), questions about the relation of Church and State in an age of new energy and danger (in the Church of Scotland, where of course no bishoprics were available to serve as the flashpoints of the conflict, there was a bitter dispute about the rights of patrons over the parish churches). In Scotland Thomas Chalmers, a figure as remarkable as any south of the Border in his time, an Evangelical of Moderate origins and lingering habits, a pastor, professor, and statesman, led the Disruption of the Church in 1843.

In England, the Nonconformist bodies and the Roman Catholics also experienced great tensions and some triumphs. The Church of England did, however, possess a special significance in the nineteenth century.

When the century began the Church of England was, proportionately to the population (all of which it married and buried), the richest religious body seen anywhere since the Middle Ages. It was able to dispose of handsome endowments to promote religion in Ireland and Wales, without any very noticeable effort to be Irish or Welsh. Its higher clergy received stipends for being connected with a splendid collection of cathedrals and other great churches, and if individual stipends were not splendid enough they held two or more together. A quarter of the Justices of the Peace in 1832 were clergymen. Comfortable parsonages belonged to the Jane Austen landscape, however great was the scandal of non-resident incumbents (about a quarter of the incumbents were pluralists), and however deep the poverty of many of the curates who did most of the work. Such a profession was attractive, more so for peaceable gentlemen than the Law, Medicine, the Army, or the Navy. Three-quarters of the undergraduates who rowed in the first boat race, in 1829, became parsons. The college chapels in Oxford and Cambridge, the city churches in London, and the elegant pulpits in the spas spoke of the consecration or the humbug of learning, wealth, and fashion. Compulsory tithes to maintain the clergy, and compulsory rates to repair the churches, were very practical expressions of the obligations acknowledged, however unwillingly, in the parishes. The attachment of the Crown to the National Church, at least nominally, had been maintained since the flight of James II. Protestants not prepared to receive Holy Communion in the Church of England were in theory excluded from public life until 1828 (although annual Indemnity Acts made it possible for some of them to hold office), and the small Roman Catholic minority was not emancipated politically until 1829. Parliament acknowledged this work for religion, or for the class system, when it handed over more than a million pounds to the poorer clergy in 1809 – 29, and a million and a half pounds for new churches in 1818 – 24; and worried bishops assumed that things would get better if only more seats could be provided in more churches. The National Society, founded in 1811, attempted to promote 'the education of the poor in the principles of the Established Church'.

This stately home of official England had many claims to be considered the most abuse-ridden Church in the world. 'The Church, as it now stands, no human power can save', wrote Thomas Arnold in 1832, knowing how the mobs had rioted against the bishops. John Stuart Mill reckoned that the only question delaying its abolition was the question what to put in its place. The Reformation of the sixteenth century had left the National Church's medieval structure virtually intact. In the next century the new discipline which swept through Catholic Europe as the Counter-Reformation was known in Protestant England mainly through the rival efforts of Archbishop Laud, who was beheaded, and the Puritans, who failed with Cromwell. The Methodist movement of the eighteenth century had been forced out of the National Church. Its shrewder friends, and all its foes, therefore now argued that if the Establishment was to survive, its many corruptions must be purged and its prevailing slackness must be invigorated. But if the Church of England was to be given a new structure and a new spirit, if it was to be no longer the Church which Arnold rightly thought doomed in 1832, who was to control the reform? That seemed to be a question of consuming interest, for with all its defects the Established Church remained a rich prize.

Ecclesiastical parties manoeuvered in order to capture this prize, with propaganda such as the militant Evangelical weekly, the *Record*, or on the other wing the Anglo-Catholic *Tracts for the Times* which gave rise to the name 'Tractarians' and to much else. Those who refused to support the theology or the tactics of the Low Church, or High Church, party found themselves classified as 'Broad Church', however indignantly they protested that they were not a party. In October 1853 an article in the *Edinburgh Review* by W. J. Conybeare attracted wide attention as the clearest analysis to date of these competing factions.

Conybeare estimated that the clergy of the Church of England (including Wales but excluding Ireland and Scotland) were about 18,000 in number in a population of about eighteen millions, and he guessed that they could be classified as follows:

| | | |
|---|---|---|
| Low Church | Normal type ('Evangelical') | 3,330 |
| | Exaggerated type ('Recordite') | 2,500 |
| | Stagnant type ('Low and Slow') | 700 |
| High Church | Normal type ('Anglican') | 3,500 |
| | Exaggerated type ('Tractarian') | 1,000 |
| | Stagnant type ('High and Dry') | 2,500 |
| Broad Church | Normal type | 2,800 |
| | Exaggerated type (concealed infidels) | 20(?) |
| | Stagnant type | 700 |

Two further groups were mentioned by Conybeare: 'about 1,000 peasant clergy in the mountain districts', largely Welsh, and 'twenty-eight bishops and archbishops

... thirteen belonging to various shades of High Church, ten to the Broad Church, and five to the Evangelical parties.' Conybeare admitted that all this was 'an approximation', but it does give us some idea of the groups arranged in the background behind the leaders whose portraits we are to paint. And we must add that in 1859 the High Church forces were mobilized – they claimed, defensively – in the English Church Union, to be followed in 1865 by the Church Association for the Low Church party. The battlefield was set.

One reason why the Church of England was a valuable prize was that the island where it had slumbered was now the world's first industrial state, while after Trafalgar the Royal Navy commanded the seas. For all its isolation and casualness, nineteenth-century England could not avoid a role in the world; it continued to influence the American ex-colonies, and as the century progressed it became the centre of a vast new imperial system. Religious ideas exported by Englishmen went all over the world, and the Church of England itself slowly and reluctantly ceased to be insular. We shall find most of the leaders of Victorian religion well aware of this global setting, and had our study begun at an earlier date we should have paid special attention to the Evangelicals' enthusiasm for the work of the Church Missionary Society, founded in 1799. These religious ideas, when they had been exported, often returned to England in the stories or legends of men who had become apostles while building the Church on new ground overseas; and England was influenced.

In 1841 an Etonian who had been a curate in Windsor sailed to New Zealand as its first Anglican bishop, at the age of thirty-two. In 1844, at Waimate, he summoned a synod of three archdeacons, four other priests, and two deacons. It was the first experiment in corporate action by nineteenth-century Anglicans outside the United States; for at this date the ancient Convocations of the clergy in the Church of England were silenced. That experiment was accompanied by others, in the course of which Anglicanism was strongly renewed. Even before his enthronement as Bishop of Lichfield in 1868, this architect of Anglicanism in New

Zealand, George Selwyn, taught the lessons which England could learn. He declared in 1847:

> The experience of a new colony convinces me that the Church of England system fully worked: 1. Under an able and pious head; 2. With sufficient clergy of one mind; 3. With no pecuniary basis; 4. With no State interference; 5. With free power of expansion ...; 6. With a *sacramentum* [oath] of obedience; 'Here am I, send me'; 'I go, sir'; as well understood as in the army and navy ... That, these postulates granted, the Church of England would speedily become a praise upon the whole earth.

Here Selwyn underrated the strength of habit and prejudice in England, but his words illustrated the new spirit of world-wide Anglicanism. Those who had found 'a Saviour for me' in England might find themselves supporting missionaries, or actually themselves preaching in the southern seas, or even being murdered there, as John Coleridge Patteson, the first and saintly Bishop of Melanesia, was in 1871; and so they might find an unexpected vitality in their Christian faith, as when the news of Patteson's death stirred all England.

In one respect, indeed, these builders of the new Anglicanism at home and overseas were more significant than could be known by anyone at the time. In efforts towards religious peace in England, the Tudor architects of the National Church had made it as comprehensive as possible. That was the reason why in the nineteenth century the Church was the battleground of rival theologies, perhaps more conspicuously than it was an army against unbelief. But most of the theological rivals were still yoked together by the system of the Church of England, which seemed to hold for them even more blessings than curses; and the system of the Established Church of England came to have a more and more distinctly ecclesiastical basis. At home and overseas, as the Tudor arrangements fell away Anglicans were stimulated to serious thought about what were the essentials and inessentials in the constitution of the Christian Church. Controversy was inevitable once this problem had been posed, but when the modern ecumenical movement tried to move towards an ideal of unity which would include much diversity within a bond of charity, Anglicans naturally found themselves involved in the reconciling trend; and when after the Second Vatican Council a new era opened in the attitude of Roman Catholics to other Christians, Anglicans were eager for this dialogue also. Thus the tensions within Anglicanism could be regarded as a training-ground for the tensions and hopes of the ecumenical struggle for Christian renewal and reunion around the world.

Its ability to produce missionaries such as Selwyn and Patteson was one of the most important of the strengths which enabled Victorian England to stumble into its imperial role. There were many more like them at home. The Church of England was then proud to breed captains of a new empire of Christ. This was in the style of the period, which with Thomas Carlyle definitely believed in 'heroes'. Nonconformist congregations were built around their preachers, and basked in the glory of princes of the pulpit such as R. W. Dale in Birmingham or Joseph Parker or Charles Spurgeon in London. Methodism produced in Jabez Bunting an administrator who was more of a dictator than any bishop, and later in Hugh Price Hughes a publicist whose commanding enthusiasm was able to create a newspaper, a network of central halls, and a whole 'Forward Movement'. Most astonishing of all was the meteoric career, flaming across darkest England, of William Booth, the ex-Methodist founding General of the Salvation Army.

The leading Anglican ecclesiastics, however, definitely belonged to the ruling class – even if some far-seeing men such as Thomas Arnold and George Selwyn had begun to say that the Church of England must broaden the social basis of its clergy and forget the 'Gentleman-Heresy'. In the shires the clergy prospered financially and socially in the Victorian age more than at any other time in English history; they were helped by the commutation of agricultural tithes in kind for money payments in 1836, since these easily collected payments provided many handsome incomes for the parsons until the whole of English agriculture began to suffer through foreign competition in the 1870's. The higher clergy of the Established Church were educated alongside the other leaders of the national life. They were nominated to their posts by the Crown on the recommendation of the government of the day. It was a convention surviving from the old days of the unity of Church and State. Although indefensible theologically, this was convenient for the time being, in that it enabled the Crown to push to the top some able men who were unpopular with, or unknown to, the parochial clergy. In the colonies, where the Crown's control of the Church was gradually weakened by geography as much as the theology, the quality of the bishops became all the more important; in the development of the Anglican Communion, few things mattered more than the Colonial Bishoprics Fund in London. And in the colonies the clergy and lay missionaries, however poor, were the recognized ambassadors of a proud 'Christian civilization'.

Were such churchmen truly eminent? They were not so eminent as their contemporaries believed. No one today could read with entire conviction such Victorian works as Frederick Arnold's two volumes on *Our Bishops and Deans* (1875), or the quarrelsome Dean Burgon's *Twelve Good Men* (1888); and no one today could plausibly write in that style about later churchmen. But it is equally true that no student of the largely frustrated life of Lytton Strachey can help wondering about a man such as that. Was he right to assume an air of bland superiority to the *Eminent Victorians* about whom he was so witty in 1918? For one thing, the Victorians were far more critical of their own failings than Strachey and other intellectuals of that generation were of theirs. Frederick Arnold in the course of his chatter observed that 'the crying necessity of our times is a sweeping Ecclesiastical Reform Bill, and unless reform is adopted we shall have Revolution or Destruction.' The Victorian churchmen at whom Strachey sneered did reform, although not enough. They fought the battles of faith, and won some of them. They led a large religious body into a new style of life. They influenced a great – by many standards, the greatest – age in English history. In the *Oxford History of England*, Sir Robert Ensor wrote: 'no one will ever understand Victorian England who does not appreciate that among highly civilized ... countries it was one of the most religious that the world has known'.

# I

# Thomas and Matthew Arnold

I

When Thomas Arnold began to reign as Headmaster of Rugby School in 1828, he was thirty-three years old and full of the ambition to educate. 'My object will be, if possible, to form Christian men, for Christian boys I can scarcely hope to make.' His own eldest son Matthew, then aged almost six, was a problem. When barely six months old he had already seemed 'backward and rather bad-tempered'. Matt had to wear irons in order to straighten out his legs; his father nick-named him 'the Crab'. The boy was not permanently lame, but he was awkward and a stammerer. He alarmed his father by being a dreamer. 'Matt does not know what it is to work, because he so little knows what it is to think.' Was his moral influence on the other children all that it might be? As a precaution, he was for a time separated from them.

Amid 'trembling' at home, Matthew Arnold was sent off to his father's old school at Winchester. His father had been happy there, but now he feared that the son might fall into vice – although the son wrote one of his first poems about the moral issues involved in entry into a public school. However, what happened was that some of the boys heard him telling a master that the work was 'quite light', and Matt was teased brutally; so, after a year, he was recalled and placed under his father's care at Rugby. When told to stand behind the Headmaster's throne for being unsatisfactory in the Sixth Form, he made funny faces at the class. His father was 'astonished' when the boy won a scholarship to Balliol College, Oxford; and Oxford was no less astonished to find Thomas Arnold's son totally unlike the young prigs emerging from Rugby. Matt was a dandy, conspicuous for the length of his hair, the colour of his waistcoats, the sophistication of his knowledge of French literature, and his habit of calling his friends 'my darling'.

Oxford meant much to father and son, the countryside even more than the colleges. The father loved that country because in it he could work off some of his energy. He took to the river, he went for immense walks, and he specially enjoyed 'skirmishes' which involved plunging over, or through, hedges and streams. For the son, however, delight in the country around Oxford was not an athlete's pleasure; Matthew Arnold sought relief from mental exhaustion. His reading in Oxford had contributed to his virtual rejection of his father's religion. For a time he found a substitute in the religion of beauty, 'all the live murmur of a summer's day'. But in the end, beauty was not enough. Was it merely that Matthew Arnold grew middle-aged? Already in 1853 he wrote to Clough: 'I am past thirty, and three parts iced over.' Or was he turning from the country to the town, from poetry to prose, because of his inheritance? Or was it the fault of a 'deeply unpoetical' age? He asked himself such questions many times, and there is no reason why we should give a clearer answer than he did.

At any rate, Matthew Arnold expressed the dilemma of his age better than anyone else – and it was a talkative age. He did it by poetic symbolism. He transfigured the Oxford (or, to be more accurate, the Cumnor) countryside by painting it in an atmosphere which he himself described in self-criticism as a 'pleasing melancholy'. 'The Scholar-Gipsy' (1853) was based on the seventeenth-century story of the Oxford man who had gone into the country in search of a secret, in his case the gipsies' skill in hypnotism. As the seasons came and went, this scholar still awaited the great secret.

> Thou waitest for the spark from heaven! and we,
>> Light half-believers of our casual creeds,
>>> Who never deeply felt, nor clearly will'd,
>> Whose insight never has borne fruit in deeds,
>>> Whose vague resolves never have been fulfill'd; ...
> Ah! do not we, wanderer! await it too?

'Thyrsis' (1866) was another lament, set amid the 'high Midsummer pomps' of the same country. It was a lament for his schoolfellow Arthur Hugh Clough, who at Rugby had been heartily admired among the heroes of the Sixth Form. Oxford and the world had proved too much for Clough, and he had become a poet of the vanished faith, the full tomb. Matthew Arnold had disapproved of this withdrawal from duty and this surrender to anxiety; 'Thyrsis', despite its melancholy, ended on a distinctly religious note. And in his poem 'Rugby Chapel' (1867), he strained language as far as it would go in order to identify himself with his father's faith. Thomas Arnold was now remembered from the days when he had led his children for great walks up the fells in the Lake District; and he was imagined among the dead whose courage had somehow earned immortality and who had taken lesser men into regions which, however misty, were higher than the workaday plain.

> Languor is not in your heart,
> Weakness is not in your word,
> Weariness not on your brow ...
> Eyes rekindling, and prayers,
> Follow your steps as ye go.

Matthew Arnold wrote 'Rugby Chapel' because in his own inner life he had been reconciled with the memory of 'dear papa'. He himself said he wrote the poem as a result of the novel by Thomas Hughes, *Tom Brown's School-days*, published in 1857; he dated the poem 'November 1857' although he did not visit Rugby in that month. The novel moved Matthew Arnold, and a hostile review by Fitzjames Stephens, leaving the impression that the Headmaster of Rugby had been narrow, bustling fanatic who spread gloom, made him indignant. The son knew, better than anyone else, how clumsy and oppressive his father could be. But he also knew – and he could say it better than any of his father's adoring pupils – how Arnold of Rugby deserved more than a coldly cynical review. This 'strong soul' still had a message of high seriousness to deliver, while nature itself proved powerless to solve the spiritual problems which emerged as the old order of mind and society declined, while

Coldly, sadly descends
The autumn-evening. The field
Strewn with its dank yellow drifts
Of wither'd leaves, and the elms,
Fade into dimness apace,
Silent; —hardly a shout
From a few boys late at their play!


2


There were many shouts when Thomas Arnold began his work at Rugby in 1828; and not only shouts of pain from the fags being bullied, or shouts of battle as Rugby football worked off young male instincts less sadistically, Thomas Arnold did much of the shouting himself. He was then at the height of his manhood, and his reputation rested on his energy. While running a small private school in the Thames-side village of Laleham, he had shared the work and the sports of his pupils with equal ardour. At Rugby he still needed hard exercise, and particularly enjoyed swimming and jumping. Although the public school cult of compulsory games was not introduced in his time, it was an important part of his policy to encourage innocent recreations, knowing that the alternatives had made public school life notorious. He also insisted, for the first time in the school's history, that the boys should sleep in separate beds.

The school was made into something more like a family. At Laleham his pupils spent their evenings in his drawing room. At Rugby he was a little more remote, but favourites such as Arthur Clough would find themselves often with Matt and the Headmaster's other children, and the system by which the boarders at the school in fact boarded in Dames' Houses in the town was abolished in favour of having the boys in School House under the Headmaster or in other houses under assistant masters. Although the boys were still allowed far more freedom than would have been tolerated under the later development of the house system in public schools, they were now under closer supervision than before. In order that they might supervise, the masters were both ordered and enabled to give up their part-time curacies in parish churches. Schoolmastering was now seen as a full-time profession, for the schoolmaster's role was parental. A flag would often fly over the Headmaster's study. It was an invitation to any boy to call and discuss anything. Other masters were expected to be similarly available.

Thomas Arnold had a lively sense of the financial implications of his policy. His insistence on adequate salaries for his staff would entitle him to be the patron saint of the National Union of Teachers, and what he demanded for his staff he was not too shy to obtain for himself: he received the then enormous salary of over £3,000 a year together with a free house. Although he entered the post in debt and brought up nine children, he reckoned that fifteen years as Headmaster of Rugby would enable him to retire for the rest of his life to the family home which he now built, Fox How, in the heart of the Westmorland fells, on a site chosen by Wordsworth. These larger salaries for himself and his staff came partly from the increase in the number of boys (he was paid per head), but mainly from raising the fees. The parents of boarders paid thirty guineas a year when he arrived. By 1834 they were complaining that they had to find at least £130 a year. Arnold did not hesitate to change the intention of its Elizabethan founder for Rugby School; at the beginning, in 1567, the school had provided education for a small village, but during Arnold's reign poor boys were effectively excluded from its benefits, despite local indignation. A local school emerged to take care of those who could not afford Rugby School's new fees.

One of the reasons why it was easier for Arnold to recruit the sons of the upper middle class on a national basis was that this was the railway age. *Tom Brown's School-days* was deliberately nostalgic in its opening chapters about Squire Brown staying at home in Wiltshire and then sending his son off to school by the stage coach. In real life the Doctor welcomed the railway to Rugby, and took regular services for the railwaymen at the new station. He also saw the railways' unification of England as part of a new age for the world. He was the son of the chief customs officer in the Isle of Wight, and his boyhood at Cowes had been spent in sight of ships and the sea. As soon as he had any money he began touring Europe with a gusto rare in his time; he made twelve European expeditions, and later his travel diaries were published. Matthew Arnold thought that this European outlook was as important as anything else in his father's legacy. At the time it seemed bold that the form masters at Rugby should be required to teach French as well as the classics, and bolder still when a man was appointed to the staff who spoke French as a native. The wandering headmaster also thought much about remoter horizons. He spoke of crossing the Atlantic if Revolution came at home, or of becoming a colonial bishop, or of teaching in Tasmania or New Zealand, or at least of sending Matt out there so that he might learn how to work. One of his disciples was his son Willy, who became the educational pioneer of the Punjab.

Thomas Arnold's formula can be made to sound like the privileged being politer to each other in a more prosperous world. But he did not regard the public school system as a bastion of privilege. The boys who flogged the guilty and used the fags as slaves were not given such rights because of their physical strength. On the contrary, boys whose physical development had outpaced their minds found themselves quickly removed from the school. 'The Doctor', we recall from *Tom Brown*, 'who had long had his eye on Flashman, arranged for his withdrawal next morning'. Nor did a boy's status in Rugby School depend on his parents' status in the world. The Doctor himself had not come from the top of the social tree. The clever boys of the Sixth form were the 'praepostors' to whom many privileges were entrusted. And Rugby School was viewed by its headmaster as part of a system which depended on the upper middle class making itself useful. Arnold had no respect for a selfish cleverness, and he applied to a public school the principles which he had shown in action at Laleham. A pupil of his from those days, who subsequently joined the Rugby staff, wrote: 'Dr. Arnold's great power as a private tutor resided in this, that he gave such an intense earnestness to life. Every pupil was made to feel that there was work for

24

him to do – that his happiness as well as his duty lay in doing that work well.'

A boy such as Arthur Clough, then a thorough convert, worked and lived in order to add to the moral glory of Rugby School. The other senior boys were all expected to share the same attitude. Many of them did, or at least they learned to echo their formidable headmaster's idealism; for one of Arnold's policies was to use to the full his right to require the parents of boys who were unsatisfactory for any reason at all to remove their offspring before they corrupted the school. It came to feel like a compliment to be asked to pay the Rugby fees. Once a boy had conformed to the system and had earned promotion to the Sixth, he seemed morally mature enough to act as judge and executioner over younger boys. There were public outcries against flogging in the school during Arnold's time, but the Headmaster refused to appease outsiders. Another reaction came from the senior boys themselves, who would often retire to the sick room with 'fatigue', but the moral pressure was maintained when the Doctor and his wife paid pastoral visits to the bedside.

The course of duty was overtly Christian. Indeed, the religious atmosphere of the whole of life in Rugby School, at least in its headmaster's eyes, was its most significant challenge to other schools. This was what 'spoiled the public schools' (in Clough's phrase, for once playful). Previously, good headmasters had been expected to concentrate on the production of classical scholars for the universities, and during the 1840s some still insisted that Greek, not morality, provided their role. While the scholars were being coached, the other boys could toughen each other up for their future lives as squires or soldiers. If in the process they hurt each other, their elders remembered how the Englishman's freedom had been defended on the playing fields of Eton. At Rugby Arnold's priorities were new: 'first religious and moral principle; secondly gentlemanly conduct; and thirdly intellectual ability'. The flogging was as religious as the preaching. The expulsions, as much as the Communions, made Rugby a school for Christian gentlemen.

Thomas Arnold's religion was a little hard to classify.

'But is *he* a Christian?' was John Henry Newman's reaction when someone quoted his views on the Old Testament prophets – whom Arnold regarded not as foretellers of the future but as proclaimers of good and evil. Doctrinal difficulties, particularly over the Athanasian Creed, had made him hesitate about entering the ordained ministry as a young Fellow of Oriel College. When friends headed by John Keble (an Oriel colleague) had persuaded him to become a deacon, he had still jibbed at taking responsibility for a parish or for the priesthood. Since he could not continue to reside as a Fellow of Oriel if he married, schoolmastering seemed the obvious profession. He never worked out a satisfactory system of beliefs. He would advise young clergymen to read the Bible, Bunyan, and the classics of Greece and Rome; the only English theologians for whom he expressed any admiration were Richard Hooker and Joseph Butler. He was one of the first to apply the Victorian remedy for doubt: work.

However, Lytton Strachey in *Eminent Victorians* may have confused Thomas with Matthew Arnold when he ascribed to the Doctor a 'puzzled mind'. Thomas Arnold experienced enough of the religious crisis to reject, or to feel uneasy about, a number of traditional dogmas, but it is impossible to read his sermons and letters with a modicum of sympathy and still to doubt his piety. Any boy's approach to irreligious levity or impertinence was checked with a glance, or a white face, or if necessary a terrible word or a judicial blow. Even adults who could not be treated in such a way sensed that the Doctor wrestled with the Devil. Keble was probably right to refuse to take his doubts seriously, and the Provost of Oriel, Edward Hawkins, probably had his religious stature in mind when he supplied the testimonial which won the headmastership for him, prophesying that if elected Thomas Arnold would 'change the face of education all through the public schools of England.'

Although still only a deacon when appointed, he promptly became a priest and a Doctor of Divinity, and he had not been at Rugby for long before he got himself made chaplain to the school. Sunday by Sunday he preached to the boys, sometimes weeping in the pulpit, sometimes denouncing their faults, sometimes warning them of death and hell, sometimes proclaiming Christ as the only Saviour for them, sometimes holding up the vision of a nobler life for man and nation. It was all in the mood of warm Evangelical seriousness, even if his desire to talk the language of common life and his independence of mind prevented him from echoing all the slogans of the Evangelical party. His sermons were authoritarian, even if his insistence on moral power and on preaching drove him to say that 'to revive Christ's church is to expel the antichrist of priesthood'. Although he wanted commentaries to be written which would apply criticism to the Bible, he had little sense of the destructive power of the new sciences on religious faith. He fell out with the one visitor who had lectured on science to the Rugby boys under his predecessor. When he published an essay 'On the Right Interpretation and Understanding of the Scriptures', it was in a volume of 1832 containing twenty-nine intensely practical sermons to the Rugby boys, whose difficulties were clearly believed to be more moral than intellectual.

Any theological hesitations got little attention in Rugby Chapel, and child psychology less.

There always are boys scattered up and down the School [Thomas Hughes remarked] who in heart and head were worthy to hear and able to carry away the deepest and wisest words there spoken. But these were a minority always, generally a very small one, often so small a one as to be countable on the fingers of your hand. What was it that moved and held us, the rest of the three hundred reckless, childish boys, who feared the Doctor with all our hearts, and very little besides in heaven or earth . . . ?

Hughes answered his own question by remembering 'the warm living voice of one who was . . . calling on us to help him and ourselves, and one another'. The Doctor who preached to them was 'a man who was striving against whatever was mean and unmanly and unrighteous in our little world'. His sermons, published in six volumes (two of these posthumously), enabled him to appeal over the heads of his enemies to more impressionable readers including Queen Victoria. It was a prophecy turned towards secular affairs (but was there a real difference between secular and sacred?); towards unrighteousness in the school, but also towards the economic and political problems of the nation. He would quote Francis Bacon: 'In this world, God only and the angels may be spectators.' When one reads about the very full life which he led with his family and his school, one is further exhausted to discover that Thomas Arnold's most passionate interests lay in the social crisis of the time. 'I must write or die' was his motto, for as he told the boys in a sermon 'this is a marked time – a time such as neither we, nor our fathers for many generations before us, have experienced'.

He was far from being a sophisticated statesman. Matthew Arnold was to recall, in the first edition of *Culture and Anarchy*, how his father had advocated flogging rioters. It had worked in Ancient Rome; it was working at Rugby, where the boys called him 'Tiger Tom' and learned to fear the bulging of the blue vein on his forehead. But because Thomas Arnold's ardent sympathies in the theory of politics were with the poor, his fellow-gentlemen regarded him as a radical. In 1831 he started his own newspaper, the *Englishman's Register*, to warn the country of the great evils which he saw coming imminently from a selfish aristocracy and a class of managers who treated workers as 'hands'. The newspaper was a flop, but other journals, in Sheffield and Hertfordshire, printed other controversial political letters which he did not sign, but which he also did not disown. His convictions about politics made him unpopular among the gentry around Rugby. At a banquet in 1835 some shouted 'No insult to the Doctor!' – but more took up the Tory cry, 'Church and King!' This partly explains his many complaints about Warwickshire and the joy with which he would leave the school for West-morland on the first day of the holidays twice a year, postponing his return until the last possible moment – although he once broke into a Lakeland holiday, making the long and expensive journey back in order to vote against the Tories.

Friends, including Provost Hawkins, deplored his en-tanglement in public controversies, for it was bound to offend those on whose goodwill and fees Rugby School depended. Observers thought his habit of seeing Antichrist in his opponents ridiculously unworldy if not intolerably arrogant. Sydney Smith was to call him 'a learned, pious, virtuous person, without five grains of common sense'. In 1836 resentment at the well-paid headmaster's social radicalism and over-zealous indiscretions came to a head because Arnold published in the *Edinburgh Review* a bitter attack on 'the Oxford Malignants and Dr. Hampden' (a title supplied by the editor, but fair enough). These 'malignants' included other Fellows of Oriel such as Newman; naturally their colleagues crowded round in nervous curiosity when Arnold dined at Oriel College in 1842, and Provost Hawkins had to say hurriedly, 'Arnold, I don't think you know Newman?' The 'malignants' also included Keble, Thomas Arnold's intimate friend when they were both undergraduates at Corpus Christi College and now Matthew Arnold's godfather. These men were denounced for their 'moral wickedness', and a comparison of them with the Jews who crucified Christ seemed to exceed even the harsh conventions of theological controversy. The article was written because Newman and others had been protesting – also in an extravagant style – against the Whig government's appointment of an excessively broad-minded theologian, Renn Hampden, as Regius Professor of Divinity. The article's passionate indignation appears to have sprung partly from Arnold's suspicion that Hampden's real offence had been to want Dissenters admitted to Oxford, and partly from his belief that by insisting on reading the worst possible meaning into Hampden's benevolent-minded ambiguities the Tractarians were throwing away the Church's best chance of survival in the new age. But one result of this article's unbalanced tone was that the Doctor nearly lost his own appointment. Of the eight trustees who voted as the governing body of Rugby School, four now wanted his dismissal.

He was already in trouble in the Church because of a pamphlet written at Fox How during the Christmas holidays of 1832–3 on *Principles of Church Reform*. This was one of a spate of pamphlets about the ecclesiastical crisis

at the time of the First Reform Act of 1832, when it looked
as if the Church of England might be reformed violently
and destructively. Thomas Arnold's purpose was conservative; indeed, he wrote in reply to a pamphlet by the
Evangelical Lord Henley urging the radical remedy of virtual disestablishment as the only medicine for the Church's
ills. Arnold wanted to see the establishment of the Church of
England secured. However, he was at that stage convinced,
as many others were, that 'no human power' could save
the Establishment as it then was. His remedy was to broaden
the Church's basis in the national life. There should be
more (but poorer) bishops, each surrounded by an advisory
council and a diocesan conference. Parishioners should have
a say in the appointment of rectors or vicars, and working-
class men should be ordained as deacons. The doctrinal
comprehensiveness of the Church, already large, should be
widened so as to include all Christians in England except
the Roman Catholics and the Quakers. Perhaps the creeds
might be revised. Presumably the sweeping legislation
needed could come only from Parliament. Such proposals
alarmed the Lord Bishops in their palaces, the incumbents
in their freeholds, all the clergy who valued their middle-
class self-satisfaction, all who feared Parliament, and all
who despised Dissent as being socially inferior as well as
religiously erroneous. Even the Dissenters were not flattered;
they were to be extinguished by comprehension. It was now
clear that Arnold could not be made a bishop, despite the
shortage of clergymen acceptable to the Whig government.
'What have Tory churchmen ever done for me,' asked the
Prime Minister, Lord Melbourne, 'that I should make
them a present of such a handle against my government?'

Arnold was not even allowed to preach at another's consecration to the episcopate. When Edward Stanley – a
liberal, but a Whig aristocrat to his fingertips – was nominated as Bishop of Norwich, and invited his friend Arnold
to be preacher, the Archbishop of Canterbury vetoed the
idea on the ground that it would anger the clergy. The
only post which the Liberals could safely produce for their
champion was a non-theological professorship. Accordingly
he was appointed Regius Professor of Modern History at

Oxford in 1841. He had confessed to being 'one of the most ambitious men alive', but had tried to take his disappointment in the Church as a chastisement from God; and he was delighted at this new and more scholarly opening for his energies. When, as he planned, he resigned from Rugby in 1844, he would sit in his study at Fox How and write history, visiting Oxford in order to lecture. Meanwhile he gave away his Oxford salary while he received his Rugby income and his first lecture in the university was a triumph. Although only a handful of undergraduates regularly studied modern history, his admirers claimed that this was the largest audience which Oxford had provided for any lecture since the close of the Middle Ages.

It is, indeed, possible that had he lived Thomas Arnold would have become a considerable historian. It is true that he wrote little about the time between the fall of Rome and the nineteenth century, although he did announce plans to cover the modern world in future lectures. But his imagination had been seized by history, and his view of the contemporary drama had been coloured by the great narratives of the social crises of the ancient world. They appealed to the preacher in him. In an essay on 'The Social Progress of States' appended to the first volume of his edition of Thucydides, he compared states with the childhood, youth, manhood, and decay of individuals; and, viewing his own age as an age of decay, he believed that Providence had acted in history like a schoolmaster. But he also loved history for its own sake. He had learned German in 1824 in order to read Niebuhr's work, and thus benefit his own *History of Rome*; and he sympathized strongly with Niebuhr's interest in institutions as well as heroes. When he published the first volume of this *History*, in 1838, he announced his hope to carry it on to the coronation of Charlemagne, although his last words, written a month before his death, were about Hannibal. His *Thucydides* in three volumes (1830 –5) was one of the real beginnings of English study of Greek history despite signs of haste inevitable in the work of a busy schoolmaster. His Sixth Form at Rugby was deeply impressed by his teaching of history, and it is possible that, given time, he might have matured sufficiently to be taken seriously by adults, ordering the past if he could not order the 1850s and 1860s

It is also possible that he would have lived down the unpopularity of the 1830s, and would have been taken from his literary labours to pour his zeal into the work of a bishop. John Keble was going to spend some of the summer holidays of 1842 at Fox How for a reconciliation. But Thomas Arnold was fated. Almost on the eve of his forty-seventh birthday, on a Sunday morning in June 1842, he died after an attack of *angina pectoris*, from which his father had also died. He took the pain as from God, quoting the text: 'But if ye be without chastisement, whereof all are partakers, then are ye bastards and not sons.' He was buried in front of the altar of Rugby Chapel.

3

His family and his pupils were stunned. When Matthew Arnold saw the dead body, the thought crossed his mind that the head had been the family's one source of information. When Rugbeians at Oxford and elsewhere heard that the Doctor was dead, an important part of their world died; and for some, nothing ever took its place. But the nation took little notice until two years later one who had been (even more than Clough) favourite among all the Rugby boys, Arthur Stanley the Bishop of Norwich's son, published *The Life and Correspondence of Thomas Arnold, D.D.* Through that book, and through the Tom Brown novels (there was a sequel, *Tom Brown at Oxford,* in 1861), the life of this frustrated and pessimistic schoolmaster, a life ended prematurely, was prolonged to form one of the major influences in the making of Victorian England.

Few biographies, if any, have been so well adjusted to their purpose as was Stanley's. The letters were printed with a minimun of editorial comment, which added to the impression that the plain truth was being told: on the surface there was scarcely a touch of emotion. But with his editorial skill, and some vivid words of his own, the young Arthur Stanley proved himself a first-class publicist. Arnold's words were selected in order to adorn a theme.

References to embarrassing matters were left unexplained. Local, political, and religious storms were played down. Enough opposition was mentioned rather vaguely, and only enough, to enable Stanley to present his headmaster as a crusader. The only long chapter in his own words was a eulogy of the Rugby system. The whole book was dominated by the courage and piety of the deathbed, which was described minutely. The man who had been known nationally as a controversialist, and locally as a boy flogger and fee-raiser, was transfigured, as he had been when the candles shone on him in the pulpit. Rugby School now felt that it was the centre of the moral universe, and parents became anxious to include their boys in the saga. Masters and Sixth Formers in other schools studied the book and resolved to make their schools more like Arnold's – or at least Stanley's – Rugby. The teaching profession found itself heroic.

Of course historians have added their notes to the legend. Some religion, as well as Latin and Greek, must have been communicated by some of the many thousands of clergymen who taught English schoolboys before 1828. Thomas Arnold's own predecessor at Rugby, John Wooll, is one of those who do not deserve total oblivion. He had built the chapel where Arnold preached; Arnold added only stained glass and burial vaults. Wooll had in fact transformed the appearance of the school, to house numbers which grew under his early rule and diminished only with his own decline. As headmasters, both Wooll and Arnold rose with the rising market of the new classes given money by the industrial revolution, wanting their sons to be made gentlemen alongside Squire Brown's son, and prepared to see them Christians too because that was better than the French Revolution. Some of Arnold's distinctive characteristics were handicaps in appealing to this market, which did not like the overflow of his exuberance into radical talk about Church and State. Certainly the popular image of the Doctor as spread by Arthur Stanley and Thomas Hughes had to suppress some aspects of the complicated reality of the living Thomas Arnold.

Historians also stress that the impact of the legend of

the Doctor was not complete. Many schoolmasters resented the Rugby ideas; many parents thought them not practical enough for a commercial life; many boys carried on as before. Even at Rugby, vast tracts of boy-life remained impervious; *Tom Brown's School-days*, although it ended in tears over Arnold's grave, indicated as much; and went far to justify Arnold's sermons against public school vice. And, despite the Doctor of Divinity in the centre of its background, it was from first to last an anti-intellectual book. When Stanley read it, he commented: 'It is an absolute revelation to me: opens up a world of which, though so near to me, I was utterly ignorant.'

Yet the legend was powerful. It probably owed its initial impact to one and half pages contributed to Stanley's *Life* by George Moberly, then Headmaster of Winchester. Moberly had taught Stanley and other Rugbeians at Oxford, and had been impressed by the school's elevating influence on them. He knew, as he confessed, 'but little' of Arnold. He was a generous, rather sentimental, man who was writing to console the mourners. He referred to the deep 'delinquencies' of the old days at Winchester and to an Oxford where 'a religous undergraduate was very rare, very much laughed at when he appeared'. He added that 'a most singular and striking change has come upon our public schools', and he attributed this mainly to Arnold's influence on Rugbeians who became 'thoughtful, manly-minded, conscious of duty and obligation'.

It was an oversimplified picture. How had a handful of Rugbeians been able to change the scene within a few years from darkness to light? Even as headmasters – and a remarkable number of pupils and colleagues did become headmasters – the Doctor's disciples could not have effected the transformation by moral force alone. Yet the picture was painted by the most acceptable kind of artist. Moberly was at the head of a famous school. He was also a High Churchman, the intimate friend and spiritual director of John Keble himself; his name carried weight in circles where Tom Arnold had been a figure of fun. The fact that Moberly was prepared to accept the Doctor impressed many who were looking for a hero; and there was enough truth in his tribute to make Arnold of Rugby a major influence in actually changing the schools after his death and the appearance of the books by Stanley and Hughes. His death was essential to his legend. How could a Professor Stanley have written so movingly about a Professor Arnold who had given up schoolmastering as soon as he had made enough money?

The essence of Thomas Arnold's theories about Church and State was that England should be made more like Rugby School. It should be changed by moral preaching and example. One defect of this approach had the merit of being usable by men who believed that the original preacher had got some of the details wrong. The aim was clear. It was to make the holders of power more conscious of their duties. Arnold felt that he had to some extent succeeded in this aim with the boys of the Sixth, and wrote his pamphlets in the hope of persuading adults such as their parents to behave themselves. There was no need to be ashamed of possessing privilege, or to be hesitant in expecting respect and conformity. But the power was to be exercised within a community, and for its benefit, under the eye of God.

Thomas Arnold's schemes to make Church and State more communal, in a sacred order, were a mixture of the shrewd and the crazy. As his friends begged him to remember, his personal experience was limited to schools and Oxford. For all his sympathy with it, the industrial revolution was what lay between School House and Fox How. (When he was offered a post in Manchester, he said that he could not afford to accept it.) This lack of realism about the social structure of the nation blinded him to the sociological necessity of Dissent, and of working-class movements. He did not see that society had changed so that there were now millions of Englishmen who did not want to be comprehended in an enlarged National Church, because they did not want leadership from Thomas Arnold and his like. However, to be fair we must add that before the 1851 religious census few Englishmen realized quite how popular Dissent was. We must also add that history showed abundantly that the basic principles of Rugby could be asserted by men eager to be involved more deeply than the Doctor in the day-to-day work of Church and State: men such as the author of *Tom Brown's Schooldays*, and subtler men.

One historian of the Victorian Church, Desmond Bowen, has picked on this as the central thread. 'This was the great accomplishment of the Church in Victorian England. Through the writing, teaching, and preaching of its creative minority, it gave to the powerful new middle classes an ethic of "service", based upon Christian principles.' Thomas Arnold helped to falsify the prediction of Marx and Engels that the English middle classes would act more selfishly, and bring Church and State down in their ruin. For he did as much as any man to teach that stern sense of duty which was regarded as sacred even by Victorian agnostics such as George Eliot, Leslie Stephen – and Matthew Arnold.

Gradually the moral development of a more democratic, and far more heavily populated, England was seen to involve the necessity of primary schooling for all. Secondary education, and even the universities, had also to be expanded. Who was to be responsible? Almost into the last quarter of the nineteenth century, many Englishmen still assumed that the Established Church must be the nation's schoolmaster, and others added that Nonconformity must educate its own. When the twentieth century began, there were still more English children in church than in state schools. The principle that Roman Catholic children should be taught in Roman Catholic schools was still scarcely questioned in the middle of the twentieth century. But the growth of the population in the nineteenth century, and the practical demands of commerce and industry, defeated the ambitions of churchmen. Heroic sums of money were raised for church schools, the most dramatic example being the work of Nathaniel Woodard in providing a chain of schools for the middle classes, with the great chapel at Lancing on the Sussex coast as the spiritual centre. Woodard argued that, given enough money, clergymen with devout assistants could educate all the middle classes. However, despite his genius for fund-raising, his hope was wild. Replying to Woodard in *A French Eton* (1864), Matthew Arnold gradually presented an eloquent, unanswerable, and influential case for massive intervention by the State; and he was strengthened in this case by some rather vague words written by Arnold of Rugby as he looked towards the nation's educational future.

Thomas Arnold also bequeathed a more direct legacy to the nation's schools. His fatal heart-attack seems to have been hastened by the emotions which arose in School House when his favourite daughter, Jane, the 'dearest K' of Matthew Arnold's letters, was jilted by one of the Rugby masters within three weeks of the wedding; the young man went on to become Bishop Cotton of Calcutta. Jane was heart-broken by this insult, followed so soon by her beloved father's death, and Matthew Arnold's 'Resignation' records the sombre emotions with which she and her brother now retraced the old walks from Fox How. But Jane survived, and she married a Liberal politician, William Forster. She remained very much an Arnold: indeed, her distinguished family took the name of Arnold-Forster. And the instrument by which the English State assumed its responsibility for the schooling of the people was Forster's Education Act of 1870.

4

Matthew Arnold was pleased when bishops spoke to him in the Athenaeum Club, and although he was known to shirk churchgoing the biblical or ecclesiastical images or quotations to be found everywhere in his poetry and prose show the religious atmosphere in which he lived and thought habitually. His wife used to dismiss talk about his heresies by saying that he was at bottom a good Christian. His inclusion in a small portrait gallery of leaders of the modern Church of England would, no doubt, have surprised him no less than his father. 'Institutions are to be judged by their great men; in the end, they take their line from their great men,' he wrote. 'The Christian Church, and the line which is natural to it and which will one day prevail in it, is to be judged from the saints and the tone of the saints.' He was not of that company. But a layman may articulate the feelings of many of his fellow-laymen in the religious community, and may more widely influence the attitudes of fellow-countrymen. The distinction of Matthew Arnold as a writer entitles us to include him in this book as a layman through whom we may get in touch with levels of religion liable not to be noticed if we fix our attention entirely on clergymen. The churches of Victorian England were revived, but a study of Matthew Arnold is the best way possible of entering into the subtler question of what was really happening in the Englishman's view of God.

The legacy of Arnold of Rugby helped to kill his eldest son as a poet. 'Sohrab and Rustum' put Matthew Arnold's personal story into a poem which, when completed in 1853, was reported to his mother as 'I think by far the best thing I have yet done ... I have had the greatest pleasure in composing it – a rare thing with me ...' The style was influenced by Homer and Virgil; the material was gathered from fragments of the geography and legends of Persia; but the passion and dignity welled up from the poet's experience. For it was the story of a father who unintentionally killed his son.

Sohrab, the son, had been brought up far from Rustum, so that he must say

> 'I seek one man, one man, and one alone—
> Rustum, my father; who I hoped should greet,
> Should one day greet, upon some well-fought field,
> His not unworthy, not inglorious son."

And Matthew Arnold is known to have been shocked by the early death of his father, particularly since it came before he had achieved a real understanding with him. His letters contain a number of confessions of his desire to vindicate himself after his father's distrust. This desire was all the stronger because he retained a great love for his mother, who survived until 1873.

When Rustum does meet Sohrab in single combat, neither recognizing the other, they talk of the possibility of reaching an understanding. Although the main purpose of this talk in the poem may be to maintain the dramatic suspense, there is at least one reference, when death has been inflicted, to the distant happiness which father and son had shared.

The castle, and the dewy woods, and hunt
And hound, and morn on those delightful hills ...

And Matthew Arnold never forgot how with their father
'the Dogs' had walked the fells. For all his sensitivity to
his father's insensitivity, for all the impatience which he
would sometimes betray when people quoted the Doctor's
verdicts, for all the dislike (dare we say it?) which he largely
suppressed, he was never finally alienated from his father,
or willing to condemn him. In the poem Sohrab spares
Rustum when he might have killed him, and he drops his
shield fatally when at last Rustum announces who he is.

What finally angers Rustum, and drives him into the
duel, is an effeminate appeal for peace from Sohrab.
Rustum thunders:

'Girl! nimble with thy feet, not with thy hands!
Curl'd minion, dancer, coiner of sweet words!'

But when Sohrab has received the mortal blow, his dying
eloquence makes his father weep. Did Matthew Arnold as
a boy dream of converting the angry father by his poetic
sweetness and light? We may guess so; yet we know that
as a man, he was himself slowly converted back to what his
father had taught. In a poem where glimpses of the story
of a heart mingle with sonorous lines of 'orientalizing',
Sohrab finally dies because he chooses to draw his father's
spear out of his side. For Matthew Arnold's were poems
of a growing resignation: first a resignation to the loss of
belief in the precise gospel preached by his father, and
then a resignation to a destiny to preach a revised version
of this gospel. When the poet finally acknowledged that
he was a prophet's son, and accepted his destiny as being
the work of education in his father's steps, the poetry more
or less ceased. As his family saw with surprise when they
opened his first book, *The Strayed Reveller* (1849), Matt's
had been a poetry of pain.

For a time the pain would be eased by nature, and his
collection of poems in 1852 included very lovely examples of
how the light of the moon over a city street, or of the grass in
a London park, would calm his heart. But his 'Calais
Sands', a poem of waiting in agitation for 'my darling', was

significantly different from Wordsworth's evening walk on those same sands, in the quietness half-hearing the pagan gods of nature. Nature did not have consolations enough for Matthew Arnold, whom Quiller-Couch aptly called Wordsworth's widow – but then, pantheism did not have enough religious value to be the permanent satisfaction of Wordsworth himself.

For a time Matthew Arnold seemed about to find a new strength in his emotional life from the love of women. While on a Swiss holiday in 1848 he was conquered at the Hotel Bellevue, Thun, by 'the blue eyes of one of its inmates', as he told Clough. The infatuation lasted barely a year, and, seeing 'Marguerite' as impossible in the role of Thomas Arnold's daughter-in-law, the poet declined into speculations about how many lovers she had already enjoyed, and whether she had become a prostitute. But his poems testify to the intensity of what seems to have been his first serious love-affair. On the rebound from Marguerite, and after the further shock of his sister Jane's marriage in 1850, he fell in love with a judge's daughter, Frances Lucy Wightman, 'Flu', whom he married in 1851. It was almost certainly to her that he wrote:

> Ah, love, let us be true
> To one another! for the world, which seems
> To lie before us like a land of dreams,
> So various, so beautiful, so new,
> Hath really neither joy, nor love, nor light,
> Nor certitude, nor peace, nor help for pain ...

But help for the heart's pain in the love of women did not lead Matthew Arnold to write poetry about it. The heart's ultimate questions were too insistent. Where was the 'bright and tranquil' sea glimpsed at the end of 'Sohrab and Rustum'? How was the individual to enter its peace? Or was it really 'the unplumb'd salt, estranging sea' of one of his poems to Marguerite?

> Dotting the shoreless watery wild,
> We mortal millions live *alone*.

It was probably from the description of the attack on Epipolae by moonlight in *Thucydides* (translated by Thomas

Arnold) that Matthew Arnold drew the conclusion to 'Dover Beach':

> And we are here as on a darkling plain
> Swept with confused alarm of struggle and flight,
> Where ignorant armies clash by night.

And the religious confusion implied in those lines was what enabled them to be linked with the great image of 'Dover Beach':

> The Sea of Faith
> Was once, too, at the full, and round earth's shore
> Lay like the folds of a bright girdle furl'd.
> But now I only hear
> Its melancholy, long, withdrawing roar,
> Retreating, to the breath
> Of the night-wind, down the vast edges drear
> And naked shingles of the world.

No countryside and no lover could permanently calm grief of the depth described in 'To a Gipsy Child by the Sea-shore'. No mortal man could possess the ultimate meaning attributed to 'the Tree' in 'Thyrsis'. The sense of 'the burthen of the mystery' was too great for his heart to rest without a religion. He had felt with a cruel intensity:

> Resolve to be thyself; and know that he,
> Who finds himself, loses his misery!

This self-conscious, self-torturing, young man had then answered his own anxiety:

> Live by thy light, and earth will live by hers!

And he had rebuked Clough for being too worried about the riddle of the universe. But who *was* he? What *was* his light?

For a time he was impressed by Hindu mysticism, but in the end Matthew Arnold's light had to be a moral tradition going back to Christ, and all his questions could be concentrated on the nineteenth-century question: was the Saviour dead?

> 'While we believed, on earth he went
> And open stood his grave.
> Men call'd from chamber, church, and tent,
> And Christ was by to save.
>
> 'Now he is dead! Far hence he lies
> In the lorn Syrian town;
> And on his grave, with shining eyes,
> The Syrian stars look down.'

Was that verdict in 'Obermann Once More' final? One of the dramatic poems, 'Empedocles on Etna', was about a despairing philosopher's suicide, and the spiritual misery of some of the others poems do suggest that Matthew Arnold (like John Stuart Mill or Thomas Carlyle) may have contemplated suicide as an end to the enigma of existence, when very near to the complete breakdown of his inner life. But if he needed a religion, the religion could not be conventional. In his pencilled notes for poems to be composed during 1849, he jotted down: 'Empedocles – refusal of limitation by the religious sentiment'. And the religious sentiment in its traditional form was never strong enough to heal Matthew Arnold's hurt. He had enjoyed the style of Newman's sermons while an undergraduate, and later he went out of his way to pay compliments to him, but the alleged discovery of the living God in the living Church always struck him as revived medievalism, and so as 'impossible' for free, modern minds. 'For God's sake, believe it then!' was the most he could say (in his poem 'Pis-Aller') to those who, like Newman, declared that life could not be lived without belief in a supernatural grace. For him the romance of the Grande Chartreuse was a retreat from reality:

> Here leave us to die out with these
> Last of the people who believe!

But one of the companions of Empedocles, Pausanias, leaves him on the mountain before the philosopher's leap into the volcano. Pausanias returns to work in the cities of the plain; and the only solution of his own dilemma that Matthew Arnold achieved was to identify the living Jesus with the 'sweet reasonableness' of a sober gospel of daily righteousness. It was not a strongly traditional, doctrinal, articulate sentiment of Newman's kind; but it seemed enough, for thus Matthew Arnold returned to the Christ at the centre of his father's religion.

In a poem first published in 1867 under the title 'Anti-Desperation', he answered the question which had paralysed Clough:

'Sits there no judge in Heaven, our sin to see?—

*'More strictly, then, the inward judge obey!*
*Was Christ a man like us? Ah! let us try*
*If we then, too, can be such men as he!'*

Another short poem of 1867, 'East London', was about the Reverend William Tyler, a Congregational minister. Tyler had moved Arnold by being, while

the fierce sun overhead
Smote on the squalid streets of Bethnal Green ...
'Much cheer'd with thoughts of Christ, *the living bread.*'

This was the spear of Rustum, *alias* Thomas Arnold.

In 'Obermann Once More', which seems to have been written in 1865-6, a revelation comes to replace the vanished certainty of the old religion. The agitation which had set up in Matthew Arnold's loyalties when he had first read in Oxford de Senancour's seductive novel of ennui in 1804, *Obermann,* was now at least more or less resolved in mid-Victorian energy.

*'Unduped of fancy, henceforth man*
*Must labour!—must resign*
*His all too human creeds, and scan*
*Simply the way divine!'*

But 'the morning' does not 'break' until the poet has accepted the commission to preach this gospel of the simple way:

'Though late, though dimm'd, though weak, yet tell
Hope to a world new-made!'

And having glimpsed the glory of the sun

Across the glimmering lake,

the poet does turn to encourage others along the way. As he remembered in 'Rugby Chapel':

> But thou would'st not *alone*
> Be saved, my father! *alone*
> Conquer and come to thy goal,
> Leaving the rest in the wild.

5

But was Matthew Arnold a Christian? His prose usually leaves a first impression of sunshine, happiness, clarity, assurance – of 'sweetness and light' in the one phrase of his (borrowed from Dean Swift) which all the reading public regarded as typical. His books are much more tranquil than his father's sermons, or his own poems; they seem like the books of a man who has found peace, because they charm like the glimmering lake. He winks while preaching. Even the rebukes seem to come from a weary teacher who will not disturb himself enough to flog us. This mood was, indeed, what the ex-poet wanted. He wanted to be a sage; more authoritative because calmer, less easy to ridicule or hurt, than Arnold of Rugby. When a sister complained that he was becoming as dogmatic as Ruskin, he pointed out in high good humour that Ruskin was dogmatically *wrong*. A more serious reply would have been that Ruskin was, in comparison, dogmatically graceless. When the remark went round that he was a Jeremiah in kid gloves, he only commented that Jeremiah was the Old Testament prophet whose style he admired least.

This appearance of a tranquil authority succeeded because the reading public was then ripe for it, and because some readers ever since have treated this prose as one of the strengths of a great age. Of course, the religious books have not been so popular as the literary criticism. Some friends doubted whether 'Flu' Arnold had ever read them, and he himself complained in 1881 that 'whoever treats religion, religious discussions, questions of churches and sects, as absorbing, is not in vital sympathy with the movements of men's minds at present'. However, Arnold set a new standard in the assessment of literature, a new standard of knowledge, discernment, and elegance, with the result that some of his *Essays in Criticism* were being studied in English schools a century after their writing. The religious books of such an eminent critic were given special sympathy, and the irony was that the prestige of the prose stimulated the sales of the poetry at a time when the poet could only edit, revise, and add inferior pieces.

His was a time which knew that it needed guides, because it knew that a new day was dawning; and its major guides left room for Matthew Arnold. Tennyson and Browning, far greater and more popular as poets, had no comparable achievement in prose. Carlyle and Ruskin, far louder prophets in prose, were known outside the ranks of their disciples to be on the brink of insanity. Although Newman fascinated, his theology was not taken very seriously. Although George Eliot, the preacher of unbelief, was a grave and penetrating moralist, she was, no less than Newman, in conflict with the Victorian Establishment. Behind such mid-Victorian sages stood the figure of another pontifical poet-theologian, Samuel Taylor Coleridge, but Coleridge's addiction to opium had been one of the reasons why his work was fragmentary, and among many Victorians his character inspired (the word was Matthew Arnold's) 'repugnance'.

Matthew Arnold with his many compromises may be viewed as the secular Newman, as the churchgoer's George Eliot, or as the respectable man's Coleridge. But his was, after all, a great moral achievement, and that mattered to a generation which shared his own view of conduct as 'three-fourths of life'. Shaken as much as anyone by the spiritual problems resulting from the collapse of the old Christian framework, he had not allowed himself to be either paralysed or attracted into an escape which would have meant the suppression of his intelligence. That moral victory in his 'buried life' runs through his poems, while the more obvious respectability of his working and domestic life was implied by his prose. His workaday morality was made more clearly and widely known when some of his letters to his mother, sisters, and wife were edited after his death with an admiring memoir by Mr. Gladstone's friend, G. W. E. Russell. (This Christian statesman, who specialized in graceful studies of eminent churchmen, loftily remarked in his Prefatory Note about Matthew Arnold that 'his theology once the subject of some just criticism, seems now a matter of comparatively little moment'.) Matt was a model of loyalty as a son, brother, husband, father, and friend; and of industry as one of Her Majesty's Inspectors of Schools for thirty-one years from 1851.

People often complained that he gave himself superior airs. They ought to have considered what arrogance an Arnold could show – as when Matthew's brother Thomas, a man of painful integrity who sacrificed much to become a Roman Catholic, criticized the social work of the author of *Tom Brown's School-days*: as 'too democratic, too content with commonplace strivings after comfort and recreation'. As it was, Matthew Arnold, when already one of the most distinguished literary figures of the day, toiled at the constant travel and petty detail of school-inspection. For his first twelve years he was almost entirely restricted to inspecting Nonconformist primary schools, and later, when allowed to visit a wider variety, he was compelled to preside over mechanical tests of reading, writing, and arithmetic. The wonder was that he did it so competently, with so few complaints; and the result was that he could appeal to the public as one of them. A family man, he could make wry jokes about going to work on suburban trains. It was a miracle of self-discipline, because many hours of boredom must have inspired his dictum that 'to the middle class, the grand aim of education should be to give largeness of soul and personal dignity' – and his sly question whether Shakespeare or Virgil would have enjoyed crossing the Atlantic in the company of the Pilgrim Fathers.

This miracle appealed to the clergy; for his involvement in their work of social uplift, together with his literary prestige, made Matthew Arnold less unpopular with parish priests than his father had been. The clergy who invited him to address them in Sion College in London could applaud his admiration of three-fourths of their work, because it was the patently sincere tribute of a lay fellow-worker.

A man who has published a good deal which is at variance with the body of theological doctrine commonly received in the Church of England cannot well, it may be thought, stand up before the clergy as a friend to their cause and to that of the Church ... Perhaps that opinion is shared by some who now hear me. I make bold to say that it is totally erroneous ... I regard the Church of England as, in fact, a great national society for the promotion of what is commonly called *goodness*, and for promoting it through the most effectual means possible, the only means which are really and truly effectual for the object: through the means of the Christian religion and the Bible. This plain practical object is undeniably the object of the Church of England and of the clergy.

Another virtue which communicated itself to the Victorians was his courage in maintaining his intellectual activities. He said in his Preface to *Literature and Dogma* that

the plea that this or that man has no time for culture, will vanish as soon as we desire culture so much that we begin to examine our present use of time ... Give to any man all the time that he now wastes, not only on his vices (when he has these), but on useless business, wearisome or deteriorating amusement, trivial letter-writing, random reading, and he will have plenty of time for culture.

And he practised what he preached. He not only read; he made notes, and meditated on them until they became parts of his own mind. It was the reason why his books contained so many texts, biblical or secular, although these might hold less meaning for his readers. The Inspector of Schools also lectured on Homer, or Celtic literature, or 'the grand style' in general, as Professor of Poetry at Oxford; and the prophet of a new religious understanding edited Isaiah for schools. One fruit of his application to his duties and books was his zeal in reconsidering educational policy. When he began inspecting he seems to have regarded it merely as a rather better-paid job than being Private Secretary to Lord Lansdowne; he wanted to marry. In 1856 he confessed to his brother Willy that he was always tempted to say to people when asked about education: 'My good friends, this is a matter for which my father certainly had a *specialité,* but for which I have none whatever.' But unlike Clough, who also drew an income at the Education Office, he came to regard it as something more than a subsidy to a poet. He gave his mind to education.

Having seen so much, read so much, and thought so much, and having transformed the distress of his soul into the eloquence of a moralist, Matthew Arnold was able to make his own brand of dogmatism almost convincing. When he defined culture as 'the acquainting ourselves with the best that has been known and said in the world', and when he said that those who had put themselves under this discipline would show it by being 'disinterested', 'calm', and 'mild', he was able to illustrate his precepts from his own behaviour. When he extolled the culture of France or Germany, his own intellectual habits were those of a European. When he admired the standards which had been set through the the influence of the French Academy and its equivalents on the Continent, he seemed to be constituting himself as a one-man academy, to be inviting the British public to see things as they really were. When he denounced the barbarism of the aristocracy, the Philistinism of the middle classes, the near-bestiality of the Populace, and the dogmatism of the National Church, he was stating both the spiritual needs of England and the superficiality of its official pastors; he was stating what the whole romantic protest had tried to say; and he was stating these things persuasively.

Yet Matthew Arnold was in his own way both as dogmatic and as unconvincing as the enemies on whom he waged war. The glimmering wit was the dance of the sunshine on a shallow lake. Take, for example, his famous parody of the Evangelical creed.

In imagining a sort of infinitely magnified and improved Lord Shaftesbury, with a race of vile offenders to deal with, whom his natural goodness would incline him to let off, only his sense of justice will not allow it; then a younger Lord Shaftesbury, on the scale of his father and very dear to him, who might live in grandeur and splendour if he liked, but who prefers to leave his home, to go and live among the race of offenders, and to be put to an ignominious death, on condition that his merits shall be counted against their demerits, and that his father's goodness shall be restrained no longer from taking effect, but any offender shall be admitted to the benefit of it on simply pleading the satisfaction made by the son; —and then finally, a third Lord Shaftesbury, still on the same high scale, who keeps very much in the background, and works in a very occult manner, but very efficaciously nevertheless, and who is busy applying everywhere the benefits of the son's satisfaction and the father's goodness; —in an imagination, I say, such as this, there is nothing degrading, and this is precisely the Protestant story of *Justification*. And how awe of the first Lord Shaftesbury, gratitude and love towards the second, and earnest co-operation with the third, may fill and rule men's hearts so as to transform their conduct, we need not go on to show, for we have all seen it with our own eyes.

There are two possible interpretations of that passage. The first is that Arnold was protesting against the crudity of the Evangelical slogans and of other popular religion. The great Christian symbols of the infinite and inexhaustibly mysterious God as Father, Son, and Spirit had been taken by the Barbarians, the Philistines, and the Populace, and had been dragged down to their level; and preachers willing to pander to this religious market had debased the currency of serious theology. Any man who has acquired some insight into the depths of religious experience, and who has preserved some integrity in the use of religious language, is bound to protest against such triviality. Thomas Arnold's son was under a special obligation to prophesy, and the weapon of sarcasm might be legitimate. But the second possible interpretation is that Arnold by telling the 'fairy tale' of the three Lord Shaftesburys was ridiculing any attempt to use analogies drawn from human experience in order to struggle to speak of that tremendous and fascinating mystery, the ineffable; and he was doing this because he did not think that it was at all possible to talk about, or to know about, any reality beyond our experience of this world. Thus any awe, gratitude, or love felt for a transcendent God was misplaced. If this second interpretation is correct, then the help which is given to 'conduct' through the imagination by the use of Christian symbols may be regarded as help which could be discarded in a happier time, in a fuller light, when men would be able to understand, accept, and enjoy their true condition without recourse to the remnants of Christianity; and the best hope of man becomes not a return to Bible reading but the growth of a new poetry to replace the Bible.

Which interpretation best represents Matthew Arnold's thought? Almost certainly the second. Arnold was shrewd enough to know why he was so often pressed from the Right and the Left, but he never offered a clear, systematic exposition of his religious thought. He excused himself charmingly by saying that he was no metaphysician, and that after his *Last Essays on Church and Religion* (1877) he would be relieved to return to the study of literature. He placated the pious by referring to their faith as 'extra-belief', as '*Aberglaube*, the poetry of life'; their preference seemed to be optional or not verifiably certain, rather than clearly wrong. He also consoled them by pointing out that he was reckoned a religious conservative on the Continent and in the United States. Above all, he identified himself with clerical conservatism in England. His *Culture and Anarchy* (1869) echoed the alarm of the upper middle class about the advent of democracy; he was suspicious of the scheme to revise the translation of the English Bible; he was opposed to the clamour for the disestablishment of the Church of England; he was contemptuous of the style of the burial services which Nonconformist ministers were at last allowed to conduct in parish churchyards. All this was a long way from *Robert Elsmere*, the bestseller of 1888 in which his niece (Mrs Humphry Ward) told the story of an Anglican clergyman who came to see clearly that he had ceased to believe and so must go into the wilderness.

Matthew Arnold amused his readers by little jokes at the expense of those who were crudely orthodox or crudely atheistic, and he impressed them temporarily by repeating his favourite phrases in the context of his favourite quotations, thus making it clear that his intention was to edify as well as to entertain. His readers gathered that religion was closer to literature than to science, but they did not gather precisely what was the status of religious knowledge – nor what were its contents. At the very moment when he would seem to be contradicting talk (such as Bishop Butler's) about the 'moral and intellegent Governor of the universe' as contrary to the modern mind, he would find a place for it in the modern heart. 'We do not think that it can be said that there is even a low degree of probability for the assertion that God is a person who thinks and loves, properly and naturally though we may make him such in the language of feeling; the assertion deals with what is utterly beyond us.'

He preferred to speak about God as 'the Eternal', airily claiming that this was the name used by the Hebrews. God was 'the stream of tendency by which all things strive to fulfil the law of their being', or more significantly God was 'the Eternal Power, not ourselves, which makes for righteousness'. But what did the capital E signify? Did 'the Eternal' lie beyond time, or was the phrase a way of describing the universe? As F. H. Bradley asked, could one equally well speak about 'the Eternal not ourselves that makes for cleanliness'? Or might 'Early to bed and early to rise' be presented as 'the Eternal not ourselves that makes for longevity'? All that Arnold said very clearly was that men have experienced something more than themselves. 'The grandeur of the spectacle given by the world, the grandeur of the sense of its all being *not ourselves*, being above and beyond ourselves and immeasurably dwarfing us, a man of imagination instinctively personifies as a single mighty and living power; as Goethe tells us . . .' The contribution of Israel was the emphasis on the moral sense, even more than on the imaginative feeling, as the most important element in this experience. 'To one who knows what conduct is, it is a joy to be alive; the *not ourselves*, which by revealing to us righteousness makes our happiness, adds to the boon this glorious world to be righteous in. That is the notion at the bottom of the Hebrew's praise of a Creator; and, if we attend, we can see this quite clearly.'

What is evident is that Matthew Arnold brought a fine spirit and a subtle mind to the discussion of abiding mysteries. In the words of a philosopher, R. B. Braithwaite, 'his keen insight into the imaginative and poetic element in religious belief as well as his insistence that religion is primarily concerned with guiding conduct make him a profound philosopher of religion as well as a Christian teacher full of the "sweet reasonableness" he attributed to Christ'. But we cannot be so clear about the relevance of Matthew Arnold's philosophy to any tradition which regards religion as primarily the worship of the ultimate reality Matthew Arnold's 'patronage of a Christianity fashioned by himself is to me more offensive and trying than rank unbelief', Mr. Gladstone told the Duke of Argyll in 1895. His two great successors as the critic-moralists in England, T. S. Eliot and F. R. Leavis, have united with the professional theologians to dismiss his theology.

There was a perpetual ambiguity in his use of the word 'God', an ambiguity which became all the stronger as he clarified and simplified:

> God's wisdom and God's goodness! —Ay, but fools
> Mis-define these till God knows them no more.
> Wisdom and goodness, they are God!—what schools
> Have yet so much as heard this simpler lore?

The ambiguity is there, we may conclude, in Matthew Arnold's heart. However nostalgically he may admire the wisdom and goodness of the Christian past, and however prophetically he may look to the spark from heaven in the new age of science, the one thing that he cannot say is: God is real.

Since every living theology is an autobiography, Matthew Arnold was perfectly entitled to say what he knew from his own life to be true. He had found his 'best self' and his happiness through the 'not ourselves' which, by proclaiming duties, makes for righteousness; and one aspect of this discovery had been his acceptance of his status as the natural heir of one of the great Christians of the nineteenth century. He could justly say that he had striven to fulfil the law of his being. What was more open to objection was his claim that nothing more had ever really existed in Christianity. For in his *St. Paul and Protestantism* (1870) he seemed to assume that Spinoza, the seventeenth-century pantheist who was prepared to bless a warmer religion for the benefit of weaker intelligences, had thought out what St. Paul had really meant. When Jesus prayed *Abba*, Father, he meant 'the best self', and any other teaching arose because Jesus was over the heads of his reporters. The religion based on Jesus could be satisfactorily rendered as 'morality touched by emotion', with the result that 'the peace of God' became 'the Christian phrase for civilization', and the following formula became the proper statement of 'the essential facts and truths' behind the legends:

What then is the miracle of the Incarnation? A homage to the virtue of pureness, and to the manifestation of this virtue in Jesus ... What does Easter celebrate? Jesus ... dying to re-live. To re-live in Paradise, in another world? No, in this. But if in this, what is the Kingdom of God? The ideal society of the future. Then what is immortality? To live in the eternal order, which never dies.

Such a free translation of Christianity was, surely, a sublime example of the very tendency that he denounced in *Culture and Anarchy* as 'Doing as One Likes'. Yet Matthew Arnold claimed that only by his method of interpretation could the Bible be retained as the basic book of English morality.

The great danger to the Bible at present [he wrote] arises from the assumption that whoever receives the Bible must set out with admitting certain propositions, such as the existence of a personal God, the consubstantiality of Jesus Christ with this personal God who is his Father, the miraculous birth, resurrection and ascension of Jesus. Now, the nature of these propositions is such that we cannot possibly verify them.

Matthew Arnold died of a heart-attack in Liverpool in 1888, and was buried at Laleham. On his grave it is recorded not that he wrote poetry or prose, but whose son he was.

# Newman and Keble

I

When John Keble preached the Assize Sermon in the
university church of St. Mary the Virgin, Oxford, on 14
July 1833, his protest against government policy in Ireland
provided the occasion for John Henry Newman to begin
leading a religious movement. Keble's views on Ireland
did not really matter. He never went there. Even he did
not find it very easy to defend the particular abuse in
Ireland which had attracted the attention of the reforming
government in Westminster: the financial support required
by twenty-two Anglican bishops in a country consisting
largely of Roman Catholic peasants. ('What are the Protestants of Ireland', as Thomas Arnold had indiscreetly asked
in a pamphlet four years before, 'but military colonies
planted by the conquering nation who can only have a
distinct existence so long as the evils of conquest are una-
toned for ...?') On that Sunday morning in Oxford, the
government's plan to suppress ten of these dioceses was
mentioned as the main item in a list of national sins by
the preacher, who was a Tory country clergyman.

Newman, who had a passion for anniversaries, kept 14
July as the beginning of the Oxford Movement, although
curiously he left behind no account of hearing the sermon.
In 1833 he had just returned from six months abroad, his
health having broken down after years of academic overwork. While in Europe he had thought constantly of
England, of himself, and of his mission to England. For
many years already he had felt himself to be a man set
apart by God. When alone in Sicily, ill with fever, his
assurance that he had a work to do had reached a new

power of introspection and self-dedication. He could not die until his work was done; he had not sinned against the light. When he returned home, his friends did not recognize him. His body was now brown and muscular, his energy exuberant. He was determined that men should know that he was back. Keble's sermon gave him his cause.

There were, of course, many others connected with the movement of 1833. Edward Pusey was to give his name to the movement, although apparently he never cut the pages of the copy of Keble's sermon sent to him when it was printed. Hugh James Rose, a Cambridge theologian more learned and even more conservative than any Puseyite, had a name to rally the High Church party until he died prematurely in 1839. But none of these possessed Newman's flair as a journalist. It was he who conceived the idea of *Tracts for the Times*, and who wrote the first: '*Choose* your side . . .'. None of the others had quite his sense of a campaign; he once said that he burned to be a soldier. Perhaps none had quite his personal reasons for fighting in defence of the Church; and certainly none had his power to fascinate both his contemporaries and the future.

Twelve years later he was at the feet of the rain soaked Father Dominic, asking to be received into the 'One Fold of the Redeemer'. Thirty-two years from 1833, he walked towards a front door where another old man, white haired and almost deaf, stood talking. The other looked at him in puzzlement. Newman silently produced his visiting card. The old man was John Keble, who grew agitated. His wife was ill (both the Kebles were to die within a year). They already had one visitor, Pusey. But Keble invited Newman into Hursley Vicarage, and the three men dined together for the first time in their lives. Pusey dominated the meal with talk, but went off to take Evensong in the village church. Newman and Keble walked in the garden, and had just begun to resume something of their old intimacy when a sound of wheels on the drive joined the sound of church bells. Father Newman's gig had come to take him on his journey.

2

It is one of the most discussed questions in church history, why Newman and Keble parted in 1845. Newman was unable to find peace outside the Roman Catholic Church, while Keble remained a country parson. The question was intensely debated at the time. England, secular as it seemed to the Oxford apostles, was still excitable by ecclesiastical controversies. Oxford was then England's most lively centre of religious thought, and Newman had cast a spell over it. For Newman to become a Roman Catholic was somewhat like a prominent Conservative becoming a Communist in the twentieth century. And Newman, knowing how many eyes were upon him, feeling in every fibre (and how many fibres he had!) that the decision would be momentous, fasting and weeping, studying and praying, kept himself and his audience in an agony of suspense, although after 1841, if not before, it was reasonably clear that this was to be the outcome of his religious development. One by one the steps were taken: Oxford abandoned for the village of Littlemore (then part of the parish of St. Mary's), the vicarage of St. Mary's resigned (but an informal kind of monastery continued in the stables which he owned in Littlemore), past attacks on Roman Catholicism publicly recanted, the Fellowship at Oriel given up, the young men allowed to make their submission, finally – as a sign that he no longer considered himself a clergyman of the Church of England – grey trousers worn. At each stage letters of advice flooded in from friends such as Keble; at each stage his explanations flooded out. Which among all these actions was decisive? Where among all these words was the vital truth?

While he was 'on his death-bed' as an Anglican, Newman wrote and rewrote a book which was to show why he was becoming a Roman Catholic, and which was to persuade others to follow. The book was broken off because he felt that he had to submit to Father Dominic and to leave Littlemore and his library. It had this address to the reader as its conclusion:

Put not from you what you have here found, regard it not as a mere matter of present controversy; set not out resolved to refute it, and looking about for the best way of doing so; seduce not yourself with the imagination that it comes of disappointment, or disgust or restlessness, or wounded feeling, or undue sensibility, or other weakness. Wrap not yourself round in the association of your past, nor determine that to be truth which you wish to be so, nor make an idol of cherished anticipations. Time is short, eternity is long.

But *An Essay on the Development of Christian Doctrine* was not, in fact, a defence of nineteenth-century Roman Catholicism. That was a subject about which Newman at the time knew very little, although he devoted some pages to analysing a collection of popular tracts recently sent to him. He used to say that he had never met a Roman Catholic in England before becoming one. The book was about the Church fourteen or fifteen centuries before: the Church of the Fathers. It was an essay in theology, with the thesis that the history of Christianity was the history of a great idea's development; and no thorough explanation was offered to convince critics that Roman Catholicism was the only development which passed the proper tests.

In 1850 he did publish *Lectures on Certain Difficulties felt by Anglicans in Submitting to the Catholic Church.* He had delivered the lectures in London, and the audience had been impressed, but the book has not retained a place in literature. It was rhetorical and rambling. As many debating points as possible were made against 'the movement of 1833' as being 'uncongenial to the National Church' and therefore barren except as a path to Rome. As many debating points as possible were made in defence of 'the Catholic Church' – almost as effectively as that same Church had been denounced by the same author in the 1830s. A few pages were autobiographical, but Newman seemed to stand too close to his conversion for the full magic of his nostalgia to be evoked. Only occasionally do his words to Anglicans sound as if spoken in a dress-rehearsal for the coming triumph of remembrance. 'Can I wipe out from my memory, or wish to wipe out, those happy Sunday mornings, light or dark, year after year, when I celebrated your communion-rite in my own Church of St. Mary's; and in the pleasantness and joy of it heard nothing of the strife of tongues which surrounded its walls?'

In 1864, while he was close to despair about his work, Newman wrote a far more personal book in order to vindicate his motives in his submission to Rome. Charles Kingsley, a clergyman in the Thomas Arnold tradition and a popular novelist, who was then Professor of Modern History at Cambridge, reviewed a volume in the *History of England* by James Anthony Froude. In the course of the article, three fatal sentences slipped from his pen.

Truth, for its own sake, has never been a virtue with the Roman clergy. Father Newman informs us that it need not, and on the whole ought not, to be; that cunning is the weapon which heaven has given to the Saints where-with to withstand the brute male force of the wicked world which marries and is given in marriage. Whether his notion be doctrinally correct or not, it is at least historically so.

Such an insult might have been ignored. But it gave Newman the opportunity to explain and justify himself to his fellow-Catholics as well as to Anglicans, and he interpreted this opportunity as an obligation. The material lay ready to hand, in the letters and journals; it was already in his mind, in the memories. Once again he threw himself into writing a book, sacrificing all comfort to it as he had done to the *Essay on Development*, and to *The Arians of the Fourth Century* which had brought about the breakdown before the foreign tour of 1832–3. He wept as he wrote. The result was one of the immortal autobiographies: *Apologia pro Vita Sua*.

Its immediate consequence was to transform Newman's place in public opinion by vindicating his integrity. Yet even this was not a complete self-portrait. In the sub-title it was *A History of His Religious Opinions*. It proved that he had sincerely sought religious truth, which was all that he thought he had to show against Kingsley. It proved that he still believed that he had found it, which was all that he had to prove against his critics within the Roman Catholic Church. But it was not an account of all the influences which had made his mind such an extraordinary mixture of courage and 'undue sensibility', shrewdness and credulity ('If I am to bandy words it must be with sane persons', wrote Kingsley, refusing a publisher's invitation to reply to the *Apologia*); it was not a full confession. More may be gleaned from a number of fragments of *Autobiographical Writings*, collected in 1956.

Later books have attempted to fill the gaps. Some of them have concentrated on the Newman family, telling the unhappy stories of the father, a bankrupt who sank to keeping a public house in Clerkenwell; of the brother Francis who, abandoning his prospects in Anglican Oxford, became an embittered recluse in a Welsh cottage (and refused to see John before he died, for he was an atheist). When John Henry Newman deviated from the *via media*, the safe middle way of Anglican conventionality, did the explanation lie in the unusual psychology of the whole family? And was the devout John simply softer than his brothers? 'You are encouraging a nervous and morbid sensibility and irritability of mind', his harassed father had warned him back in 1822. 'Religion, when carried too far, induces a softness of mind. Take care, I repeat.' And when John inclined towards religious authoritarianism rather than his brothers' scepticism, did another bitter taunt come true? When the young John had defended the conduct of George IV, the father had sneered: 'Always stand up for men of power! And in time you will get your promotion!'

John Henry Newman's emotions have been probed from other angles. In his lifetime men detected a feminine quality in his sensitivity and in his very looks. One visitor thought of him as an old lady washed in milk. As a boy he vastly preferred his mother, who could be idealized, to the blundering father. When he was a young man, the only woman who meant much to him was, so far as we know, his sister Mary, who was aged nineteen when she died. Towards men he had a great gift for friendship; Henry Tristram has reminded us of this by a delightful study of *Newman and his Friends*. Some of the Oxford friendships with men were passionate, although all the evidence suggests that he had an innocence perhaps

possible only in that pre-Freudian time. He was devoted to
John Bowden, Hurrell Froude, Henry Wilberforce, and
Frederic Rogers, one after the other. But Bowden married
and died, Froude grew consumptive and died, Wilberforce
married, Rogers (later Lord Blachford) grew alarmed at
Newman's intensity. Each parting was bitter. When Henry
Wilberforce hoped that their friendship might continue,
Newman wrote back that 'you ask me to give you my heart,
when you give yours to another', and that he was resolved
'to make my own mind my wife'. Fortunately he had the
sense not to send the letter (although he kept it), and they
remained friends. When Newman became a Roman
Catholic, it was always clear that he would live surrounded
by a community of younger admirers; his entourage went
with him. In this circle one emerged prominently, and not
only because he helped Newman by translating German or
was in mind as Newman's eventual biographer; he was the
best friend. The *Apologia* ended with a tribute to 'dear
Ambrose St. John; whom God gave me, when He took
everyone else away'. When Ambrose St. John died,
Newman is said to have spent the whole night on the bed
beside the corpse, sobbing; and when Newman died he
was buried in the same grave. It was a generation which
accepted friendships between men as friendships; these
were a mark of the Evangelicals as well as of the Oxford
Movement. The death penalty for sodomy remained on the
statute book until 1861, and the word 'homosexual' was
not coined until 1897. In such circumstances Newman's
nature, which all acknowledged to be pure, was left in some
obscurity, at least until Sir Geoffrey Faber's study of 'vir-
ginity and friendship' in the Newman circle (*Oxford
Apostles*, 1933). But it was no accident that the attack by
Charles Kingsley, an aggressive heterosexual, included the
two words 'male' and 'marriage'.

What, then, was Newman's secret? He refused to put his
'reasons for becoming a Catholic in a teacup'. He recorded
parts of the intricacy in his journals, and hoarded every kind
of souvenir. He communicated aspects of his personality to
correspondents – more easily, it would seem than in conversation; and about twenty thousand of his letters were

preserved. He, of all men, knew that the truth about him could never be presented simply. The only book apart from his novels which he ever wrote without a driving controversial necessity, his *Essay in Aid of a Grammar of Assent* (1870), was a subtle analysis of the complexity of the forces behind 'real apprehensions'of a living religion and 'real assent' to it. In the course of that book Newman quoted some of his own words, written in 1841: 'Life is for action. If we insist on proofs for everything, we shall never come to action: to act you must assume, and that assumption is faith.' The truth about his faith and action must be complex – and more complex than even he knew. He should not be taken solely as he put himself on the printed page; that would be like the mistake, which he came to acknowledge, of believing in Anglicanism as a paper religion. But in the final analysis Newman's genius was religious, so that his psychology should be explained in terms of the thirst for God as well as in reductionist categories. Sixty years later Newman still remembered 'with what feelings I went up . . . in November 1817 for my first communion – how I was in mourning for the Princess Charlotte, and had black silk gloves – and the glove would not come off when I had to receive the Bread, and I had to tear it off and spoiled it in my flurry'. Richard Church, Dean of St. Paul's, wrote in an obituary that Newman had wanted a New Testament kind of holiness – and had not found it in the Church of England. If a single explanation has to be offered as the key to Newman, that surely must be it.

## 3

> Lead, Kindly Light, amid the encircling gloom,
> Lead thou me on!

So Newman prayed in his famous poem, written when becalmed on his homeward voyage from Sicily, a month before Keble's Assize Sermon. This light came to him as the inner light of conscience. It cannot be emphasized too much that what ended in Rome and ecclesiastical miracles began for him at the same tribunal that was revered by the moralists who wished to stay within the limits of reason. In the *Grammar of Assent*, he took the religious witness of the conscience for granted. 'Even philosophers, who have been antagonists on other points, agree in recognizing the inward voice of that solemn Monitor, personal, peremptory, unargumentative, irresponsible, minatory, definitive. This I consider relieves one of the necessity of arguing with those who would resolve our sense of right and wrong into a sense of the Expedient or the Beautiful, or would refer its authoritative suggestions to the effect of teaching or of association.' Here, in every child, was the 'external Master'. In the pamphlet where he defended the infallibility of the Pope against Mr. Gladstone in 1875, he could still remark that if he had to give a religious toast at the end of a dinner, he would propose Conscience before the Pope. In his *Apologia* he recalled how as a boy his mind had already rested 'in the thought of two and two only absolute and luminously self-evident beings, myself and my Creator'.

He could never remember a time when he had not felt certain about the reality of the Creator, although he spoke about this as the most difficult part of the Christian creed. 'I know that I know.' He seems to have been naturally religious, influenced by his mother's simple Bible piety but chiefly by his own conscience and imagination: 'I thought life might be a dream, or I an Angel, and all this world a deception, my fellow-angels by a playful device concealing themselves from me, and deceiving me with the semblance of a material world'. The experience which came to him when he was fifteen, in 1816, the experience sometimes referred to as his 'conversion', was the direct connection of this early religious sense with life's moral drama, under the influence of a schoolmaster, Walter Mayers, who had himself recently become a convinced Evangelical. But Newman's was not the full Evangelical conversion. For better or for worse, it left him still seeking. Evangelical readers wrote to point this out when he told the story in his *Apologia*, but any perceptive student of his *Justification* could have seen it some thirty years before. For Newman in that theological treatise showed no sympathy with Luther. The essential Protestant idea of 'justification by faith' seemed a psychologically meaningless formula, because he had never had Luther's experience of finding peace with God through trust in him. Not faith, placed in God once and for all, but the Church's sacraments must be the key to Christianity, for they at least were objectively real while the experience of faith was an unreliable condition. Because the heart was deceitful, its conversion could not be enough.

When he was elected a Fellow of Oriel at the age of twenty-one, he seemed a priggish, narrow-minded, tongue-tied Evangelical, and Richard Whately, the endlessly argumentative logician and hearty dog-owner, was entrusted by the Common Room with the task of bringing their new colleague out of his shell. Whately succeeded; so much so that Newman became his factotum and Vice-President of Alban Hall under him, adding up his accounts, drafting a book on logic for him, and running around like one of his dogs. But no logic could efface Newman's sense of the presence of God, or his wish to obey the will of God. Indeed, the study of logic only served to increase his emphasis on the role of the will in the formation of opinions and lives. He was ready to risk or to sacrifice all, and he knew that there was for him no guarantee of earthly comfort – or of transcendent assurance. In a conversation with Wilfrid Ward in 1885, he could look back and allow himself to half-wonder: 'Is not the ideal Christian life a very risky venture, based perhaps on a conclusion due to prejudice and fanaticism?' But after 1816 it was his way, his life.

> And with the morn those angel faces smile
> Which I have loved long since, and lost awhile.

He first saw the angels in the gardens of Grey Court House in Ham. All through his life he dreamed about those gardens and about the beautiful house. They were always his image of heaven. His father was then a banker, able to afford two elegant homes, at Ham and nearer the centre of London, for his pretty wife, his three sons and his three daughters. The children seem to have enjoyed an exceptionally happy childhood, although John, the eldest, was his mother's favourite. But the bank was ruined in March 1816. The father then tried to manage a brewery in Hampshire, but his self-confidence was gone – and was not restored on the many occasions when his wife urged him to follow John's advice in money matters. The family's status sank until all their furniture, including John's music, had to be sold. When John graduated at Oxford, it was to the immediate need to earn enough to give Frank a university education. So the 'conversion' a few months after bankruptcy was, in part, the turning of an ultra-sensitive adolescent from his feckless, now shabby-genteel, family, from the ruins of his childhood, to the Communion of Saints. Those who supported the Church, but who had their own families, could never understand the passion of Newman's devotion. As Richard Church noted: 'With Mr. Newman, his cause was identified with his friendships and even his family affections'.

The books which Mr. Mayers lent him shaped his mind for ever. Joseph Milner's *History of the Church of Christ*, with its extracts from the Fathers, introduced him to the fourth and fifth centuries, always his sacred age – a 'paradise of delight' as he wrote in 1850. Thomas Newton's *On the Prophecies* stamped Rome on his imagination, for Newton argued that the Pope was the prophesied Antichrist. Other Evangelical books showed the boy what serious, personal religion was, and he now grew convinced that he was called to lead a single life. From one of these authors, Thomas Scott, Newman drew the essence of Trinitarian orthodoxy ('Manhood taken by the Son') and with it two proverbs which expressed the pattern of his own search until it ended on a summer's evening in 1890: 'Holiness rather than peace' and 'Growth the only evidence of life'.

> The night is dark, and I am far from home—
> Lead thou me on!

His real home was now the holy city of his imagination and of the theology which he began to learn, but Newman gradually abandoned the Evangelical simplicity of the schoolboy under the pressure of Oriel College. Oriel was then the cleverest college in England, for it threw open its fellowships to examination on intellectual merit alone and not on parentage. If Oriel thought that they possessed the promise of men, such as Newman himself, who had failed to gain Firsts in the university's examinations. (Newman's own failure came because of unwise overwork – and also perhaps because the private school at Ealing had not been as efficient as Winchester or Rugby.) Newman's colleagues, almost without exception, became devout clergymen; the college was no hotbed of heresy. But in that firmly clerical Oxford the Oriel circle which included Richard Whately and Thomas Arnold was thought to be daringly liberal and reforming, and was dubbed the 'Noetics', from a Greek word suggesting 'Intellectuals'. Under Whately's tutelage the young Mr. Newman forced himself to argue as they did, and to read and write more than they did.

The college made Newman a thinker – and a pastor, for it was Provost Hawkins who persuaded Newman to gain some parish experience as a curate among the poor around St. Clement's in Oxford. Hawkins and other Fellows of Oriel explained the real Church to the young man. The Evangelicals tended to view the Church as an invisible society of saved individuals. All other men were outside; there were, as Newman noted, 'two classes, the one all darkness, the other all light'. Oriel showed Newman the visible Church, a society with a long history, a 'mixed multitude' of good and evil. It was a great corporation, responsible for the moral education of the country; but Thomas Arnold's teaching that this was its chief role – 'like a Mechanics' Institute' in Newman's phrase – could, Newman came to think, be avoided. From Whately's own (but anonymous) *Letters on the Church by an Episcopalian*, in 1826, he learned that Church and State should be independent of each other, and that in separation the Church should retain not only its mission but even its property. From other Fellows of Oriel, principally Keble and Froude who had at first been suspicious of him as an Evangelical or (worse) a Noetic, he learned to see the Church as a society of saints and sinners, believers and doubters; a society recruited and united not by its feelings or opinions but by its sacraments and creeds. His rejection of the Noetics' Protestantism in the end set up echoes far beyond the Oriel Common Room. One who looked back on the Noetics' Oxford many years later sadly concluded: 'Newman beat and supplanted them, winning the great majority of the clergy and through them of the devout but half-instructed laity, by his maintenance of a sacerdotal as against a national Church.' Not the intellectuals but the priests should decide the faith of Christians.

In his lectures published as *The Idea of a University*, Newman was to put into urbanely splendid prose, transmuted by the tears of an exile, the spell cast by Oxford through a quarter-century. It was a vision of a complete civilization with a rational and humane, but authoritative, theology at its centre; a vision of a university which was a community of talk between equals preparing to seek God as gentlemen in Church and State. But if as a Fellow of Oriel he was drifting into liberalism, preferring intellectual to moral excellence as he himself put it, his sister Mary's death in 1828 recalled him to his own vision of life. 'What a veil and curtain this world of sense is', he wrote to another sister some months later; 'beautiful, but still a veil'. His vocation was, after all, to pierce the veil, not to study the world's beauty; to be a priest, not a scholar; to renew the Church in holiness, not to reform Oxford. Years afterwards truly academic minds such as Mark Pattison's would still grow bitter with the thought of how irrelevant the whole Oxford Movement had been to the true business of a university. Oxford, Pattison held, should be dedicated to teaching, and above teaching to research in order that there might be more knowledge to teach. But what was all this to Newman? 'Now by Liberalism', he explained in the *Apologia*, 'I mean false liberty of thought, or the exercise of thought upon matters, in which from the constitution of the human mind, thought cannot be brought to any successful issue, and therefore is out of place. Among such matters are first principles of whatever kind; and of these the most sacred and momentous are especially to be reckoned the truths of Revelation.' His heart lay beside the veil – and that was one of the secrets of his fascination. Mark Pattison, now a sceptic who faced death, wrote to

him in 1883: 'I can still truly say that I have learnt more
from you than from anyone else with whom I have ever
been in contact'.

The world always lay in darkness for Newman; or rather,
the world was unreal in comparison with the Creator and
the soul. The soul was purged by the Creator's holy love, and
finally sent by the Creator to endless bliss or endless torment behind the veil. Nothing else mattered ultimately.
That was why 'I have never seen Oxford since, excepting its
spires, as they are seen from the railway' (as he wrote at
the end of the *Apologia*). Richard Whately, who became
Archbishop of Dublin but remained a formidable Noetic,
used to say that Newman had become a Roman Catholic
because the alternative for him was to have no religion at
all. Whately considered such a sacrifice to be treason to
the mind, and refused to meet Newman during all the
time when the two men were in Dublin. Of the two men,
however, it was Newman to whom his own proud words,
preached before the University of Oxford on 22 January
1832, could be applied: 'A few highly-endowed men will
rescue the world for centuries to come.'

> I loved the garish day, and, spite of fears,
> Pride ruled my will: remember not past years.

Newman remembered that once, when his mother had
pointed out that he had not got his way over some triviality
as a child, he had replied: 'No, but I tried very hard!'
Many noted that as an adult his will was imperious. That
was why he so enjoyed organizing the Tractarians, with
what he called a 'mixture of fierceness and sport'. The
strange truth about this man who wrote so exquisitely was
that he thought of himself as an activist. His grief in the
Roman Catholic Church was that he was not given 'work'
to do; he was doomed to spend his life 'indoors'. As an old
man he put up a newspaper map of General Gordon's
journey in the Sudan on the wall of his Birmingham room,
and there it remains to this day. The general *manqué*, the
donnish Caesar: that was the old Adam in him, and he
knew it. Knowing the temptation, his crucial objection to
'popular Protestantism' was that it encouraged 'private

judgement'. It failed, as he claimed in his lectures on *Justification*, to subdue the soul 'to receive the Divine Presence ... and to be made a Temple of the Holy Ghost'. Often in his early and best years as a preacher, he preached against pride.

His sermons while Vicar of St. Mary's were mostly addressed in theory to his parishoners, a few shopkeepers and college servants in the centre of Oxford. But he always found it difficult to talk with lower middle class people as contrasted with visiting the grateful poor, and everyone including Newman admitted that 'I do not know my Oxford parishoners' (as he wrote to Keble in 1840). The response came gradually, from undergraduates and young men recently elected to fellowships. They heard the message; it was so simple, but it was so tense because heartfelt, so eloquent because austerely restrained. A sentence would rush out; then a pause; then another sentence, like a nail hammered into the heart. Pride was sin. Christians must be humble before the Church. Christians must be humble before Christ, the incarnate God who had humbled himself to the death of the cross.

Like other preachers, Newman did not always find it easy to hear his own message. When he was so ill with his fever in Sicily in the spring of 1833, he reproached himself with being in Sicily at all. It was an example of his remaining wilfulness, for it had been wrong to insist on exploring Sicily instead of returning to England from Rome with his companion Hurrell Froude (and with Froude's father, a grim archdeacon). The need to obey was bound up with Newman's very idea of God, apprehended by the conscience. On his return to Oxford and the *Tracts*, he often professed his devotion to the Bishop of Oxford, Richard Bagot. 'My own Bishop was my Pope', he recalled in his *Apologia*. When Bishop Bagot criticized Tract Ninety, Newman's whole position in the Church of England was shaken, and he began to move on.

> So long Thy power hath blest me, sure it still
> Will lead me on
> O'er moor and fen, o'er crag and torrent, till
> The night is gone.

Newman felt deeply that the man of God must grow in holiness; everything except this road was a waste. When he was made a tutor of the Oriel undergraduates, he taught his favourite students with a devoted care but made no secret of his contempt for the rowdies – who were still making a noise when Thomas Hughes arrived from Rugby, as *Tom Brown at Oxford* shows. However, this intensely pastoral conception of a don's duty alarmed Provost Hawkins, who in 1828 refused to send Newman any more pupils; and Renn Hampden took over the tutorship. St. Mary's, Tractarianism, and theology became the only outlets for Newman's energies, and he hoped that his writing might earn a professorship. When the chair of Moral Theology fell vacant in 1834, he was so confident that he recorded his appointment on the title page of a new volume of sermons, but Hampden was appointed and Newman again turned back to stony paths.

But *was* the Church of England the road to holiness? It was all very well to say that an individual or a religious body must depend on creeds and sacraments, not on feelings, but as Newman's knowledge of the Establishment grew he saw to the full its weakness. Few of the clergymen who after some years adorning the university progressed with their brides to country vicarages had much of Newman's otherworldliness. In his first tract, he put to them a serious, practical question. 'Hitherto you have been upheld by your birth, your education, your wealth, your connexions; should these secular advantages cease, on what must Christ's minister depend?' His immediate answer was that they depended on 'our apostolical descent'; they were 'assistants, and in some sense representatives' of the bishops who were successors to Christ's apostles. But few of the bishops of England in 1833 were amused when Newman in that Tract wished for them the 'blessed termination' of the first apostles: 'the spoiling of their goods, and martyrdom'. (The fate which came to Bishop Bagot was a nervous breakdown resulting from the unprecedented excitements of the Oxford Movement.) Nor were they much more attracted by the theological role in which Newman had cast them. They were the spiritual lords of a Protestant country; mitres were on their silver spoons in palaces, not on their heads in parish churches. And the reluctance of the bishops to see themselves in the mirror held up by Newman was matched by the refusal of others to agree with Newman's episcopalian challenge. Evangelicals, and even liberals such as Arnold, showed that they, too, had ideas to offer.

As the contemporary scene grew more alarmingly confused, the Tractarians penetrated more deeply into the past for the ideal of the Church. Pusey's historical scholarship changed the *Tracts* from pamphlets into treatises, and he first made his mark by citing the Fathers of the Church to show that all sin after Baptism was very grave. Pusey had already bought copies of the works of the Fathers for Newman in Germany, at a shilling a volume, and Newman's *Arians of the Fourth Century*, dedicated to Keble, had attempted to display the purity of doctrine from the beginning. It was the traditional High Anglican line: orthodoxy had been accepted always, everywhere, by everyone until heretical minorities had challenged it and had evoked its definition by the great councils. It echoed the boast of Lancelot Andrewes about 'two Testaments, three creeds, four general councils, five centuries'. But gradually Newman found himself less able to take refuge from his disillusionment in the pure womb of the Patristic past. The Tractarians launched an immense series to bring back the Fathers in translation. But nowhere in these volumes did Newman find what his heart needed. The Church of the Fathers turned out to be full of controversy and confusion, like the Church of England; and Antiquity had the further disadvantage of being dead.

In the Introduction to his lectures on the *Prophetical Office of the Church* (1837), Newman wrote: 'We travel by night; the teaching of the apostles ... which once, like a pillar in the wilderness, was with the children of God from age to age continually, is in good measure withdrawn; and we are, so far, left to make the best of our way to the promised land by our natural resources.' All his arguments against Rome's authority in those lectures crumpled under the impact of his religious need. For he came to believe that he needed a pillar of fire by night, that it was not enough that the light had once shone in the darkness. There were too many quarrels in the nineteenth century about who held the light, and what it was; and dead men, as he used to say, could not decide the quarrels of the living. That applied even to his beloved Fathers; it applied also to the Anglicans whose teachings about the Church of the Fathers he attempted to bring into a synthesis in *The Prophetical Office*. 'It still remains to be tried whether what is called Anglo-Catholicism, the religion of Andrewes, Laud, Hammond, Butler, and Wilson, is capable of being professed, acted on, and maintained on a large sphere of action and through a sufficient period, or whether it be a mere modification or transition-state either of Romanism or of popular Protestantism, according as we view it.'

It was to be Newman's own developing view that Anglicanism was a transition-state – but not to popular Protestantism. As he said in *The Prophetical Office*, 'the essence of revealed religion is the submission of the reason and heart to a positive system, the acquiescence in doctrines which cannot be proved or explained'. He wanted 'an infallible oracle of truth' teaching a dogmatic system, but always the truth he wanted was a truth supporting a holy life. He edited yet another series, this time of the lives of the English saints. But those volumes could not make him a saint. He needed a living voice which he could venerate as Christ's own; a pillar moving on through the wilderness.

4

We can trace the path to Rome at two levels, emotional and intellectual. When he first saw Rome on 2 March 1833, it fascinated him more than Oxford itself. He still disapproved of its religion. Lecturing on *Justification* in 1838, he thought that the charge was 'not unfounded as regards popular Romanism, that it views or tends to view the influences of grace, not as the operation of a living God, but as something to bargain about, and buy, and traffic with, as if religion were, not an approach to things above us, but a commerce with our equals concerning things we can master'. But he slowly grew out of the idea that the Pope was Antichrist; and from his travels in Sicily he remembered a crowded village church at Mass early one morning, or the cool, dark peace of the churches in sunbaked Palermo. It has been suggested that the course of religious history might have been different, had Newman known German. He was cut off from the most important theology of his time by this lack; for example, Schleiermacher's *The Christian Faith*, first published in German precisely when Newman was forming his mind, was not to be translated until 1928, although it related Evangelical feelings to the formal Christian doctrines and to the culture of the world at a level deeper than any nineteenth-century book in English. Yet it seems improbable that the thought of Schleiermacher, or any other variety of Protestantism, would have satisfied Newman's dependence on the Holy Church – or that Germany would have satisfied his highly visual imagination. There was only one place in the world with the religious authority and glamour which he needed.

> Oh that thy creed were sound!
> For thou dost soothe the heart, thou Church of Rome,
> By thy unwearied watch and varied round
> Of service, in thy Saviour's holy home.

His friendship with Hurrell Froude at Oriel drove deeper into Newman the religious spell of Rome. Froude was clever and energetic, 'bright and beautiful' as he was remembered by his friends. He was also a dying man, in a hurry to do battle for his chosen cause. And he was odd. He brooded secretly over the sins of youth: sado-masochism appears to have been among these. He found consolation in romantic thoughts about the Church of the Middle Ages. 'Really I hate the Reformation and the Reformers more and more.' The Reformation was 'a limb badly set, it must be broken again to be right'. In 1838–9 Newman and Keble published Froude's *Remains*, including a number of such quips amid more innocuous letters and sermons. The spiritual journal now given to the world showed that

Froude was ashamed because he enjoyed being admired for his bold sailing and other athletic vigour; so he slept on the floor. He was ashamed because he liked roast goose or buttered toast; so he fasted in his college room. He wanted to impress a companion on a walk, he pretended to have read a book, he could not keep his mind fixed on the chapel services; he accused himself of many faults. Newman and Keble seem to have cut out the graver sins, which might have explained the pervading sense of guilt, but the general verdict was that they had betrayed their friend's memory by not burning the morbidly scrupulous confessions which remained.

Newman continued to brood over the mystery of Hurrell Froude. Had he or the Reformers been right? If the Reformers had been wrong, could grace still be left in the Church of England, grace which had nourished Hurrell Froude himself, grace such as that still given to the ten rebellious Northern tribes of Israel? James Anthony Froude also thought and re-thought about his dead brother, whose bullying had made his boyhood miserable. His *Nemesis of Faith* (1849) was an incoherent but moving novel about a clergyman's loss of faith. In a Preface to the second edition, he insisted that the story was not autobiography (he had never been ordained), but he added his own poignant cry: 'We seek for God, and we are sent to find Him in the words and thoughts of other nations and other ages about Him ...' Eventually he tore himself away, to become the disciple and biographer of Carlyle and the historian of the English Reformation. William Froude, the youngest brother, became a leading scientist and agnostic. He would say that he had been taught by Hurrell to apply a bold mind to Butler's theology, and had reached the conclusion that the truth of Christianity was improbable.

Newman's own thoughts went another way. He carried on an argument by letter with William Froude over thirty-five years, and rejoiced when William's wife and son (named Hurrell) were received into the Roman Catholic Church. An accident at the beginning seemed to show the path. Asked to choose a book from Hurrell Froude's library as a keepsake, he selected the Roman Catholic

*Breviary*, and was so impressed that he published a translation as Tract Seventy-five. In 1841 he published Tract Ninety, which argued that the doctrine of the Church of England had not been changed fundamentally at the Reformation, despite the evidence printed in every Prayer Book: the Thirty-nine Articles. He sought to persuade others (and himself) that the Articles, although 'the offspring of an uncatholic age', had not been intended to exclude the Catholic doctrines which he had come to regard as parts of Christian holiness. He did this by applying his logical and debating power to the Articles. Could they not be stretched to include much in Catholicism? Indeed, had not the framers of the Articles intended this in order to include Catholic-minded Englishmen in the National Church? 'The Protestant Confession was drawn up with the purpose of including Catholics; and Catholics now will not be excluded.' Almost half a century later, Gladstone – who took more trouble than Newman did to investigate the history of the Elizabethan settlement of religion – remarked to Lord Acton that Tract Ninety had been basically correct. 'The *general* argument of that tract was unquestionable, but he put in sophistical matter without the smallest necessity.'

The condemnation of Tract Ninety by the heads of the Oxford colleges, and later by the bishops, awoke Newman to the unreality of his version of Anglicanism. The Oxford Movement since 1833, he now saw, had been a defence of a Church which did not wish to be defended by his arguments. Like an indignant *prima donna*, he recalled in his *Apologia*:

I was quite unprepared for the outbreak, and was startled at its violence . . . I saw indeed clearly that my place in the Movement was lost; public confidence was at an end; my occupation was gone. It was simply an impossibility that I could say any thing henceforth to good effect, when I had been posted up by the marshal on the buttery-hatch of every College of my University, after the manner of discommoned pastry-cooks, and when in every part of the country and every class of society, through every organ and opportunity of opinion, in newspapers, periodicals, at meetings, in pulpits, at dinner tables, in coffee-rooms, in railway carriages, I was denounced as a traitor who had laid his train and was in the very act of firing it against the time-honoured Establishment.

This was Newman's way of acknowledging that Oxford now held little or no scope for his spiritual and intellectual ambition. To be sure he was still Vicar of St. Mary's; but he had never deceived himself about his effectiveness in his parish, and his prestige with the undergraduates seemed to have been broken. The defeat of Isaac Williams as a candidate for the Professorship of Poetry in succession to Keble (on the ground that he was a Tractarian) was now a reminder to Newman that he was unlikely to receive academic promotion or to be reinstated as a tutor in his college. He had assumed that he would 'live and die a Fellow of Oriel', and seems never to have seriously considered any post in the Church of England outside Oxford. In his life the Oxford chapter, and with it the Anglican chapter seemed to be closing. At bottom the necessity which drove him to challenge the Church of England with Tract Ninety was suicidal.

The ambition, however, was very far from being crude. He had been purged. On 8 April 1843 he was meditating

that God put into my heart, when 5 or 6 years old, to ask *what* and *why* I was, yet now I am forty-two, and have never answered it in *my conduct*; that if disobedience is *against nature*, I am, in the sight of Angels, like some odious *monster* which people put out of sight; that I have acted hardly ever for God's glory, that my motive in all my exertions during the last 10 years, has been the pleasure of energizing intellectually, as if my talent were given me to play a game with (and hence I care as little about the event as one does about a game) ... Various great trials struck me, 1. the having to make a Gencral confession to some one in our Church I not having full faith that our Church has the power of Absolution. 2. having to join the Church of Rome. 3. having to give up my Library. 4. bodily pain and hardship. I considered that God is used to accept offers, but I think He will not exact such.

Why, then, did he delay until 9 October 1845 his submission to the Rome where he could find light? Why in April 1842 did he retreat to Littlemore? Perhaps he was sulking; certainly he was watching. What he saw confirmed the Protestant character of Anglicanism. The Church of England co-operated with the Prussian Lutherans, who were undeniably Protestants, to sponsor a joint bishopric in

Jerusalem. To Newman it seemed a move in power politics; and it was the kind of thing Thomas Arnold would have liked. In Oxford Pusey was dropped from the list of university preachers and a dramatically public and vindictive move was made to strengthen the university's formal condemnation of Tract Ninety, although the move was vetoed by Richard Church as one the the proctors for the year. And part of the explanation of the years in Littlemore is that Newman was praying for light; no longer in a game.

Although he had never talked with a Roman Catholic in England, he knew enough about their communion to be realistic. In a few years' time, in his *Lectures on the Present Position of Catholics* (1851), he would show why 'we Catholics are so despised and hated by our countrymen'. His mood would then be defiant; and his hectic gaiety nearly landed him in prison, for a jury held that he had libelled the ex-priest, Achilli. But to decide to adopt this despised and hated position was not easy for a Fellow of Oriel. In the 1840s he knew well that the Roman Catholic gentry had been excluded from higher education for centuries, and that Roman Catholicism in England was unlikely to attract many fresh recruits except from Ireland, and that if illiterate and drunken Irish peasants were driven by hunger to make roads, canals, railways, and slums in a Victorian England full of prejudice against them the result would not be beneficial to the old Catholic gentry. In the summer of 1845, as Newman prayed and read at Littlemore, the future of Roman Catholicism in England was largely hidden from him, for it was the failure of the Irish potato crop through disease that autumn (and in 1846-7) which decided that future. But by the summer of 1845 the unpopularity of the Roman Catholic Church in England was already great enough to draw the heart of England's most accomplished theologian.

Had the Roman Catholic Church been more successful in England, it would have been less attractive to Newman. For its very weakness could now be taken as showing that it was no idol. In his lectures on *The Prophetical Office of the Church*, the danger of idolatry had been his key argument against Rome. The heart of Lecture III, on 'Doctrine of

Infallibility Morally Considered', had been this sentence:
'When religion is reduced in all its parts to a system, there
is hazard of something earthly being made the chief object
of our contemplation instead of our Maker.' Released from
this fear by the thought of the Church of Rome's ill-repute,
Newman now found what he needed in his longing for
self-sacrifice as the gate to holiness. He had found the
humble Body of Christ, to be adored because thus the Maker
might be worshipped. He had ended his articles which were
reprinted as *The Church of the Fathers* (1840) with a story
about St. Martin. The saint saw a vision of Christ; he knew
it to be a false vision, when this Christ failed to show the
the print of the nails.

In the *Essay on the Development of Christian Doctrine*, there
are three magnificent paragraphs which compare the
Roman Catholic Church in the 1840s with the Church of
the Fathers. These paragraphs were necessary to explain
why if St. Athanasius and St. Ambrose were to come to
Newman's Oxford, that 'fair city, seated among groves,
green meadows and calm streams', they would 'turn from
many a high aisle and solemn cloister which they found
there, and ask the way to some small chapel where mass
was said in the populous alley or forlorn suburb'. Two
of these paragraphs provide the climaxes to Sections II
and III of Chapter VI. The first comes at the beginning
of the chapter.

There is a religious communion claiming a divine commission,
and holding all other religious bodies around it heretical or
infidel; it is a well-organized, well-disciplined body; it is a sort of
secret society, binding together its members by influences and by
engagements which it is difficult for strangers to ascertain. It is
spread over the known world; it may be weak or insignificant
locally, but it is strong on the whole from its continuity; it may be
smaller than all other religious bodies together, but is larger than
each separately. It is a natural enemy to governments external
to itself; it is intolerant and engrossing, and tends to a new
modelling of society; it breaks laws, it divides families. It is a gross
superstition; it is charged with the foulest of crimes; it is despised
by the intellect of the day; it is frightful to the imagination of the
many. And there is but one communion such.

However, Newman himself possessed one of the best intellects, as well as the most magical style, of his day. Much of his time in the late 1830s and early 1840s was spent on the academic study of the Fathers; much of his *Development* was occupied by the assembly of this historical material, and by its adjustment to the central theme of the 'one communion'. His intellectual need was to show that the Rome of the 1840s was a legitimate, and indeed the best possible, development of the doctrine and holiness entrusted by Christ to his apostles. He began where his Anglican reading of the Fathers had left him; with the truth that if one confined oneself to what all the Fathers had taught, one was left with a creed which was too brief if one had developed a strong taste for dogma. The shrewder Anglican apologists, acknowledging this, had argued that matters such as the government of the Church by bishops had been left by the apostles for decision by others, but the absence of a strong link with the apostles had proved religiously intolerable for Newman and other High Churchmen. Newman's studies had increased the problem by revealing to him a lack of a clear agreement among the earlier Fathers – whatever the older Anglican theologians, such as Bishop Bull, had pretended. 'They make mention indeed of a Three; but that there is any mystery in the doctrine, that the Three are One, that They are coequal, coeternal. all increate, all omnipotent, all incomprehensible, is not stated and never could be gathered from them.' The Fathers then, were inadequate guides not only to ecclesiastical government but also to the most important mystery in Christianity – unless the Fathers could be interpreted by being developed. So the whole Church had in practice acknowledged by accepting the decrees of the Ecumenical Councils beginning with Nicaea. But if the earlier councils were obeyed, why not the Council of Trent which had defined modern Roman Catholicism?

The standard Anglican answer to this last question was that Rome had developed the tradition too enthusiastically and in the wrong direction. As he looked back over the pilgrimage of his own life, Newman was able to suggest a new mood by writing a general chapter on the development of ideas. He was wiser now than as a schoolboy; growth was the evidence of intellectual life.

It is indeed sometimes said that the stream is clearest near the spring. Whatever use may fairly be made of this image, it does not apply to the history of a philosophy or belief, which on the contrary is more equable, and purer, and stronger when its bed has become deep, and broad, and full ... In a higher world it is otherwise, but here below to live is to change, and to be perfect is to have changed often.

Of course not all change led to perfection: Newman knew how his own brothers Charles and Francis had developed away from orthodox Christianity. He thought he knew how his rival, the Professor of Divinity in Oxford, was going the same way without being aware of it; that had been the theme of his pamphlet of *Elucidations* of Renn Hampden's theology. But at least it could be agreed, after this introductory discussion, that all bodies of Christians, whether orthodox or not, in practice develop the doctrines of Scripture. Since the good development must be distinguished from the bad – *must*, because the soul of religion demanded it – Newman could invite all readers to agree also that 'there is a strong antecedent argument in favour of a provision in the Dispensation for putting a seal of authority on those developments'.

It must be a very strong authority, for Newman's studies of the history of the Church had shown him what a battle had been necessary to defend Christian doctrine and holiness against human error. Christianity might easily have been lost. 'If Christianity is both social and dogmatic, and intended for all ages, it must humanly speaking have an infallible expounder.' Anglicans solved this problem by pointing to the authority of the Church represented by the bishops assembled in Ecumenical Councils. But the Thirty-nine Articles had declared that great churches such as Antioch or Alexandria might err, and Newman's historical researches had confirmed the point. The Articles had added that the Church of Rome had also erred; this Newman could not now grant. His argument included emphasis on the importance of the representatives of the Popes, and of the Papacy's one theological treatise in the ancient doctrinal controversies, the short *Tome of Leo* of 446. Anglican theologians admitted that high honours had been paid in the Church of the Fathers to the see of Rome as the custodian of the memories and teachings of Peter and Paul; Newman turned the admission of Papal dignity into an insistence on Papal supremacy (although this had in fact only clearly developed from the time of Pope Leo the Great – and then only in the West). But was obedience to the nineteenth-century Papacy the right development of such early honours? Newman appealed to Butler: probability had to be the guide where conclusive proof was impossible. He found enough probability by pointing to the evidence of the holiness bred in the Church of Rome, before moving on to the more intellectual arguments that a true development of doctrine must not contradict itself and must exhibit certain 'notes': preservation of type, continuity of principle, power of assimilation, logical sequence, anticipation of its future, conservative action on its past, chronic vigour. These 'notes' could all be found in Rome.

How far, then, had the Papacy made *additions* to the creed of the apostles? Newman avoided the sharp questions about innovation, partly because the Roman Catholic definition of Papal infallibility was not clear until the Vatican Council of 1870, and partly because his style was more rhetorical than logical. But the second half of the book, unclear as it was, was definite enough that any changes in Rome had not distorted the tradition. An exhausted author broke off his discussion: 'Doctrine is where it was, and usage, and precedence, and principle, and policy; there may be changes, but they are consolidations or adaptions...'

Newman did not think that the question of the extent of the 'consolidations or adaptions' developed in Rome was crucially significant. After all, as an Anglican he already held almost all Roman Catholic doctrines, and used many Roman Catholic customs; and even in 1845 he did not intend to break completely with the spirit of Anglican Oxford. As a Roman Catholic the reserve which he felt towards Italianate or 'Ultramontane' teachings and devotions was enough to make him suspect as a crypto-Anglican, so that for years his reputation lay under a cloud in the Vatican. Newman, who would declaim that 'you must accept the whole or reject the whole', liked to speak about throwing himself into the Anglican or the Roman Catholic system, but as his critics noted in practice he largely chose what to believe and to do, after as well as before 1845; his quest for authority stopped just short of fundamentalism. His choice was for the Church of the Fathers, brought alive by the 'chronic vigour' of the Church of England or of Rome. What was crucial in his decision between England and Rome was a factor which, curiously, was not listed among the 'notes' of true development. It was the factor of Catholicism or universality.

When studying the history of the fifth century, Newman was struck by the thought that most of the bishops had wished to compromise while rejecting the heresy of Eutyches about the nature of Christ. They had made the damaging admission that Christ had only one nature; in a word, they were Monophysites. Rome had been a stronghold of the doctrine, later judged to be orthodox, that two natures, divine and human, were united in Christ. Newman asked himself: in that summer of 1839 might not Anglicans be imitating the compromising bishops, backed as those had been by political forces, instead of the orthodox Pope? 'I saw my face in that mirror, and I was a Monophysite.' That September an article by Nicholas Wiseman, later Cardinal Archbishop of Westminster, was put into Newman's hands. The article compared the Anglicans not with the heretical Monophysites, but with another ancient movement, the Donatists who were Puritans guilty of the sin of schism; and it included an anti-Donatist quotation from St. Augustine, *Securus judicat orbis terrarum*: 'The world judges safely'. As Newman later recalled, these four words 'absolutely pulverized' the Anglican appeal to Antiquity. If an infallible expounder was needed to preserve and develop Christian doctrine and holiness, his basis must be global. Authority would not be safe in the hands of local bishops in the East, who might be heretical; or in North Africa, who might be schismatic; or in England.

It would be possible, but pointless, to protest that Angli-

cans were not officially Monophysites or Donatists; that the
Church of England did not stress too exclusively the divine
nature of Christ or the holy nature of the Church. It
would also be possible to remark that *Securus judicat orbis
terrarum* was, on the face of it, not a defence of the Vatican
but a call for a public opinion poll, which Newman would
have derided. Newman knew very well that men could interpret history differently; he knew his Gibbon. It was
enough for him that historical study provided a mirror, to
help him to see his nineteenth-century face with its puzzlement and its belief. It was enough for him that history
could add precedents, when he had decided that the authority of his Anglican bishop was uncertain in comparison with the authority of the Bishop of Rome. His story,
he knew, was the story of his heart, and the motto which
he chose when he was made a cardinal summed up both
his prayer to God and his influence on men: *Cor ad cor loqui-
tur*, 'Heart speaks to heart'. He wrote in his own *Apologia*:
'It was not logic that carried me on. The whole man moves;
paper logic is but the record of it.'

5

Newman in 1845 did not see the distant scene. He believed
that at the age of forty-four his creative days were over. Now
that he had submitted to the teachings of 'the Church of
Christ', for some years he had no thought of writing another
book of theology. Who was he, to teach the teachers? If
he was to lecture in public, it would be in order to ridicule
the Church of England as the creature of the State, as
hopelessly worldly and compromising, and in order to
vindicate the Roman Catholic Church in the face of
Protestant ignorance and prejudice; here he could speak
out of experience, and he enjoyed doing so, publishing three
books based on such lectures in 1849–51. He also wrote
two propagandist novels, one (*Loss and Gain*, 1848) a
narrative of an Oxford man's conversion to Rome, the
other (*Callista*, 1856) a romance about a third-century
martyr. His chosen work was that of an educational

organizer. With other Oxford converts he founded in Birmingham a centre for prayer and study, an Oratory of St. Philip Neri (a seventeenth-century saint who reminded Newman of Keble). A school was attached to it, 'on the plan of the Protestant public schools, Winchester, Rugby, etc'. Neither the Oratory nor its school grew large, and neither escaped personal tensions around Newman; but here in Birmingham was his home.

He undertook two other adventures. Both of them were failures, both of them parts of his convert's martyrdom that gradually refined his thought until it reached the pure essence of the *Apologia*.

He became rector of a new Catholic university in Dublin, envisaging it as a centre for the higher education of Roman Catholics from all over the English-speaking world. It was to be another and better Oxford, to teach 'all knowledge' while retaining the Lord as its light and theology as its queen. It was to be an 'Alma Mater, knowing her children one by one, not a foundry, or a mint, or a treadmill'. He worked for the success of this idea of a university, with a command of detail which astonished. But the idea was stillborn. The Irish bishops had no intention of blessing the debates of another Oxford; the parents of young Irishmen wanted them to be equipped with some of the 'utilitarian' skills upon which the rector of this new university poured such elegant scorn; and the English and American Catholics saw little reason to go to Dublin. Newman received the insignia of a bishop from enthusiastic friends, for he had been promised this status, but the final appointment never arrived from Rome. This university, although equipped with a university church with many regulations, with many inspirations from Newman's eloquence, and with the nucleus of its future buildings and professoriate, never attracted more than a hundred students at a time and was not chartered to award a degree. A medical school remained from the wreckage.

His second adventure was the editorship of the *Rambler*, a magazine dedicated to the encouragement of culture among the English Catholics. When he had edited two numbers, bishops fearful of its unsettling effect persuaded him to resign. He was as helpless in this controversy as he had been in the battle of Dublin, for while believing that it was his mission to edify and educate Catholics he had no stomach for a fight with the reactionary bishops and no aptitude for intrigue. A cold dislike existed between him and Henry Manning, another Oxford convert, who became Archbishop of Westminster in 1865; but Newman was unwilling to lend his support openly to the opposition to Manning's religiously reactionary and socially progressive policies. When Manning twice frustrated a plan for Newman to open a branch of the Oratory House in Oxford, his victim kept silence although he had confessed to dreaming of another Oxford Movement. Newman had said when the Roman Catholic hierachy was restored in 1850, 'we want theology, not bishops' – and now they had Manning. When Manning's insistence that the infallibility of the Pope should be decreed carried the day at the Vatican Council in 1870, Newman's attitude was that this doctrine was true, but that it was not expedient to proclaim it. He refused to be a consultant at the council, but in a private letter which was leaked to the press he branded the party demanding the decree as an 'insolent and aggressive faction'. He also let slip a complaint about the 'Roman malaria' at the foot of the rock of St. Peter.

A vague idea that Newman might supervise a new translation of the Bible came to nothing because the bishops declined to be sponsors. Meanwhile Newman did not produce any major defence of Christianity against the new secularism. He was sensitive to the censorship, or at least displeasure, of Rome; 'it is like the Persians driven to fight under the lash'. He wrote privately in 1864 that 'unless one doctored all one's facts one would be thought a bad Catholic', and his cowardice in accepting this situation angered Lord Acton, the English historian who led the fight against his fellow-Catholics' dishonesty. Part of the trouble was that, unlike Acton, he was not really in touch with the best thought of the day on an international basis, although his praises of Christian scholarship were sincere enough. His *Essay in Aid of a Grammar of Assent*, although it appeared in the same year as the infallibility decree, could be published because in it Newman did not need to get involved in too many embarrassing discussions of specific dogmas. The book had an inner integrity; he had been saying much the same thing while an Anglican, and the developed form of the *Grammar* was the emotion of his successive religious crises recollected in the tranquillity of his mature philosophy. He pondered it, and struggled to write it, at intervals over twenty years. It had two targets. On the one hand, it rebuked sceptics who refused to acknowledge the seriousness and subtlety of religious decisions; and on the other hand, it rebuked theologians who fancied that the acceptance of a creed was a simple matter of logical inference – because they, too, had never been through the slow pain of making such a decision. Yet, for all the force of its analysis or 'real assent' to religious doctrines, it was not a definitive work of philosophical theology. It would be more accurate to classify its exposition of the 'illative sense' under 'psychology' or 'phenomenology' of religion. It was not likely to exert a profound influence on the revival of deep studies of St. Thomas Aquinas which began in the Roman Catholic Church after Newman's day. Nor was it likely to convince the sceptics, for they would dismiss Newman as a man credulous from boyhood. It cannot be denied that Newman gave his real assent to legends which most educated Roman Catholics a century later would despise.

It is a record of disappointment after the brilliant promise of the 1830s. Pusey commented shrewdly that the Church of England had not known how to employ Newman, and if we take 'employ' in the rather subtle sense which Pusey must have intended we can see that the Church of Rome was equally at a loss. We cannot be surprised that before the *Apologia* the rumour spread that Newman was about to become an Anglican again. He contradicted this report, adding for good measure that 'the thought of the Anglican service makes me shiver'. Such bitterness came, however, from unhappiness. Newman wrote in his journal for 15 December 1859:

I am writing on my knees, and in God's sight . . . When I was young I thought that with all my heart I gave up the world for Thee . . .

When I was older and in Anglican Orders I prayed absolutely and without condition against rising in the Church ... I knew what I was saying, and how it is Thy way to grant, to fulfil such petitions and to take men at their word ... O my God, not as a matter of sentiment, not as a matter of literary exhibition, do I put this down. O rid me of this frightful *cowardice*, for this is at the bottom of all my ills. When I was young, I was bold, because I was ignorant — now I have lost my boldness, because I have advanced in experience. I am able to count the cost, better than I did, of being brave for Thy sake, and therefore I shrink from my sacrifices.

Next month he again wrote at length in his diary about his failures and his loneliness. 'O my God, I seem to have wasted these years that I have been a Catholic. What I wrote as a Protestant has had far greater power, force, meaning, success, than my Catholic works, and this troubles me a great deal ...'

The success of the *Apologia* four years later brought him out of that particular depression. But disappointment remained. Thomas Arnold's biographer was among the Anglicans who renewed their contacts with Newman as a result of the self-disclosure and the charity of the *Apologia*; and Stanley recorded a long conversation with Newman in the autumn of 1864.

It left the impression, not of unhappiness or dissatisfaction, but of a totally wasted life, unable to read, glancing at questions which he could not handle, rejoicing in the caution of the Court of Rome, which had (like the Privy Council) kept open question after question that he enumerated as having been brought before it; also, although without the old bitterness, still the ancient piteous cry. 'O my mother! why dost thou leave us all day idle in the market place?' Studiously courteous, studiously calm.

Even when Stanley's touch of complacency as the literary and popular Dean of Westminster has been discounted, this impression remains representative of the thoughts of observers who remembered the past (as Newman himself did so thoroughly). And the disappointment remains for those who have experienced that world-wide crisis of religion which Newman expected. 'My apprehensions are not new, but above 50 years standing', he wrote in a letter of 1877. 'I have all this time thought that a time of widespread infidelity was coming, and through all those years the waters have in fact been rising as a deluge. I look for the time, after my life, when only the tops of the mountains will be seen like islands in the waste of waters.' Against that day, what had Newman done?

In 1879 he was made a cardinal by Pope Leo XIII; Leo was an imaginative aristocrat who had quietly groaned under the reactionary Pius IX. A last-minute manoeuvre by Manning to prevent the honour failed. Newman was allowed to remain at the Birmingham Oratory and was too old to play any part in the politics of the Church, but he was delighted, feeling that 'the cloud is lifted from me for ever'. Two years previously he had been made an Honorary Fellow of Trinity College, Oxford, which pleased him almost as much.

Even now, however, Newman did not foresee the nature of his posthumous destiny. When he received the red hat of a cardinal in Rome, he restated the purpose of his life. 'For thirty, forty, fifty years I have resisted to the best of my powers the spirit of liberalism in religion.' He explained such liberalism as

the doctrine that there is no positive truth in religion, but that one creed is as good as another . . . Revealed religion is not a truth, but a sentiment and a taste; not an objective fact, not miraculous; and it is the right of each individual to make it say just what strikes his fancy. If a man puts on a new religion every morning, what is that to you? It is as impertinent to think about a man's religion as about his sources of income or his management of his family. Religion is in no sense the bond of society.

Newman saw that education was spreading this attitude. It was 'a universal and thoroughly secular education, calculated to bring home to every individual that to be orderly, industrious, and sober is in his personal interest', instead of being based on the supernatural sanctions or religion. And Newman concluded by bidding his hearers not to fear this movement. 'Christianity has been too often in what seemed deadly peril, that we should fear for it any new trial now . . . Commonly the Church has nothing more to do than to go on in her own proper duties, in confidence and in peace; to stand still and to see the salvation of God.'

This was a suitable speech for an old man on being made a cardinal. It was a suitable speech for a Christian who was a lifelong conservative. But it was not a speech which hearers in Rome would regard as special for anything more than its beauty. Its dogmatism was precisely the cause which had been invoked against the new cardinal by Manning and the other fanatical or foolish guardians of religion; and outside Manning's Church, it was a lost cause in England. When he had regarded Rome as Antichrist, Newman had been logical in believing that an Englishman should not be allowed to vote if he was of the Roman Catholic religion; but even in 1829 Newman had reluctantly accepted Roman Catholic emancipation, and religious liberty and toleration were now established. Back in 1841, Newman had written seven long letters to *The Times* brilliantly ridiculing Sir Robert Peel's support of popular education when opening the Tamworth Reading Room, on the ground that Sir Robert had not mentioned God enough, and had trusted in education to improve the morality of the people; but history had not laughed at Peel. Was Newman, then, merely trying to put the clock back? Was his nostalgia irrelevant to the hard questions which Thomas and Matthew Arnold had asked (if not answered): what kind of a truth was in religion, and how should the Churches while trying to teach it view each other, and how was it to be apprehended by the conscience, and how was it to be related to a democratic society? If the speech at Rome in 1879 had represented Newman's only contribution to the coming Catholicism, the opening sentence of Chapter V of his *Apologia* would have had a truth fatal to his significance for the future: 'From the time that I became a Catholic of course I have no further history of my religious opinions to relate.'

As it was, Newman was able to add immediately in the *Apologia*: 'I do not mean to say that my mind has been idle, or that I have given up thinking on theological subjects.' And that was one of his winsome understatements. It was true that he could write in complete sincerity: 'I never have had one doubt'. But he did not attempt to maintain a rigid dogmatism, at least not by Roman standards; and his degree of flexibility was to be influential precisely because his intention to submit his mind to the mind of the Roman Catholic Church without one doubt could be questioned even by the malignant, because his achievement of orthodoxy could not be assailed except in details or by the ignorant, and because no one could look on his old age without realizing that here was a man who, mistaken or not, lived for God. His legacy thus remained available to those whose task in the twentieth century would be the updating of the Roman Church, to the delight of the 'separated brethren' of other Churches. The *aggiornamento* around the Second Vatican Council, with all its ecumenical fruit, grew from loyally Catholic roots, and it would be both an insult and an error to call it a concession to Protestantism. However, among all the theologians of the Roman Catholic past John Henry Newman seemed most symbolic of the spirit of that Council of Renewal, Aquinas himself being read in his light; and those accused of innovating could always appeal to his name. We may conclude that although he so dramatically left the Church of England, and so eloquently and so often denounced it, John Henry Newman always embodied, and in the end spread, much of what was best in the spirit of Anglicanism. It was his destiny that he, who depicted the chasm between the devout and the liberal, was to be valued later by his fellow-Catholics as a bridge-builder; that he, who came to be at ease only among the faithful in Birmingham, was later, after his death, to be admired widely as the voice of Oxford in Rome.

An article by Newman in the *Rambler* in 1859, which was delated to Rome for heresy (without result), advised the bishops to consult the faithful in matters of doctrine. Newman did not completely explain what he meant by 'consult', but the principle that the laity as well as the hierarchy could, and did, guard the faith was a principle to be acknowledged by the Second Vatican Council. The importance of sober and honest theology, for which Newman contended in his day according to his lights, was acknowledged by that council's method of work, involving consultations between the bishops and distinguished and articulate theologians – who, unlike Newman, did not refuse to be consulted. The *Development*, which no theologian in Rome could understand when Newman took it there in 1846, was being widely used in a theological renaissance more than a century later to show Catholics how it was not heretical to suggest that doctrine had indeed developed – and might develop again, for even orthodoxy must be seen as coloured by its historical background, and thus opened to future change. The *Grammar of Assent*, which had survived the reign of the scholastic textbooks with their cold 'proofs' of the faith, was being expounded in order to show that some men's minds could be profoundly aware of the mystery of religion, and aware of the difficulties involved, and yet could hold Christianity as true. Newman's attitude to the Bible, where he acknowledged human elements but found the source of the river of tradition and the food of prayer, was being studied to inspire both the scholarship and the devotion of the biblical revival. *The Idea of a University*, all that survived from the dream of Dublin, now provided a golden text preaching the freedom and vitality of man's mind to Christian humanists. Even where men did not read any of his books, Newman's name was invoked as patron by graduates. It could even be pointed out that Newman was not a complete Tory in politics. He was cynical about all states, whether Liberal or Papal; his name could be cited by those who wanted a renewed Catholic Church to stand on its own spiritual feet.

The name of Newman also became acceptable to Anglicans. One day in 1862 he met in a London street a former curate of his, a priest who was still an Anglican, W. J. Copeland, and pressed him to talk at the Oratory: he did not wish to convert, but to remember. Out of their renewed friendship came the idea that Copeland would edit anew Newman's *Parochial and Plain Sermons*. As a Roman Catholic Newman had tinkered with them, but in vain: they had stopped selling. Now republished without censorship, they – or extracts from them, or the vague reputation of them – recovered for Anglicans the sense which undergraduates had felt in St. Mary's: the sense that through Newman the Christ of the gospels spoke, and through the Christ of the gospels the eternal God. Stanley said about these sermons: 'They belong, not to provincial dogma, but to the literature of all time'. Gladstone, although he considered Newman 'no philosopher' in comparison with Bishop Butler, said boldly in 1866 that 'since the days of Butler the Church of England has reared no son so great as Newman', and gave the style of Newman's sermons as his reason. 'I find myself constantly disposed to cry aloud ... It is like the very highest music, and seems sometimes in beauty to go beyond the human.'

On Monday 25 September 1843 Newman preached his last Anglican sermon, in the little church which he had built at Littlemore. Twenty-five years later, a passer-by found Newman at the same church, 'leaning over the lych gate crying. He was to all appearances in great trouble. He was dressed in an old grey coat with the collar turned up and his hat pulled down ...' But in 1843 his congregation did the weeping, as they heard:

And O my brethren, O kind and affectionate hearts, O loving friends, should you know any one whose lot it has been, by writing or by word of mouth, in some degree to help you; if he has ever told you what you knew about yourselves, or what you did not know; has read to you your wants or feelings, and has comforted you by the very reading; has made you feel that here was a higher life than this daily one, and a brighter world than that you see; or encouraged you, or sobered you, or opened a way to the inquiring, or soothed the perplexed; if what he has said or done has ever made you take an interest in him, and feel well inclined towards him; remember such a one in time to come, though you hear him not, and pray for him, that in all things he may know God's will, and at all times he may be ready to fulfil it.

In the Church of England as in the Church of Rome, many have granted that request. In his tribute at his death, Richard Church could 'almost say' that Newman was 'the founder of the Church of England as we see it'. This direct influence of Newman the preacher an Anglican spirituality – or the more blurred image of Newman the man in the Anglican imagination – was part of the whole triumph of the Oxford Movement, which raised the spiritual level of parochial, diocesan, and national life, and expanded the Anglican Communion in prayer as well as geography. The fiftieth aniversary of Thomas Arnold's death found the Archbishop of Canterbury, E. W. Benson, reflecting in his journal: 'It is impossible not to see that everything almost which distressed Arnold in Church life is changed for the better but mainly by the agency of the Oxford Movement which he opposed.'

6

There have been some who have remembered Newman's disclosure of the secrets of human hearts and his pointing to a 'higher life', without thinking the nineteenth-century dogmatism of the Roman Catholic Church an absolutely necessary safeguard.

In 1876 a religious novel by a Birmingham manufacturer of chemicals became a best-seller. The author of *John Inglesant*, J. H. Shorthouse, was an Anglican, and his book ended with a discussion about the Church of England, set by the river in Worcester one evening in the seventeenth century. John Inglesant expounded the Anglican position to a doctor, Valentine Lee.

I am not blind to the peculiar dangers that beset the English Church. I fear that its position, standing, as it does, as a mean between two extremes, will engender indifference and sloth, and that its freedom will prevent its preserving a discipline and organizing power, without which any community will suffer grievous damage; nevertheless, as a Church it is unique: if suffered to drop out of existence, nothing like it can ever take its place.

His companion protested that such a compromise was not enough. 'If there be absolute truth revealed, there must be an inspired exponent of it, else from age to age it could not get itself revealed to mankind.' 'That is the Papist argument', answered John Inglesant; 'there is only one answer to it – Absolute truth is not revealed.' 'But if absolute truth is not revealed', Dr. Lee inquired, 'how can we know the truth at all?' Inglesant gave a long answer, in which the key quotation was: 'the Kingdom of God is within you'.

John Keble was not among the Anglicans who accompanied Newman to Rome. He stayed loyal to the Church of his baptism and ordination because the Kingdom of God was in it. That loyalty became even more than Pusey's refusal to move, the focus of a very English variety of Catholicism. The popularity of his *Christian Year* in his lifetime made him the most humanly appealing exponent of this happy Anglicanism, for Victorians at many different heights of churchmanship and social status loved and used the book – 'without equal, the Bible excepted, in the English language', as Thomas Arnold roundly declared. The most popular poems in that collection were harvested for the hymnals, so that since Keble's death innumerable Anglican congregations have continued to sing his explanation of where his heart found peace and the Kingdom:

> Old friends, old scenes, will lovelier be,
> As more of heaven in each we see ...

> We need not bid, for cloistered cell,
> Our neighbour and our work farewell,
> Nor strive to wind ourselves too high
> For sinful man beneath the sky:

> The trivial round, the common task,
> Would furnish all we ought to ask,—
> Room to deny ourselves, a road
> To bring us daily nearer God.

It was a domestic creed. Keble's father was altogether more stable than Newman's; he had the same name as his son, and much the same nature. Born at Court Close, Fairford, in one of Gloucestershire's most delightful small towns during the year of the last Jacobite rising, John Keble senior died in the same house in 1834, having married a parson's daughter who bore him five children, and having done his own duty as a clergyman by ministering as the incumbent of the village of Coln St. Aldwyn, two or three miles away. For a time he was also a Fellow of Oriel. This tranquil life was a glimpse of heaven to John Keble junior, and nothing broke his loyalty to it. He remained at heart what he was as a boy, never seeking the second birth of the Evangelicals, never tempted towards the modernism of the liberals. He was one of the most elegantly accomplished scholars in the university, but his education had been entirely at home until he had won a scholarship to Oxford at the age of fourteen, and his heart never left home. He gave the best years of his life, 1823 –35, during which by his own account there was a major crisis in Church and State, to looking after his father and Coln St. Aldwyn. One of the most influential priests in Anglican history, in his maturity he used to say about a theological proposition with which he agreed that it was exactly what his father had taught him.

Some letters, and some poems in *The Christian Year*, hint at moods when the son contemplated the possibility that he might be wasting his life in his father's house, and when the round in Gloucestershire seemed too trivial. But such depressions were soon brought under his dominant feeling that by denying any worldly ambitions – by refusing the Archdeaconry of Barbados which was offered to him in 1824 and which was then worth '2,000 a-year, &c., &c.', and by so behaving that no official dignity was even offered to him in England – he would be brought nearer to God amid old scenes. Newman, on the other hand, could never get back to that security after the loss of the angel-faces in the garden of Ham. When Newman stayed with the Kebles in 1828 (the visit had been arranged by Hurrell Froude) he saw 'Keble's verses, as it were, written on all their faces'; but he saw this family life as an outsider. When Keble published a book of poems about children in order to raise money for building a new church at Hursley (*Lyra Innocentium*, 1846), Newman never acknowledged the copy which the 'always your affectionate and grateful J. Keble' sent him, but instead published in the *Dublin Review* an article in which he argued that a man of Keble's poetic temperament should not rest content with the dreary scene of Anglicanism, where the royal arms had replaced the crucifix. 'Poetry is the refuge of those who have not the Catholic Church to fly to and repose upon; the Church itself is the most sacred and venerable of poets.'

Another contrast between Newman and Keble arose from Keble's dependence on women. Keble did attract sensitive men; there was a beauty in his looks and his whole life, and he could be light hearted (but so could Newman). But he never needed the devotion of men. He fell in love with a young lady in Devon; later he set his heart on Cornelia Cornish. His 'humdrum marriage' (Newman's phrase) with Charlotte Clark after his father's death in 1835 may have begun as an affair of convenience (Charlotte's sister had married his brother Tom), and they had no children; but his love for her deepened as he nursed her through various illnesses, until by the 1860s it had become all that a Christian marriage should be. He was also devoted to his sisters; one of them who had an artificial leg lived gently in his vicarage. A very frequent visitor to his vicarage, and to the homes of deserving poor in his parish, was Charlotte Yonge, whose novels were to do almost as much as his poems to spread the aroma of Tractarian piety. These women in Keble's life were delicate creatures, spending much time on the sofa, but to see them in church for daily Evensong when they were able to manage the little excursion meant more to Keble than to see the Fellows of Oriel polishing their logic over their port.

Continuity marked his affections to the moment when he was wheeled silently away from his wife's sickbed because his own time had come to die, and his spirituality never wavered. In Holy Baptism, the baby was filled with a supernatural life; in Holy Communion, as the little congregation held out empty hands Christ was really present (in the heart and, as he came to add after a long conservative hesitation, also in the hands). The whole countryside was an extended church, where nature preached. The bishops were remote from this idyllic scene, and Keble never bothered much about them; when his bishop refused to ordain his curate as a priest because the young man's theology was suspect, Keble carried on with him as a deacon. But the absent bishops could be regarded through the golden haze as in some sense heirs of the apostles, and therefore their defence against the politicians seemed part of one's religious duty. What mattered here was not so much episcopacy as the belief that the Church depended on Christ's presence, not the State's favour. John Keble used to say that, whatever happened outside, the Church of England would always be found in his parish.

For almost twenty years he had no full-time job of his own, but alternated various curacies with periods in Oxford (where he was Professor of Poetry 1831–41, lecturing in Latin, praising Wordsworth but disparaging Shelley, Byron, and even Milton on moral grounds). As a position to take in nineteenth-century life, it was too mild even for the Fellows of Oriel, who did not elect Keble when the provostship fell vacant in 1827. 'We are not electing an angel but a provost', remarked Newman, for whom Keble resembled 'something one put under a glass case and kept on one's chimney-piece for one's children to admire'. The parish where Keble settled instead was not a complete paradise; the Baptism register shows how many of the girls were pregnant as they came to be married, and some of the boys delayed touching their caps to the Vicar until they received his stick across their shoulders. And he was not completely content. His lack of theological power during what he habitually referred to as the Church of England's 'very great and continued distress' grew painfully apparent, to himself as to others (when presenting the correspondence to Keble College, Oxford, Newman censored as too embarrassing the many passages where Keble blamed his own inadequacies). But as Vicar of Hursley for thirty years, he still lived under something like a glass case, for the squire, Sir William Heathcote, who had been one of Keble's most admiring pupils, virtually owned the village and would allow no Dissenter, let alone an atheist, among his tenants.

Keble refused to expose himself either to Oriel (where Newman learned the logic which he was to deploy in Tract Ninety and the *Apologia*) or to Birmingham (where, at least in his early years, Newman spent a good deal of his time hearing the confessions of the poor). And Keble paid a price. He became the editor of Richard Hooker, the compiler of a life of the saintly Bishop Wilson, an unwearying student of the Fathers; but he was incapable of intellectual creation. In handling his own time, his ignorance of the world crippled his judgment. He would refuse to discuss 'infidelity', saying briefly to a young inquirer in 1851 that most of the men who had difficulties as to the inspiration of Holy Scripture were 'too wicked to be reasoned with'. He even lacked insight into how the minds of other Oxford clergymen were likely to react to theological events. His advice was often sought by the young Newman, who took a long time to get over his sense of awe on that first evening as a Fellow of Oriel. How difficult it was to call the great Mr. Keble by his mere surname! But how charming he was to the gauche newcomer at dinner! On at least two occasions, however, Keble's advice to Newman proved disastrous: when he strongly encouraged the publication of Froude's *Remains* and of Tract Ninety, apparently not expecting the indignation which would be aroused by these major indiscretions. We cannot wonder that Newman, while he wrestled with the Fathers and his own soul at Littlemore, depended no longer on Keble, although they exchanged friendly letters; nor that the two men, once such intimate allies, ceased to correspond after the crisis of 1845.

Why, then, was Keble College founded as a national monument to this escapist country priest? Because many believed that the system of values illustrated by Keble and his parish ought to be preserved in an Oxford dominated by Matthew Arnold and worse. Because Keble's stability at Hursley symbolized what was steady in the Anglican revival of clerical duty and church life; he fasted and was humbly penitent, he happily saw God in the countryside and the villagers, he was constant at daily services in church, he prayed for his people and 'waited on' them in their homes regardless of his personal convenience, he prepared young people for Confirmation in twenty or thirty classes for each, he taught for two hours a day in the village school. Because his quiet work as a director of souls made it less thinkable for another devout Anglican soul such as Hurrell Froude (or Newman) to struggle for Catholic holiness without a guide. And because it all added up to a spiritual revival. The Tractarians, in the judgment of Professor Owen Chadwick, 'weakened the Church in politics by dividing; and in dividing, by loosening its grip on the Tory party and the crown ... [They] weakened the Church in popular esteem by making laymen suspicious of clergymen ... But beneath the popular disesteem and public weakness they strengthened the soul of the Church of England.'

Keble's sermon had been the beginning, and his *Christian Year* had been the poetry, of this movement; he had been its saint. Accordingly Richard Church, who eyed with alarm some of the strange men coming as mourners and claiming a share in the legacy, found his funeral 'more like a festival than anything else, with the sun and the fresh keen air, and the flowers just coming out, and the beauty of the place and the church, and the completeness of that which had come to its last stage here'.

# 3

# Wilberforce and Tait

I

Anthony Trollope's *Barchester Towers* (1857) began with speculation around a bishop's deathbed. 'The illness of the good old man was long and lingering, and it became at last a matter of intense interest to those concerned whether the new appointment should be made by a conservative or liberal government.'

There was such an incident in 1868, when the *Last Chronicle of Barset* had only recently come out with its hints that Archdeacon Grantly or his successors would probably not be dominating many more dinner tables in the county, and that the hidden influence of the saintly Septimus Harding was also in jeopardy. In such a time of crisis, the mortal illness of an Archbishop of Canterbury aroused interest. It was an age of 'improvement' and it was commonly thought that there was room for improvement at Lambeth Palace. Newman, for one, believed about the Anglican Church that 'as her prospects have opened and her communion extended, the See of Canterbury has become the natural centre of her operations'; he drew the conclusion that 'no Church can do without its Pope'.

Who, then, would make the new appointment?

As Archbishop Longley lingered with bronchitis, Disraeli's Conservative government was tottering under the impact of Gladstone's new cry that the Church of Ireland must be disestablished. If Gladstone became Prime Minister in time, it was understood that he would move Samuel Wilberforce, Bishop of Oxford, a moderate High Churchman, to the Primacy. But Disraeli had in mind Charles John Ellicott, Bishop of Gloucester and Bristol, a moderate Evangelical. He was an industrious pastor, and healthy enough to work as a bishop until 1904. A Cambridge scholar, and the tireless chairman of the company of the scholars revising the English version of the New Testament from 1870 to 1881, he obstinately upheld the infallibility of the Bible in its original tongues. And he was a Conservative, strong in the defence of the Church of Ireland and likely (Disraeli reckoned) to rally to the Conservative candidates in the forthcoming general election all who distrusted Gladstone either as a Liberal or as a High Churchman. He struck most men of the world as a talkative ass. Could he be as silly as he seemed? 'He has a foolish voice and manner which make him appear weaker than I believe he really is', Lord Derby wrote. Disraeli, who did not care for clerical society, had not taken the trouble to get to know him.

In the end, neither Wilberforce nor Ellicott was promoted. Archbishop Longley died on 27 October. Disraeli remained Prime Minister until 1 December, but Queen Victoria refused to consider Ellicott or Disraeli's other ideas. Only one man was possible in her eyes: Archibald Campbell Tait, Bishop of London, 'an excellent, pious, liberal-minded, courageous man, who would be an immense support and strength to the Church in these times', as she told Disraeli on the day when she heard of the death of the 'worthy and amiable' Longley. Disraeli did his best to persuade her that Tait was too Broad Church to be a strong churchman, and too sympathetic to be a leader.

Acknowledging his abilities and virtues, Mr. Disraeli finds him as an Ecclesiastical statesman obscure in purpose, fitful and inconsistent in action, and evidently, though earnest and conscientious, a prey to constant conflicting convictions ... This is to be observed of the Bishop of London, that, though apparently of a spirit somewhat austere, there is in his idiosyncrasy a strange fund of enthusiasm, a quality which ought never to be possessed by an Archbishop of Canterbury, or a Prime Minister of England. The Bishop of London sympathises with everything that is earnest; but what is earnest is not always true; on the contrary, error is often more earnest than truth ... Is this the Prelate who can lead the Church? The Church *must* be led: gently, but firmly and consistently. It will not do any longer merely to balance opposing and conflicting elements.

Privately he lamented that Tait's appointment 'will please only a few clerical freethinkers' and 'some Romanizers'. Was it not a tragic waste of a political opportunity? But Disraeli had already betrayed his ignorance of ecclesiastical personalities by his suggestion of Ellicott. He had no convincing alternative to offer ('I could win if I had a man'); and he had to give way to the insistent Queen.

On 13 November 1868, therefore, Tait received Disraeli's 'desire, if it meet your own wishes, to recommend Her Majesty to elevate you to the Primacy'; and he promptly replied with an acceptance. Wilberforce did not even get the vacant London; any question of a move for him was settled at this point by the announcement that his daughter was becoming a Roman Catholic. Disraeli moved the colourless Jackson to London from Lincoln, and Wilberforce contented himself with writing about Disraeli as 'a master of selfish cunning and unprincipled trickery' – and with advocating concessions to Gladstone's ecclesiastical policy.

Tait had been almost certain that Disraeli would choose William Thomson, Archbishop of York, for Canterbury, and would send Samuel Wilberforce to York. And this forecast reveals his opinion of Disraeli, for Thomson's career had been an example of energy rather than earnestness. While an undergraduate William Thomson wrote a textbook on philosophy which compensated for his Third in the examinations and ensured his return to the Queen's College, Oxford, after brief curacies. As a don he was a success: he was Tutor, Chaplain, Dean, Bursar, Provost, active and reforming. He was also much in demand as a preacher in London. He was consecrated Bishop of Gloucester and Bristol at the age of forty-two in 1861, and his first episcopal act was to preach about the death of Prince Albert. Within a year he was telling his handsome wife, 'My dear, I am the Archbishop of York'. She replied: 'Oh, *do* go and lie down.'

He was an active archbishop for more than a quarter of a century, promising to hold a confirmation in any village which could muster ten candidates, consecrating a hundred new churches, and specially liking to deliver vigorous, common-sense addresses to the working men of Sheffield.

(Sheffield did not have its own bishop until 1913.) He certainly did better than, for example, Vernon Harcourt, who was Archbishop of York for forty years from 1807. But despite all his pleas for the reconciliation of religion and science, it could not be pretended that he had any very convincing theology of his own. Nor, for all his addresses in Sheffield, could it be pretended that he had a clear view of the emerging democracy, In 1886, four years before his death, he plunged into a major controversy with the churchwardens of St. Mary's, Beverley, who wanted to open all the seats in the church to all parishioners. This shocked Archbishop Thomson, who threatened legal proceedings and invited the parishioners to inform him of their social status so that he could personally distribute the seats in their parish church 'according to their degree'. Neither Ellicott nor Thomson as Archbishop of Canterbury would have been reckoned among Disraeli's more brilliant coups.

Wilberforce and Tait better deserve our study, for they were better examples of the industrious clergyman in Victorian England. Tait himself quoted Wilberforce's example when he spoke to the clergy: 'No men have greater means of guiding their fellows then we have, if we learn from those who have gone before us to sanctify whatever gifts God has bestowed upon us, by devotion to His service, by making the study of His Word the great object of our lives, and by giving ourselves to unwearied toil.' On that occasion, Tait could not resist adding a jab at his dead rival. 'He had doubtless his faults – some say they were grave ones – but who has not?' This was more than an unkind aside. Wilberforce and Tait, united in their power of self-dedication, were dedicated to different policies.

An important issue was decided for the time being when the powerful Tait was preferred above Ellicott or Thomson; and another issue when Wilberforce was defeated by Longley's bronchitis. For Tait, now the Primate of All England, believed in liberty for Protestants, under the protection of the Crown and the law. He adhered to the Reformation of the sixteenth century, and was sympathetic with those who wanted a second Reformation to respond to the new knowledge and the new society. He regarded the work of the Church as a work of quiet education and moral improvement, and in order to preserve the Christian character of England wanted good relations with Nonconformity. In more ways than one, he was the successor of Thomas Arnold. His own speciality in this work was influence on Parliament in order to secure ecclesiastical legislation and to counteract the secularizing tendency of the age. He partly succeeded, because he had learned the art of managing men, and because the Queen and many of her people thought him wise; but the majority of the clergy in the parishes distrusted him as being too liberal, and it may be doubted whether he ever really understood clergymen any more than Thomas Arnold understood boys.

Wilberforce, on the other hand, believed in the faith and order of the Catholic Church, safeguarded by the bishop. He exhibited an apostolic zeal which made the House of Lords nervous. Gladstone warned him in 1862: 'I seem to observe that the character you have got with politicians among whom I live is that of a most able Prelate, getting all you can for the Church, asking more, giving nothing.' But the clergy became fascinated by the energy and eloquence which he threw into their favourite causes. Men who were opposed to him, or embarrassed by him, wished to emphasize a flaw in him, and they found it easily enough in his snobbery – which they attributed to ambition, and connected with a basic humbug. When Disraeli came to portray an Anglican ecclesiastic in his novel of 1870, *Lothair* (which he wrote to relieve his financial problems on his fall from power), he had Wilberforce in mind.

The Bishop was high-church, and would not himself have made a bad cardinal, being polished and plausible, well-lettered, yet quite a man of the world. He was fond of society, and justified his taste in this respect by the flattering belief that he was extending the power of the Church; certainly he was favouring an ambition which could not be described as moderate.

More soberly, Dean Wellesley, her confidential adviser on ecclesiastical personalities, told the Queen that 'there is a want of moral strength in Wilberforce which prevents him being really dangerous in the Church whilst his brilliant and popular talents prevent him being hated in the country'.

The fatal nickname stuck to Wilberforce, in his lifetime and later: 'Soapy Sam'. He was not, however, a hypocrite. Gladstone was not easily fooled by clergymen, and Gladstone always treated him as a serious Christian, although he disapproved of some aspects of his complex character. The remarkably frank biography, using indiscreet journals and letters, which shocked many when it appeared in the 1880s, was judged by Gladstone to be 'edifying'. It seemed to confirm what Gladstone had written to the living bishop in 1869. 'Thank God it has not been in the power of jealousy or cowardice or spite, or any other evil creature, to detract one jot from the glory of that truly great episcopate, the secret of which you have written alike in the visible, outward history of the Church and in the fleshly tablets of the hearts of men.' Samuel Wilberforce had distinct thoughts of becoming Archbishop of Canterbury on Howley's death in 1848, and recorded them in his journal. He wanted to be Bishop of London in 1856; he wanted to be an archbishop again in 1862; he would have liked Canterbury or London in 1868. What happened was that Gladstone made him Bishop of Winchester in 1869. But he left behind the memory of a man who put all his many talents into the renewal of the parish and the diocese.

2

Samuel Wilberforce was the son of William Wilberforce, the Member of Parliament for Yorkshire famous for his leadership of the campaign which led to the abolition of the slave trade in 1807 and of slavery in the British Empire in 1833, the year of his death. William Wilberforce, this Great Emancipator, was also famous as the author of *A Practical View of the Prevailing Religious System of Professed Christians in the Higher Middle Classes in the Country, contrasted with Real Christianity*. When published in 1797, this at once became the Evangelical manifesto against the eighteenth century – and against the French Revolution which did much to encourage the higher and middle classes in England to look with favour on this call for personal loyalty to Christian doctrine, morality, and stability. William Wilberforce was a leader in Parliament by his eloquence and his intimacy with the younger Pitt; a leader in society by his charm and wealth, earned from trade in the Baltic; and a leader in the Church by the zeal with which he organized evangelistic and philanthropic societies, converted individuals, and spread 'seriousness'. But he was nowhere more remarkable than in his home. He resigned his seat in the Commons in order to devote himself to the education of his four sons and two daughters, and when his unsatisfactory eldest son got into financial trouble he produced the money and did without a home of his own.

Such a devoted father inevitably aroused some rebellion, despite his sons' gratitude and the willingness of three of them to be ordained. Henry, the youngest, was a vicar in Anglican parishes and married (to Newman's dismay, as we saw), but he became a Roman Catholic and an ecclesiastical journalist. Robert, who had been Archdeacon of the East Riding in Yorkshire and an impressive theologian, followed Henry; had he not died in Rome in 1857, Newman would have been less isolated. Samuel's only deviation from his father's position was to embrace moderately High Church views – and that was not a real deviation, for his father was responsible for enrolling him at Oriel College in 1823. Samuel's ambition was in keeping with William Wilberforce's precepts, for the father ended many of his letters to him with the single word REMEMBER. It had been the last word of Charles I, but William Wilberforce meant by it 'all a father's (let me say a Christian parent's) wishes and prayers for a dearly-loved child's temporal and eternal happiness'.

The very temporal tinge in Bishop Wilberforce's ambition was also not totally opposed to his inheritance, for his father, although he sacrificed public office to his causes and refused a peerage, taught the young Samuel the social arts as part of his duties in the Lord's temple. He urged him to bring together all Men who are like-minded, and who may probably at some time or other combine and concert for the public good. Never omit any opportunity, my dear Sam, of getting acquainted with any good man or any useful man (of course, I mean that his usefulness, in any one line, should not be countervailed by any qualities of an opposite Nature from which defilement might be contracted). More perhaps depends on the selection of acquaintances than on any other circumstance in life, except, of course, still more close and intimate Unions. Acquaintances are indeed the raw materials from which are manufactured friends, wives, husbands, &c ... O my dearest Boy, *Aim high*. Don't be satisfied with being hopeful, still less with being merely 'not vicious'. How little do you know to what Services Providence may not call you.

Samuel aimed; and twenty years later, he wrote the outcome in his journal. 'Afternoon at 6, while sitting with Mrs. Sargent, arrived a messenger from Sir R. Peel, with offer of Bishopric of Oxford. I had wished for this, and now that it comes it seems *awful*. Wrote to Sir R., whose letter was remarkably cordial, and accepted.'

Samuel Wilberforce confided to his journal about the prospect of episcopal work: 'My soul is penetrated with a thrilling sense of it.' It was more than the thrill of a clerical Disraeli at the sweet smell of success. The sons of William Wilberforce belonged to a generation, the generation of Arnold and Newman, which was fascinated by the mixture of glamour and slovenliness in the Established Church. Six months before offering him Oxford, Sir Robert Peel had made him Dean of Westminster. Instantly the young man's mind had been filled by the excitements of reform. 'The school is in a dreadful state ... the choristers are a grief of heart to me ... the openings for exertions all round are most numerous.' In Samuel Wilberforce's itch to reform the Church of England, as in Newman's zeal to defend it, we can see the touch of Gladstone's mixed metaphor: 'The Evangelical movement filled men so full with the wine of spiritual life that larger and better vessels were required to hold it.'

William Wilberforce's campaign for the abolition of the slave trade set a new moral tone, and gave a new example of efficiency, for the whole of English politics; but a new chapter was also opening in the history of parishes and dioceses. Had not Charles Simeon, the greatest name among the Evangelical clergy (who died in 1836), set the example by his firm loyalty to the Church of England and by his enterprise in buying up advowsons (the right to appoint clergy to parishes)? And many self-effacing Evangelicals were now at work in the parishes; one had even been made a diocesan bishop in the year of Waterloo. Yet precisely because he grew to be so fascinated by the Church, and by himself as an agent of its revival. Samuel Wilberforce grew dangerously apart from Protestant Englishmen who distrusted bishops as well as priests; and he came to reflect that his Catholic conception of the Church and the episcopacy had cost him the supreme honour of the clerical profession. In 1857 he burst out to a correspondent, Golightly: 'You do not suppose that I am so blind as not to see perfectly that I might have headed the Evangelical party and been seated by them at Lambeth.' But, he went on, he believed in 'the Spiritual presence of Christ and the Personal presence of God the Holy Ghost' in the Church of England.

However, we have first to glance at Samuel Wilberforce's years of preparation. After taking a First at Oxford and a tour of Europe, he failed to join his brother Robert as a Fellow of Oriel. Instead he was married (by Charles Simeon) to Emily Sargent, with whom he had been in love since he was a boy of sixteen. After a curacy in a pretty village by the Thames, in 1830 he moved to the pleasant rectory at Brightstone in the Isle of Wight, and remained there for ten years of great happiness. With Robert he compiled his father's *Life and Letters* in seven volumes; but like his brother he was already a man with his own opinions, so much so that the seven volumes failed to make clear exactly what his father's Evangelicalism had been. He opposed Newman's attempt to dominate, but Hurrell Froude was an intimate friend. It was equally in accordance with the trend of the time that Henry Manning, the curate from Oxford who lived in Lavington Rectory in Sussex (Emily Wilberforce's old home), also became a High Churchman in the 1830s – and married Emily's equally devout, equally beautiful, and equally delicate sister,

Caroline. It was natural, too, that the two other Sargent girls were carried off by two young clergymen who were Newman's disciples, George Ryder and Samuel's own youngest brother, Henry – although old Mr. Sargent had been an Evangelical.

Unlike Keble, Samuel Wilberforce rapidly attracted attention as a fluent speaker, pleading for new churches or missionaries. At one meeting in Winchester he thought that a speech by the great Palmerston was insufficiently enthusiastic about the Church, and he said so with such passion that the Duke of Wellington, who was also present, observed that he would sooner face a battery. (Thereafter Palmerston never liked Wilberforce.) Offers of larger parishes came in, and he shared none of Keble's hesitations about preferment; but he was not willing to leave his base in the Isle of Wight until, during 1839–40, he was made a Canon of Winchester, Archdeacon of Surrey, and Rector of Alverstoke. Despite his many outside interests, he was diligent both in organizing his curates and in paying warmly personal visits to his parishioners. In January 1841 he was also appointed Chaplain to Prince Albert, and while looking forward with pleasure to his future sermons at Court he settled down to write Bampton Lectures for delivery in Oxford, on the Holy Spirit. He was as happy as could be.

Then the blow fell. His Emily had given birth to a fourth son, Basil, later the eloquent Archdeacon of Westminster. Her many pregnancies cannot have helped her weak heart, and she now developed a fever. He held her through the night in his arms, thinking that the deep breaths might mean sleep. She died, and the next evening he wrote up his journal:

*March* 10, 1841. A day of unknown agony to me. Every feeling stunned. Paroxysms of convulsive anguish – and no power of looking up through the darkness which had settled on my soul. O Lord have mercy upon me. *March* 11. In some degree, yet but little, able to look to God, as the smiter of my soul for healing. Oh, may HE enable me to lead a life more devoted to His glory and my Master's work. May ye utter darkening of my life, which never can be dispelled, kill in me all my ambitious desires and earthly purposes; my love of money and power and place, and make me bow meekly to Christ's yoke.

Again and again around Good Friday 1841 he told himself that his Emily had been taken away because the service to which he was called was a '*desolate* service'. 'Domestic happiness not for me, or why taken away?' And again and again through thirty-four years as a widower, particularly on each anniversary of Emily's death, he told himself that she had been taken from him in order to teach him to pray more earnestly and to work less selfishly. It had come, as he had foreseen in his journal in 1838: 'I fear being scourged into devoutness'.

This was the bitter completion of his character. He naturally found it difficult to keep his vows to speak less to enthusiastic audiences and more to God, and to take no thought for the morrow. He never remarried, and found it impossible not to ache for Emily. Thus on 21 May 1867 his journal recorded that he went to church in London, to the the French and British Institutions, to a debate in the House of Lords, for a ride with Bishop Ellicott, and to dinner at the Admiralty with the Prince of Wales and Disraeli; and the entry for the day includes these words: 'That unspeakable depression last night and to-day which sometimes visits me. A longing for satisfied affection, which is not satisfied. O Lord, let it bind me to THEE in whom is all my spirit longs for!' But to the end, there was a burning passion for the Church which was now his bride. Before Emily's death he had already formed the habit of many absences from home for preaching engagements. Now he was incurably restless and incurably communicative. It was his habit to write forty or more letters a day, and Tait justly spoke about his 'aptitude for business and a devotion to the details of business such as no man in this generation ever showed'. Perhaps the psychological key lay in Emily's grave.

There were connexions between deaths and doctrines in Victorian England. One reason why Edward Bouverie Pusey became such an austere champion of the High Anglican kind of fundamentalism was the death of his wife Maria in 1839. Obviously it was not the only reason; his

stern *Tracts for the Times* on Fasting and Baptism dated
from before 1839. But as a rich young man he had been
more at home in the world and a strong sportsman, and as
a young Fellow of Oriel he had mastered Oriental languages
in order to equip himself splendidly to be Professor of
Hebrew. More, he had published a sympathetic account
of German theology at a time when most English Churchmen, if they knew anything about Germany, knew only
about its decline into rationalism (one of Newman's stock
themes). Pusey had been shaken by the English reaction to
that publication, and had hastily turned back to the
Fathers; but now the death of his wife plunged him into
a deep and permanent melancholy. Sport, objective
scholarship, and liberal sympathies were all laid aside. He
imposed on himself such morbid mortifications that Keble,
his spiritual director, had to beg him to take care.

One reason why Henry Manning, Archdeacon of
Chichester, ended up as the Cardinal Archbishop of
Westminster was the death of his wife, Emily Wilberforce's
sister, in all her beauty at the age of twenty-five, in 1837.
He tried to console himself with Anglican work, writing
his sermons by her grave, but his refusal of the invitation to
follow Samuel Wilberforce as Sub-Almoner to the Queen
(in charge of the Royal charities) in 1846 was an indication
that Anglican honours would not heal his hurt. Wilberforce once shocked Prince Albert by remarking breezily
that Manning would never have left the Church of England
if they had made him a bishop; but it was not a perceptive
remark.

Wilberforce himself stiffened in his churchmanship. As
a young archdeacon he encouraged that obscure thinker,
F. D. Maurice, and even when a bishop he tried to suggest
a formula of concord to help Maurice out of his troubles at
King's College, London; but later Maurice came to regard
him as an enemy of serious theology. Maurice thought that
this was because the bishop was drunk with the applause
of churchmen. But there seems to have been another factor
at work. Men around him often thought that his work was
his consolation for his grief, but Wilberforce told himself
over and over again that it must not be selfish work. To

the Church as his bride he sacrificed his leisure: that was
nothing. To her defence he sacrificed his career: that was
a great deal. And to the faith of the Church as he understood it while a young man, he sacrificed also his intelligence.

## 3

Tait was among the many observers who agreed that Samuel Wilberforce's twenty-three years as Bishop of Oxford
had changed the face of the Church of England. 'I cannot
doubt that a new idea of a Bishop's work was set before the
Church by your father's appointment', he wrote to Reginald
Wilberforce in 1879. The tribute is the more remarkable
because Tait, had he given way to his jealousy of Wilberforce, might have maintained that the remodeller of the
episcopate was his own predecessor in the great see of
London. Charles James Blomfield, the man who was accused
by Sydney Smith of an 'ungovernable passion for business'
because he wanted to reform St. Paul's Cathedral, was
Bishop of London, 1828–56. Blomfield was, indeed,
indefatigable in building churches and church schools, in
raising money to pay for hard-working clergy, in promoting
public health, and in sponsoring many public charities
at a time when London's growth (doubling and more in
the forty years from 1801) was creating the slums of
Dickens and Mayhew. He had been a brilliant mathematician and classical scholar at Cambridge, and the razor-
sharpness of his proud mind, contrasting with the flowers
of Oxford scholarship studied in the last chapter, cut
through administrative problems. More important still
was his work for the Church of England as a whole. He
was the ally and agent of Sir Robert Peel in the beginnings
of the administrative reconstruction of the Church, and
was the indispensable businessman among the Ecclesiastical
Commissioners who had emerged as a permanent body in
1836. Why, then, did Tait, and public opinion, not put
Blomfield first? Because there was about Blomfield a love
of money or a lack of unction or a lack of theology (however
one put it) which belonged to the eighteenth century. When

he read in a tract from Oxford that he was a successor of the apostles, he did not quite know what to make of it. His spiritual or theological defiances opened him to the satire of Disraeli in *Tancred*. 'There is a great spirit rising in the Church ... a great and excellent spirit. The Church of 1845 is not the Church of 1745. We must remember that; we know not what may happen. We shall soon see a bishop at Manchester.' To which Tancred replied: 'But I want to see an angel at Manchester'.

To a greater extent Samuel Wilberforce's style of pastoral zeal was anticipated by his own patron and second cousin, Charles Sumner, Bishop of Winchester for forty-two years, and by Charles's elder brother John Bird Sumner, who was translated to Canterbury in 1848 after twenty years as Blomfield's successor at Chester. But the Sumners, although they set new standards of conscientious work as diocesan bishops and stirred up the parochial clergy, also had about them something of the eighteenth century. Charles, for example, was given the then immense revenues of Winchester at the age of thirty-seven and at the suggestion of Lady Conyngham, the Prince Regent's mistress.

The truth was that neither Blomfield nor the Sumners possessed Wilberforce's infectious liking for people whether they were fashionable or poor. (In this, Samuel Wilberforce's predecessor was his father's friend, the saintly Henry Ryder, the first Evangelical to be a bishop – at Gloucester in 1815 and at Lichfield, 1824–36.) None of these bishops, however hard-working, combined as he did the talents of a manager with those of an orator. None knew so well what he wanted, or was so ruthless in getting it. None was responsible for Oxford, then the storm-centre of English religion; and while the Sumners and Ryder were ornaments of Evangelicalism, the Oxford Movement prevailed in the form in which Samuel Wilberforce accepted it.

Obviously many unwilberforcian bishops such as Edward Stanley at Norwich, or William Thomson at York, were among the instruments of the revival. This was the Gothic Revival, which all over England seemed to be restoring the zeal as well as the architecture of the Middle ages. But there was an angel at Oxford, magnifying his office, and because all the other bishops except Tait were in comparison rather dim, Wilberforce could be called (as he was by W. F. Hook, then Dean of Chichester) 'the Great Lord Bishop of England'. He certainly knew how to make the best of his privileges as a pioneer. Compared with a modern bishop he would seem single-handed, for he had no professional secretary and (although he had himself been an active archdeacon) he took care that his diocesan officials were cyphers. He applied the personal touch to everything, and in the course of his paternalism spent far more money than a modern bishop could. He was so far from being the slave of any machine that he was for long periods away from his diocese, as an ecclesiastical statesman or social lion in London or as the squire of Lavington; such absences often accounted for nearly half the year. But everyone knew who was Bishop of Oxford.

When he was appointed at the age of forty, he received from Prince Albert a long letter about his duties in the House of Lords. He was to abstain from party politics 'beyond giving a general support to the *Queen's Government*', but 'he should come forward whenever the interests of Humanity are at stake'. 'As to religious affairs', wrote the Prince, 'a bishop cannot but take an active part in them; but let it always be the part of a *Christian*, not of a mere *Churchman*.' Albert clearly hoped that in Wilberforce he had found an eloquent ally in the causes of liberal uplift and social progress. But gradually Albert and Victoria came to understand that the young Bishop of Oxford had some High Church principles, with the result that Wilberforce noted in his journal in 1849 an 'evident withdrawal of Royal favour'. 'The Queen', she wrote to Gladstone on hearing of his death, 'admired and liked him *most before* he became a Bishop, and before he leant so much to those High Church views which did harm, and which are so great a misfortune to the Church.' He could not even enjoy the nobility of martyrdom, for the Prince and his obedient wife concluded that they had been tricked into trusting Soapy Sam. 'He does everything for some object', said the Prince to Lord

Aberdeen, whom Wilberforce tried to use as a peace-maker in 1855; and the Prince could not be persuaded by Lord Aberdeen that Wilberforce's object was good.

It was not that he alarmed the Court by developing much sympathy with any High Church extremes. A few days after his consecration, this young bishop wrote to Professor Pusey rebuking 'a subtle and therefore most dangerous form of self-will ... This seems to lead you to judge the Church which you ought to obey.' But he did seem too much the High Churchman in his handling of the crisis caused in Oxford by the Crown's (more accurately Lord John Russell's) nomination of Renn Dickson Hampden, Newman's rival and enemy, as Bishop of Hereford in 1847.

Wilberforce joined with Charles Sumner, Blomfield, and ten other bishops in a Remonstrance against this appointment which, they claimed, would excite 'apprehension and alarm' in the minds of the clergy. Other bishops protested privately. Lord John Russell brushed all this aside, forcing Hampden's clerical opponents to institute proceedings for heresy against him in his capacity as Vicar of Ewelme in the diocese of Oxford. Under the Church Discipline Act of 1840 Wilberforce had to agree to this lawsuit, and he did so, hoping that Hampden would be so alarmed as to avow his orthodoxy and withdraw the writings which had been censored by the guardians of orthodoxy in Oxford. As Keble noted with the cattiness to which that saint could yield, the new and young Bishop of Oxford had an 'earnest desire of peace joined to a fancy that he was the person to make it'. He wrote to Hampden urging all this, but Hampden in reply took the same line as the Prime Minister who had nominated him. Wilberforce's doctrinal questions were an insult; legally he was entitled to be Bishop of Hereford. At the same time Hampden pointed out (in a letter addressed to Provost Hawkins but passed to Wilberforce) that a pamphlet written by him in 1834, on which his accusers were relying, had not been reprinted and was not now being sold with his sanction, and that he was intending to revise the Bampton Lectures.

This skilful reply unnerved Wilberforce, who brooded over the Bampton Lectures more carefully than he had done before. As he read, he saw how difficult it would be to nail the learned but obscure lecturer down as a heretic. Only the pamphlet exposed Hampden to the law; and now Hampden had denied that it had been circulated according to his wish during the years to which the Church Discipline Act limited his responsibility to the Bishop of Oxford. Wilberforce therefore withdrew his consent to the case, and with his desertion the campaign against Hampden sputtered out. Pusey was left complaining that the Bishop of Oxford's conduct had caused a greater scandal than the original appointment. By opposing and yet allowing Hampden's consecration, Wilberforce had in fact got the worst of both worlds. The Court now regarded him as a traiter to Prince Albert's conception of liberal Christianity, while High Churchmen regarded him as unstable. Newman had long been calling him a humbug. Not many observers shared the insight of the charitable Arthur Stanley: *'He had nothing to gain by it*, any more than he had when he jumped out of the carriage to pick up geological specimens, so I cannot but think it is equally sincere; and any act of undoubted sincerity in him is worth ten times as much as it would have been in another person.' As he mulled over the situation, Wilberforce thanked the God who had removed the snare of ambition from him, and consoled himself with the thought that justice had been his aim throughout the negotiation. But obviously he was now in no position to dominate ecclesiastical politics, and he threw himself with all the more zest into diocesan work.

Berkshire had been added to the diocese of Oxford only in 1836, and Buckinghamshire only on his own appointment, so that Wilberforce's task was to unite as well as to renew the Church in the great area over which he now presided. His very first ordination gave the clue to his policy. Where before there had usually been only the academic examination, a brief interview, and the service, Wilberforce made the occasion intensely devotional, intensely personal, and, to the young men who knelt before him, intensely moving. He also transformed the service of confirmation, which had previously tended to be a formality conducted for large numbers in a few centres by a bishop with his mind in the House of Lords. Wilberforce would go to a village and confirm there, taking pains to make the occasion memorable for each candidate on whom he laid his hands. He seemed to be ubiquitous by means of horses or the new railways. He set himself to inspect the clergy, and to charm the leading laity; and visit by visit, year by year, in six hundred parishes he built up a triumph for himself and for his idea of the Church.

The results were solid. Over a hundred new churches and seventy new parsonages were built in the diocese in his time, and over 250 churches were rebuilt or thoroughly restored. A theological college for ordinands was opened next to his palace at Cuddesdon, a village seven miles from Oxford, in 1854. It was intended to be primarily diocesan, although Cuddesdon College soon achieved a national status. His control over his clergy was increased by the fact that he managed to obtain the right to appoint the incumbents of over a hundred parishes in the diocese, instead of thirteen when he arrived. He used his rural deans and his own energy to obtain and act on detailed reports about the preaching, visiting, and general life of the parish priests. The office of rural dean had been revived in the 1830s and 1840s (by Blomfield among others), but it was Samuel Wilberforce who taught them to gather their clergy regularly and who assembled the rural deans themselves annually at Cuddesdon. He led his clergy personally in spiritual retreats, and his lay people in missions. And at Culham he founded another college, this time for training schoolmasters for the church schools which were regarded as indispensable parts of the mission of the parish churches. The kind of advice which he gave may be illustrated from this letter to a priest who was sad because his parish seemed to be stagnant. Wilberforce reminded him that 'I know by eighteen years' experience as a parish priest so many of the parish priest's *difficulties*'; but he also pointed out that stagnation 'is a rare and exceptional thing in my diocese', and he frankly attributed it to the parish priest's idleness. 'Pray for the outpouring of the Spirit on your own soul and on your ministry, and then live in your parish, live for your parish, work in it as a man only can work who has come to his work from intercession for his people.'

Naturally a great challenge came from the need to fit the disciples of the Oxford Movement into the limits of the law and public opinion of England. He had to keep an eye on Cuddesdon College lest Romanizing ritual should destroy the confidence of Church of England people, and for this reason Henry Liddon, the first Vice-Principal, was eased out. He had to keep an eye on the new sisterhoods, lest the revival of the religious life in the Church of England should be wrecked on Protestant suspicion. A later generation might think Wilberforce an over-fussy administrator, but it testified to his wisdom that he was able to hold in his diocese formidable Anglo-Catholic activists such as W. J. Butler the founder of the Wantage Sisters, T. T. Carter the founder of the women's community of St. John the Baptist at Clewer, and R. M. Benson the founder of the men's society of St. John the Evangelist in Cowley.

Such an achievement cannot be appreciated without recalling the circumstances. Newman became a Roman Catholic a fortnight after Samuel Wilberforce became a bishop. Samuel's brothers Henry, Robert, and William, his sister-in-law Mary, his brother-in-law George Ryder, and his daughter Ella, all took the road to Rome, and his darkly tragic view of such moves did not arise solely from acute embarrassment. In 1853, after Robert's conversion, he thought of resigning the bishopric, 'in order that without the reproach of remaining in the English Communion for the sake of my preferments, I may testify with what little strength is given me for the rest of my life against the cursed abomination of the Papacy'. He did not resign, but he did testify.

He would argue that no healthy Englishman of the nineteenth century would stand for the imitation of Rome. Any tokens, however small, that the great Protestant decision of the sixteenth and seventeenth centuries was being undermined were condemned. Wilberforce hated any signs of affectation among clergy or ordinands, any crucifixes above the fireplace or sorrowful Madonnas on the walls, and above all any thought that a young person might discuss sex with a priest in confession. When the eccentric J. L. Lyne ('Father Ignatius') proposed to found a new monastic order wearing the old monastic dress, Wilberforce warned him: 'You are sacrificing everywhere the great reality for which you have sacrificed yourself to the puerile imitation of a past phase of service which it is just as impossible for you to revive in England as it would be for you to resuscitate an Egyptian mummy and set it upon the throne of the Pharaohs.'

Tait, who sympathized with the religious earnestness and social usefulness of the revived sisterhoods, uttered similarly patriotic warnings. But Wilberforce added an argument which was not nearly so clear or so prominent in the teachings of Tait. It was the argument which replied to Newman and to all who had followed him: if you want to see a system which is no paper religion but manifestly, holy, manifestly Catholic, manifestly apostolic, you can take a look at my diocese.

4

But how was the holy, Catholic and apostolic character of the Church of England to be shown at the national level? In January 1852 Gladstone stayed with Wilberforce and immediately afterwards wrote a private memorandum recording their joint alarm about the ecclesiastical situation. The heart of the danger, as seen by these two churchmen, lay in the bishops' unwillingness to trust and defend traditional Christian doctrine authoritatively. Since 1833 the power to define the Church of England's doctrine had moved to the Judicial Committee of the Privy Council as the final court of appeal (previously there had been a special 'Court of Delegates'); on this body the Archbishops of Canterbury and York and the Bishop of London were outnumbered by the lay lawyers. The committee had recently ordered that Charles Gorham, an Evangelical who believed in conversion, should be instituted to a parish in Devon. Such an order was needed because the extremely conservative and combative Bishop of Exeter, Henry

Phillpotts, whose appointment had been the Duke of
Wellington's last act as Prime Minister, had gone to all
possible lengths in order to show that Gorham did not
believe the Prayer Book's teaching that infants were
regenerate (born again) in Holy Baptism.

The bishops appeared indifferent to this danger; yet when
in 1850 the Pope gave English titles to the bishops whom he
sent to 'govern' the Roman Catholics in England, the
bishops of the Church of England were prominent in the
general outcry of Protestants against Papal Aggression.
Romanizing stirred the bishops, but heresy – was not the
Gorham Judgment heresy, when the Apostles' Creed
included belief in Baptism 'for the remission of sins'? – left
them unmoved. This stirred the Bishop of Oxford to the
depths. The Gorham case was the reason given by his
brother Robert, and by his brother-in-law Henry Manning
for their renunciation of the Orders of a church under the
control of laymen who flouted Catholic doctrine.

By the end of the year 1852, however, the situation had
begun to brighten for Wilberforce and Gladstone. Lord
John Russell's ministry fell, to be replaced for a few months
by the Conservatives under Lord Derby; and Derby
turned a blind eye to the Convocation elected by the clergy
of the Province of Canterbury when it debated for three days
instead of the usual one. Specially since the Gorham case,
Wilberforce and other churchmen had grown convinced
that the Convocation must be revived. It was older than
Parliament, yet for 135 years it had been in virtual sus-
pension because successive governments had not wanted
the nuisance of clergymen arguing in public. In 1852 the
Archbishop of Canterbury was very nervous about the
whole affair, and the Archbishop of York refused to have a
Convocation in his Province, so that York did not copy
Canterbury until 1861. But the 'proctors' elected by the
parochial clergy in the Southern Province – together with
the deans, archdeacons, and some other dignitaries who
greatly outnumbered them in the Convocation – did now
meet for business. Although no layman was included, this
step represented the beginning of the self-government of
the Church of England. In 1861 'letters of business' enabling

the Convocation to amend a canon (or ecclesiastical law) were issued by the Crown; and Tait, while he still regarded Parliament as the chief forum for debates and the chief instrument of legislation on ecclesiastical issues, made no attempt to undo the Convocations. Although a layman, Henry Hoare, had organized the Society for the Revival of Convocation, Wilberforce's indomitable advocacy of this revival gained, and deserved, the chief credit.

So the Gorham Judgment had led to the revival of the Convocation as the clerical forum. The next doctrinal crisis, because its chief figure was a bishop overseas, led to the creation of another feature in the modern Anglican scene; the Lambeth Conference of the bishops of the world-wide Anglican Communion.

The bishop concerned was Colenso of Natal, who had begun in the right road: he had decided to become a missionary as a result of one of Wilberforce's sermons and Wilberforce had preached at his consecration as a bishop. The story of Bishop Colenso's alleged heresies, and of the volume of liberal *Essays and Reviews* which preceded that sensation, belongs to our study of Tait. Wilberforce was passionately convinced that Tait was wrong to defend Colenso's legal position, as he was wrong to defend the legal position of the contributors to *Essays and Reviews*. The arguments between the two men in these years were so heated that once, when Wilberforce threw a note across the table to him, Tait expected it to contain a debating point, only to find that Wilberforce was recommending a better make of boots for the sake of his health. Wilberforce was also convinced that his brother-bishops, not the English State, should decide whether or not Colenso was fit to be Bishop of Natal, and he threw his oratory and political skill behind the request which came from the Anglican bishops and clergy in Canada for a synod to uphold 'the truth of Religion' against critics of the Bible.

It was his own view, expressed to the House of Lords, that 'the Church of England in the colonies was a purely voluntary body, like the Wesleyans or any other body of religionists'. He was keenly interested in the Protestant Episcopal Church in the United States, about which he wrote a book (1844). So he agreed with the Canadians, despite the suspicion of the more Establishment-minded divines in England such as Tait. Archbishop Longley used him to negotiate with Colenso's principal accuser, Bishop Gray, and to write the message of the First Lambeth Conference which eventually met in September 1867. 'Keep whole and undefiled the faith once delivered to the saints', wrote Wilberforce to the faithful on behalf of the bishops. 'We beseech you to hold fast, as the sure word of God, all the canonical scriptures of the Old and New Testament.' Privately, Wilberforce reckoned that gathering 'a very great success. Its strongly anti-Erastian tone, rebuking the Bishop of London and strengthening those who hope to maintain the Establishment by maintaining, instead of by surrendering, the dogmatic character of the Church, was quite remarkable.'

Wilberforce thus discharged some of the most important duties of national leadership while Archbishops Sumner and Longley occupied Lambeth Palace. He hoped to go to York in 1862, and he received many letters of sympathy when William Thomson was appointed over his head; he accepted the pointed invitation of the Dean of York to preach in York Minster on the first public occasion after Thomson's enthronement. And it seems clear that he also hoped that Gladstone would reach power before Archbishop Longley reached heaven. From Disraeli he knew he could hope for little, for Disraeli no less than the Queen thought High Church views dangerous, and warned Wilberforce a month before Longley's death that 'it is all over with the Church of England, if she be disconnected with the State'. By September 1868, however, Gladstone was able to offer the see of Winchester, which old Charles Sumner had at last resigned (while continuing to draw a pension from the revenues of the see and to live in Farnham Castle). The work would be harder, for the diocese then included South London with the whole of Surrey, Hampshire, the Isle of Wight, and the Channel Islands. But for Samuel Wilberforce it meant being enthroned in the city where Emily had died and living at Lavington in her home, near her grave.

He plunged into all the work, but it brought severe heart

attacks and he could no longer conceal his constant tiredness and depression. Then deliverance came. On 19 July 1873 he was far more cheerful as he went for a ride on Abinger Common. He was going to stay with his companion, Earl Granville. The summer's day was fine. The horse stumbled, he was killed instantly; and he was buried beside his wife.

What, then, was wrong with him? Within the terms of the religion which he acknowledged, not much was. Yet something was. 'The late Bishop of Winchester', wrote Matthew Arnold in his Preface to *God and the Bible*, 'was a man in high office and dignity, a man at the same time of great gifts; he spoke to the English public with authority and with responsibility proportionate to that authority; yet he freely permitted himself the use of clap trap.' The justice of this rebuke is shown when we turn to the story of an incident which later came to seem symbolic of the whole Victorian crisis of faith.

At Oxford on a Saturday morning in June 1860 there was a meeting of one of the sections of the British Association for the Advancement of Science, to discuss some of the wider aspects of the new theory of the descent of man from the lower animals. The Bishop of Oxford spoke, with his genial charm and wit, with his eloquence about the dignity of man, with his stream of half-digested science. And as had happened before, one of his jokes was unfortunate. Surely it could not be on his grandmother's side that the evolutionist claimed descent from the apes? So a dedicated widower appealed to the Victorian sense of gallantry to the ladies; and so the proud son of the Wilberforces aroused the cheers and the laughter – now, as on innumerable other occasions. But in the audience (very reluctantly) was the scientist T. H. Huxley, the man who coined the word 'agnostic'. 'The Lord hath delivered him into my hands!' he whispered to his neighbour – for agnostic mid-Victorians were biblical. In a quiet, dignified reply, he annihilated the bishop, declaring that he would rather be descended from an ape than from 'a man highly endowed by nature and possessed of great means of influence and yet who employs these faculties and that influence for the mere purpose of introducing ridicule into a grave scientific discussion'. The undergraduates present led the applause for Huxley.

After that reply, even the laughing clergy, the ladies, and the fundamentalist admiral who had attacked man's evolution must have sensed they would have done better not to put around the story in advance that the Bishop of Oxford would 'smash Darwin'. And those among them who knew Archbishop Tait must have known that in such a debate he might have bored, but would not have exposed Christianity to a smash.

## 5

Archibald Campbell Tait was born and educated in Edinburgh, the son of an eccentric and impoverished gentleman. Since his mother died when he was three years old, in 1814, he owed everything to his nurse, Betty Morton; and since he was born club-footed, he owed his ability to climb in life to the strange tin boots which a doctor made him wear in boyhood. The pale-faced, pathetically serious young scholar, knowing that scholarship was the only path upwards, entered Glasgow University and then (with a scholarship) Balliol College, Oxford.

He was called 'the little bishop' at home – a strange title, for the family was Presbyterian. Even more ominous was a conversation which took place during his first visit to London, in 1830, when on his way to Balliol at the age of nineteen. One evening he returned from a walk. 'Where have you been to, Archie?' he was asked. 'Walking through Lambeth', he replied. 'Through Lambeth!' was the astonished answer; 'why, what ever possessed you to walk through Lambeth?' 'Well, I wanted to see how I shall like the place when I get there.' When he reached Oxford he obtained one preliminary qualification. He was confirmed as a member of the Church of England.

His success in Anglican life began with a fellowship at Balliol in 1834. A year later he was appointed a tutor of this, one of the two foremost colleges in Oxford. Stanley and Jowett were among his first pupils; others included Frederick Temple and Matthew Arnold. In the course of his teaching he would urge his pupils to study the Bible with the honest care which they were expected to give to the Greek and Roman classics. (Later on, some of his former Balliol pupils embarrassed Tait by reminding him of this.) But he was very far from being too critical in religion. (When he delivered his 'charge' to the diocese of Canterbury in 1880, published under the title *The Church of the Future*, he was still urging his hearers, as he had urged undergraduates at Balliol, to turn to Bishop Butler.) It was in relation to slumbering institutions that he would be a reformer. He published a pamphlet in 1839: *Hints on the Formation of a Plan for the Safe and Effectual Revival of the Professorial System at Oxford*. This was based partly on his first-hand knowledge of Germany. (Later on, Tait made use of his knowledge of other universities with an effect momentous for Oxford.) Soon he was ordained and after the week's work in Balliol would ride over to a neglected village, to sleep in a cottage before taking the Sunday services.

This hard-headed Scot was never charmed by Newman. Evening by evening he would argue in the Balliol Common Room with W. G. Ward – a fat little man, in many ways like a character out of the comic operas which he adored, who would kick off his shoes and settle down over the port under the candles to enjoy his own brilliance as the *enfant terrible* of the Oxford Movement. Ward, who used to say that he was made a deacon as an Arnoldian and a priest as a Newmanite, was now a frequent contributor to the *British Critic*, which Newman edited, and many of his articles were more or less anti-Anglican. One February morning in 1841 he handed to Tait Tract Ninety, which he had challenged Newman to write. 'Here is something worth reading.' Tait, already goaded by Ward, was shocked by Newman; and when a clergyman named Charles Golightly (an embittered ex-disciple of Newman's) organized a protest, Tait's name was the most weighty of the four college tutors who signed. And when Thomas Arnold died, it seemed fitting that Tait should carry on the Doctor's work, although other candidates for Rugby were his superiors in scholarship, notably C. J. Vaughan, one of Arnold's favourites.

As Headmaster of Rugby, Tait was never able to over-come the three sad facts that he was not a classical scholar of the first rank, that he had no previous acquaintance with an English school, and that he was not Thomas Arnold. He seemed dull, cold, and aloof. But Rugby in his time did not collapse, although a hundred extra boys came to the school as a result of the publication of Stanley's *Life*. The effort needed to maintain the Arnold tradition when all around knew that the glory had been buried beneath the chapel made the headmaster weary and drowsy. Eventually, in 1848, he was so ill with rheumatic fever that he was thought to be dying. His nurse was his wife Cath-arine, an archdeacon's daughter, Samuel Wilberforce's cousin, herself sweet, efficient (she supervised the Rugby School accounts), and High Church, all to Tait's advantage.

What was to be done for Tait, who clearly could not carry on as the sick and not entirely successful successor to Arnold? The answer seemed to be a cathedral, where in dignified retirement he could try to develop himself as a scholar. Accordingly in 1850 Lord John Russell sent him to the half-ruined cathedral of Carlisle and to a Deanery which one more fashionable clergyman (Arthur Stanley, the future Dean of Westminster) had refused as 'so remote'. On his first Sunday there, Tait found only ten communi-cants; there were only seventy-two on his last Sunday, more than he had ever seen before. Yet in the Lake District he recovered his health, although the action of his heart was always irregular. More, in Carlisle he fought his canons, cleaned up the cathedral's worst abuses, reorganized its grammar school, handed over its estates to the Ecclesi-astical Commissioners (Carlisle was the first cathedral to do this), and emerged as a pastor and teacher of the poor – at that time an astonishing role for a dean. More yet, he accepted Lord John Russell's invitation to serve on the Royal Commission appointed to recommend reforms at Oxford.

He became the most active member of that Commission, which (with Stanley as secretary) was the instrument in sweeping away much of Newman's Oxford. The powers of the Heads of Houses were to be cut down; the status of the professors was to be raised; the insistence on ordination for fellows of colleges was to be relaxed; Gentlemen-Commoners were to be abolished (these were rich, and normally idle, undergraduates); scholarships were to be thrown open for a far wider competition; and undergraduates who could not afford to belong to a college were to be admitted to the university. This great Blue Book on Oxford, published in 1852, caused there the greatest sensation to follow Newman's conversion. The iron Duke of Wellington took it to bed with him on the night of his death, and gradually the reforms proposed were effected. Tait added to the official report a boldly personal recommendation: that undergraduates should no longer be made to sign the Thirty-nine articles.

He never wrote the scholarly book for which his friends hoped. Indeed, Gladstone once remarked: 'I doubt if he ever read a theological book in his life.' Like Wilberforce, he was a man of action – but what action was there in Carlisle? He was in exile. 'At times', he wrote, 'I feel greatly depressed here by the uncongenial spirits amongst whom I am thrown.' But escape came through a bitter ordeal.

His consolation during the strain and illness at Rugby, and through the quarrels at Carlisle, was his family. Six daughters brought life and merriment to the Deanery. But between 10 March and 10 April 1856, five of them were laid in a single grave in Stanwix churchyard: first Charlotte ('Chatty'), then Susan, then Frances, then Catharine ('Catty'), then Mary ('May'). It was scarlet fever. At the time, Tait wrote in the Journal to which he had confided so many anxious prayers against depression or ambition: 'When last I wrote I had six daughters on earth; now I have one, an infant. O God, Thou hast dealt very mysteriously with us ...' Almost a quarter of a century later he arranged for the printing of his wife's detailed description of their piety, their innocence, their gaiety, their loveliness, and their deaths. In writing it, she had found some relief for the agony which remained with her and with him to their own deaths.

With their one surviving child, the baby Lucy, they spent the summer in a borrowed house on Ullswater. They sought comfort in the hills and in the knowledge that their tragedy had aroused the sympathy of the whole English upper class including the Queen. But how could they return to the empty Deanery among the quarrelling canons? Then the royal sympathy combined with the Liberal government's gratitude for that report on Oxford, and with Lord Shaftesbury's gratitude for that moderation in theological liberalism. There was another entry in the journal.

*Sept. 17th*, 1856.—I have this morning received a letter from Lord Palmerston saying that he has the Queen's command to offer me the See of London. I am now (11a.m.) about to take an hour of prayer. The subjects on which to pray are these—That I may not act rashly, seeing that I have no doubt about accepting the offer . . . This is certainly not a post which I should ever dreamed of for myself. The preparation which Thou hast given me for it has been deep affliction.

## 6

Tait wrote truly when he wrote that his agony as a father had been his main preparation as a Father-in-God. He certainly had little practical training to succeed Blomfield at the head of a thousand clergy in London. Neither Oxford, nor Rugby, nor Carlisle had familiarized him with ecclesiastical problems or personalities. Gladstone was indignant that he had been chosen instead of the tested Wilberforce, and so was Wilberforce. Twenty-six years after his first visit, Archie Tait of Glasgow returned to London with the equipment of a broken heart – which, added to his strong Scots mind, was enough.

'The only advice I should venture to offer is that you should do as little as possible', wrote Benjamin Jowett from Balliol. But to Tait, as to Wilberforce, work was the great consolation in grief. He became as efficient as Blomfield had been, and in his eagerness for new churches launched an appeal for half a million pounds. But he was more earnest than Blomfield, for he knew that the Gospel had to match its strength against death. When people protested that this Bishop of London was not so dignified as his predecessors, his retort was that the Church of England might 'die of its dignity'. He preached in Covent Garden, from a railway train, and on the streets. He even encouraged Church of England services in theatres. Amid great excitement he presuaded Westminster Abbey and St. Paul's Cathedral to hold popular evening services. He gathered his clergy in St. Paul's and read them his 'charge'. It grew dark under the dome, but the bishop had some candles; through five hours Tait's voice went on, urging the clergy to efficiency and evangelism. The Evangelicals, although they still suspected him because of his associations with Balliol and Rugby, were compelled to acknowledge that he was a Christian.

The High Church ritualists of London – who in their desire to take the Oxford Movement into the imaginations of the poor were now indulging in practices which had held little interest for Newman, Keble, or Pusey – felt the lash of the ex-headmaster's pen as a disciplinarian. 'I must, therefore, lay my commands upon you to discontinue the practice you have introduced without my authority ... of lighting the candles on the Communion Table in broad daylight.' 'As to the green vestments, stoles, or whatever they may have been ... I very deeply regret that you should think it right to assume the unusual garments you described to me ... If you continue with this, it is against my express order.' Most conservative High Churchmen (for example, Pusey) applauded such commands – especially when the alternative might be the riots seen Sunday after Sunday in the dockland parish of St. George-in-the-East, when these illegal Roman ornaments were seen in church.

Was he overtaxing his strength? Lord Palmerston thought so, and in 1862 offered him the lighter work of York, intending to move Wilberforce to London. But Tait was enjoying London too much; he stayed on, despite a severe heart attack, for some of the most stormy years of Victorian religion.

Because he was Bishop of London, and because he was the canny Archie Tait, he could not do everything which his fellow-liberals wanted done to bring in a new era. In 1860 Benjamin Jowett and six other Broad Churchmen, including H. B. Wilson who had been one of the tutors against Tract Ninety and Frederick Temple who was now Headmaster of Rugby, published a volume of *Essays and Reviews*. For a time there was a lull. Then Wilberforce fiercely denounced the volume, called for replies to it, and increased its circulation amid the excitement. Tait did not leap to the defence of these 'seven against Christ'. Indeed, he signed his name to the reply made by the Archbishops of Canterbury and York and twenty-four diocesan bishops to a very agitated protest from some country parsons in Dorsetshire. The bishops expressed 'the pain it has given them that any clergyman of our Church should have published such opinions as those concerning which you have addressed us. We cannot understand how these opinions can be held consistently with an honest subscription to the formularies of our Church, with many of the fundamental doctrines of which they appear to us at variance.' This statement was drafted by Wilberforce. Connop Thirlwall of St. David's, whom Tait called 'the most learned man of the century', was among the twenty-three bishops (out of twenty-six) who supported its condemnation of *Essays and Reviews*.

Tait's feebleness in signing Wilberforce's condemnation of *Essays and Reviews* brought wounding letters from his Broad Church friends. Stanley reminded him that he had already cleared his own opinion that the essays by Jowett and Temple, if not the others, had nothing seriously wrong with them; 'what can I say in your defence?' Temple was so deeply embittered that he never entirely forgave Tait. He, too, recalled that in private Tait had raised no great objection to his own contribution. Yet now Tait had condemned the whole book, and had virtually demanded that its authors should recant or resign.

'If you do not wish to alienate your friends, do not treat them as you have treated me', Temple wrote in his fury. 'What you did had not the intention, but it had all the effect, of treachery. You will not keep friends if you compel them to feel that in every crisis of life they must be on their guard against trusting you.' In his next letter Temple poured salt into the wound. 'You ought not to make it impossible for a friend to calculate on what you will do. I do not care for your severity. I do care for being cheated.' In a third letter Temple added vinegar, by referring to Tait's wish to appease the Evangelicals. 'Your friends complain that they cannot count on you: your enemies say that they can, and that you will always do what is popular with the Low Church party.' Thirty years later, when he was himself Bishop of London, Temple allowed Tait's biographer, Randall Davidson, to print these letters in full. But Davidson in his own life suffered from Temple's unalterable suspicion of Tait and his men, as traitors to the cause of intellectual honesty.

In his replies to his wounded friends Tait insisted that the volume as a whole was dangerous, and that any of its contributors who did not wish to be associated with its tendency and fate should withdraw their contributions. Jowett and Temple refused to desert their colleagues in this way, although they let it be known that they had had no idea about what was in the other essays until the printed book had reached them. Tait's second line of defence was to plead his responsibility as a bishop. Despite that, could he not keep his friends? 'It is the misery of an official position', he wrote to Temple, 'that if a man is determined that his private friendships and public acts shall never appear to come into collision, he must give up his friendships.' Jowett and Temple were little moved by the pathos here. But Tait argued that what was really needed was a doctrinal restatement, instead of the critical and negative tone of *Essays and Reviews*. 'It is a poor thing to be pulling down; let them build up.' This was the one argument which eventually convinced Temple.

Tait, however, soon seized the opportunity to vindicate himself as a friend of honest thinkers. Two of the contributors were brought before the Judicial Committee of the Privy Council, on which he sat with the two archbishops and four lay judges. They were accused of publishing views on the inspiration of the Bible, and on the everlasting punishment of the wicked, which were too liberal to be compatible with the doctrines of the Church of England. The two archbishops agreed with this accusation.

The laymen thought the charges 'not proved'. Tait voted with the laymen.

Another storm of abuse now fell on his head. 137,000 laymen congratulated the archbishops. Eleven thousand clergymen signed a declaration that the Bible was to be regarded as divinely inspired 'without reserve or qualification', and that punishment in hell would be 'everlasting'. And it was not merely an outcry from the mob. Gladstone, while thanking Tait for sending him some sermons and while expressing 'cordial respect for your pastoral zeal and labours', made it clear that he agreed with the archbishops in dissenting from the judgment in favour of *Essays and Reviews*. 'It appears to me that the spirit of this judgment has but to be consistently and cautiously followed up in order to establish, so far as the Court can establish it, a complete indifference between the Christian Faith and the denial of it.' Tait's only ally among the bishops was Connop Thirlwall. But his vote had made it possible for Broad Churchmen to remain parsons of the Church of England. By so voting in defiance of clerical opinion Tait had recovered his integrity, and had discovered his vocation. He wrote privately at this time: 'I feel my own vocation clear, greatly as I sympathize with the Evangelicals, not to allow them to tyrannize over the Broad Churchmen' – despite their alliance with the High Churchmen for this purpose. He would protect the ewe lamb of theological liberalism against the beasts once described by Matthew Arnold as 'the High Church rhinoceros and the Evangelical hyaena'. But Tait, who still felt that the publication of *Essays and Reviews* had been foolish, and some of its contents dangerous, added: 'What is wanted is a deep religious liberal party, and almost all who might have formed it have, in the alarm, deserted ... The great evil is that the liberals are deficient in religion, and the religious are deficient in liberality.'

Next year Tait further angered many clergymen by supporting a campaign led by his friend Arthur Stanley for a relaxation of the terms on which the clergy accepted the Thirty-nine Articles. It did not escape notice that Tait, whose protest had been the instrument to break

Newman's Anglican career because Newman had placed a dishonest interpretation on the Articles, was now the patron of Article-evading liberals. When the Clerical Subscription Act of 1865 was passed to satisfy the consciences of the mid-Victorian liberals, Tait was blamed, and he became no more popular in the next doctrinal crisis.

John William Colenso was a Cambridge mathematician (*Colenso's Arithmetic* was known to countless schoolboys), and a tough minded man who battled with poverty. Having been a Norfolk vicar and a disciple of the great theologian F. D. Maurice, he sailed out in 1853 to become the first Bishop of Natal. This was at the invitation of Robert Gray, Bishop of Cape Town and a disciple of Samuel Wilberforce. All seemed to be going well and quietly until in 1861 there appeared *St. Paul's Epistle to the Romans: Newly Translated and Explained from a Missionary Point of View*. This small commentary, printed by African converts, expounded Pauline theology in the light of the Maurician doctrine that all men were united to Christ from birth. To be a missionary in Natal, Colenso was saying, was to place before the Zulu the fact that he was already redeemed. This book profoundly shocked Robert Gray; it shook Maurice himself. For when Maurice's message was clarified like this, what became of the contrast between the heathen's blindness and the Church's salvation? And what became of the contrast between heaven and hell? Gray wanted the Church of England to dissociate itself from the heresy, and Wilberforce wrote to Colenso ('one very dear to my heart') that surely the loneliness and autocracy of a colonial bishop's position 'cannot be the most favourable position for the discovery of religious truth'. But Tait shrewdly refrained from reading the book, explaining that when he had time to read, the book must be a good one. 'London was strong against action as action', wrote an indignant Wilberforce to Gray. ' "Was not prepared to say," etc.'

Colenso now added to his offence by publishing a discussion of the first books of the Bible. Zulu converts had asked him whether the Old Testament was truer or more moral than their own ancestral fables. Colenso, who had already shown his capacity for quick study by becoming the leading authority on the language and literature of the Zulus, set himself to work through the sacred scriptures in the light of such German commentaries as he was able to acquire and with the mathematical equipment which he already possessed. He concluded that the writings traditionally attributed to Moses and the Book of Joshua were not free of mathematical, historical or moral error. Urged on by Wilberforce, Gray now determined to depose him from his bishopric. For Robert Gray nursed solemn ideas about his responsibilities as the Metropolitan of South Africa. A curate who admired these ideas, S. J. Stone, wrote a hymn about them: 'The Church's one foundation'. Gray was building a new part of the Catholic Church, but at the same time he was studying the Fathers and wishing to revive their orthodoxy and discipline. He would contend for the Faith once delivered to the saints, whatever the cost. His aged father's episcopal palace had been burned down by the mob in Bristol, in 1831; old Bishop Gray had nevertheless insisted on appearing in his cathedral. Robert Gray in Cape Town was not the lesser man.

This move drove Tait to take a firm stand, for he shared the conviction of most Victorian churchmen that Gray had no legal power to take such a step against Colenso, who had been appointed by the English Crown through Letters Patent. Already in 1858 Tait had opposed Wilberforce's plea that Gray should be encouraged to consecrate more bishops to work with him and Colenso (then his ally). Wilberforce and Gray had wanted these bishops 'to head aggressive missions in the parts of South Africa which are exterior to the Queen's dominions', but Tait had conveyed to Wilberforce a belief that 'bishops in Roman Catholic countries should be sent by the Pope; in our country the Bishops should be sent by the Queen, who stood in the same place as the Pope'. Now the fact that the Queen had appointed Colenso was decisive for Tait. He was the author of an appeal from the English bishops to Colenso to resign if he could not share the Church's acceptance of the whole Bible as the Word of God; among the bishops only Thirlwall refused to endorse this appeal. But he knew that Gray was reluctant to have the doctrinal issue decided by English lawyers, that the Privy Council had ruled that Gray had no right to depose him, and that Colenso had refused to go quietly. So Tait was unwilling to take actions which would acknowledge the authority of Gray (or of Gray's ally Wilberforce) to decide who was to be Bishop of Natal. Tait did not inhibit Colenso from preaching in London, although much pressure was brought on him to make this gesture, and he led the majority of the English bishops in refusing to arrange for a new bishop to be consecrated for Natal. When the timid Archbishop Longley refused to ask the overseas bishops what they thought about the problems of maintaining doctrinal unity and the royal supremacy in the colonial churches, Tait issued a questionnaire on his own responsibility, and armed himself with many replies which were gratifyingly hostile to the Gray – Wilberforce solution of these problems.

When the first Lambeth Conference was convened, Tait was expected to join the bishops who boycotted it as a Gray – Wilberforce plot. Instead, he and Thirlwall agreed to be present. By their attendance they hoped to make sure that Archbishop Longley fulfilled his promise to keep the Colenso affair off the Lambeth agenda. When Longley failed in this, Tait resisted the plan of Gray and Wilberforce to get the bishops' conference to approve the consecration of a new bishop for Natal, and won. Gray 'made my blood boil', he wrote in his journal. Tait spoke in 'severe rebukes' to Bishop Selwyn of New Zealand who attacked the establishment of the Church of England. When other bishops urged him to be a disciplinarian against the Colenso type of Broad Churchmanship as he was against the Anglo-Catholic ritualists, he 'let it be distinctly understood that I thought the Romeward tendency more dangerous for our clergy than the tendency towards free-thought.'

7

As Primate Tait established an ascendency over the Victorian mind, and when he died Queen Victoria asked for a lock of his hair. It was an honour that she did not bestow upon Disraeli. Men and women in many different walks of life, belonging to many different schools of thought, trusted him, and they knew that his devotion to duty as he saw it made Lambeth Palace resemble a government office. No Archbishop of Canterbury had exercised such influence since the Middle Ages. For the nearest equivalents men had to go back to William Laud and John Tillotson in the seventeenth century – but Laud the High Churchman owed his execution to his unpopularity, while Tillotson the Broad Churchman (Tait's hero) had to see most of his ideas frustrated by the clergy. And Tait was entirely frank in his delight to be Archbishop in such an age. 'Look abroad,' he urged the Church Congress of 1877. 'What other country in the world would you change Churches with? Look at home; which of the denominations would you prefer? Look back; what age are you prepared to say it would have been more satisfactory to have lived in?'

Unfortunately much of Tait's Primacy was consumed by the battle against the ritualists, with the Public Worship Regulation Act of 1874 as the weapon. Tait knew that when appointing him Archbishop of Canterbury the Queen and Disraeli intended that he should enforce the law against the small number of Anglican priests who were imitating Roman Catholic practices. When the Pope was declared infallible in 1870, anti-Catholic prejudice in England found a fresh cause for alarm; even Gladstone, who deplored the attempt to regulate religious life by Act of Parliament, was stirred to write at length against the menace of 'Vaticanism'. In 1871 the Judicial Committee of the Privy Council clearly condemned an Anglo-Catholic priest in Brighton, Father Purchas, for wearing the medieval priest's vestments, for adopting the eastward position to face the altar not the people, for using wafers instead of ordinary bread, and for mixing water with the wine ceremonially. Lord Shaftesbury was bent on legislation to enforce such a prohibition of ritualism, and 60,000 people signed a 'memorial' to the Archbishops organized in 1873 by the Church Association. Above all the Queen insisted, and talked of abdicating if she did not get her way. It became inevitable that voices such as Maurice's, appalled by the prospect of a religious persecution, should be drowned, and that Tait should sponsor legislation. If he had not been willing to do so, more extreme laymen would certainly have pushed legislation through, either out of a passionate Protestantism, as in the case of Lord Shaftesbury, or out of a sense of the electoral advantages to be gained by appeasing the popular clamour, as in the case of Disraeli.

Tait's first idea was that the diocesan bishops should be strengthened as judges in liturgical matters, with diocesan councils to advise them. He optimistically believed that the few mule-like Anglo-Catholic priests would soon be brought to their senses by a combination of the stick of this new legal discipline with the carrot of pastoral kindness. However, such episcopal action was unlikely to be stern enough to satisfy the Protestants under Lord Shaftesbury, who amended Tait's Bill so that there should be only one judge, and he a layman. Tait spoke against this amendment but, sensing the power of the anticlerical suspicion, voted for it. The one point on which he would not give way was his insistence that the diocesan bishop should have the power to veto any proceedings. This combination of Shaftesbury's zeal with Tait's caution was presented to a cheering House of Commons by Disraeli as a 'Bill to put down ritualism'. But Shaftesbury's amendments resulted in more problems for the Archbishop than he realized at the time. They created a further impression that the English State was attempting to override the theological convictions of Anglo-Catholic churchmen, as in the Gorham and Colenso affairs; but more: since the new lay judge turned out to possess, and to be willing to exercise, the power of imprisoning for contempt of court, Shaftesbury's amendments gave to Anglo-Catholic churchmen the fertile boon of martyrdom.

The greatest error of Tait's life was his failure to foresee these dangers in 1874. His experience as Bishop of London had taught him to respect the pastoral earnestness of some of the ritualists, and to hate the Protestant bigotry and violence of some of their opponents (usually from outside their parishes), which was why he insisted on the right to veto prosecutions. But Anglo-Catholicism to him still meant the logic-chopping of Tract Ninety or the sentimentally medieval antics of the first London ritualists. He completely underestimated the spiritual power of the movement.

Such a movement was not going to be blackmailed or bludgeoned into conformity with the Protestant Establishment. Instead, it was a movement which operated with a Victorian energy and self-righteousness like Tait's own, and which was looking for martyrs as mascots; and in this atmosphere the Public Worship Regulation Act was a very foolish measure. Its new lay judge was Lord Penzance, an eager Protestant who had previously specialized in divorce cases. Tait was genuinely distressed when there were five cases of imprisonment at Penzance's orders under the Act (Tooth in 1877, Dale and Enraght in 1880, Green in 1881–2, and Cox in 1887). And he had every reason to be distressed. Quite apart from a bishop's embarrassment at the spectacle of priests in prison for obeying their consciences, and quite apart from the agitation among the clergy whose organs were the newly founded English Church Union and the *Church Times*, these punishments turned public opinion away from the witch-hunt against the ritualists. By the end of Tait's Primacy the Public Worship Regulation Act was doomed, and he knew it. He changed his mind to a greater extent than either he or his admirers cared to admit. Gladstone, for example, told Pusey that in the Tait of 1881 he could scarcely recognize the man who had allied himself with Disraeli against the ritualists in 1874.

Was this futile battle such a blot on Tait's government of the Church that it ought to overshadow everything else? Certainly the details of Anglo-Catholic ritualism in conflict with mid-Victorian law make tedious reading today, and there is a natural tendency to conclude that the archbishop who presided over such petty excitements was a man so entirely Victorian as to be of no permanent interest. But at the time Tait, for all his mastery of the historical and legal precedents in England, was not excited himself. This came out when a consecrated wafer was produced in Lord Penzance's court and retained as a piece of evidence. Protests against this blasphemy poured into Lambeth

Palace, to Tait's dry amusement. He quietly asked for the wafer to be brought to him, and ate it. Thanks now poured in, but Tait was still contemptuous.

A man with such a low estimate of the controversies which fascinated the average clergyman or the devout churchgoer may easily be reckoned a bad appointment as a Father-in-God, and it is probable that had Tait been born a century later he would have ended up in university life as a Vice-Chancellor; certainly no system of electing bishops would have produced Bishop Tait. Yet his inner remoteness from the battles did have its compensation. He shared both the layman's dislike of parsons in strange clothes and the layman's dislike of priests in prison. It became his ambition to leave the Church of England in peace. He secured the appointment of a Royal Commission on Ecclesiastical Courts in 1881, and chaired its laborious and largely fruitless investigations. One practical step he could take. In 1882 he knew that he was dying, and he deliberately used this status in order to persuade one of the most publicized and most prosecuted of the ritualists, Arthur Hugh Mackonochie, to leave his church, St. Alban's, Holborn. Father Mackonochie clung to his church when Tait first suggested an exchange with another Anglo-Catholic priest, Father Suckling of St. Peter's, London Docks; but he could face anything except a dying bishop who was a fellow-Scot, and eventually agreed.

Tait concentrated his attention on what, writing to Mackonochie in his last month of his life, he called 'the prevailing sin and unbelief'. The only aspect of Anglo-Catholicism that impressed him was its hold on the loyalty of certain congregations including working-class folk. Because of that, even ritualists might eventually be considered on the right side in the real battle. But in the main, Tait pursued these great issues whatever might be the reactions of the clerical mind. Thus, while opposing secular funerals, he was convinced that it was both charity and justice to allow fellow-Christians to be buried in the parish churchyards with the benefit of a Nonconformist service if that was their wish. He supported the Liberal government's legislation to this effect in 1880. The greatest clerical outcry in Tait's whole life followed. Three-quarters of the clergy petitioned against the concession. Bishop Wordsworth of Lincoln called it an 'Act for the martyrdom of the National Church', and Bishop Ellicott announced that he would not consecrate any new churchyards. The Archbishop most courteously dismissed all that as hysteria; and within a few years, when the parish churches were seen to be standing although a few Nonconformist funerals had approached their hallowed walls, even clergymen acknowledged that he had been right.

In some other reforms which he advocated, Tait was defeated. An example was his wish to see a relaxation of the public use of the fifth-century Athanasian Creed.

The Prayer Book ordered that on each day of the main Christian festivals, including Christmas Day, Easter Day and Whitsunday, parson and people at Mattins should together profess:

Whosoever will be saved: before all things it is necessary
  that he hold the Catholick Faith.
Which Faith except every one do keep whole and undefiled:
  without doubt he shall perish everlastingly.
And the Catholick Faith is this ...

A comprehensive summary of Trinitarian and Christological doctrine followed. Various churchmen, including Archbishop Tillotson, would have been glad to see a creed so detailed and so damnatory removed into obscurity, but the Oxford Movement had encouraged obedience to the Prayer Book's directions and the later ritualists were enthusiastic about *this* part of the Book. By the 1870s, few thoughtful members of the Church of England were willing re-open the Trinitarian and Christological questions in theology, but equally few shared Newman's enthusiasm (in the *Grammar of Assent*) for the Athanasian Creed as 'the most simple and sublime, the most devotional formulary to which Christianity has given rise'. More practically, few wished all churchgoers on all the festivals to hear the Church teaching the everlasting damnation of all who did not answer the mysterious questions with a complete correctness. Lord Shaftesbury, that pillar of orthodoxy, organized a petition of 6,000 leading laymen against the compulsory use of the creed.

In 1870 a Royal Commission accordingly recommended that in the Prayer Book a new rubric should be printed, explaining 'that the condemnations in this Confession of Faith are to be not otherwise understood than as a solemn warning of the peril of those who wilfully reject the Catholic Faith'. Tait believed this explanation to be inadequate, and announced his view that the creed 'should not retain its place in the Public Service of the Church'. But then the most respected Anglo-Catholic spokesman, Henry Liddon, let it be known that he would retire from the ministry of the Church of England if any damage were done 'to this most precious creed', and Dr. Pusey sent in a similar threat from Oxford. Liddon never forgave Tait; he would always absent himself from any service or meeting where Tait was to be prominent. But in the end all that happened was that the Convocation of Canterbury passed a resolution containing the words suggested in 1870 and adding (without producing evidence) that the creed 'doth not make any addition to the faith as contained in Holy Scripture'. So the Athanasian Creed was saved. 'And there,' commented Arthur Stanley, 'it will go on standing until it carries off the other two creeds on its back'. But Stanley was too gloomy, for the creed gradually fell into disuse while the Apostles' and Nicene Creeds continued in daily or weekly use.

Tait, while lacking the theological courage of a Colenso, possessed some understanding of the challenges to belief. 'When I was young', he said in his charge at Canterbury in 1876, 'we were told there was no such thing as an atheist in the world, but all that is changed.' Yet his own religion was not primarily intellectual. It was a defiance of the grave – of five small graves. He said about sceptics in 1876: 'We must reach their hearts in hours of sickness and approaching death and when friends are taken from them; then we may find their consciences awake and their hearts open, ready to return to the faith of their childhood, and to believe in the great Redeemer.' Four years later, in an outspoken review of Mozley's *Reminiscences of the Oxford Movement,* he was still insisting that Newman's influence had been disastrous in trying to stiffen the great National Church 'after an alien and antiquated model', whereas Arnold's influence had appealed to the consciences 'of the vast majority of intelligent persons throughout the Kingdom'. What he really cared for was that the Church of England should remain established as the national recognition that the Christian promise of eternal life was true.

The defence of the Establishment was for Tait no light matter. No sooner had he reached Lambeth than Gladstone became Prime Minister with a mandate for Irish disestablishment. Tait and his ally Queen Victoria had to content themselves with securing some financial concessions to the Anglican clergy in Ireland, and with some pacifying tactics which slightly lessened the bitterness of the Parliamentary debate. But it did not amount to much, and the anxiety of that first year's negotiations brought Tait once more face to face with death. Another heart attack left him partially paralysed in November 1869, and his left arm never truly recovered. His resignation or death was expected, but he convalesced through 1870, and spent the next winter on the Riviera. His illness alarmed the Government into allowing the consecration of a Bishop of Dover, to carry the main burden of the episcopal work in the Canterbury diocese. (It was part of a move to increase the number of bishops: in 1874 Parliament allowed the creation of new dioceses of Truro, St. Albans, Liverpool, Southwell, and Wakefield – provided that the money could be raised for the new bishops, which caused some delay.) Tait then devoted himself to the central administration of the National Church, for which, as he believed, his life had been spared.

He defended the National Church both by the shrewdness of his leadership during successive crises, voicing the instincts of thoughtful laity by never driving the clergy too much, and by the zeal with which he did his duty as a spiritual peer. When newspapers arrived, he always had the foreign and domestic political news read to him first; ecclesiastical controversies, which in those days could fill many newspaper columns, could wait. He treated the House of Lords with great seriousness (he was scandalized by Disraeli's *Endymion,* which viewed politics as a game), and the compliment was repaid. Distinguished lawyers used to reckon him a first-class judge, and there were those who believed that he would have made a powerful Prime Minister. In 1879 he even impressed a delegation from the Trades Union Congress with the breadth of his political insight. In a role which was less dignified, he was an indefatigable, cunning, and remarkably successful lobbyist for ecclesiastical legislation. Like every other politician, he often had to compromise or to admit defeat; he could not preserve the compulsory collection of the 'church rate' to repair the parish churches (this was made illegal in 1868), and he could not preserve the full position of the Church of England in the nation's universities or schools. But partly because Tait was now so often crossing the river from Lambeth to Westminster, the complete severance of Church and State seemed an idea more improbable in the 1870s than in the 1860s.

This achievement had international repercussions, for Tait used his prestige at home to build up the position of Canterbury in the whole Anglican Communion. He did this without ever echoing the Wilberforce-Gray line about Anglicanism overseas as an exciting adventure in English Catholicism free from the shackles of the Establishment; his approach was pragmatic. When Bishop George Selwyn persuaded the American bishops to ask for another Lambeth Conference, Tait replied that he was willing to convene such a gathering provided that the bishops thought that they had enough subjects to discuss. In the end a hundred bishops assembled in 1878. He dominated the meeting not by holding up any new vision of the Church, but by his mastery of the problems of the existing mixture of constitutions and theologies within Anglicanism. 'I believe', he told his brethren, 'that there are not more than three persons in England who can give you a definite idea of what the constitution of a Colonial Church is. I rather pride myself on being one of the three . . .'

That second Lambeth Conference took place little over a month after the death of Tait's only son, Craufurd. Before the year was out, he had buried his wife. Now that death had touched him once more, all around him noticed that the Archbishop had been purged of most of the lingering traces of arrogant impatience. His chief domestic happiness in the years which remained to him was watching his chaplain, Randall Davidson. This young man, a rising Scot, who reminded him of his own youth, married his daughter Edith and handled most of his letters and many of his interviews under his general instruction. Craufurd Tait had been ordained amid his proud father's hopes. After the son's death, the son-in-law became the heir of the whole legacy of Tait's life and work.

Archibald Tait from Glasgow was buried in the church-yard of Addington Park, the country house of the arch-bishops, four miles from Croydon. If religion be defined as an excitement over the glamour of the Church, or as a facility in devout emotions, it is true to say, as the *Church Times* said in 1877: 'What music is to a man with no ear, that religion is to Archbishop Tait.' But C. J. Vaughan, whom he had defeated for the headmastership of Rugby forty years before, wrote the inscription on his monument in Canterbury Cathedral:

A GREAT ARCHBISHOP,
JUST, DISCERNING, DIGNIFIED, STATESMANLIKE,
WISE TO KNOW THE TIME AND RESOLUTE TO REDEEM IT,
HE HAD ONE AIM:
TO MAKE THE CHURCH OF ENGLAND MORE AND MORE
THE CHURCH OF THE PEOPLE:
DRAWING TOWARDS IT BOTH BY WORD AND GOOD EXAMPLE
ALL WHO LOVE THINGS TRUE AND PURE,
BEAUTIFUL AND OF GOOD REPORT.

# 4

# Shaftesbury and Maurice

I

'Revolutions', he wrote in his journal for 25 March 1848, 'go off like pop-guns!' Yet Lord Ashley, who three years later was to become the seventh Earl of Shaftesbury, did not believe that the explosions rocking the Continent must be followed by a violent class struggle in England. On 13 April, rejoicing over the collapse of the Chartist demonstration in London, he wrote: 'The middle classes are content, and so are nineteen-twentieths of the working people; but this will be of no avail against indistinct terrors, ignorant uneasiness, and speculative, not social, policies.'

His basic confidence in the social order is the more interesting because his knowledge of the defects of capitalism was far from indistinct. As he inspected the mills in Yorkshire where the 'hands' were slave-armies of women, children, and labourers bewildered by their uprooting from the soil, or as he visited the hovels which provided some kind of shelter to the new London poor, or as he poked into the places (one was inside the lawn-roller in Regent's Park) where filthy, verminous, and illiterate children huddled, Shaftesbury was walking where all too many of his fellow-Englishman lived. Consequently he saw legislation as sacred; he saw inexhaustible agitation and negotiation to secure reforms as necessary; and he saw the inspection of the enforcement of laws as a daily task worthy of all the energy of a Christian gentleman.

It was the vision of Tory Democracy, with 'social' aristocrats leading the 'ignorant' people against the 'speculative' merchants; the heady vision of the Young

England of noble scions around the climbing Disraeli. The theory was summed up when in 1848 Lord Ashley produced his answer to the Chartists. He persuaded Prince Albert to inspect some working-class dwellings and then to take the chair at a meeting of the Labourer's Friend Society, despite the hesitations of the politicians. This man whose indignation swept through so many factories always disliked trade unions. He also disliked the idea of life peerages as a blow to the aristocracy; he publicly opposed Disraeli's notion of adding to the Queen the title 'Empress of India'; and he attacked the Salvation Army as another vulgar innovation.

Later generations have forgiven his prejudices as an aristocrat born in 1801, but his fame has seemed more badly tarnished by his fundamentalism. The causes which he led to the incalculable benefit of his age were upheld by him on the basis of a religious faith opposed to that age's whole intellectual life; 'Satan rules in the intellect'. He was a man of God, but he never wearied of arguing that to be a man of God meant to be a man of the infallible Bible. 'The blessed old book is "God's Word written", from the very first syllable down to the very last.' He was a Christian who had compassion on the crowds – and who believed that the essence of Christianity was a narrow creed, because only in that creed had he found his own escape from black depression and the sense of failure.

Again and again in his journal Shaftesbury complained that he was virtually alone in his struggles. It became his habit (in and after 1838) to sacrifice leisure to these secret moans, the egoism of an exhausted man, and although he nearly destroyed the journal he decided in the end to let his biographer use it. The real tragedy of these passages is that, while his fellow Evangelicals were often open to Shaftesbury's condemnation, there were others in England who had a social conscience, but who were not rigidly Evangelical. The Chaplain of Guy's Hospital, F. D. Maurice, warned him in a pamphlet of 1843 of the dangers of admitting only fellow-Evangelicals into his crusades. But the pamphlet breathed sympathy. 'The intercourse into which your Lordship's benevolent labours have brought you, with the middle class of our countrymen, must have made you sensible of the very strong Protestant feelings which pervade it. Take away its Protestantism and it becomes a trading class indeed; that and nothing else.' Such pacifying words were wasted. Shaftesbury had taken the chair at a meeting to demand that Pusey – who was his cousin – and other Tractarians should be more firmly disciplined by their university; and Maurice, who disagreed with Pusey's views, had been stirred to defend Pusey's freedom. But now Maurice's sympathy was repulsed, and Shaftesbury united with Pusey only once, when the two orthodox partriarchs denounced Frederick Temple for liberalism. It was a tragedy, because, although Evangelicalism and liberalism were doubtless destined to collide, in its early stages Tractarianism had not been anti-Evangelical. Shaftesbury's personality on the one side seems to have been as significant as Hurrell Froude's on the other in widening the breach and increasing the bitterness.

Yet this bigoted man was in many ways the embodiment of Christian mercy. He was so overwhelmed by the problems and pains of his contemporaries that he believed the only solution to be the Second Coming of Jesus. He printed a prayer in Greek, 'Even so, come Lord Jesus!', on his envelopes, and he declared that he advocated the Anglican–Lutheran bishopric in Jerusalem, which to Newman was the 'ultimate condemnation 'of Anglicanism, in order to hasten the Coming. When he died, they erected as a monument to him the statue of Eros in Piccadilly Circus, so that the Greek god of desire might shoot his arrows into the idlers, the shoppers, and the pleasure-seekers. It would be hard to think of a more inappropriate memorial. Had he not been such a stalwart Evangelical, they could have put in the heart of London a sign of the love which he did practise: a crucifix.

2

The centre of the old Evangelical scheme of salvation was the experience of alienation from God the Father, without virtue or hope until one accepted the good news of the

146

perfect sacrifice offered on Calvary to appease the just wrath of the Father and to reconcile the Father to sinners. Inevitably many who accepted the Evangelical doctrine had not gone through this experience with much intensity. They had taken the doctrine from parents or teachers with whom they were on good terms. Samuel Wilberforce, for example, was a young Evangelical because his father was William Wilberforce. Sometimes people experienced something like the Evangelical conversion in connection with a shock to their position on earth, as John Henry Newman did in 1816, without having been thoroughly miserable. It was relatively easy for such people to drift away from a strict Evangelicalism.

But for some this Evangelical doctrine expressed, as no other available theology could, escape from the mire. When John Wesley felt his heart 'strangely warmed', it was after a long failure to reach holiness as an Oxford don or effectiveness as a clergyman. Thomas Scott, to whose writing Newman owed so much, was a dim curate of Unitarian views until he was converted by John Newton, the preacher and hymn-writer who had formerly lived in sin as 'white trash' in West Africa and as the captain of a slave-ship. Such men knew that they had been ransomed. And for some, deliverance had come in childhood through a Christian whose love did something to compensate for the absence, indifference, or hostility of parents. We have just seen how the orphaned Archie Tait got his faith from his nurse, Betty Morton. The seventh Earl of Shaftesbury was a Christian because of his nurse, Maria Millis, whose love was more or less the only comfort he knew as a child. He always carried Maria Millis's watch about with him, but also something timeless. To a man who had been miserable because his earthly father and mother had showed no love, the Evangelical doctrine about the angry God, the doomed race, and the propitiating Saviour was now more than theology out of books. Such a man really felt himself to be saved and anything that touched this Gospel touched such a man's heart. Broad as he was, Tait accordingly thought *Essays and Reviews* not religious enough, while Shaftesbury, with his narrower mind, campaigned against that volume vehemently. Shaftesbury also denounced Seeley's prosaically and moralistically liberal portrait of Jesus, *Ecce Homo* (1866), as 'the most pestilential book ever vomited from the jaws of Hell'.

Such experience of a personal salvation in manhood or childhood lay behind the doctrinal inflexibilities of many Evangelicals, and it was natural that the young Lord Ashley should identify himself with the Evangelical party, as he gradually did while he was learning his own mind in the 1830s, without, so far as we know, any great crisis of conversion. Those who had not shared Shaftesbury's bitter youth now tended to notice only his rigidity and gloom (but great Evangelicals such as John Newton and William Wilberforce had not been gloomy); just as those who did not find churchgoing irresistible, and who were not particularly anxious that everyone should have the opportunity to go to church and to be quiet before and after, were depressed by the Victorian Sunday, which owed much to Shaftesbury. Shaftesbury's own eldest son, Anthony, was a rebel who reduced him to despair and who shot himself in a London cab less than a year after inheriting the title.

In an age when many holy men such as Newman felt little obligation in the social field, and when many devout Evangelicals insisted that the poor whom they helped should be the 'deserving' poor, Shaftesbury helped those who were powerless to earn or reward help.

As an ambitious young Westminster politician he did not acquaint himself with factories or slums, but not much pressure on his conscience was needed to send him there. He would in this connexion recall another experience as a boy. After a terrible school at Chiswick – which he afterwards compared with Dotheboys Hall in the no less bitter mind of Dickens – he enjoyed a happier four years at Harrow. While there he saw a pauper's funeral; those who carried the coffin were all drunk. An Indian prince, Guatama the Buddha, when he had a similar shock as a young man resolved to find the path of liberation from a world of suffering, but the English boy who had heard the Gospel of Christ from Maria Millis formed a resolve (dormant, admittedly, for years) to relieve suffering. This eventually meant being prepared to take endless trouble to bring practical help to those in physical or mental distress. Having been miserable himself – lonely, insulted, hungry, and cold although heir to the earldom, for his parents left him to contemptuous servants – he came to identify himself with the broken-hearted and the captives. When he had come into the family honours, he still could not banish a boy's nightmares or a man's memories from his mind, and each summer, while he took his own family to country houses or to fashionable spas on the Continent, he would cut cruelly into his own relaxation by remembering those in the slums for whom sunshine meant heat and stench.

His parents gave him the means, as well as unintentionally the impetus, to live this life of piety and service. His feckless mother, who was dedicated to the pursuit of fashion, was a daughter of the Duke of Marlborough, but at least she provided Maria Millis, who had been a maid in Blenheim Palace. His brutal father – from whom he was estranged for ten years until formally reconciled in 1839, only to be estranged again – was prominent in the House of Lords; he was the chairman of its committee work for forty years. The young man marked his independence by gaining a First at Oxford, yet when he was elected to Parliament at the age of twenty-five it was as member for the Duke of Marlborough's pocket borough, Woodstock. When he was noticed by both Canning and Peel, and appointed to a junior office in Wellington's government, it was because he was a promising Tory. When he was elected for his father's county town of Dorchester in 1830, the election was expensive. When he married, it was to the most admired beauty of the year. Only the deep misery of his childhood could have scarred him enough to make him more than an ornament of this Tory world. In these early days he grew passionately interested in astronomy, and might have become an amateur of science, as his ancestor, the third earl, had been a philosopher and man of letters; but he turned away from the stars, and his first important speech to the Commons was on the treatment of lunatics. Once he had decided what battle to enter, he hit out to the end with an obstinacy recalling the death of his younger brother in a schoolboys' fight at Eton.

His life was determined when in 1833 he took over the Parliamentary sponsorship of the Ten Hours Bill from Michael Sadler, who had lost his seat in the election. At this stage Lord Ashley was the handsome, sensitive, and religious heir to an earldom. A committee went to Westminister to seek a new advocate for the restriction of the daily working hours in the factories, initially in the interests of the women and children employed as cheap labour (but everyone knew that working men would benefit); this committee was recommended to try him, but he had almost no knowledge of industrial conditions apart from what he had picked up by reading *The Times*. It says much for his developing strength of character that his wife, the beautiful Minny, was already converted to an Evangelical seriousness and was foremost among those who now urged him to take up the cause.

He paid for his courage. He could still boast to Peel, 'I know that I have conciliated thousands of hearts to our blessed Constitution'. And he still wanted office, for despite his growing family his father refused him a proper allowance and he hated living in debt to money-lenders who lent at a high interest rate on his expectations; 'my finances are very, very low'. But he was marked as radical, or at least as unreliable. Although Peel at one stage thought of putting him in charge of the Irish problem, all that was offered to him was a seat on the Admiralty Board, and then a post at court. It was clear that he would never now be entrusted with power by Peel: 'he wanted my name, and *nothing* but my name. Had he desired anything else he would never have pressed on me a department in which I could exhibit nothing good but my legs in white shorts . . .' Being very human, he often felt the contrast with his youthful visions of political glory. One journal entry reads: 'I have laboured almost incessantly for four-and-twenty years, and I have never received an honour, or notice of any sort or kind, great or small, from the Crown, the Minister, or the public, except the citizenship of the small borough of Tain, in

Scotland.' But he made it a point of honour to refuse the offer of the Garter in 1854 and the possibility of becoming Home Secretary in 1866.

He paid another penalty in his fight with the factory owners over the Ten Hours Bill. He represented an agricultural constituency and would inherit a large estate. These facts were embarrassments when the industrialists made legitimate propaganda out of low wages and insanitary housing in Dorset. Why did not Lord Ashley do something for farm labourers doomed to bring up families on ten or eight shillings a week in filthy cottages, instead of interfering in the far better paid work of Lancashire or Yorkshire mill-hands? All that Ashley could do was to utter a guarded warning against the neglect of the labourers when addressing the Sturminster Agricultural Society in 1843; and that speech was enough to end his reconciliation with his father, one of the worst employers in Dorset, itself one of the most backward counties. Finally, when Peel deserted the protection of the landowners by proposing the repeal of the Corn laws (which had kept the price of bread high), the industrial employers of labour rejoiced and Ashley, although their enemy, found himself converted to their side and compelled to resign as M.P. for Dorset. So it was that when prolonged agitation behind the Ten Hours Bill at last secured an Act of Parliament, in 1847, Lord Ashley had no seat in Westminster and the honour of sponsoring the Act fell to John Fielden, himself one of the largest cotton-spinners.

There was also an epilogue which emphasized Lord Ashley's ambiguous position. It was found that the limitation of working hours by the 1847 Act was not tight enough because the factory-owners now worked 'relays' or a shift system. Parliament must brace itself to legislate again. At this stage, in 1850, Ashley suggested a compromise to the working men's committees whose battles he had fought so faithfully: a sixty-hour week. He was rewarded by their fury. 'I won for them *almost* everything; but for the loss of that very little, they regard me as an enemy!' In fact it was a Conservative government that finally accepted the full Ten Hours demands in 1874. Many historians – for example the Hammonds in their *Lord Shaftesbury* – have criticized him for not being thorough in his attention to the problems of industrial workers; but that is to misunderstand the man. He had entered the campaign not because he was a man of the Left, but because he was a Christian aristocrat who took pity on women and children. As such he lived down the controversy of 1859, becoming known universally as the Working Man's Friend.

His exclusion from office did not deter him from the work which now commanded his conscience. He had found his vocation in the Parliamentary advocacy of social reform, in tours to gather evidence for it on the spot, in endless duties to inspect its enforcement, and in personal philanthropy to supplement it. Now, one by one, he took up the causes of the oppressed.

As early as 1828 he had been made a Commissioner in Lunacy; six years later he became Chairman of the Commission. He was the chief architect of the Lunacy Act of 1845, and at the time of his last sickness in 1885 was still active in detailed labours in the oversight of the treatment of lunatics. This cause alone would have secured him a true glory, but he also shouldered heroic burdens of work on the Public Health Commission formed in 1848 to force sanitation into one town after another. He did more than any other man to regulate the lodging houses where so many working-class people had to live. He befriended the blind, the cripples, the destitute incurables; the women and children wearing their bodies out in the factories or underground in the mines or as 'gangs' at work on the farms; the boys made to climb chimneys as sweeps; the children beaten into being acrobats; the vagrant boys or the adult thieves whose only hope of escape from a life of crime was the scarcely believable luxury of emigration or training; even the cabmen who needed cheap and respectable clubs. He was not interested in the sufferings of Englishmen only. He insisted on denouncing the British profit from the opium trade imposed on China; he probed into the conditions of factory labour in India; he defended the liberties of Italians and Poles; he fought to restrict the vivisection of animals in laboratories. The older school of politicians was very slow to accept the possibility of action by the State in such fields, and slower still to accept its desirability. 'Is the House prepared to legislate for all these people?' asked Peel in a debate about the factories in 1844. 'Yes!' was the answer shouted back, but Peel threatened to resign if it did.

Until he was fifty years old this courageous reformer was hindered financially by his father's survival and emotionally by his father's hatred; while he habitually referred to his mother as a 'fiend'. When eventually he became Earl of Shaftesbury his work increased, for his creditors demanded the repayment of his own debts and the estate's, and his conscience drove him to improve the disgraceful conditions of his labourers and tenants. The confusion in the estate's affairs plunged him into piles of paper; he then turned back to philanthropy in London only to find that his agent in Dorset swindled him and had to be sued in protracted and expensive legal actions. At no stage did he have a competent secretary or assistant, yet as his fame and involvements increased his hand-written correspondence exhausted him. 'My mind is as dry as a gravel road, and my nerves are sensitive and harsh as wires', he was writing in 1857. His chief pleasure became not his estate but the Ragged Schools, small charitable institutions for very poor boys and girls. He would ask for the prayers of the children, boast of their successes, and treasure their letters. He also found consolation in the work of the Young Men's Christian Associations, then on a strong Evangelical foundation.

Another form of public service which would have brought some pleasure to many other men seems to have been regarded by him as a burden: he was chairman of innumerable missionary and charitable meetings. Nearly five hundred of these were represented at his funeral in Westminster Abbey. The most influential on the home front was the Church Pastoral Aid Society, founded with the young Lord Ashley as President in 1836 in order to supply Evangelical curates and 'lay agents' in 'popular' districts. The most scholarly was the Parker Society founded with the same President in 1840 in order to reprint the divines of the English Reformation. But there were many others – too many – from the Bible Society downwards. In addition there were many rallies or special services in theatres or in Exeter Hall in London (the scene of much of this oratory, built in 1831). He was expected to dignify the proceedings, to read a lesson, to speak. He was always applauded, yet he allowed himself so little time for rest or preparation that he knew that his speeches were usually stale and often they bored him.

'Is he thinking more of the clubs of St. James's Street than the audience of the Heavenly host?' he asked about Lord Raglan's conduct in the Crimea. The question never arose about him; and he was as indifferent to the universities as to the London clubs. He had not endured the abuse of the factory-owners, or the learned arguments of eminent doctors produced to testify to the beneficial effects of machine-minding on the health of women and children, in order to capitulate to scholarly critics of the Bible. He had not spent so many hours unravelling the case histories of people thought justly or unjustly to be lunatics, in order to have others hint that his religion had damaged his mind. Once a lady appeared before him while he was acting as a Lunacy Commissioner. 'Are you aware, my Lord, that she subscribes to the Society for the Conversion of the Jews?' 'Indeed! And are you aware that I am President of that society?'

The one mundane reward which this austere man enjoyed was some taste of power in making ecclesiastical appointments. His was the most momentous word in the creation of three archbishops, sixteen bishops, and thirteen deans. This came about because his mother-in-law took Lord Palmerston as her second husband, and his own wife Minny was widely rumoured to be Palmerston's daughter (her nominal father was the fifth Earl Cowper). Palmerston knew almost nothing of theology or clergymen, but respected Shaftesbury. Shaftesbury on his side approved of 'Pam', who had supported factory legislation when Gladstone had fumbled, and who had raised high the reputation of Britain for a moralizing interference in the affairs of European nations. While Palmerston was Prime

Minister (1855–65, with one year's interruption) Shaftesbury therefore became the eminence behind the scenes. Despite the lamentations of Samuel Wilberforce and others, he used his power well on the whole. The Prime Minister's only instruction was that the bishops should be men who got on with the Nonconformists. Shaftesbury, although he naturally preferred to produce an Evangelical for promotion, did not exclude all Broad Churchmen. For example, he recalled: 'I suggested to him Dr. Tait for London ... believing that the Broad Church ought to be represented ... and selected Dr. Tait as the mildest among them.' He often gave vent to impatience with the dignitaries of the Church, mainly because they did not support him enough in social reforms, and as an anti-Tractarian he declared that 'nothing would more tend to induce great numbers of people to join our Church than the putting an end to a state of things under which Ordination is left in the hands of a single individual.' But, being an aristocrat, he did believe very firmly in the usefulness of strong leadership. Palmerston persuaded Shaftesbury to accept the Garter and as he lay dying, and was asked by Shaftesbury whether he believed in redemption through Christ, replied: 'Oh, surely.'

3

To Frederick Denison Maurice, the revolutionary dramas of 1848 went beyond any sphere to be covered by Prince Albert's benevolence. When he preached on Advent Sunday that year his excitement was still intense:

The flourishes and exaggerations of rhetoric, puerile always, become absolutely ridiculous when they are set side by side with the experiences through which Europe has been passing and is passing. Do you really think the invasion of Palestine by Sennacherib was a more wonderful event than the overthrowing of nearly all the greatest powers, civil and ecclesiastical, in Christendom?

The year seemed to Maurice a veritable Apocalypse. When, later on, he came to lecture on the last book in the Bible, he was to compare the Babylon of St. John the Divine's vision with Victorian London; and now in 1848 he heard the thunder of destiny.

He was also stirred, more than Lord Ashley was, to do something for – and with – healthy, male workers. One practical result of the agitation was that he became President of the Society for Promoting Working Men's Associations, and one great achievement of this society was to promote legislation which made it far easier for such 'associations' to register themselves against fraud, and in general to establish themselves as legal entities. With the backing of John Stuart Mill and lesser economists, with the blessing of a Conservative (Derby–Disraeli) government which wished to court the workers, and with remarkably little opposition, an Act to protect 'Industrial and Provident Societies' was passed by Parliament in 1852. It was the charter of all modern co-operatives. Although its terms were modest enough (it did not grant limited liability), Shaftesbury refused to sponsor it, and the M.P. whose name was associated with this measure was the otherwise obscure Robert Slaney.

The only occasion when Maurice and Shaftesbury collaborated seems to have been the launching of one of the associations – a short-lived experiment to help women skilled at needlework. Maurice sent £25 with a letter saying that his name as one of the sponsors was 'likely to disgust Lord Shaftesbury and his friends'. It was just as well that he was not present at the inaugural meeting in Shaftesbury's home, for the proceedings included a proposal from Thomas Carlyle that the problems of distressed needlewomen should be solved by shipping them to California, where they would find husbands. It was also just as well for the needlewomen that Shaftesbury was not made more aware of the philosophical implication of their 'association' in the minds of the Christian Socialists who looked to Maurice as their prophet. One of these, John Malcolm Ludlow, who was present at the meeting, was still smarting under the peer's patronage when he wrote retrospectively in 1868: 'Lord Shaftesbury's ideal was one of dumb instinctive obedience, not of self mastery in the harmonious fellowship of work. Substantially he had to work *de haut en bas*. He delighted in raising the humble, and the humbler the better . . .'

It was in Maurice's house that Charles Kingsley composed his placard during the evening of 10 April 1848, after the failure of the Chartist demonstration: 'The Almighty God, and Jesus Christ, the poor Man who died for poor men, will bring freedom for you, though all the Mammonites on earth were against you . . . Workers of England, be wise, and then you *must* be free, for you will be *fit* to be free.' To be sure, the courage of this manifesto has been exaggerated by later writers who have pretended that the whole religious world of the day was hostile. In fact preachers and religious journalists seem to have sympathized on the whole with the early attempts of Maurice and his friends to get alongside the workers, just as the reaction of Chartists to such support seems to have been favourable on the whole, although no great notice was taken in any quarter. But those few who like Kingsley could stammer out at a meeting 'I am a Church of England clergyman . . . *and* a Chartist' were doing more than sympathizing. Telling the workers to be wise was no novelty. The courageous innovation lay in working alongside them so that they might raise themselves; and it was this that in the 1850s brought on Kingsley, and on Maurice, the wrath of the religious Tories of the *Record* and the *Quarterly Review* – and of secularists such as Karl Marx who feared competition from the Christian Socialists' 'holy water'.

Interference in the workings of the new industrial society was, indeed, so daring for a Church of England man that, just as Lord Ashley did not identify himself with factory reform until 1833, so Maurice did not become a Christian Socialist until 1848. Of course neither man had been totally oblivious before his conversion to reform. The young aristocrat had already undertaken his work for lunatics; the young clergyman had ministered to the sick of London as Chaplain of Guy's Hospital, and had welcomed Carlyle's *Chartism*. And of course other examples of practical sympathy with the workers could be found in the Church of England (specially in the North). But it is significant that Ashley could feel so isolated in his social crusading. The Tractarians were more worried about the suppression of bishops in Ireland than about the deaths of babies in the slums which Oxford colleges owned. Samuel Wilberforce was advised by his father that a Northern industrial parish was no place for a young clergyman to cultivate his devotional life. Many churchmen were worried by the fear of revolution which had contributed to the appeal of William Wilberforce; some were worried into urgent words, such as the semi-radical Arnolds (or the romantically Tory Poet Laureate, Robert Southey, whose hatred of the barbarism in the new manufacturing towns impressed both Shaftesbury and Maurice). But fewer were worried into effective sympathy.

Therefore when a movement called itself 'Christian Socialist', it was combining the two words in a startling paradox. By the end of the century, the Christian Social Union was to be a nursery of bishops, and the rise of the Labour Party was to owe much to the work of the local churches and chapels in training men to concentrate, to combine and to speak up for idealistic purposes. Ludlow lived to speak at the Pan Anglican Congress of 1908, rejoicing in that scene of social idealism at the age of eighty-eight. But in the 1840s not only were most Christians unsocial: all Socialists were thought by respectable property-owners to be atheistic and violent. Maurice joined the two words with his usual educational purpose, for the paradox would make men think. To encourage men further, he edited the penny tracts, *Politics for the People,* and Ludlow edited the journal, the *Christian Socialist.* The idea of tracts had been in Maurice's mind for years, and he had also had the idea of calling them Cambridge Tracts. However, neither the tracts nor the journal reached a large audience, or lasted long. As a journalist Maurice was no Newman, and Christian Socialism never possessed the intellectual coherence of Oxford Tractarianism.

Much of the material which it sponsored was diffuse, aimed at making churchmen sympathetic and workers wise. Kingsley emerged as the movement's only vigorous popular publicist, with his novels about farm labourers and tailors (*Yeast* and *Alton Locke*) and his shorter writings as 'Parson Lot'. The political thrust, when this emerged,

the Maurice of my own imagination'. Perhaps
ght to have been warned in the very day of
demonstration, when Maurice, who had
olled as a Special Constable in order to pro-
stayed at home because he had a cold and
erve his voice for his Sunday sermon. Certain-
hile he was wrecking the Christian Socialist
Ludlow conceived it, he gave a convincing
did not merely say that he was more interested
han in politics, although his work for King's
he Queen's College for women, and (in the
or the Working Men's College might have
fficient alibi. Nor did he merely disclaim the
ratory and business of, say, Shaftesbury. (He
lecturing with his eyes closed which, we are
ed disorder when his audiences were present
lsion, and we may gather that when his
e voluntary they might be small.) It could not
, as it could be said of Shaftesbury, that he
controversies because he had a large vested
economic order; nor was personal ambition
ike the Oxford Tractarians he had pledged
id ecclesiastical preferment and the favour
In 1849 he had written, and had meant it:
s with the discontented, weary, hopeless, with
debt, and disgrace, with outcasts and rag-
e different bodies.' But Maurice knew that
as not limitless. His integrity as a spiritual
d to demand refusal to get involved in argu-
e division of the political and economic in-
ng the discontented.
f 1849 had hinted at the foundations. 'I have
things can be kept going upon our present
tual hatred and suspicion. The end of that
must be at hand, and the only work I desire
ring people for it, by showing them that there
tand upon when the rains descend and the
ow in 1852 he wrote to Ludlow:
cause I am a theologian, and have no vocation
ogy, is not to build, but to dig, to show that

162

was towards 'associations' – co-operative workshops where
the capital would be provided initially by well-wishers and
subsequently by ploughing back profits. The idea was in
the air of early English Socialism, but Maurice himself
owed it to a letter from Ludlow (now lost) which passed on
some of the excitements of the French experiments and some
of the warnings of the French disturbances. Ludlow's own
strong personality reinforced this dramatic message from
Paris. He had been left fatherless and had been taken by
his mother for a first-rate education in France. He had
become a conveyancer (solicitor) in London because his
mother had told him that his father would have wished him
to be an Englishman, but had felt lonely and near suicide
in a strange land. He had met Maurice because he wanted
advice about how to do social work in his spare time;
Maurice had referred him to the nearby parish priest, but
had kept in touch with Ludlow because he gave to this
work some of the collections in Lincoln's Inn Chapel,
where he was Chaplain. Now in 1848 Ludlow virtually
appointed Maurice his spiritual father, and summoned
him to lead a crusade. When the crisis was over, it was
Ludlow who kept up the pressure on the London group to
produce something like the newspaper he had envisaged
for France (it was to have been called *La Fraternité Chré-
tienne*) and something like the working communities he had
glimpsed there, notably Fourier's scheme for college-like
*phalanges*.

Many small producers' co-operatives were founded in
England during and after 1850, and conferences of their
representatives were gathered. Ludlow believed passionately
that they pointed to the salvation of the society, and was
never completely disillusioned. In the twentieth century the
banner was handed on to the Guild Socialists such as G. D.
H. Cole, and to many later advocates of 'partnership',
'co-ownership', or 'profit-sharing' schemes for industry.
But the main emphasis in the powerful Co-operative Movement derived from the Toad Lane Store in Rochdale, not
from the idealists of the London workshops. Producers' co-
operatives ran into many difficulties. Some of their members
were fraudulent, and others inefficient. Wages were a prob-

lem, once it was agreed that it was unrealistic to make these equal, and prices too, until consumers were regenerate. All the time it was difficult to secure the orders and to market the goods. Not surprisingly, most workmen preferred to get regular wages from capitalists. On the other hand, consumers' co-operatives found competition with the capitalist system easier, for they paid dividends to purchasers and could with relative ease manufacture their own goods for sale to their own members. Consumers' co-operatives never enjoyed the sacred ideology which Maurice and Ludlow bestowed on the workers whose associations they promoted, yet few could deny their economic benefits, nor the advantage to them of the 1852 Act. Even they, however, did not lay down the high road of Socialism. That road was provided by state interference, growing in England almost continuously during and after the 1870s. Ludlow, who was appointed Chief Registrar of Friendly Societies in 1875 and who encouraged many steps towards social security either as a civil servant or as a writer, would say to the end of his long life that to him Socialism was a faith, not a business. He often struck men of the world as being doctrinaire, perhaps because his mind was French. He thought it vitally important that Maurice, the only major prophet he knew, should guide the advance, and should be supported by 'a true and holy Jesuitry'. When Maurice abandoned the leadership of Christian Socialism Ludlow did not attempt to take it up, although he often looked back and asked himself whether he should have done more.

The immediate cause of Maurice's withdrawal from 'politics for the people' was his concentration on his Principalship of the Working Men's College, first housed in the premises of the defunct Needlewomen's Association, but many tensions had arisen before 1854 among the Christian Socialists. They were tensions between those who regarded the work as primarily political or economic, and those who regarded it as educational. Maurice was in the latter group, Ludlow in the former, although he loyally became Maurice's chief lieutenant in the college. Another leader of the work now emerged: Vansittart Neale, a barrister with no clear theological views but with a grasp of the practical problems

economy and politics (I leave physics to dear Kingsley ...) must have a ground beneath themselves, that society is not to be made anew by arrangements of ours, but is to be regenerated by finding the law and ground of its order and harmony, the only secret of its existence, in God.

Both Ludlow and Maurice agreed in the aim of the Society for Promoting Working Men's Associations: 'to diffuse the principle of Co-operation as the practical application of Christianity to the progress of trade and industry. To Ludlow, however, the associations were the first steps in a political programme, putting capital into the hands of the workers. To Maurice these small experiments were prophetic signs, declaring against every economist's emphasis on general or corporate or class selfishness that men were brothers, tied by blood not money in a Divine Order which already existed. The profits of the co-operatives interested him less than their brotherhood; their value as pointers to the future less than their value as revelations of present facts. He was a little more practical over the management of colleges, but when he came to expound his philosophy of adult education, in his lectures on *Learning and Working* (1855), he showed a similar contempt for commercial considerations. We cannot wonder that some of the Christian Socialists who referred to him as 'the Prophet' privately found him maddening. On the other hand, Maurice the visionary has held a more permanent interest than Ludlow the reformer. The hard times of the Hungry Forties passed, thanks in part to reforms but mainly to the unregulated expansion of the economy, although much distress remained in the shadows of Victorian life. But Maurice's reforms in the kingdom of faith and the imagination have continued to command attention.

John Stuart Mill himself witnessed to the primacy of the theological debate. In the last chapter of his *Autobiography* he noted that the reforms after 1848 'had been attended with much less benefit to human well-being than I should formerly have anticipated' because they had not altered the average Englishman's confused habits of mind. Mill, writing about 1861, added:

When the philosophic minds of the world can no longer believe its religion or can only believe it with modifications amounting to an eventual change of its character, a transitional period commences, of weak convictions, paralysed intellects, and growing laxity of principle, which cannot terminate until a renovation has been effected in the basis of their belief, leading to the evolution of some faith, whether religious or merely human, which they can really believe: and when things are in this state, all thinking or writing which does not tend to promote such a renovation, is of very little value beyond the moment.

## 4

'The world', wrote Tom Hughes, 'has only had three great theologians, Augustine, Luther and Maurice, and the greatest of these is Maurice.' Since the second world war several books have offered enthusiastic introductions to the thought of Maurice, whose published writings may be said to need summary, for another commentator, Claude Jenkins, reckoned that they contained nearly five million words. Yet in his own lifetime Maurice knew that he was often regarded as a 'muddy mystic', and after his death Leslie Stephen's memoir in the *Dictionary of National Biography*, while describing his character as 'very fascinating', left the impression that the only interest of his mind lay in its confusion. Matthew Arnold observed that Maurice passed his life 'beating the bush with deep emotion and never starting the hare', while John Stuart Mill paid the wry tribute that 'there was more intellectual power wasted in Maurice than in any other of my contemporaries'. Part of the blame attaches to Maurice's habit of dictating some of his books, walking up and down, hugging a pillow, and furiously poking the fire. But, even when he did not dictate, the style was the man: his manuscripts show the haste with which he wrote. He was essentially a preacher out to warn or comfort, who did not mind if the fire was scattered or if the pillow induced mental sleep. In this he was like Augustine and Luther, but although Maurice was the greatest English theologian of the nineteenth century he did not attain their greatness, for he did not have their ruthless clarity or the world-transforming courage of their radicalism.

Like Shaftesbury, he had an experience as a boy which eventually shaped his life. He owed much to Plato and to Coleridge, because he found in their philosophies echoes of his own experience, but he gained few of his theological insights from the Cambridge tutor who took him through Plato (Julius Hare, who became his brother-in-law), and he was too shy to meet Coleridge. He was, like Shaftesbury, a man of the Bible – and was more truly biblical, for he objected to the Evangelical (or Tractarian) 'system' of 'notions' which tended to prevent the Bible from speaking for itself; yet this exposition of the Bible was full of pet ideas and reiterated jargon. We are told that he borrowed many of these special meanings for common theological terms from his mother. Essentially his thought was home-made. His was a home intensely pious and intensely intellectual, and at first it seemed that on leaving it he would concentrate on the enthusiasm for current affairs which he inherited from his father. After leaving Cambridge he tried his hand as a London journalist and as a novelist (his *Eustace Conway* was published in 1834). But the novel showed that what really stirred him was the drama of a conflict of religious opinions in a family, and it hinted at a deeply theological solution.

His father was a Unitarian minister, insisting on the reality and unity of God but teaching mainly about morals and politics. With his tolerant liberalism, Michael Maurice baptized in the name of the Father, and of the Son, and of the Holy Ghost; 'in the name of an abstraction, a man, and a metaphor' as a friend remarked pleasantly. (Who would have ventured on such a pleasantry with any other member of the family?) Such a religion was not enough for his three eldest daughters, who had themselves baptized again and who wrote to him in 1816: 'We do not think it consistent with the duty we owe to God to attend a Unitarian place of worship.' One of these girls became a Baptist, although the others were Anglicans. Nor was it enough for his wife; she soon became an earnest Calvinist in the Church of England, sending letters of religious advice to her husband but believing that she was not herself numbered among the elect of God.

Nor was it enough for Frederick. But the boy was loyal to his father's example which combined integrity with broad mindedness, and probably he also noticed the patience with which his father received letters about theology from the women living under his roof. He therefore refused to undergo a thoroughly Evangelical conversion in his boyhood, or to sign the Church of England's Articles in order to proceed to a Cambridge degree and a career. What crisis there was came to a climax when he was aged twenty-six, in 1831, feeling the need of a 'personal deliverer'. He was baptized in Oxford as a member of the Church of England, and spent almost the whole of the next three months at the deathbed of his sister Emma, conversing mainly on Evangelical themes. That winter he was able to inform his father that he had found the satisfying answer to 'the one great cry of human nature in all ages'. 'If the Infinite, Incomprehensible Jehovah is manifested in the person of a Man, a Man conversing with us, living among us, entering into all our infirmities and temptations, and passing into all our conditions, it is satisfied; if not, it remains unsatisfied.' By moving beyond his father's position he had found his own faith to proclaim, and he spoke the Trinitarian blessing as his last words early on Easter Monday, 1872. But he could never say that he had passed from secular darkness into Evangelical light, for the Christ whom he had found as the one Redeemer was a Christ who preached a message not utterly remote from Michael Maurice's.

The discovery of Christ as the shining centre of the universe, and this refusal to banish anyone to outer darkness, provided the message, reached after countless hours of theological argument in his family, and after years spent like Jonah trying to escape his destiny to be a preacher. No attack by agnostics or Evangelicals could ever move him. Yet he was so assured as to be tolerant. The whole of a personality deeply Christian lay behind his refusal to place the Socialists, or his pragmatic collaborator Vansittart Neale, beyond the pale of Christianity. His greatest scholarly work was a history of *Moral and Metaphysical Philosophy*

(1861), designed to show how a Christian might learn from the intellectual life of mankind. He went far towards saying that each nation's history was its own Old Testament; not only England's or Germany's, but also the Eastern nation's (about which he, naturally, knew far less). When in 1845–6 he delivered the Boyle Lectures on *The Religions of the World*, he was clear both that Christ was the Revelation of God and that Muslims or Buddhists were seeking God in sincerity and with some success. Maurice dared to express this wide vision at a time when Reginald Heber was hymning the religion of Buddhist Ceylon in these terms:

> The heathen in his blindness
> Bows down to wood and stone.

The nature of Maurice's own spiritual pilgrimage also determined the nature of his vision of the Church. Unlike Newman, he did not see the Church as the substitute for, and therefore effectively the enemy of, the natural family and the normal life. On the contrary, Maurice proclaimed – like Keble, but with a passionate conviction which never lost its urgency however often he repeated himself – that men entered the Church through the family. If they were faithful to the duties of family life, they would be faithful also to the duties of national citizenship, and if they understood themselves properly as members of families and nations they would enter into their heritage as members of the Church, the universal family.

Maurice expounded his vision of the Church to a Scotsman, Thomas Erskine, whose own generous views had provided a large influence and encouragement.

The Church—it seems to me—is a part, the highest part, of that spiritual constitution of which the nation and the family are lower and subordinate parts; implied in the acts we do and the words we speak, established before all worlds, manifested as the true and everlasting kingdom when the Son of God died, rose, and ascended on high, testified as the common property and inheritance of men by certain forms and ordinances which convert it from an idea for the mind into an actual reality for all who will enter into it and enjoy it, and which prove God to be true though all men be liars.

Maurice went so far as to deny that Christianity was 'a religion'. To call it a religion was to limit or to corrupt its message about God the Father of all. 'We have been dosing our people with religion, when what they want is not this but the living God.' And the living God, the God of Jesus Christ, was not remote. 'The revelation of Christ', he wrote to his sister Esther (Mrs Julius Hare), 'must be the revelation, however gradually, of all these hidden principles and secret powers, and directing laws, which men in all directions have been seeking after; must be the revelation of all the relations in which they stand to each other and to God's universe.' In the same letter he envisaged 'the Son of God vindicating the name of the carpenter's son which He bore upon earth by asserting every energy of man's bodily frame, every natural machine as His.'

This vision of Christ as 'the Ruler over the universe now' arose from a boy's protest against the theological quarrels which were tearing his father apart from his mother and which were dividing his seven sisters. The vision was strengthened by his early experience as a clergyman. He served as a curate under an incumbent who had a theory about the Revelation of St. John the Divine. There was nothing extraordinary about that; stranger, however, was the nature of Mr. Stephenson's theory, as recalled by his curate. At an early stage

he maintained that the hills and valleys of this earth, redeemed, purified, and regenerated, were to be the scene of the felicity of the ransomed children of God ... This opinion he never changed, but deeper study and meditation ... led him to conclusions very different from those which are adopted by modern readers of prophecy generally ... He became convinced that the greater part of those Scriptures which are usually referred to a far distant period, were actually accomplished when the Jewish polity passed away and the universal Church rose out of its ruins ..., that these events were nothing less than the actual manifestation of Christ's Kingdom, the actual establishment of a communion between the two worlds, the creation of a new heaven and a new earth.

It was a version of the old millenarian belief that Christ and his saints would reign on the earth for a thousand years; but it added that they were *already* reigning. In the midst of such speculation Mr. Stephenson's curate heard the one message he needed. When Maurice, still suffering from shyness and a 'great depression of spirits', moved to London and Guy's Hospital, he remembered the message and lived by it. He found courage to approach the sick, or to lecture to the medical students, only because he now believed that the goodness which he found in them (among much else) pointed to the fact that they, too, were already citizens in Christ's Kingdom, for they had been baptized. 'It seemed to me that except I could address all kinds of people as members of Christ and children of God, I could not address them at all.'

He therefore shared the Tractarians' insistence that the Church was constituted not by feelings or 'notions', but by objective realities. What, however, were the sacraments? In 1837 he was crossing Clapham Common on his way to an Evangelical meeting and reading Dr. Pusey's immense Tract Sixty-seven on Baptism. 'The baptized child was holy for a moment after its baptism, by committing sin it lost its purity. That could be recovered by acts of repentance and a system of ascetical discipline.' So he understood as he read, and the apparent denial of the sure status of all the baptized horrified him. He now publicly broke with the Tractarians, who had previously been hoping that he would join them in Oxford as Professor of Political Economy, and in 1841 he published an open letter to Archdeacon Samuel Wilberforce, entitled *Reasons for Not Joining a Party in the Church*. But he did not prefer the Evangelical view of Baptism, which tended to imply that the service mattered little in comparison with the emotions of the 'second birth'; and he was soon to incur the wrath of that party by his open letter to Lord Ashley against the persecution of Pusey. What he did believe he poured out in a book which was published in 1838 as a series of Anglican tracts for Quakers. He revised these chapters in 1841, to form his most important work, *The Kingdom of Christ*.

He chose to address the Quakers because he believed that the Society of Friends was 'likely to perish by a slow decay' unless its members would move beyond the spirituality of its founder in the seventeeth century, George Fox.

The decay had come because the Quakers had fallen victims to the disease of the age, 'money-getting', but this itself could be traced to Fox's trust in an 'inward light' when he ought to have been humble enough to receive the only light and power greater than the appeal of 'money-getting'.

For a description of this light and power Maurice turned to Luther, who 'told men that union with Christ was deliverance from sin and condemnation; that that union was claimed and maintained by faith; that faith was therefore justification'. Maurice understood the heart of Lutheranism as very few other Englishmen did; yet he rejected the 'mysteries' which had corrupted the 'principles' of the Reformitaon. What he offered in the place of Lutheran orthodoxy was a series of 'hints' about the nature of the Catholic Church with this experience of faith at its heart. To him as much as to the Tractarians, the Church was 'built upon the very nature of God himself, and upon the union which He has formed with His creatures'; yet, true to the way in which he had experienced faith, he preferred to begin with the natural family, 'the true order of the world'. In the Church there were certain 'signs' which pointed to Christ as King and God as Father. These were Baptism itself, the sacrament which asserted the 'constant union' between God and his children; the creeds which were confessions of 'the Name' of our salvation; liturgical forms of public worship, the family's praise of the Father; the Eucharist, the family's communion, nourishing body and spirit with its witness to the finished work of Christ; the orders of ministry including episcopacy, signs of the universality of Christ's Church; and the Scriptures. So the Church George Fox had dismissed as 'steeple-houses' was idealized by Maurice, but also identified with the world as it 'really' was.

When you go into the town to market, look up at the churches and say,—'This, too, is my Father's dwelling place; these are witnesses that I am a citizen of the New Jerusalem, that I belong to an innumerable company of saints and angels, and that all these men who are about me, are of the same family. The city and the men in it are holy.'

It is not difficult to see how the experience reflected in *The Kingdom of Christ* enabled Maurice to prophesy with a vision of the City of God in 1848, and to persevere with his message. 'The desire for unity, and the search after unity both in the nation and in the Church, has haunted me all my days', he told his son Frederick when he was near the end, after confessing that 'I have laid a great many addled eggs in my time'. He ascribed parties in the Church to the devilish spirit of sectarianism and refused to be the leader of a Broad Church party, as he had refused to organize the Christian Socialists. 'I am sure the Liturgy will torment us so long as we continue selfish and divided, therefore I would cling to it': that was one of his ways of extolling the Prayer Book. He defended the Thirty-nine Articles on the ground that they preserved the Church from the 'superstitions' of the nineteeth century. He was reluctant to abandon the use of the Athanasian Creed, claiming that it had never made him feel uncharitable. And he magnified his clerical office, writing: 'If we called the four Gospels "The Institution of a Christian Ministry," we might not go very far wrong.' But the desire for unity which made him for practical purposes a conservative in ecclesiastical politics also made him a preacher of social reconciliation and joint progress, and a High Statesman. 'The State is as much God's creation as the Church, even as the body is just as much his creation as the spirit.' On this basis he struggled to reassert Richard Hooker's theme of the unity of Church and State. To him, this seemed as appropriate in Victorian as in Elizabethan England; but he also looked forward to the time when the Episcopal Church in the United States would have earned establishment as the National Church. (Until then, were the United States a true nation?) He was not greatly interested in those privileges for the Church of England's bishops and clergy which might be affected by Parliamentary pressures, but he declared: 'The duty which the State owes to the Church . . . is simply this: to give the Church free scope to educate the people.'

Maurice had little sympathy with the Dissenters' protests against an Anglican monopoly in state-supported schools: 'you, not we, are the exclusionists.' His failure of imagination here was one of the indications that his zeal for Anglicanism was the zeal of a convert from Unitarianism. It was his experience that the Church of England meant liberty of spirit, and he could not understand those for whom it would be a prison. After his restless years in Cambridge and London he had enrolled at Oxford, again as an undergraduate, in order to prepare for Anglican ordination; and even Oxford's insistence on the signing of the Thirty-nine Articles on entry (Cambridge required it only on graduation) had seemed glorious to him, as he declared while a curate in his pamphlet *Subscription No Bondage*. Thomas Erskine once observed that his friend could find a good reason for *anything*, and Maurice came to admit that it had been a mistake to require undergraduates to subscribe to the Articles. We must confess that his detailed arguments often amount to 'vague generalities' or 'declamations', the very things which the Utilitarians sought to expose. But no Christocentric vision could be, in principle, more inclusive.

## 5

Maurice's experience led him to attack the Evangelicalism of his day. He rebuked its whole atmosphere as shown in Shaftesbury's life: both the emotionalism of its introspection and the bitterness of its polemics. He rebuked it with a wider vision of the People of God, and in the fifteenth of his *Theological Essays* he poured forth his vision in tumbling paradoxes: 'The world contains the elements of which the Church is composed. In the Church, those elements are penetrated by a uniting, reconciling power. The Church is, therefore, human society in its normal state; the world, that same society irregular and abnormal. The world is the Church without God; the Church is the world restored to its relation with God, taken back by Him into the state for which he created it. Deprive the Church of its Centre, and you make it into a world.'

Maurice disliked the Evangelicals' obsession with the depravity of mankind. Maurice's own mother believed that she had no hope of salvation, and a letter to her in 1833 was typical of his efforts to lift her out of her gloom.

My text is this, 'Know ye not that Jesus Christ is in you?' ... The truth is that every man is in Christ; the condemnation of every man is, that he will not own the truth; he will not *act* as if this were *true*, he will not believe that which is the truth that, except he were joined to Christ, he could not think, breathe, live a single hour. This is the monstrous lie which the devil palms upon poor sinners. 'You are something apart from Christ. You have a separate, independent existence.'

The Evangelicals started from the sin of Adam, and some of them like poor Priscilla Maurice fixed themselves there. Priscilla's son knew why, and as late as 1845 he wrote to his sister Esther: 'How thoroughly one knows that the Devil is the spirit of despair!' But he was convinced that Christian theology should start with the original righteousness, with the Lordship of Christ, and when he wished to arouse a sense of sin he said: 'You are under a law of love; you know you are, and you are fighting with it.'

It was fatally easy to present the Evangelical scheme of salvation in such a way as to suggest that the Father's justice demanded the Son's sacrifice as a transaction to be completed before the Father's love could be shown. Indeed, the second of the Thirty-nine Articles which Maurice extolled declared that Christ died 'to reconcile his Father to us'. Maurice believed in the sacrifice offered by Christ, but he preferred to speak of Christ as men's representative – as 'the Head and King of our Race' into whom we are incorporated as one Body – rather than of Christ as the substitute for men's sins. He saw Calvary as the supreme manifestation of the love of the Father: 'Christ satisfied the Father by presenting the image of His own holiness of love'. And he saw the sacrifice of Christ as a sign of the eternal relation of love between the Persons of the Trinity: 'we must not dare to speak of Christ as changing that Will which he took flesh and died to fulfil'. Indeed, he saw all human life as founded on love, and love as founded on self-sacrifice; sacrifice is 'the law of our being'. He repeated such phrases often, bringing together the Trinity, the nation, and the family; and he repeated them sincerely. He poured himself out for others in a life which reflected his doctrine of the Trinity. In particular his second wife Georgina, whom he married in 1849 four years after Annie's death, was a Victorian invalid who needed, or seemed to need, his constant self-sacrifice.

When consigning obstinate sinners to everlasting punishment Evangelical preachers were only echoing the belief of Christendom, but they seemed to sentence more people to this fate, since many concluded that the only members of the human race with a hope of escaping it were those few who before their death had put their trust in Christ's sacrifice as the substitute to appease the wrath of God. Calvinists limited the numbers escaping hell to those predestined by God. In the last of his *Theological Essays* (1853), Maurice repeated an argument which he had made public in his earlier writings, to the effect that the Greek word *aionios* in the biblical description of hell meant not 'endless' but 'eternal'. His conservative instincts battled with his human sympathies here as in Christian Socialism, and he denied that he was a universalist who believed that all men were bound to be saved. But he also denied that sinners would experience everlasting tortures, and as he lay dying he thought about the mysterious passage in the First Epistle of Peter on the harrowing of hell. 'As the ark saved the eight souls as a promise that *all* should be saved', he mused, 'so baptism saved those who were baptized, thus figuring God's salvation of all.' When he wrote on everlasting punishment in his *Theological Essays* he knew, as he said, that he was writing his own death-sentence as a professor at King's College. But he could do no other. 'I am obliged to believe in an abyss of love which is deeper than the abyss of death: I dare not lose faith in that love. I sink into death, eternal death, if I do.' Modern theologians have tended to comment that Maurice's conviction that the Kingdom of Christ was already present on earth, and his conception of eternity, both reflected Platonist idealism rather than biblical doctrine, but that has not prevented the very widespread acceptance of his protest against the old pictures of hell.

Punishment on earth came soon. King's College, London, had been founded as an Anglican reply to the 'godless' University College; power over it was vested in trustees who were mostly devout peers, and in the Principal, who was then the unimaginative Dr. Jelf (Maurice had refused to be a candidate for the post). Maurice's supporters rightly believed that the peers were not deeply involved in the metaphysical foundations of the intellectual problem of conceiving eternity. But during the first three months of 1852 there had been a major industrial dispute in the shape of a national lock-out, marking the rise of the first of the modern trade unions, the Amalgamated Society of Engineers, to whom Ludlow gave legal advice. The trustees of King's College, as they turned over publications such as Charles Kingsley's exposure of the conditions of tailors in *Cheap Clothes and Nasty*, saw what might be the consequences of a decline in the lower orders of belief that strikes and other rebellions against authority would bring everlasting punishment. Professor Maurice at that stage occupied two chairs in King's College, one on English Literature and Modern History, the other of Theology. The majority on the trustees' council refused the suggestion of Bishop Blomfield that competent theologians should examine the professor's writings. Instead the trustees felt 'it to be their painful duty to declare that the continuance of Professor Maurice's connexion with the college as one of its professors would be seriously detrimental to its usefulness'. They also felt competent to declare the two chairs vacant; but in so doing they made the ex-professor an underdog, and dramatized for the British public the moral iniquity of the old belief. (Tennyson wrote a poem about it all.) When Maurice was elected Knightsbridge Professor of Casuistry and Moral Philosophy at Cambridge in 1866, his name seemed to have been cleared at the expense of the everlasting punishment of the wicked.

What, then, of the mid-Victorian Evangelicals' belief in the verbal infallibility of the Bible? Maurice in the pulpit, in the Bible classes which he loved to conduct, and in private conversation breathed an intense reverence for Holy Scripture, 'I am conscious of just as much unbelief about the books of the Bible, as I am about the facts of nature and my own existence,' he boasted when writing 'On Inspiration' in his *Theological Essays*. When he said that 'the Bible itself forces us to ask a multitude of questions', he had in mind not so much questions arising out of science as moral questions; this remark was made in connexion with Elisha's cursing of the impertinent children. When Colenso applied criticism to some of these books he took fright, telling him that 'Samuel must have been a horrid scoundrel if he forged the story about the I AM speaking to Moses'. Later he refused to meet the heretical bishop. His own references to the problem of the authority of the Bible have not retained much value, because he understood so little of the problem. But while Shaftesbury (or Pusey) believed that Christianity depended on questions about the authorship and authenticity of the books of the Bible, Maurice's orthodoxy (somewhat like Newman's) had a certain flexibility. Newman depended on the Church for his religion, and Maurice, the Christian Platonist, depended on a direct insight into the transcendent meaning of the life recorded in the Bible and in every family's and nation's history as well as in the Church. Their hearts were not where Shaftesbury's was; and while neither was much interested in scientific or historical criticisms of the biblical text, each shared Coleridge's conviction that Christianity could, and should, survive without the Bibliolatry which pretended that all the Bible's facts must be accurate and all its opinions divine. 'I leave critics to discourse about documents, what their value is, or whence they came. I merely take what I find.' So Maurice declared in one of his last books, *Social Morality*. At least such an attitude was better than Shaftesbury's (or Pusey's) hysteria against the critics.

In comparison with the academic negatives of the theological liberals, Maurice could claim that the Bible had 'found' him (to use Coleridge's phrase) as profoundly as it had found Shaftesbury. At one discussion in London after *Essays and Reviews* and Colenso, a Member of Parliament raised an easy laugh by remarking: 'sometimes one would like to know what the clergy *do* believe nowadays!' Maurice arose and seemed to be on fire as he recited the Apostles' Creed. He added that he was bound to protest against all attempts to set up money or other idols in place of the teaching of the living God. The discussion abruptly ended.

Such a display of prophetic emotion made it easier for later theologians to work quietly, thus bringing nearer the day which he had seen from afar in a letter of 1849: 'I cannot but think that the Reformation in our day, which I expect to be more deep and searching than that of the sixteenth century, will turn upon the Spirit's presence and life. . . .'

Maurice had one other major controversy, and he looked back on it with the conviction that it had been the most important of his life, although also with the knowledge that in his 'great heat and vehemence of spirit' he had mismanaged it. One Sunday in 1858 William Thomson, who was soon to grace the throne of York, earned his Sunday dinner with Maurice after the Lincoln's Inn service by a horrifying account of the current series of Bampton Lectures in Oxford. In essence, he declared, they were atheism. Actually they were some very shrewd remarks by Henry Mansel on *The Limits of Religious Thought*, anticipating many modern objections to 'natural religion' or 'metaphysics' on the convincing ground that the human mind cannot understand the eternal or divine. To Mansel the Unconditioned was inconceivable, and the German philosophical tradition as echoed by Thomas Carlyle, speaking so volubly about the Infinite or the Absolute, was so much confusion or humbug. Theology was concerned not with God in himself, but with our symbols of him, for 'the primary and proper object of criticism is not Religion, natural or revealed, but the human mind in its relation to Religion'. Mansel accepted orthodox Christianity, to him a religion of revelation and miracle. 'For the infinite, as inconceivable, is necessarily shewn to be non-existent; unless we renounce the claim of reason to supreme authority in matters of faith by admitting that it is our duty to believe what we are altogether unable to comprehend.' But he added disconcerting warnings that his arguments in support of 'God manifest in the flesh' were not demonstrations and that the contents of the revelation were 'regulative', not simply descriptive. What was revealed was what God had chosen to reveal, so that man might think about him in that way 'for the sake of action'.

These Oxford Lectures seemed designed to appeal to

infidels and to the irrational 'orthodox', but they did not appeal to Maurice. In an elaborate onslaught through sermons and open letters published as *What is Revelation?* (1859), he attempted to undo the damage. He tried to vindicate reason as leading to revelation, and the revelation in Christ as unveiling the mysteries of God. He thundered against those 'who make orthodoxy an excuse for denying the Union of the Father with the Son, the perfect Manifestation of the Father in the Son, the desire of the Father and the Son by the Spirit to bring all men into the obedience of the Truth'. He proclaimed that God's self-revelation communicated God's reality authentically; it was not merely 'regulative'. He did not possess the training or the temper to deal satisfactorily with the philosophical problems involved – cognition, analogy, and so forth – any more than he could write authoritatively about biblical criticism. W. R. Matthews (one of Mansel's successors as Dean of St. Paul's) observed of this controversy that it 'resembles what one might imagine to have taken place had a discussion ever happened between Aristotle and one of the Minor Prophets, except that Mansel wrote much better than Aristotle and Maurice more copiously than any Minor Prophet.' But Maurice said enough to help later theologians such as William Temple who, while distinguishing the event (of the personal revelation of God in action) from human speculations, were to argue that truth was thus surely apprehended – and was compatible with other truth reached in other ways.

Maurice was at one with Newman in finding the cold, clear tone of Mansel, or before him Butler, religiously unsatisfactory. More than this was needed if there was to be a barrier against unbelief. In the tenth of his *Theological Essays*, he suggested that perhaps Butler's talk about probability had been due to the wish of that 'great and good man' to talk in their own language with fashionable gamblers. But Butler's basic appeal to the moral sense also dissatisfied him. His Cambridge lectures on *The Conscience* (1868) showed him as the honoured veteran who was still aware that 'the more there is of conscience in me – the more I confess a higher law – the greater will be my degradation and the sense of it'. It seems clear that his shyness and depression as a young man, morbidly interpreted by him as degradation, resulting in part from the theological tempests which had wrecked his home, made him turn for shelter to the Church of England with a rather extravagant loyalty, combined with a rather extravagant hatred of all religious parties and sects. John Stuart Mill wrote that Maurice's 'great powers of generalization, rare ingenuity and subtlety, and a wide perception of important and unobvious truths' had led him to the conclusion that 'the Church of England had known everything from the first, and that all the truths on the ground of which the Church and orthodoxy have been attacked (many of which he saw as clearly as any one) are not only consistent with the Thirty-nine Articles but are better exposed in those Articles than by any one who rejects them'. And Mill attributed this waste of a mind to 'that timidity of conscience, combined with original sensitiveness of temperament, which has so often driven highly gifted men into Romanism'. Mill's verdict was only slightly unfair. It is therefore worth seeing what separated Maurice from Newman.

Revelation was not for him, as it was for Newman, 'the substitution of the voice of the Lawgiver for the voice of conscience'; for his Christ came to strengthen, not condemn. Revelation was, indeed, no system, moral or dogmatic, to which 'assent' must be given; it was the Father shown by the coming of Christ even when Christ was not named, and the right response could only be the obedient love of a son. Of course Maurice lived in awe of the Holy One, but his most characteristic reaction was one of a confident, if humble familiarity. Characteristically he replied to Newman's *Essay on Development* in an enormous Preface to a book of sermons on the Christ, the eternally sympathetic high priest of men, as pictured in the Epistle to the Hebrews; and privately he wrote about the *Essay* that 'of all the books I ever read it seems to me the most sceptical' (but this was before he read Mansel). Maurice's essential answer to Newman was to invite men to turn again to the Christ of the Scriptures. They would find there the manifestation of the loving power of God as the crown of their daily experience; and they would receive the Spirit of God in their own hearts, to cry *Abba*, Father. In yet another of those Victorian references to Bishop Butler's *Analogy of Religion, Natural and Revealed, to the Constitution and Course of Nature* (1736), Maurice told a correspondent in 1865:

I go great lengths with you in your bold saying that Butler's 'Analogy' should be written over again in our time ... Revelation must be the discovery of God to a creature formed to know him and to be like him ... I own that I never have been, and never will be, content with probable evidence when it is opposed to demonstration. I ask for a demonstration of the Spirit with power to my spirit.

It was Maurice's task to answer his own challenge; and much of his answer, as this was perceived through his own jargon and emotionalism, did persuade many people in Victorian England, as the circulation of his writings showed. It was foolish of Newman to dismiss it: 'to use general terms and glowing words is to Mauricize'. For in 1837 Maurice hinted what such a demonstration of the Holy Spirit might mean to the nineteenth century. He told a friend:

The Oxford Tracts are, for the most part, more unpleasant than I quite like to acknowledge to myself or to others. Their error, I think, consists in opposing to 'the spirit of the present age' the spirit of the former age, instead of the ever-living and acting Spirit of God, of whom the spirit of each age (as it presents itself to those living in it) is at once the adversary and the parody. The childlike spirit of the fathers, say they, must be brought in to counteract the intellectual spirit of these times —the spirit of submission to Church authority against the spirit of voluntary association. Nay, I contend, but the spirit of earnest and deep reflection is that which God would cultivate in us to oppose the superficial intelligence of the day, the spirit of Christian or Church liberty (the service which is freedom) to counteract the lust for independence, the spirit of unity to overthrow the spirit of combination.

# 5

# Gladstone and Benson

In May 1898 the body of William Ewart Gladstone lay in state in Westminster Hall, and was then buried in the Abbey. He had died in his eighty-ninth year. Almost as much as the funeral of Queen Victoria three years later, those obsequies stirred reflections about the nineteenth century; and much more than the Supreme Governor of the Church of England (who really preferred Prince Albert's fellow-Lutherans or the Presbyterians around Balmoral), Mr. Gladstone was correctly identified as an Anglican.

He seemed to many to have betrayed the Church's cause by disestablishing Anglicanism in Ireland and by allying himself – with whatever hesitations and obscurities – with those who wished to see it disestablished in England. During the last thirty years of his life he was, indeed, thought by many to be the enemy of all English institutions. The Queen grew to hate him. In 1880 she told her private secretary that 'she will sooner *abdicate* than send for or have anything to do with that *half-mad firebrand* who would soon ruin everything, and be a *Dictator*'. It was not merely that his speechifying irritated her (while Disraeli had the tact to address her as the stupidly conservative and obstinately lonely widow, susceptible to flattery, that she was); nor was it merely that she was alarmed by the politics of 'the People's William'. She also seems to have thought that his eloquence about the moral imperatives of democracy was so much humbug. Gladstone himself attributed her attitude to her acceptance of the rumours that, after a day's administration and oratory at a very exalted level of ethics, he would take his pleasure with prostitutes met in the London streets.

However, neither the guarded support which he gave to disestablishmentarians nor the lavish friendship which he gave to prostitutes really justified the Queen's hatred of him. While they were undergraduates at Oxford, he and some friends resolved to undertake a definite work on behalf of the outcasts, and they drew lots to decide which particular category of outcasts would fall to each member of this group. Gladstone's efforts which were begun as a result of this lottery continued when he became the most eminently respectable statesman in the world. No aspect of his life was more extraordinary. While in the cabinet, loaded with work and worry, even while Prime Minister, he would give hours in the late evening to this task. Armed only with a stick, he would enter alleys where the police feared to go, knowing that the brothel-keepers maintained a small army of thugs for the protection of this thriving and lucrative trade. He would speak to prostitutes with a courtesy which constantly exposed him to blackmail or suspicion; the wonder is that there were not more incidents of blackmail, and that the rumours about his intentions were not used more freely by his potential rivals. He would invite the prostitutes back to his home, and take endless trouble with those who were willing to be reclaimed. He spent £83,500 of his own money on them. In his eighties he still gave detailed attention to this work, although he thought that it had cost him the Queen's confidence and although some of his closest associates had been courageous enough to warn him of its other dangers.

Why did he do it? Whatever may have been the truth about the undergraduates' lottery, his persistence in this particular form of charitable activity, when almost anyone else in his position would have excused himself on the grounds of official duty and dignity, is the most dramatic possible illustration of his energy. Just as he walked mountains or felled trees during his holidays, so during Parliamentary sessions he was out on the streets of London while his colleagues dined or intrigued or slept. Just as he addressed Members of Parliament with a unique blend of copious emotion and exactly mastered and massed detail over a period of sixty-one years (until the day of his last speech

came in 1894, and that speech was a passionate attack on the House of Lords), so he took infinite pains in innumerable conversations with brainless women. If only he had treated the Queen like a prostitute!

A later generation, accustomed to Freudian analysis, will point to the charms of the sinners who attracted Gladstone's zeal. It is clear that Gladstone was highly sexed. Perhaps this contributed to his lack of censoriousness, astonishing in one who habitually spoke like an Old Testament prophet. He got on well with that frank hedonist the Prince of Wales, and even smoked cigarettes at his table. While he did good to them, he seems to have enjoyed the company of two ladies whose virtue was far less secure than his own: Lillie Langtry who was the friend of the Prince of Wales, and Skittles Walters who was the toast of Englishmen in Paris. Although he insisted on his Irish ally Parnell resigning when he was cited in a divorce case, he had previously corresponded with Parnell's mistress, Kitty O'Shea, in attempts to drive a political bargain. He knew perfectly well that Lord Hartington, who succeeded him as Liberal leader in 1875 (but made way for his return to power in 1880), was more intimate with the Duchess of Manchester than with Lady Hartington. He was a man of the world. What made him break Parnell, and therefore end his own hope of solving the Irish question, was not Parnell's immorality but Parnell's refusal to see that he must bow, at least for a period, before the public indignation which had been aroused by the public scandal.

Gladstone was eager to marry Caroline Farquhar, and when that young lady refused him (protesting that 'the terrifying intensity of his eyes makes one go cold'), Lady Frances Douglas. We can gather what Caroline Farquhar suspected from her action when, many years later as a married lady, she found herself kneeling near him at the rail to receive Holy Communion. She immediately got up and left the church. But she was wickedly wrong. This man with such a rare energy was never suspected by anyone who knew him of being unfaithful for a second to Caroline Glynne, with whom in the end he made a perfect marriage. Nor did he ever think of betraying his Lord, with whom he spoke in daily prayer, and for whose sake he kept a daily journal to account for his expenditure of time. 'We should deal with our time', he advised his eldest son in 1855, 'as we see in a shop a grocer deal with tea and sugar, or a haberdasher with stuffs and ribands: weighing or measuring it out in proportions adjusted to that which we are to get for and by it.'

While an undergraduate he thought very seriously that he should, and would, consecrate the extraordinary energy of which he was already aware to work as a priest. He wrote long and solemn letters to his father in 1830, with this theme: 'I do not see how I am to persuade myself that any powers, be they the meanest or the greatest, can be *so* profitably or *so* nobly employed as in the performance of this sublime duty.' His father persuaded him to aim at public life rather than the narrower sphere of a parochial clergyman. 'You will allow me to doubt whether the picture your perhaps too sanguine mind has drawn in your letter before me, would ever be practically realized.'

William Ewart Gladstone seems always to have believed that his father was right, and that it was also God's will that he should be a statesman. However, he was delighted when his second son, Stephen, became a clergyman and when his daughter Mary married a penniless curate. In 1850, in a letter to the future Cardinal Manning, he was still able to speculate about what his task might have been, had he been ordained himself. 'My course would be set to work upon the holy task of clearing, opening and establishing positive truth in the Church of England, which is an office doubly blessed, inasmuch as it is both the business of truth, and the laying of firm foundations for future union in Christendom.' These were not empty words. In his earlier years he enjoyed reading his own sermons to a congregation composed of his own servants. He read more theology, and wrote more, than most clergymen. His appetite for ecclesiastical facts and his sympathy with Christian believers were truly ecumenical. And the courageous tenderness of his work for prostitutes showed that he not only might have been, but actually was, a great pastor.

Inevitably such a Prime Minister regarded the responsibility for the key ecclesiastical appointments as one of the most important of the duties attached to the supreme political office. He took great pains over his own nominations to bishoprics, deaneries, and canonries, and he was interested enough to care what other patrons did. He was far too acutely aware of his responsibilities to confine his patronage to High Churchman or to supporters of the Liberal Party; anyway, there were not many leading church men available who combined the roles as he did. Two of his most successful episcopal appointments were of men who were not quite gentlemen, but who attracted him because they were Liberals, and above all honest thinkers and hard workers: Frederick Temple, and James Fraser the second Bishop of Manchester.

Gladstone made St. Paul's Cathedral what it was to mid-Victorian London. When the Deanery fell vacant through the death of Mansel in 1871, he offered it first to W. F. Hook and then, when Hook refused, to Richard Church, who was then the 'High' and scholarly pastor of a village of two hundred souls. Had Church shown any taste for ecclesiastical politics and administration, the Primacy might have been his on Tait's death, for although acknowledging that he was a recluse in poor health Gladstone revered Church. Gladstone also appointed Henry Scott Holland, then a don under forty years of age, to a canonry of St. Paul's in 1884. He thus gave Scott Holland a pulpit from which he fascinated vast congregations until another Liberal Prime Minister, Asquith, moved him back to Oxford in 1910. Scott Holland combined a magician's flow of rhetoric with a Catholic sense of the sacramental life of the Church and a Socialist sense that the life of society ought to be a sacrament of the reign of Christ. Through such appointments, Gladstone preached by proxy.

During his first period as Prime Minister, 1868–74, he filled no fewer than twelve bishoprics and eight deaneries. At the time he jotted down what qualities he looked for in bishops.

Piety. Learning (sacred). Eloquence. Administrative power. Faithful allegiance to the Church and to the Church of England. Activity. Tact and courtesy in dealings with men. Knowledge of the world. Accomplishments and literature. An equitable spirit. Faculty of working with his brother bishops. Some legal habit of mind. Circumspection. Courage. Maturity of age and character. Corporal vigour. Liberal sentiments in public affairs. A representative character with reference to shades of opinion fairly allowable in the Church.

'Who is sufficient for these things?' may well be the reaction of a later generation; yet Gladstone and his successors at Downing Street did find Victorian churchmen who passed most, if not all, of these tests of character. There can be no doubt that Gladstone would have passed all of them himself, and would have filled the throne of St. Augustine with high distinction, had it been possible for Queen Victoria and Disraeli to combine to appoint him Archbishop of Canterbury in 1868. A twentieth-century scholar, A. R. Vidler, has permitted himself to speculate along that line. 'After all, would not Gladstone's political achievements have been carried out, in one way or another, even if he had not been at the political helm? Whereas, if the Church had been under his leadership, history might have pursued a very different course, and it might be in a very different condition to-day.'

As it was, Gladstone's most decisive connection with the Archbishopric of Canterbury came when he appointed E. W. Benson to it in 1883, having been deprived of the chance of appointing Samuel Wilberforce in 1868. Benson entirely lacked Gladstone's Parliamentary gifts and certainly had few 'liberal sentiments in public affairs.' But he was a High Churchman, admired by Gladstone for his piety, his sacred learning, and his eloquence. In his life we glimpse a little of what Archbishop Gladstone might have been.

2

The story of the connections between Christianity and democracy in the Victorian age cannot be other than tangled, until that story issues in the supremely Gladstonian idea of the politics of democracy as the politics of morality.

In his last speech to the Commons, Gladstone boasted

that the electorate was now six millions, of whom two millions had been added by his own Reform Act in 1884. But the numbers of the new electors were not the key fact in the politics of the end of the nineteenth century. What mattered even more was the 1884 extension to the electorate in the county constituencies of the principle on which Disraeli had based the electorate for the borough seats; and that mattered not only because the counties had tended to vote Conservative in the period 1867–84. The crucial change made when workers in the villages were included in the electorate under Gladstone in 1884 was the acknowledgement of the principle which he had suddenly laid down during a Commons debate twenty years before (to the dismay of Lord Palmerston, who was then Prime Minister). Gladstone declared in 1864: 'I venture to say that every man who is not permanently incapacitated by some consideration of personal unfitness or political danger is morally entitled to come within the pale of the Constitution.'

That proclamation of the democratic principle shocked Palmerston; and it had to be explained away by Gladstone at the time, because he was in so many ways a conservative Chancellor of the Exchequer. Palmerston then, and the Queen later, could regard him as a traitor to the governing class. Indeed, Gladstone often surprised himself by his radicalism. In his heart he was a conservative to the end of his days. This came out when he spent a week at All Souls College in Oxford in 1890, reading the lessons in the chapel and lamenting innovations. As he lay dying in great pain from cancer, he would recite the first verse of Newman's 'Praise to the Holiest in the height', and dictated a reply to one message which reached him. 'There is no expression of Christian sympathy which I value more than that of the ancient university of Oxford, the God-fearing and God-sustaining university of Oxford. I served her, perhaps mistakenly, but to the best of my ability. My most earnest prayers are hers to the uttermost and to the last.'

That might be assessed as an old man's nostalgia for the scenes of his youth, or his youthful Toryism might be pardoned as immature; but even at the height of his powers Gladstone lived by the old values. He is so securely fixed in

English history as an architect of democracy that it is important for us to remember that as late as 1858 Gladstone was begged to take charge of India or the other colonies in the Conservative administration. On that occasion Disraeli wrote to Gladstone, assuring him that if he joined Lord Derby's cabinet he would find that 'all its members are your admirers' and some of them 'warm friends'. Disraeli acknowledged that 'our mutual relations have formed the great difficulty', but he appealed to Gladstone to accept his own leadership of the Commons for the time being, on four grounds.

Don't you think the time has come when you might deign to be magnanimous? ... I may be removed from the scene, or I may wish to be removed from the scene. Every man performs his office, and there is a Power greater than ourselves, that disposes of all this ... Whatever office you filled, your shining qualities would always render you supreme ...

Gladstone replied to this flattery with the warmth of ice, but it was then possible for men to think that his hatred of Disraeli, rather than any political principle, was the main reason why he did not announce himself as a Conservative. (His attitude to Dizzy resembled the Queen's attitude to him: this rhetorician had debased the currency of public life.) At the age of forty-nine he could not be classed as an ardent reformer, except in the dismally technical fields of taxation and tariffs. The one master whom he owned in politics was the Conservative Prime Minister who had given him his chance to develop and display his outstanding skill for finance, Sir Robert Peel; and if we ask why Peel gave Gladstone such a great chance at such an early age, when he fought shy of Shaftesbury, we get the answers that Gladstone's administrative capacity was reckoned stronger than Shaftesbury's – and his conscience less dangerous. Hounded from office by Disraeli's unscrupulous rebellion, Peel had died in 1850, but eight years later Gladstone still needed to be warned by his closest political ally, old Sir James Graham, that 'the reconstruction of the fossil remains of the old Peel party is a hopeless task'. And as it was, Gladstone did accept a colonial assignment from the Derby–Disraeli administration. He went out to the Ionian Islands, which were then under British rule, as Lord High Commissioner.

One main reason why he obeyed that temporary call to the isles of Greece was that they reminded him of Homer; and one main reason why he gave a lifetime's devotion to the poetry of Homer was that the ancient Greek bard (in this so unlike Disraeli) constantly pictured human nature in heroic proportions. In the words of Gladstone with which Morley concluded his biography: 'Be inspired with the belief that life is a great and noble calling; not a mean and grovelling thing that we are to shuffle through as we can, but an elevated and lofty destiny.' Gladstone often added that Homer *was* Homer, and not a committee – and how relevant that seemed, as an answer to the German critics who were trying to abolish Moses! He would insist, too, that the noble glories of Homeric Greece had been a preparation for the Gospel – as surely as the glories of Israel, or, as he would sometimes bring himself to confess, even more surely. He did not remain a Conservative statesman after the fall of Peel, but in politics or in Homeric studies as much as in his more directly theological work, he was always a conservative preacher.

Like many other preachers, he was able to cast a prophetic mantle over causes which history has judged more cynically. He entered politics in 1832 as M.P. for Newark; this borough was then in the pocket of the Duke of Newcastle. Before casting their votes in his favour 887 electors had consumed more than two thousand pounds' worth of encouragement, half contributed by the Duke and half by Gladstone's father, who was a millionaire slave-owner. The M.P., then aged twenty-three, was properly expected to defend both the aristocracy and the slave-owning on which his whole position depended. This he did with such eloquence that in 1834 Peel gave him a junior ministerial post, and next year made him Under-Secretary for the Colonies. When Gladstone followed Peel in the repeal of the Protectionist corn laws, the Duke of Newcastle was so incensed that another seat had to be found; and so Gladstone came to represent in Parliament the Oxford University which

Newman had just abandoned. It was now his duty to resist proposals to change Oxford, and this he did until the report of the commission including Tait and Stanley persuaded him that some changes were inevitable. He preserved copies of 350 letters written in his own hand as the pilot of the 1854 Act which reformed the university; but the admission of Dissenters to degree courses was not included in the Bill as first presented to the Crown, and even after the Act the Anglican monopoly of the teaching posts was protected. This conservatism coincided with Gladstone's own idea of a university as well as with the interests of his constituents, and it was not until 1871 that he sponsored an Act to abolish all religious tests at Oxford. He was proud to represent Oxford; he worried about the effects on the dons of the reforms which, after initial horror, he gradually came to support; and when he was defeated in the university's Parliamentary election in 1865, he wrote in his journal: 'A dear dream is dispelled. God's will be done.' It is also worth remembering that he fought with great passion against the passing of the 1857 Divorce Act, the first clear departure of the laws of England from the laws of the Church. Although divorces were already obtainable by the rich who could procure special Acts of Parliament, Gladstone argued that the general provision of such facilities by the State threatened public morality; and he was specially indignant that clergymen were to be compelled to lend their churches for remarriages.

He had to appeal to morality in his defence of privileges, imparting a sacred air to those who owned land, or slaves, or an educational monopoly. To the end he maintained that a landowner's influence could be greatly beneficial, and perhaps the proudest achievement of his life was to rescue the Hawarden estate in North Wales for his family after a financial disaster in 1848 for which he was in no way responsible. He shared Disraeli's own liking for dukes in politics, and like Disraeli at Hughenden (but more convincingly) he believed that an M.P., even a Prime Minister, ought to spend as much of his time as possible as a country gentleman. Accordingly he spent about half the year at Hawarden through half a century. In this rural retreat he

remission of sins' out of the creed of the Church of England on the authority of the Judicial Committee of the Privy Council, he searched his near-broken heart to see whether it was possible to remain loyal. Yet Gladstone never abandoned his *Church Principles*.

When Gladstone came to acknowledge that the balance of the argument was against the continuance of the Anglican Establishment in Ireland and Wales (if not in England), and against the Presbyterian Establishment in Scotland, he expressed his change of view in terms as moral and as theological as any which he had used in his early books, as well as with inexhaustible statistics.

The argument was never a cool one, based on utility. When he saw that the State could not be expected to endow the Church of a minority, he counted it a duty to God to crusade for the disestablishment and partial disendowment of that Church. When he saw that the spiritual life of the Church was hindered rather than helped by the patronage of the State, he prophesied (correctly) that the Irish and Welsh Anglicans would gain by independence. He spent much time and money on ensuring that his vast collection of books would be preserved for the use of the clergy and other students at St. Deiniol's Library at Hawarden in Wales. There generations to come would equip themselves for the battle against unbelief. Already in the 1840s his interest in the religion of Scotland (his father and mother were of pure Scottish descent) had caused him to think deeply about the spiritual benefits of independence. He was devoted to the small Episcopal Church in Scotland and took the lead in founding Trinity College, Glenalmond, as a public school for the sons of the Episcopalian gentry. During its early years this school was combined with a tiny college to train priests. He also greatly admired rebels against state control over the Established Church of Scotland, and lectures in London by the chief of these, Thomas Chalmers, drove him to develop his own views of Church and State; Chalmers was admired all the more because he never became a simple disestablishmentarian.

Through all the changes in Church and State, however, Gladstone never gave any support to the common view that the State was a mere police force for the protection of property, and the Church a mere convenience for the spread of respectability. 'We are still a Christian people', he announced firmly in his *Chapter of Autobiography* in 1868. He had been moral as an aristocrat, and he would be moral as a democrat. He was a Tory and he became a Liberal, but he was never a Whig; he never venerated 1688. He used to say that the rejection of the philosophy of John Locke was the beginning of wisdom. That meant that although he abandoned as hopeless the old Tory battle for Church and State, he never abandoned the old Tory ideal of the State as a kind of church; he admired the philosophy as well as the eloquence of Burke.

After his rejection at Oxford in 1865, he became M.P. for South Lancashire, declaring in Manchester: 'At last, my friends, I am come among you, and I am come among you unmuzzled.' So he turned to the people. But even now it was not a complete turn. During the American Civil War he got into trouble by a public indiscretion which showed that he thought that the gentlemen of the South, slave-owners as some of them were, had made a nation in arms against the egalitarian but industrial North. What he needed for his almost complete conversion to democracy was an inner conviction that the British people was moral and even religious at heart, like Oxford University. This conviction came as he watched the courage of the workmen of Lancashire when the cotton industry was depressed by the American war. He now believed that the people could be trusted, and that its voice could be heard as the voice of God. The privileged class to which he himself belonged (although he never consented to join the House of Lords) could now be denounced if it was deaf to this voice, the voice which his own oratory in its organ-like plenitude echoed and magnified.

Another development came with his Midlothian campaign, nearly twenty-one years after he had formally joined the Liberal Party. By the series of speeches (developing earlier pamphleteering) which he made against Disraeli's evil policies while he was contesting that Scottish seat in 1879, he awoke the enlarged electorate to the excitement of the issues at stake, and he awoke his own potentialities not only as the Liberal Prime Minister on Disraeli's fall but also as a mob orator; the public chose him as Prime Minister. Many historians have regarded that campaign as one of the decisive dates in the emergence of the politics of democracy. However, the Midlothian campaign was couched in moral terms on a theological basis, as his books had been in 1838 and 1840. Its tradition went back to the anti-slavery agitation led by William Wilberforce. Gladstone had come to acknowledge the justice of William Wilberforce's aim, and he now related the same style, a lay preacher's, to a democracy which would have shocked the great emancipator of the slaves. People in politics laughed at him, as they had laughed at Wilberforce. But 'the People' did not laugh. Believing that the State still had a conscience, he treated the electors of the late 1870s, and the six millions who later became possessors of votes, as a congregation which he summoned to crusades against Turkish atrocities in Bulgaria or against English oppression in Ireland. He always assumed that his vast audience constituted a moral personality; and his attitude did much to make it one, with results which became apparent in 1914 and 1940.

3

There were many disadvantages in this idea of politics, aristocratic or democratic, as public morality. Gladstone's imagination was not aroused by subjects which he did not regard as intensely moral. Fortunately for England, finance did become moral in his hands, for he came to regard the reform of taxes and tariffs as a great work of righteousness. But education, for example, seems to have bored him, except in so far as Oxford University could be regarded as an educational establishment.

The great 1870 Education Act was passed while he was Prime Minister; it marked the assumption by the State of responsibilities for the education of the people, and incidentally, while it provided for religion as part of this education, it also provided that no 'denominational formulary' (they were thinking chiefly about the Church of England's Catechism) should be taught at the public expense. Gladstone showed remarkably little interest in it. He allowed W. E. Forster to prepare the Bill with only the vaguest supervision, and the legislation about religion (the 'Cowper–Temple clause') which was so fateful for the future of English Christianity was adopted almost casually by the government during the course of the Commons debates. Gladstone's personal view, to the end of his life, was that undenominational religion in the schools was an 'imposture' or 'moral monster', and he would have preferred to put religious education on an entirely voluntary basis, leaving the Churches to instruct their own children. He did not press this view, however, because the topic did not rank high among his priorities. He paid for this casualness when at the next General Election, in 1874, neither Anglicans nor Noncomformists believed that the souls of England's children were safe in his hands; and Disraeli was recalled to power. When Gladstone retired from the leadership for the first time, one reason was that 'I felt myself to be in some measure out of touch with some of the tendencies of the Liberal party, especially in religious matters'. He wished then to concentrate on religion in an interval between Parliament and the grave, but he also indicated that he would be willing to return to Westminster at any time 'with a view to arresting some great evil or procuring for the nation some great good'.

Another subject which failed to command Gladstone's best attention was the Empire. He never liked paying for the Army or Navy. He was Chancellor of the Exchequer during the first period of the Crimean War, but partly because the war embarrassed him he busied himself with domestic matters (notably the Oxford reforms). He liked to think of the Ionian Islands being under British protection, and criticized Palmerston for handing them back to Greece in 1865; but he had no clear views about India or Africa, except that Disraeli's imperialism was immoral. The weakness of his Middle Eastern policy brought bitter criticism to his later years in office. He authorized the British fleet's bombardment of Alexandria as an act of justice, but when he wanted to evacuate the Sudan he chose as his agent an imperialist soldier who became a religious martyr, General Gordon; so that Egypt and the Sudan had to join the Empire.

His taste for moral crusades could lead him to pick up the wrong end of a stick. While Chancellor of the Exchequer he proposed that the earnings of charities from investments should be subject to income tax, because he believed that the exemption of charities from this public duty was immoral – and also that many charities used their assets in an immoral way. The outcry surprised him. Again, when the Pope's infallibility was decreed by the Vatican Council in 1870 he expected many Roman Catholics to share his moral indignation and predicted that the split in the Roman Catholic Church would be far greater than the trouble which had been brought on the Church of England by the Romanizers of 1848 and 1851. He wrote a great pamphlet against the Vatican decrees, and it became a best-seller, but both Newman and Manning were able to answer it because it directed most of its fire at a non-existent enemy. Gladstone argued that every Roman Catholic who was a patriot should denounce the Vatican Council's attempt to interfere with his civil allegiance. But it was precisely in 1870, when the Pope was declared infallible in matters of faith and morals when teaching *ex cathedra*, that the Papacy's temporal power was buried. The real issue, which was whether the Pope was infallible when teaching faith or morals *ex cathedra*, did not receive the attention which it deserved because it did not chiefly engage the eminent pamphleteer's wrath.

Few people in public life thought that Gladstone was insincere, but some criticisms of his style were made by almost everyone. Henry Labouchere's complaint that Gladstone believed that Almighty God had hidden the ace of trumps up his sleeve was widely quoted. Another complaint, made on many occasions in Gladstone's Parliamentary career, was that his speeches closely resembled many sermons in that, however long they might be, the audience was left wondering what the speaker had meant to say. The explanation was advanced that Gladstone had no clear purpose, but was in Disraeli's famous phrase 'inebriated by the exuberance of his own verbosity'. People also complained that, dwelling as he did in this pulpit-like elevation, he did not take the trouble to get to know *them*. He far preferred business to parties, and although he would reply to critics that he never neglected business for the sake of Homer or theology, he could not pretend that he was adept in the social arts of a politician. He could not get interested in the unheroic men who sat on the benches of the House of Commons behind him or who were expected to vote for him in the constituencies. At least, he could not get interested in them one by one. Only when he was addressing them as a mass did his energies quicken and the heavens open. In his old age he was more than ever insistent on his political mission, and refused to give either himself or others the luxury of companionable relaxation. The breaking of the Liberal Party in his closing years was not due solely to disagreement about policies.

Yet what a life it was! When he died men felt that they would not look on his like again, and the psychological secret of his official biography, by John Morely, was that here a comparatively ineffective politician (and an agnostic) was consoling himself by writing about a personality able to shape events to a will forged like steel in the fires of a faith both inherited and acquired. Both Gladstone's parents were devout Evangelicals. A religious influence was also exerted on him by his elder sister, Anne, who died in 1828. Much of that year was spent by Gladstone at home, before he went up to Christ Church; and he had many memorable talks about religion with her. She urged him to read Hooker's *Ecclesiastical Polity* and spoke to him about baptismal regeneration, for she was able to include that belief in her mainly Evangelical theology. In 1832, during a long holiday in Italy, three shocks added to the force of such pleas for sacramental element in Christianity. In January he came across the Italian Protestants, who were venerated by Evangelicals because they had been the first to be reformed in the sixteenth century; and he found the reality unimpressive. In March he was in Rome, and in St. Peter's he had a vision of the unity of Christendom as the historic Body of Christ. Six weeks later in Naples he happened to be examining the Book of Common Prayer, when his sister's doctrine struck home into his heart: Christians, converted as they must be, were born again in Baptism and were fed by the Eucharist. Three years later he wrote: 'I am entirely convinced that in substance the movement termed Evangelical and that falsely termed Popish are parts of one great and beneficent design of God, and that in their substance they will harmonize and co-operate.' In that comprehensiveness of a religious conversion, both Evangelical and Catholic, his vast natural assurance was doubled.

In an essay on 'The Place of Heresy and Schism in the Modern Christian Church', included among his posthumously published *Later Gleanings*, he placed his trust in the fact that 450 millions were already loyal to the great central truths of the Gospel. This was better than 'spurious undenominationalism'. It was 'this mighty modern miracle, this marvellous concurrence evolved from the very heart of discord'. And that was the faith by which he lived. He insisted on climbing out of his deathbed in order to receive Holy Communion from his son Stephen, who was then Rector of Hawarden.

4

Edward White Benson, chosen by Gladstone as Archbishop of Canterbury, was born in 1829, the son of a Birmingham manufacturer of chemicals. His father was an Evangelical, a total abstainer from alcohol and totally unworldly. He did not gain much from his inventions, and what money he did make he invested in the British White Lead Company, which went bankrupt. He died the next year, 1843. His partners graciously allowed his widow to remain in the little, insanitary house next to the abandoned works with a small annuity, in exchange for a profitable patent for manufacturing cobalt. The son reacted to all this by developing a grasp of details and by accepting the High Church influence of an uncle. In a tiny office in the silent factory he established his own oratory, where he said the monastic offices every day. The practical sense was to ensure his success in life; the High Church piety was a release into the Christian centuries out of orphanhood and poverty.

He found his escape through King Edward's School, Birmingham, and he found his hero in his headmaster, James Prince Lee, who had taught at Arnold's Rugby. When Prince Lee began his (disastrous) time as Bishop of Manchester, Benson organized the gift from his pupils, and in the same year, 1847, he planned while at Cambridge a society for holy living and for the Christian education of the poor. 'Let us determine while our hearts are still warm, and unchilled by the lessons of the world, to teach the *Poor*.' 'Doubtless there is high and holy week for heads and hearts and hands in the generation to come,' he told his journal. But he sent his mother a shocked remonstrance when she suggested that she might take part in the manufacture of cobalt herself.

His work was almost frustrated when his mother died in 1850; with her, his slender financial backing ended. The house in the Birmingham Lead Works had killed off his sister Harriet by typhus, and his mother, who had nursed her, had died of heart-failure the next night. He returned to Trinity College, and his face, always pale, told his story; but a bachelor don, the Bursar of Trinity, Francis Martin, spotted him walking disconsolately across the Great Court. He invited him to his rooms and assured him that he would be responsible for financing the rest of his undergraduate course; he also supported the rest of the boy's family. So his life proceeded, and fortunately for him it was untroubled by religious doubts. On his mother's death he refused to allow his youngest brother to be made the heir to a rich uncle, for that uncle was a Unitarian. He was appointed to a well-paid post on the staff at Rugby; elected a Fellow of Trinity (but he did not reside much in Cambridge); and ordained as a schoolmaster.

In 1858, the chance of a lifetime came to Benson. A fund to perpetuate the memory of the Duke of Wellington, under the close patronage of Albert the Prince Consort, was devoted to the education of the sons of army officers. On the recommendation of Frederick Temple, Benson was appointed the first headmaster of Wellington College. He was sent to Germany, to study the best methods. He returned convinced that, whatever Prince Albert might think, the ecclesiastical and classical tradition of Rugby already provided all that was wanted to make a school out of the new red-brick imitation of a French château on Bagshot Heath, to which the nearest building was the Criminal Lunatic Asylum at Broadmoor. He made only one last-minute preparation for the battles which would be needed to build this new Rugby. He married his cousin Mary Sidgwick, a girl whom he had loved for years while he had been boarding with her parents in Rugby. She was aged eighteen. She would make a home for him in what he called the Master's Lodge at Wellington College; and she would be his first pupil.

He had, or took, the entire control of the new school in his hands. He defied his governing body, and was habitually on the brink of resignation. The building of the chapel was his first love, but every detail of school life received his stern and often angry attention. He ruled through terror; 'he had a violent temper,' wrote one of his pupils, 'and would turn perfectly white sometimes when flogging a boy.' But he knew his masters and boys thoroughly and could be intimately gracious when he chose. He and his young bride would say good night to them all. Long afterwards the boys would remember his theatrical entrances into the chapel, his mingling with the mighty on Speech Day; and the masters would remember his rebukes and tearful reconciliations. 'He saw so vividly the beautiful thing he meant to create.' 'No one could see Benson at Wellington without feeling that he loved his position. He loved, as he loved all through his life, the work of organizing down to minute detail. He loved and idealized the place . . . He passionately loved teaching', wrote his successor in the headmastership. Benson made Wellington College, in conception a monumental charity, one of the most distinguished and most expensive schools in England.

But what had become of his dream of a society for holy living, 'to teach the *Poor*'? In 1869 his appointment as an honorary Prebendary of Lincoln Cathedral revived the prayer in him. 'Lord,' he wrote in his journal, in the

Victorian manner, 'Thou knowest how from a child Thou hast put into my heart deeply to love the beauty of Thy house – and how earnestly in all the minsters of England I have prayed that Thou wouldst raise up once more the Spirit whereby they were once builded . . .' In the same year he refused to follow Temple as Headmaster of Rugby, feeling that his next post ought to be one where he could 'give manhood to men – if God only fit me to do so'. Three years later the call came, and he was Chancellor of Lincoln Cathedral. The income was half his salary as a Headmaster, the duties were vaguer, he left Wellington in tears; but at last he was a canon of a cathedral, with an opportunity to teach the poor. And he was free of the school's governors, whose worldliness had recently almost broken their head-master's strained nerves.

He threw himself into Lincoln, instructing ordinands, preaching in a crowded cathedral, befriending the humbler citizens who had previously known little contact with the great church up the hill. His power of vision once more glowed. A cathedral should be the centre for an evangelism which reached into all the world.

I firmly believe [he wrote in 1873] that there is now no greater need for the Church of England, which (so far as I can see) is now charged with the world's Christianity, and must make herself truly Christian first, than this English order of Missioners in close filial union with Bishops and Mother Churches . . . We want the social dispersion and the central fire.

So much was involved beyond a new theological college or a new night school. And by now many others knew it. He was asked to return to Cambridge, to be Bishop of Calcutta, to be the first Bishop of Truro. He accepted the last call. After four years at Lincoln, it was once again what he need-ed: a call to inaugurate. Disraeli commented, 'Well, we *have* got a bishop !' Dean Church, who arranged his consecration at a great service in St. Paul's, wrote to him: 'I hope you may be permitted to add in Cornwall another of the many victories which the revived English Church has achieved, and which, in spite of disasters and menacing troubles, make it the most glorious Church in Christendom.'

Carving Cornwall out of the ancient diocese of Exeter was, in fact, ideal work for one who thus combined a romantic heart with a love of administration. Many of the Cornish parish churches had slept through the centuries, while Methodism had recently provided what religion there was. Benson did all that he could to put new life into them and into their usually poor and lonely, often broken-hearted or odd, parsons. His optimism was like the sunshine on their moors, his eloquence like the incessant sea on their rocks; and everywhere he expounded the examples of the local saints. His daughters needed educating, so he founded Truro High School for girls, and was at work on a similar grammar school for boys. 'You have no idea what life is becoming to me', he wrote to a friend; 'a humming top is the only thing that resembles it: perpetual motion, very dizzy, hollow within, keeping up a continuous angry buzz.'

At the centre of this buzz was a wooden shed, his first cathedral. There at 10 p.m. on Christmas Eve 1880 he presided over a Festival of Nine Lessons and Carols, designed on medieval precedents but intended to get the men out of the pubs. He already had Truro Cathedral in his heart. He was his own dean at Truro, and he was not likely to neglect the opportunity. (It had been the prospect of building up Anglican cathedral life in India that had most tempted him to become Bishop of Calcutta, until he had realized the difficulties of educating his children.) J. L. Pearson designed Truro Cathedral's granite and marble, an admirer gave £40,000, and the foundation stone was laid in 1880. 'People are saying, "the first Cathedral founded since the Reformation" ', he boasted in his journal. 'Has any been founded (one or two have been translated) since the Conquest?' He consecrated it seven years later.

But black clouds of depression still rolled over him. He was desolated by the death in 1878 of his eldest son, the brilliant Martin, while a boy at Winchester. He never fully recovered. 'Martin's death remains an inexplicable grief – every day – to see into that will be worth dying,' he wrote ten years later. In his journal for 16 September 1882 he noted: 'Such reasons for thankfulness and yet this invincible depression within. Maybe these very short nights of sleep, but scarce seems so.' The years at Truro also had their depressing side for Benson in his professional life. As the junior bishop he could not belong to the House of Lords, and in more specifically clerical discussions he was frustrated under Archbishop Tait, who used to sink back in his chair with a good-humoured smile when Benson was ecstatic with some Wilberforce-type vision of ecclesiastical revivalism.

On Tait's death he was moved to Canterbury at Gladstone's insistence. One trouble about Benson was his age: he was only fifty-three. Would the other bishops, who were all older, work under him? Both the old Archbishop before his death and the Queen after it expected the appointment of Bishop Harold Browne of Winchester. Yet Browne was seventy-two and unwell; Gladstone wrote to assure him that only his age had prevented his promotion. His comparative youth having been accepted, Benson's temperamental handicaps remained. Tait had been an administrator; Benson was a creative pioneer. Tait had enjoyed a fight; the more artistic Benson was easily thrown by opposition into another of his depressions. The post of Archbishop of Canterbury had been made by Tait into a Parliamentary office, and at that time Parliament was still the only effective instrument of ecclesiastical legislation; Benson had no Parliamentary experience. After hesitations which seem to have been genuine and to have persisted, Benson accepted Gladstone's offer. His son Arthur commented some forty years later: 'I am by no means sure that it was not the greatest mistake of his life. He yielded perhaps to what had always been a temptation of his, the love of ruling. But I do not think that he had by then a wide enough outlook upon the world; indeed, I do not feel that he was interested so much in life as in the mould of institutional religion into which it could be run.'

From now on, however, he ruled in the House of God. He slept about five hours a night, with many vivid dreams of ecclesiastical subjects. He slaved and fussed over the details of administration. His recreations were a landlordly life at Addington Park, tours of historic (and if possible, ecclesiastical) sites in Europe, and work on his *Cyprian*. He

entertained lavishly. His servants were many and dedicated.
'His feeling about the splendours of the Church was that
they were a stately heritage, which it was right and proper
to enjoy, and he had not the faintest sympathy with – only
horror for – Socialistic ideas,' Arthur Benson recalled. But
Arthur also remembered that his father was seldom happy
except when immersed in work. 'His thoughts naturally
turned to what was unsatisfactory or painful, in prospect
and retrospect. He would reflect how little use he had made
of his opportunities, or sink beneath the oppressive thought
of some difficult or delicate task which overshadowed him.'
Another glimpse of his father was left by Arthur. 'Papa
always felt the need of economy at an inn. . . . He would
have liked to be comfortable, but didn't know how, I think
his fear of waste was so strong.' What scars had been left by
the Birmingham boyhood?

5

'The Church of England has to be built up again from the
very bottom,' the new Archbishop of Canterbury wrote in
his journal in June 1883. 'It is the lower and lower-middle
classes who must be won.' It was the 1848 dream, to see the
people in the cathedrals, 'to teach the *Poor*'. But in fact
Benson did little in this direction. Instead, he took to the
ceremonies surrounding the old Queen like a duck to water,
and grappled less successfully with his new role in the House
of Lords, a body which, we are told, seldom loves one who
is either prelatical or schoolmasterly in manner. He was
uneasy in the sphere where Tait had excelled, lamenting
in 1891, when Parliamentary difficulties delayed a Clergy
Discipline Bill: 'I know so little of how any of these things
are done.' This lack of Parliamentary skill was a serious
deficiency in the circumstances. For example, urgently
needed reforms in the patronage system in the parishes were
not enacted by Parliament until 1897, despite Benson's
pleas throughout his Primacy. His first Parliamentary
defeat came during his first year as Archbishop. Men were
to be allowed to marry their deceased wives' sisters, despite

the Church's prohibition founded on the Old Testament. Then came the threat of something worse. On 13 June 1884 he found Gladstone 'surely "advancing" fast into revolution'. Would the radical old man, or Joseph Chamberlain who seemed to be his destined heir as the Liberal prophet, disestablish Anglicanism in England as well as on the Celtic fringe? On 12 December 1886 the Archbishop observed 'the Church steadily losing ground with the Crown, with Cabinet, with the House of Commons, while she is steadily winning the people and the poor.' Even the Conservatives slighted him. On 15 August 1895 he lamented that Lord Salisbury had failed to consult him about who should be the new Bishop of Rochester; indeed, the new bishop himself had not discussed the matter with him.

Benson, however, took care to win the friendship of sympathetic aristocrats. Adeline, Duchess of Bedford, became one of his closest friends, and under her marshalling ladies of high social position gathered regularly for devotions in Lambeth Palace Chapel. In July 1888, while staying with Lord Carnarvon, the Archbishop meditated in his journal:

One has nowadays great heartaches in these glorious homes, with their strong heads, real pillars of the civilization that now is, and their most delicate stately women, and children whose sweet proud curves of feature show the making of many generations and readiness for responsibility from almost tender years: are all these glories going to keep together? If not how will they go down? By brute force, or by silent self-exilings?

Next year he had to record a rather less generous tribute to the Church from 'an old Duchess', who laid hold of his arm in the garden of Marlborough House, saying: 'I shall hold by the Church – until you are disestablished – which you will soon be.'

Despite the changes which he labelled Socialism and Agnosticism, Benson was on the whole master of his familiar ecclesiastical world, and anxious to build up the Church as a bulwark against these menaces. What he wrote about St. Cyprian in his big book was true of himself:

We need not look to him for theology proper, for doctrinal refinement, for the metaphysic of Christian definition. We shall find him busy with moral conditions, the work of grace, the bonds of union: the sanctification of life through the sacraments, the remodelling of life through discipline; the constitution of the Church in permanence, the transforming social influences which are to control the application of power and wealth, to charge science again with the love of truth, art with the love of beauty, and to create a new benevolence.

What the Archbishop found in his hero, others found in him: 'the devotion of his gifts, acquirements and positions to the work and life of the New People as they grew in Christ.'

A typical act was his opening of the House of Laymen in 1886, a consultative body without legislative power, but one drawn by election from all the Diocesan Conferences in the Province of Canterbury. (York followed in 1892.) It was an innovation which had resulted from a 'memorial' from Cambridge theologians headed by Westcott, and which Benson in his inaugural address justified by a reminder that 'before the Italian Church over-rode all such promises, St. Cyprian promised the faithful laity that he would without their assent do nothing'. It was a turning point in the history of the Church of England, this summoning of just over a hundred laymen; for it was the beginning of the recognition by the Church of England that Parliament was no longer the adequate voice of the laity.

Another innovation Benson contemplated, but without result. Willing to imitate Rome in this at least, he wanted a body of cardinals for the Church of England: 'the appointment of four or five bishops, to give at least an annual fortnight of conference, with nothing else to do, on matters proposed by the Archbishop – or otherwise found necessary. These to be named by the Archbishop.' One difficulty here was that the most desirable cardinals disliked the thought of such meetings; Lightfoot was reluctant to leave Durham, and Temple in London was reluctant to treat others as equals. Benson, after abandoning the idea that men who were not bishops might be included instead, was left alone to carry the burden of leadership in a situation which he described in his journal for 1888: 'so full of fears, self-misgivings, anxieties, perplexities—such sorrows threatening, such sorrows present, such openings for great mistakes . . . the clergy so depressed'.

Benson could probably have done little to lift this depression, even with the aid of a college of cardinals. The psychology of the clergy reflected a sombre mood in the nation, where the boom which had brought prosperity to the 'workshop of the world' had receded with the slumps of 1876-9 and 1883-6. The agricultural depression distressed the countryside where most of the clergy lived. The operation of the Education Act of 1870 was by now making it clear that the Church of England was no longer the nation's schoolmaster, and the Liberation Society pressed for disestablishment while party strife tore the Church apart. In brief, Tait's prestige had not removed the real problems. However, in his self-pitying journal, which served much the same purpose as Shaftesbury's, Benson certainly exaggerated the dangers of the Church because of the depression of his own spirit. On public occasions the Church could show sheer arrogance, as when the bishops met in the Lambeth Conference in this same year, 1888. 'We have realized, more fully than it was possible to realize before', they declared in their Message, 'the extent, the power, and the influence of the great Anglican Communion. We have felt its capacities, its opportunities, its privileges.' And there were some solid grounds for sober confidence. When Gladstone was talking with Lord Morley at Biarritz on Christmas Eve 1891, he made a remark which reflected the true situation in England. 'The establishment', Morley noted, 'he considers safer than it has been for a long time.' And that something was due to Benson was implied by Gladstone's grumble (to his son) in 1894: 'painful indeed is the Archbishop's establishmentarian fanaticism'. In Benson's time as Archbishop of Canterbury, as in Tait's, the Church of England was still a very powerful institution. For all its worries, it had immense resources – including Gladstone.

In answer to the dangers which did confront the Church, Benson was able to do something characteristically his own. His own sympathies were obviously High Church, but he was determined 'not to make the Evangelicals feel uncomfortable' – for fear, as he confessed to his friend A. J.

atins in Hawarden parish church, and soon after
ing of the service had a fatal heart attack. He
sixty-seven. He was the last archbishop to be
hin Canterbury Cathedral, where his grave
h the carved list of the chief pastors of England
ugustine.

## 6

y it was a life as successful as Gladstone's although
r sphere. But there was a disturbing epilogue.
ounds did Benson inflict on the minds of the wife
en whom he adored? His beloved Minnie, to
ad written an ardent love-poem when she was
l whose life was to be largely emptied of meaning
was widowed at the age of fifty-five, wrote a
he did – but hers was more intimate, and more
n that journal, she looked back on her disastrous
i:

ild, I danced and sang into matrimony with a loving
g, a believing and therefore expectant spirit, twelve
much stronger, much more passionate, whom I didn't
But let me try and think how hard it was for Ed. He
is passionate nature for seven years and then got *me*,
g, weak, unstable child! I know how disappointing
to him, how evidently disappointed he was. How hard
l of all religious and emotional thoughts and yearn-
ad never really awoke in me. How I cried at Paris!

ngton College this ill-matched pair bickered, but
submitted, blaming herself when she failed to
ith his ecclesiastical and physical vitalities, or
lared not offer comfort when he was irritably
Gradually, through this self-giving humility, she
e Victorian 'good wife' and developed into the
stress of his palace at Truro, then of Lambeth and
. Her intelligence was certainly high. When the
andell Creighton met her in 1884, he described
. Benson, wife of the Archbishop of Canterbury,
ge to say, is one of the wittiest and most amusing
r talked to'. But her journal shows that she never

Mason, that the Evangelicals would leave, and with them
the Establishment would be lost. He seemed to his intimates
nervous and ashamed about his own love for ritual and
about his great knowledge of its history. But as it was, his
scholarship enabled him to pluck the nettle of the problem
about what practices connected with the celebration of the
Holy Communion were, or were not, lawful in the Church
of England.

Edward King, Bishop of Lincoln, was now accused by the
Church Association of illegal liturgical practices. It was the
most dramatic lawsuit in this field in this century – and not
only because Edward King was a bishop. For King was
Keble's successor as the High Anglican saint. As Benson
himself noted, 'he is adored at Lincoln'. Scott Holland
wrote about this man who was accused of having candles
lit on the altar:

It was light that he carried with him, light that shone through him,
light that flowed from him. The room was lit into which he entered.
It was as if we had fallen under a streak of sunlight that flickered,
and danced, and laughed, and turned all to colour and gold. Those
eyes of his were an illumination. Even to recall him for an instant
in the bare memory was enough to set the whole day alive and
glittering.

The trial of Bishop King was also dramatic because
Benson reluctantly decided to turn the complaint into a
legal case where he would himself be judge, with other
bishops as assessors. Rather to everyone's surprise, the
Judicial Committee of the Privy Council recognized his
right to do so, although there had been no precedent for
an archbishop trying one of the bishops since a scandalous
Bishop of St. David's had been deposed in 1699. The deeply
learned historian William Stubbs, who was then Bishop of
Oxford, muttered to himself that this was merely an archbishop sitting in his library, but most churchmen were delighted by Benson's judgment when it came. This delight was
not because all churchmen proposed to act on every word of
the Archbishop. To the pleasure of the Anglo-Catholics he
accepted candles on the altar, the Eastward position of the
priest facing the altar, the singing of *Agnus Dei* ('O lamb of
God') after the consecration, and the reverent ablution of

the vessels, but he ruled against the other High Church practices of mixing wine and water ceremonially, standing so that the people could not see the consecration, and making the sign of the cross when absolving or blessing; and these practices continued. The main effect of the Lincoln Judgment, delivered in November 1890, came because this compromise was well argued legally, and was well illustrated on a theological and liturgical basis, by an archbishop known to be in love with ecclesiastical tradition. In particular, High Churchmen were delighted that Benson reversed a judgment of the Judicial Committee (against the priest's Eastward position in 1871) because careful consideration had persuaded him to set the history of Church higher than the Privy Council.

'It is the most courageous thing to have come out of Lambeth for the last two hundred years', said Dean Church. More important still: the Judicial Committee accepted it. Ever since 1871, if not before that, the committee's competence in liturgical questions had been denied or doubted by many churchmen, so that the Church of England had in practice possessed no final court. The acceptance of the Lincoln Judgment now opened up the prospect of the Church putting its own house in order through a system of ecclesiastical courts, although no further step could be taken at the time because Parliament was as yet unwilling. Benson, who had made the decision to try the case himself before he had been sure of the Judicial Committee's attitude, was showered with congratulations.

Randall Davidson said after his death: 'I have often asked myself what was the secret of his great power. . . . I should put first . . . his peculiar grasp of the great underlying religious principles of the Church's life.' Davidson had in mind the Archbishop's ability to use church history as the touchstone of nineteenth-century problems; it was all very different from Tait. Next to the Lincoln Judgment, the most notable display of this power was Benson's *Cyprian*. Begun as a safeguard against rusting as a scholar while he was running Wellington College, it was continued as a hobby; but the minute examination of the problems of the scholarly Bishop of Carthage, a high episcopalian and rigorous disciplinarian

who was martyred in 258, was
Truro or Canterbury. As his
Larpent, wrote later: 'Cyprian
schism, conciliar assemblies, ap
discipline, even of ritual, and
question of our day – the reunio
had argued that one's eternal sa
loyalty to the local branch of the
each branch depended on its bi
Bishop of Rome) had inherited
Peter. These ideas were scarcely
under Queen Victoria; but Be
them in hours snatched from t
when tempted to depression du

St. Cyprian had stood up to I
had urged on him the validity
and Benson used that fact in hi
century as essentially Anglican.
wrote, 'were as innocent of p
ational, as they were of papal,
1896 Benson received his own
shape of Leo XIII's Bull *Apost*
the ordinations of the schisma
null and utterly void'. Benson
arrangements for a scholarly
could be published, and also
ence of 1897 could be held as
ponse. He had planned to cele
anniversary of the landing
Archbishop of Canterbury, by
from all over the world, and
that this conference would for
status for the throne of St. Au

But his was a perfect end. A
touches to his labour of thir
conducted a successful tour
disestablished Church in surp
way back he stayed with the
enjoyed animated conversatio
called him to Canterbury. On

21

went to M
the begin
was aged
buried w
lies benea
since St.

Apparant
in a smal

What v
and child
whom he
eleven, an
when she
journal as
poignant.
honeymoc

An utter c
but exacti
years older
really love.
restrained
this unlovi
this must b
for him, fu
ings. They

At Wel
mostly sh
keep up
when she
depressed
became t
capable m
Addingto
brilliant N
her as 'M
who, stra
ladies I ev

lost her fear of her husband. She longed 'for *harmonious* life and all those years it had not been'. Fifteen years after her marriage she passed through a crisis of personal faith. She confided her doubts in a woman friend, not in her husband; and the simple, calm religion which she then worked out for herself seems to have owed little to his excited church-manship, although she always supported and honoured the Church of England. Her diary records a series of loves (she was bold enough to use the word herself) with other women. Her longest lasting intimate friend was Lucy Tait, the other archbishop's daughter; 'it was impossible to think of them apart'.

The children were devoted to her, while they could never entirely relax in their father's always educational and moralizing company. But something went wrong in their formative years; and although all three boys, Arthur, Hugh, and Fred, wrote many books which seemed to be self-revealing, and although both Arthur and Fred wrote about their sister Maggie, we are in the position of not knowing exactly what was the trouble. We can only make psychological guesses. None of the children married. Arthur, the don, was subject to his father's fits of manic depression, but more acutely and for years at a time. Hugh was another strange creature, uneasy as a parson and monk in the Church of England and as a curate of the Roman Catholic church in Cambridge; he came alive when he poured out his dream of the Catholic past as a preacher and as a novelist. Fred (E. F.) was the most sociable and successful of them all, and some of his novels were best-sellers, but he became serious when treating the romantic days of male youth. Maggie, intellectually as able as any of the sons, was confined to an asylum with a persecution complex and homicidal mania. While insane, her special hatred was reserved for her mother.

We know also that none of the children ever lost their fascinated interest in their father. Arthur wrote his biography in two large volumes, and had vivid dreams of him throughout his life. Hugh, who edited a posthumous collection of his prayers and hymns, kept much of his library (unopened) in his home, and when he died he bequeathed that home, Hare Street House, Buntingford, in Hertfordshire, to be the country home of the Roman Catholic Archbishops of Westminster; he remembered what Addington Park had meant to an Archbishop of Canterbury. Fred supervised the posthumous printing of the Archbishop's *Cyprian* although he knew nothing whatever of the subject, and more than thirty years later wrote some lighter-hearted reminiscences of him. Maggie made herself responsible for the publication of the Archbishop's book on the Revelation of St. John the Divine, grew absorbed in interpretations of the Divine's visions, and set herself to imitate her father in as many little ways as possible, before she went mad. So in the grave Benson continued the dictatorship which had elevated or darkened life for his family.

It was not a rule which convinced them about the religion so dear to his heart. Two of the children (Martin the devout schoolboy, and Nellie) died immature. The others did not grow up as orthodox Anglicans. Maggie wrote a strange *Venture of Rational Faith* (1908) before madness overtook her. The happier Fred was worldly, while Hugh expressed in fiction the very spirit of Rome at its most romantically arrogant, thus fulfilling the forebodings which the Archbishop poured out in his journal on Christmas Day 1887:

How do I know that the grumbling at the pressure of sermons, of speeches, all God's holy works of different kinds, or correspondence on church matters and clerical details (and I *do* express myself too freely on such matters and all the faults of the clerical character as they *deploy* before me) may not be the cause of my not having the greatest joy of all joys – the seeing my own sons devote themselves to Holy Orders? This is what I always most wished, and this seems little likely to come to pass. Have I myself to thank that *we* do less for God's service than many, many placed in positions where such service would be impossible to procure?

Arthur Benson, Hugh's elder brother, taught at Eton but would not be ordained. He would not even consent to stand for the headmastership when virtually assured of election. Instead he retired to Cambridge, where he found a new life as a popular essayist with a tone of gracefully sympathetic melancholy, and as a Fellow (later the Master) of Magdalene College. 'To the last of his days he was nowhere quite so much at his ease . . . as with the Church.' But he could not carry out the work which his father had designed for the dead Martin and which Hugh had now laid down; for he could not bring himself to believe the full orthodox creed. His own personal beliefs were expressed in a nostalgic and vague whimsy. He remembered how alarmed his father had been when any wind of scepticism had come near by accident; and how he had himself been distressed by religious doubts when an undergraduate at Cambridge in the early 1880s. And he concluded that his father had sent his sons into the world unprepared for this battle because he had himself refused to face the full challenge of the modern world's alienation from the historic Church.

# 6

## Lightfoot and Westcott

On Ascension Day 1878, and again on Ascension Day 1889, a new Bishop of Durham was put in the lofty throne in the great Norman cathedral. Each of these two men had been a boy at King Edward's School, Birmingham (which had also been Archbishop Benson's school). Each had been a professor at Cambridge. And now they were taking over a diocese which on the face of it was completely unsuitable for a shy scholar. The hills around the cathedral and the ugly little town below it both set the problem. Much of the life of Durham Diocese was then sleepily agricultural and feudal; and to suit it, its bishop was handsomely financed and housed in two castles, one near the cathedral, another (really a palace) out at Auckland. But much of the diocese was heavily industrial in the mid-Victorian style. Shipbuilding flourished on the coast. Inland the collieries were creating new red-brick mining villages, each with its Methodist chapel; and the Church of England was under challenge. The whole scene made a world which scarcely belonged to the same universe as the libraries and lecture-halls of Cambridge.

The experiment made in enthroning such men worked magnificently. A century later, the time of these two scholar-bishops is still remembered in County Durham as a golden age. It is still worth while for anyone who would understand the meaning of Victorian Anglicanism to reflect on the story of Joseph Barber Lightfoot and Brooke Foss Westcott.

2

The son of a Liverpool accountant, Lightfoot found himself orphaned like Benson, but in more comfortable domestic circumstances when the family moved to Birmingham. At Trinity College, Cambridge, Westcott who had been his school-fellow in Birmingham supervised some of his classical studies, and, like Westcott, Lightfoot obtained the highest classical and mathematical honours. He never married, and in academic peace from 1852 he was a resident Fellow of Trinity, becoming in Tait's words 'a man of really humble mind, of great learning, and perfect scholarship'.

He worked for his college as a tutor and for his university as a professor, but his real work was done in his study in the Great Court as the light burned by night during term, and as he read and wrote steadily through the vacations. From this Cambridge base he made contact with all learned Europe, almost entirely by reading and writing. He was fluent in Hebrew, Latin, Greek, French, German, Italian, and Spanish, and had a working knowledge of Syriac, Arabic, Ethiopian, and the Coptic dialects. 'Does it not sometimes happen to you', he once innocently asked a young clergyman, 'that when you have read a book you forget in what language it was written?'

His manner of life was that of a recluse, apart from excursions to cheer the college boats, to sit on university committees, to preach before Queen Victoria, or to examine ordinands for Tait. He had, so far as we know, no dark doubts about the Christian faith or about the scholarly life. In his scholarship he had no pet theories. In the composition of his lectures and books he suffered no inhibitions. He set himself to recover the history of Christianity in its first three centuries. He wished to get at the facts, and incidentally he was confident that the facts would vindicate everything that mattered in Christianity's historic faith. But he would not get entangled in the controversies of the day, and he made his only extended contribution to doctrinal theology by leaping to the defence of Christian scholars such as Westcott when they had been attacked in an anonymous best-seller called *Supernatural Religion*. Seven articles by Lightfoot in the 1870s pulverized that showy but ill-informed work by a retired Bombay merchant, W. R. Casels.

This dry student was encouraged to develop more of a preacher's fluency – although he was never really fluent – when Gladstone gave him a part-time canonry at St. Paul's in 1871. He became attached to his colleagues, Dean Church and Canon Liddon, much as he deplored their Tractarian interpretation of church history. He was more than ever assured about the Church of England's mission by their success in both spiritualizing and filling Wren's cathedral 'at the centre of the world's concourse' – the words with which he dedicated his work on St. Ignatius to Liddon.

His commentaries on St. Paul formed another Anglican glory. 'The prevailing characteristic', as his Cambridge colleague F. J. A. Hort later noted, 'is masculine good sense unaccompanied by either the insight or the delusion of subtlety.' In addition to their detailed scholarship they were generally significant, in two ways. First, they answered the Tübingen school, which under Ferdinand Christian Baur had reconstructed the life of Paul in order to emphasize a profound conflict between him and the other apostles under Peter and James. Lightfoot's (and Westcott's) tendency was to sustain the theme of the Acts of the Apostles that Peter, James, and Paul had been fellow-apostles of the one Lord, with differences but with a common Gospel. And Lightfoot's commentaries were also conceived as a reply to innovators who claimed the label 'Catholic'.

Lightfoot brought a new wealth of equipment to the traditional Anglican answer to Rome: the apostolic Gospel was simpler and stronger than the developed Roman Catholic system of dogmas, and apostles such as Paul had certainly not regarded Peter, let alone any Bishop of Rome in the centuries to come, as the infallible Vicar of Christ. Without naming them Lightfoot also answered men such as his own colleagues at St. Paul's, who held that the 'apostolic ministry' had been handed on by the apostles to the bishops and by them to priests and deacons episcopally ordained.

Lightfoot taught that the government of the Church by bishops had emerged out of a more fluid situation. The crucial points for him were that the 'elders' or 'presbyters' mentioned in the New Testament were not called priests, so as to avoid confusion with paganism; and that they *were* also called 'bishops'. The Church described in the New Testament was, Lightfoot believed, a new start in the history of religion. It was a start made by Christ alone, who had, however, not laid down a detailed church order. As Jerusalem fell to the Romans, the Jerusalem church over which James the brother of the Lord had presided was scattered; and James, Peter, and Paul were all martyred. Thus it became necessary to have a new focus of Christian leadership, to replace Jerusalem and the apostles. The local churches had already imitated the Jewish synagogues in appointing 'elders', and gradually, under the pressure of circumstances, one of these elders became overseer or bishop in each place. As Lightfoot put it: 'the episcopate was formed not out of the apostolic order by localization but out of the presbyteral by elevation: and the title, which originally was common to all [the presbyters], came at length to be appropriate to the chief among them.'

When Lightfoot was elevated from the presbyterate, the shrewder Nonconformists took pleasure in pointing out that as a bishop he was not the successor of the apostles. Lightfoot, could, however, reply that he had always maintained that the development of episcopacy had been under divine guidance and in 'the Apostolic Age'. He thought it had first developed in Asia Minor, where the apostle John had given firm leadership to the churches. The succession of bishops had first been thought of as succession in the work, not in the laying on of hands. Lightfoot recalled how the presbyters of Alexandria for long consecrated their own bishop, and how it was not until a church council in 314 that this practice was forbidden. Moving to more recent times, he deprecated any extravagant claims for episcopacy. He was glad that at various points in its history the Church of England had been very friendly with non-episcopal churches, and until 1662 had allowed some ministers not episcopally ordained to be incumbents of parish churches and cathedral dignitaries. Lightfoot's conclusion for the nine-teenth century was clear. It was both possible and necessary to preach the apostolic Gospel in the apostolic Church. The Church was based on the Gospel, not on government by popes or bishops; but the bishops should lead the Church.

3

Despite the credit which came to him for these scholarly labours, Lightfoot refused to stand for the senior (Regius) Professorship of Divinity at Cambridge in 1870. He wanted to see Westcott elected and thus able to return to academic work after years of frustration.

Three years older than Lightfoot, Westcott was the son of a leisured, if not particularly affluent, capitalist. It was remembered that his father was a man of retiring dispos-ition, and lived for the most part a quiet home life, being devoted to scientific pursuits. Chartist demonstrations in Birmingham awakened a boyish interest in social questions; and at King Edward VII's School James Prince Lee gave him the intellectual equipment needed for a contribution to social progress.

'A schoolmaster or a clergyman?' the young man wrote to his future wife. He became both. After a period recalled as 'torturing scepticism', he was ordained by Prince Lee as deacon and priest in 1851, although he was disappointed by the coldness of the proceedings. Next year he finally gave up his life as a tutor in Cambridge, to teach classics at Harrow under C. J. Vaughan. The cause was 'Louey' Whithard, with whom he had fallen in love while at school. They had met when he had rescued her brother from a bully. She took the extra name Mary at his request when she was confirmed, and he always called her Mary, in a married life of great devotion and fertility. Seven sons and three daughters were born, and they lived frugally. Westcott, who dreamed of founding some sort of monastic order for Christian families, spent little on himself. It was only when his sons had pooled their pocket money for this gift that he was persuaded to fulfil his ambition to buy a tricycle, on which, followed by the boys on bicycles, he would visit nearby churches.

He published some theology, in addition to the work which he now began with Hort on the Greek Testament. He expressed alarm to Hort lest their revision of the Greek text should encourage a new theology; but Hort persuaded him to work on. However, his was an orthodoxy enriched by a golden setting – or (as his critics used to say) obscured by a dense fog of rhetoric. To the end of his life Wescott maintained that 'the whole life of men points to the answer which Christianity has given'. He could not argue that Greek thought was identical with Christianity; for 'the assumption of humanity, not for a time, but for ever, by the Word who is God, was a truth undreamt of till it was realized.' But he did believe that the thought as well as the language of the New Testament was close to Plato's, so that 'the work of Greece . . . lives for the simplest Christian in the New Testament.' One of his favourite theologians was Benjamin Whichcote, the gentle Christian Platonist of seventeenth-century Cambridge. When Newman remembered in his *Apologia* how he had been 'carried away' as a young man by the Christian Platonists of third-century Alexandria, he might have been summing up Wescott's own theology: 'The exterior world, physical and historical, was but the manifestation to our senses of realities greater than itself. Nature was a parable: Scripture was an allegory: pagan literature, philosophy, and mythology, properly understood, were but a preparation for the Gospel.'

Other books of the Harrow years reflected the young Westcott's power as a teacher of the New Testament, and one, *The Gospel of the Resurrection* (1866), showed the personal faith which he had reached through his period of doubt. It was a book which announced not a dogma but an experienced mystery, the mystery of the flesh of Jesus common with ours, yet in resurrection lifted above our limitations. 'Wild as my doubts are, I cannot but feel that the N. T. "finds" me', he had written in his journal for 1849, 'and that with its deepest mysteries – but as *mysteries*, not as *dogmas*. Why should we be surprised at the fiery trial of scepticism? I should more reasonably doubt my safety, if I did not doubt.' A little later in the same journal, Westcott noted: 'Faith is an intuition – a momentary acknowledgement of the heart, spontaneous and perfect.'

For the ultra-orthodox, this could not be enough. The great Canon Liddon dismissed Westcott as 'a thoughtful Latitudinarian, covered all over with a thin pietistic varnish, which has the effect of leading the *Record* and other Low Church persons to suppose that he is a variety of Evangelical'. But this was the Gospel which he preached to the Harrovians – and which he implied in a private talk with a despondent Prince Lee during 1865. Lee had been talking about Arnold (whole letters to him he had just burned, explaining enigmatically that they witnessed to great differences between them), about Newman (who had 'trifled with his reason until he had lost it'), and, with his eyes filled by tears, about death. 'People quote various words of the Lord as containing the sum of the Gospel', he said to Westcott, but to him the best was the text: *Fear not, only believe.* What Prince Lee had in mind was a fundamentalist belief. But 'Lord I believe', Westcott quoted in reply; 'help thou mine unbelief.'

He was thankful to accept a canonry at Peterborough in 1869. He would unlock the cathedral at night and pray, the only mortal man in it; and one fruit of the peace of Peterborough was his commentary on St. John. He argued that the fourth gospel, and before it the last book in the printed Bible, were both written by the apostle John to convey his vision of the cosmic, triumphant Christ. The teaching in the gospel was authentically Christ's, remembered although not at first understood. St. John, as he meditated on it, found it correcting his own over-hasty teaching that the Lord Jesus would come back to the earth soon. Westcott, however, left Peterborough suddenly in 1883, when the Bishop complained that he was neglecting his duties in the diocese. Gladstone came to the rescue with a canonry of Westminster.

His Cambridge professorship was his main task for twenty years. He believed that the university was called 'to inspire men with a sense of their sovereign grandeur' and that 'no nation, no church . . . was ever called to fulfil a greater work than that to which the English nation and the English church are now summoned'. He became a Fellow of King's where he used to hold a religious discussion on a Sunday afternoon, and a Cambridge University Church Society was founded under his patronage. But his chief interest was in the red-brick Divinity School, which was built in his time. There he presided over the teaching of the Bible and the early Christian centuries and over the beginning of the Theological Tripos as an examination for undergraduates. Accepting much of the work himself, he persuaded a growing number of bishops and Oxford theologians to institute a standard examination for those to be ordained, virtually replacing the tests by the Examining Chaplains which had greatly varied from diocese to diocese. His initiative also led to the formation of a Clergy Training School in Cambridge; it was his wish that ordinands should do all their work based on their own colleges, but after his time the scheme developed into a seminary, Westcott House. He also did all that he could to encourage both the new Cambridge Mission to Delhi for dialogue with educated Hindus and the 'university extension' movement for adult education in England. It is, however, clear that in Cambridge as at Harrow many were confused by his actual teaching. if they had the patience to listen. When he died Scott Holland, who loved him, recalled his famous conversation with a pupil. 'Thank you! Thank you, Dr. Westcott! You have made that perfectly clear to me!' 'Oh! I hope not! I hope not!'

Always Westcott returned to the thought that the humanity of Jesus drew 'all men' and took all humanity into God. Everywhere in history there was self-sacrifice and a priestly prayer, but these were perfectly consummated in Jesus. When he read the biography of Maurice he wrote: 'I never knew before how deep my sympathy is with most of his characteristic thoughts'. But he shared, too, Maurice's sense of the inadequacy of words, and wrote: 'Lord Shaftesbury's has been a noble life, and complete in its way, though I wish he had left theology alone. To study that we want an unusual endowment of modesty.'

4

When Lightfoot became Bishop of Durham at the age of fifty-one, he turned Auckland Castle into an informal college. Under his eye an Auckland Brotherhood of young men from Oxford and Cambridge read, talked, played football, visited homes, and said prayers in the great chapel in preparation for a curacy. Some of them could afford to be a curate without any stipend, just as Lightfoot refused all payment for them; six or eight at a time were his guests. Not many of these young men stayed long in County Durham, but Lightfoot ordained 323 deacons in ten years.

He also brought his scholarly work to a splendid completion. He was resolved to set in order the materials for the history of the Church in the century after the apostles' deaths. This task involved a minute examination of the evidence, much of it fraudulent, much of it discovered only in his lifetime, before a lucid narrative could be made. No difficulty daunted him. He had published an edition of the Epistles of St. Clement (one authentic, the other not) in 1869, with the same care as he had lavished on the Epistles of St. Paul, and he was revising his *Clement* to the end of his life, as fresh evidence came to light. The scholarly work of his Durham years was to complete this Cambridge material, particularly by an examination of the seven letters attributed to St. Ignatius of Antioch, who was martyred in Rome at the beginning of the second century. These were documents of importance to theologians. 'As to the Episcopal system, I founded it upon the Epistles of St. Ignatius', Newman remembered; on the other hand, radical Germans detected forgery. With an unprecedented thoroughness in studying both these letters and their background, Lightfoot established their authentic text and placed it in the context of an account of the whole period, including an equally careful edition of the story of the martyrdom of Polycarp, Bishop of Smyrna. Two volumes of his *Apostolic Fathers* were published in 1885, and the third in the year of his death. In an act of thanksgiving he paid for the building of a new church in

Sunderland, dedicated it to St. Ignatius, and consecrated it after a sermon by Westcott.

None of this achievement surprised anyone who knew the orderly power of his educational influence and academic work, or the resources of his library and memory. 'From strength to strength' had been the text upon which Westcott had preached at his consecration as a bishop. Nor was Cambridge surprised when young men felt a reverent affection for this ugly, shy, endlessly learned bishop. A member of the Auckland Brotherhood recalled: 'Lightfoot had no beauty of face or form, but he had a most gorgeous smile, and when this came, it lit up his face like a glory. . . .'

Less expected was his effectiveness as a Victorian apostle. His pastoral work in County Durham interested him far more than the national problems of the Church. He never seems to have hesitated to sacrifice to it any prospect of becoming Tait's successor or Benson's closest counsellor at Lambeth. Under his predecessor, Charles Baring, the population had grown, and with it the number of churches. The policy of church-building now flourished: forty-five were erected in ten years. Lightfoot's *Leaders of the Northern Church* (1890) was a series of portraits of Aidan, Hilda, Bede, and other early English missionaries based on sermons preached at churches dedicated to them. But what had been lacking was a strong diocesan organization, and this Lightfoot set himself to supply. He successfully carried through the division of the diocese when the new see of Newcastle was created (with Samuel Wilberforce's son Ernest as its first bishop). Within the more manageable area left to him, he threw himself into confirmations in a style astonishing in a scholar who was heir to the Prince Bishops of Durham. He created a new archdeaconry, multiplied the rural deans, reorganized and increased the finances, confirmed tirelessly, and encouraged the laity both to speak in the councils of the Church and to assist the clergy in preaching and visiting, then a startling innovation.

The combination of diocesan and academic work was fatal. During Lightfoot's journeys about his diocese, or in his August holidays, his mind would be at work on his writing. He would write before Matins and breakfast; he would write late at night, falling asleep at his desk. His studies of Ignatius and Polycarp turned out to be his own martydom; yet his recreation was to write a history of Auckland Castle, the oldest episcopal residence in England. When the strain of the Lambeth Conference of 1888 was added to such overwork, his heart collapsed. After a brief recovery, he died next year.

5

So it was that, against all his own expectation, Westcott was summoned to spend the last years of his life in carrying on his friend's leadership of the diocese of Durham. And he, too, was far more successful than others expected. He succeeded partly because he limited himself. He did not attempt to create a new organization; he did not attempt to write books of original scholarship; he did not often trouble to read other men's books. Although he kept up the Auckland Brotherhood, he did not live with the young men as Lightfoot had done. But he succeeded also because the humility of this elderly professor made its impression. His favourite drink was weak tea, and when he had to use the episcopal carriage he sat miserably with his back to the horses. When he addressed the privileged, he could preach what he practised, describing 'anything which costs more either in money, or in time, or vital energy than it contributes to his power of service' is, for a Christian, a 'culpable luxury'. His devotion to duty was such that he preferred a meeting of rural deans to Archbishop Benson's funeral in Canterbury. When his wife lay dying he had left her bedside because he had an engagement to consecrate a churchyard in the presence of a miners' brass band.

He could be down-to-earth, and was fed with practical information about social conditions by the Vicar of Gateshead, but it may be doubted whether the eloquence of Westcott was understood much more readily by the workmen of County Durham than it had been by the schoolboys of Harrow. (Had the congregations understood everything in the sermons which Lightfoot had written out with such care?) What counted was what he was. In his old age Westcott's leonine head and eager eyes conveyed a memorable impression of the attraction of the unseen world; yet he, a man of books, loved to quote the dictum of Benjamin Whichcote: 'I act, therefore I am.' In his first address to his Diocesan Conference, he said: 'I know the attractions of the pursuit of speculative and of historical criticism, but these are wholly subsidiary to action, which is the characteristic of man. The Gospel which is committed to believers claims to have the power to deal with every practical question of human conduct for the manifestation of God's glory; and friends and foes alike have a right to demand that this claim should be vindicated on the broad fields of life.' He never became a man of action, but men were impressed by his feeling that he ought to be one.

On 1 June 1892 Bishop Westcott's reputation proved to be already strong enough to win for him his most memorable success on the 'broad fields'. A fall in the price of coal had led the colliery owners to reduce wages by 12½ per cent, but the trade union, the Mining Federation, had insisted on 7½ per cent as the maximum. The result had been a stoppage of work by about 10,000 men, reducing most of them to destitution and damaging the whole of the North. Ignoring cynical protests that he was a capitalist but no economist, Westcott proposed a compromise. Work should be resumed on two conditions: that there should be an immediate reduction of only ten per cent in wages, and that the question of any further reduction should be referred to a Wages Board, to be established with full powers to deal with this and all future differences as to the increase or reduction of wages. Although both sides were by now desperate for a compromise, the formula was far from being obvious; the owners had increased the reduction to 13½ per cent, and the bitter miners did not trust the idea of a Board for conciliation. Westcott went from group to group, mediating, during a Saturday afternoon when representatives of Capital and Labour conferred together and separately in Auckland Castle. A crowd around the palace set up a mighty cheer for the bishop as well as for the miners' leaders when the end of the strike was announced.

His success as an arbitrator spread Westcott's reputation so widely that he was asked to be the chief speaker at a demonstration of the unemployed in Trafalgar Square. He refused, but he was glad to be President of the more middle-class Christian Social Union founded in 1889, and his preaching was now borne along on a tide of a reforming optimism. In a preface to a book of sermons, he announced that 'there is a growing tendency to judge conduct by reference to the whole, and to the eternal; to subordinate personal to social interests'. The sermons breathed an atmosphere of trust. As the reviewer in the *Yorkshire Post* noted: 'He is not content to explain Christian duty and urge its performance: he always suggests in some subtle way that men only want to know their duty to discharge it.' Two other collections of sermons (*The Incarnation and Common Life* and *Lessons from Work*) appeared, in the same mood. Various challenges to the Church were mentioned, only to be classed as opportunities, for the Gospel could never be defeated. The nineteenth century seemed to be ending in an evening of glory. Typical was the parable of the Alpine sunset which closed a Whitsun sermon in 1891:

We gaze on the vast bare rocks and snow-slopes transfigured in a flood of burning light. In a moment there falls over them an ashy paleness as of death, cold and chilling. While we strive to measure our loss a deepening flush spreads slowly over the mountain side, pure and calm and tender, and we know that the glory which has passed away is not lost even when it fades again from our sight.

Westcott was surprisingly popular both with the miners and with the gentry of County Durham. This very popularity indicates that he was not ruthless in his demands for change. On the contrary, he was a scholar in his seventies, 'pure and calm and tender', who had not been particularly interested in social questions while a schoolmaster or professor. The Christian Socialism which he expressed was something of an enigma to comtemporaries. They knew that it was not the Socialism of Karl Marx or the Independent Labour Party. They also knew that public control was increasing now that politics increasingly depended on the working-class vote, and they wanted to know how a churchman who was in favour of this kind of semi-socialism differed from, say, Joseph Chamberlain. Westcott could be as disappointing as Maurice himself when he had to answer political questions. He, who had so often preached about peace between the nations, refused to follow Pope Leo XIII in condemning the British attack on the Boers. 'It was impossible for us to submit to arbitration the fulfilment of our imperial obligations.' Yet it would be wrong to conclude that this elderly bishop caused no alarm among conservatives. The 'Socialist tendencies of the speeches which he has made since he became a bishop' were enough for Lord Salisbury to scotch the Queen's suggestion that he should be made Archbishop of York in 1890. The fact – heartening or alarming, according to one's taste – was that this theologian with one foot in heaven was prepared to preside at conferences about social questions drawing both managers and workers to Auckland Castle, to inspect the housing of the poor as he went about his diocesan duties, and to praise the motives of trade unions and co-operatives. Many of the tributes after his death in 1901 came from manual workers, and many of the Christian Socialists who were far more radical than he was knew what their cause had gained from the glamour of his name.

At the annual miners' service in Durham Cathedral a week before his death, he summed up his message, explaining that 'it is not likely that I shall ever address you here again.' It was a message about the love of Christ.

Try by its Divine standard the thoroughness of your labour and the purity of your recreation, and the Durham which we love, the Durham of which we are proud . . . will soon answer to the heavenly pattern. If Tennyson's idea of heaven was true, that 'heaven is the ministry of soul to soul', we may reasonably hope, by patient, resolute, faithful, united endeavour, to find heaven about us here, the glory of our earthly life.

# 7

# Creighton and Davidson

I

On St. Mark's Day in 1891 two bishops were consecrated by Archbishop Benson in Westminster Abbey. One was Professor Mandell Creighton, to be Bishop of Peterborough. Six years later, when Benson died, the Prince of Wales, the Archbishop of York, and others wanted to see this brilliant man at Canterbury. He was appointed instead Bishop of London. A little less than ten years after his consecration, however, a stomach ulcer killed him. The other new bishop kneeling beside Creighton at that service in 1891, Randall Thomas Davidson, rather disapproved of him, and wrote some severe words about him privately after his death:

A great many people who knew him well found it difficult not to believe him to be a cynic, and there were those who doubted his real hold upon the dogmatic side of Christianity. This last was probably due to his endeavour, mistaken and unsuccessful as I personally think it was, to appear as a finished man of the world with social experience and social gifts, who could meet other men of the world on equal terms.

Creighton, unlike Davidson, was reluctant to become a bishop, for the simple reason that he wanted to read. Two years after his consecration he wrote: 'My life has been that of a man who tries to write a book, and is the object of a conspiracy to prevent him from doing so. It is quite true that no one cares to read my book, but that has never interfered with my pleasure in reading for it.' When a lady attempted to console him with the remark that 'after all, men are more interesting than books', he commented: 'Doubtless this is true, but you choose your own books, and you must take your men as you find them.' He used to say that he wanted his epitaph to be: 'He tried to write true history.' In fact, after his death men said more flattering things, and the chorus of praise swelled when his widow published his *Life and Letters* in 1904. Randall Davidson added after his comment just quoted: 'I know of no instance in which the publication of a public man's biography has so greatly raised him in the estimation of good and thoughtful people.'

Creighton's great book was on the Renaissance popes, and he resembled them in some ways. He shared all their love of learning. 'The formula which most explains the Church of England is that it rests on an appeal to sound learning' was one of his many donnish sayings. He was close to them in his love of Italy, tradition, art, and ceremonies. The Archdeacon of London described him sniffingly after his death: 'Although in doctrinal opinions a very Broad Churchman, he had great sympathy for medieval ritual and all kinds of pomp and magnificence'. Yet Bishop Creighton was out of tune with his own age, as the popes had not been out of tune with theirs; for in the last days of Queen Victoria an effective churchman had to be thoroughly earnest. 'He's too clever', chuckled Archbishop Frederick Temple after one of Creighton's after-dinner speeches. To Creighton, the essentials of Christianity seemed simple and sure, so that everything else could be treated as material for objective research or donnish humour. This should be remembered as the context of his remark about the Anglican appeal to sound learning. He said:

The Church of England seems to me to have a very decided position of its own – the noblest which can be taken by any institution, but through its very loftiness easily capable of misrepresentation and of misunderstanding ... The Church of England puts to one side all that is irrelevant, it shuns definitions about questions which arose from mere human curiosity, it is chary of denials in matters where affirmation and denial are alike impossible ... It is this characteristic which has led to the groundless assertion that the Church of England expresses a compromise. Sound learning must always wear the appearance of a compromise between ignorance and plausible hypotheses ... It is the function of learning to assert what is known, and to leave perverse ingenuity steadily alone.

Randall Davidson, although a Broad Churchman like Creighton, had developed a manner always 'good and thoughtful', consistently 'earnest and reverent' (another of his favourite phrases). Wickedly Frances Stevenson, Lloyd George's secretary-mistress, referred to him in her diaries as 'God's own Butler'. He took seriously what churchmen took seriously, although he also took seriously the English layman's dislike of medieval magnificence in the clergy. He was, as a result, trusted in the Church as Creighton never was. If he was somewhat ponderous, so were they. If he was no scholar, their own churchmanship did not rest on the appeal to sound learning.

The charge usually made against him during the first half of his life was not that he was too clever, but that he was too ambitious. After a slow start he had gone to Lambeth as Archbishop Tait's chaplain at the age of twenty-nine. Since then he had remained at the centre of Church and State, and in 1891 he was being consecrated as Bishop of Rochester. He had already developed a stomach ulcer, and eleven days after his consecration it confined him to his bed. (The next six months were the only period after his ordination when he found time for systematic reading.) He was transferred to the less arduous see of Winchester after four years. Weak health was the reason why he was not made Bishop of London in 1897, and why he refused to be Creighton's successor there in 1901. However, after Creighton's death Davidson's was the only possible name for Canterbury. 'I do know the ropes', as he said. He was the pope of the Anglican world for a quarter-century, and he died full of honours at the age of eighty-two.

2

Mandell Creighton was born in Carlisle, and wrote a book about its history. His father and grandfather had been carpenters, and his father's furnishing and decorating shop was a few yards from the cathedral over which Tait presided as dean. His mother died when he was seven years old, and the home over the Castle Street shop now possessed few signs of happiness, or books, pictures or other inducement to the young Mandell. The boy's chance came through the grammar school close by the cathedral. There he was nicknamed 'Homer', and from there he won a scholarship to the King's School which was part of Durham Cathedral. It seems to have been the historic beauty of Durham and its choral services that turned his thoughts to ordination. In 1864, having recently left school, he wrote an immense letter to his successor as head of the school, thus recording his eloquence as a young moralist in the high Arnoldian style.

He won a scholarship at Merton College, Oxford, and a further nickname: 'the Professor'. He was now a definite High Churchman, with severe views about the slack ritual in Carlisle Cathedral; he was also a passionate friend of fellow-undergraduates. 'Of course at a certain age', he wrote to a fellow-student, 'when you have a house and so on, you get a wife as part of its furniture. . . .' He took the orthodox classical course, and after his Firsts turned to history, becoming a Fellow of Merton in 1867 and hastily reading history books in the evening in order to lecture on them next morning. He was by now a clever, flippant, and sarcastic talker, with a taste in wine, in silk ties, in Morris wallpapers, and in blue china plates. He went through no religious crisis in an Oxford which was now growing more and more lay and sceptical. He did not trouble to read Darwin, and considered the controversy 'amusing'. The fellowship which he held entailed an obligation to be ordained, but he was not made deacon until 1870, and then he made little specific preparation. He said about this time that it was the habit in Oxford to assume that a man who took Holy Orders must be either a fool or a knave; and people could not call him a fool. But perhaps he exaggerated his wisdom.

At one of Ruskin's lectures next year he noticed a girl wearing a yellow scarf. The fellow-aesthete was Louise von Glehn, the daughter of an Esthonian merchant who had settled in England. Three weeks later he was engaged. It was now that his life began to be more than the life of an ordinary Oxford tutor. His bride was enthusiastic about Italian art, and with her encouragement he formed the intention to write a history of the subject, at a time when the Italian Renaissance was only beginning to be familiar to educated Englishmen. He taught her Italian; she taught him German; they visited Italy in a shared ecstasy. He explained religion to her, and found it difficult. He grew uneasy, but impressed, when Louise proposed to visit the poor. By the time he was ready to be a priest, in 1873, he was so nervous about the examination before ordination that he wrote to the archdeacon offering to withdraw.

The don's life continued for another year, until a vicarage where his college was the patron, and where the income was exceptionally good, fell vacant. He decided to go. He was growing bored with being a 'teaching drudge', and wanted to put all his energy into the study of one historical subject. Somehow he would buy or borrow the necessary books. The place was Embleton, on the coast of Northumberland, a quarrymen's village notorious for immorality and consisting of six hundred people, almost all in one-room cottages, with about eleven hundred other souls in the bleak countryside around.

The success of Creighton's ten years as a parish priest was both academic and personal. He finished two volumes of his history, and did most of the work for three more. He added a study of the Elizabethan Age, a biography of Simon de Montfort, many book reviews, and some coaching of pupils for the sake of the money. And in the afternoon he and his wife would visit the parishioners, entering into their lives with a human, pastoral kindness which few had suspected in the Oxford historian. The vicarage with its fortified peel tower, built as a protection against raids from Scotland, was a home where an adequate domestic staff functioned and a young family grew up in happiness – although Creighton insisted that his was the will around which the home revolved. The ancient church was the place where Creighton learned to preach extempore, usually with a moral application, but based on a simple exposition of the Bible, avoiding critical and controversial questions; it was a pulpit style to which he adhered for the rest of his ministry. He acquired other duties, but he had no ambition to take a prominent part in ecclesiastical business or theology. 'I don't like talking about religious matters', he would protest.

His work on the Papacy from 1378 was based on some original sources, but the Vatican's archives were still closed. He used mostly German scholarship, so that Embleton's distance from the conversation of historians did little harm. Enough of Creighton's original intention to write about Italian art remained to give a special zest to his descriptions of the cultural background in the Renaissance, but his down-to-earth history belonged to another world than Walter Pater's *Renaissance* (1873). 'When events are tedious, you must be tedious' was his motto. Enough of his worldliness remained to make him a master storyteller of the politics in which the Papacy was all too deeply involved, and to make him refrain from denouncing the popes – although he freely denounced idle undergraduates or debauched villagers. About the Borgia family, Creighton wrote that 'they have become legendary as types of unrestrained wickedness and it is difficult to judge them fairly without seeming to palliate iniquity.' But he did judge fairly, even tenderly, and thereby shocked many Victorians.

One of those most shocked was the Roman Catholic historian, Lord Acton. Acton knew more about the subject than any Englishman except possibly Creighton himself, but he approached it with a passionate commitment to a cause. Precisely because he was a devout Roman Catholic, he was ashamed of the Renaissance popes; and his indignation about their immorality and their rejection of reform got mixed up with the despair which he felt (with his friend Gladstone) at the insistence of the nineteenth-century popes on being both infallible and obscurantist. Creighton seemed to him, as to Davidson, insufficiently serious.

Acton reviewed the first two volumes quite favourably, but in a private letter of 1882 the peer condescendingly warned the vicar that more theology was becoming inevitable as his history progressed towards Luther. 'You will not escape theological exposition when you come to the explosion at Wittenberg, the negotiations of Ausberg, the debates of Trent. . . . There are two questions, What made Luther? and What made him so strong? which occur in the introductory period, and have never been satisfactorily answered.'

When Creighton published his next two volumes, five years later, he was a professor editing the *English Historical Review* and he sent the volumes to Acton, expecting (no doubt) similar treatment. Instead, Acton wrote a review which was an outright attack. One charge was intellectual superficiality. 'The author prefers the larger public that take history in the shape of literature, to scholars whose souls are vexed with the insolubility of problems and take their meals in the kitchen.' With this went a moral accusation. 'He is not striving to prove a case, or burrowing towards a conclusion, but wishes to pass through scenes of raging controversy and passion, with a serene curiosity, a divided judgment, and a pair of white gloves.' Creighton was angry in response to Acton's 'furious passion', but then cooled off and persuaded Acton to remove some of the more personally hostile passages from the review. He did not, however, persuade Acton to modify his condemnation of the history's indulgent description of the popes on the eve of the Reformation.

In particular, Acton was furious that Creighton appeared to condone the Papacy's involvement in the Inquisition, and he wrote to rebuke Creighton privately.

You say that people in authority are not to be snubbed or sneered at from our pinnacle of conscious rectitude. I really don't know whether you exempt them because of their rank, or of their success and power, or of their date. . . . I cannot accept your canon that we are to judge Pope and King unlike other men, with a favoured presumption that they did no wrong. If there is any presumption, it is the other way, increasing as the power increases. . . . Power tends to corrupt, and absolute power corrupts absolutely. Great men are almost always bad men, even when they exercise influence not authority: still more when you superadd the tendency or the certainty of corruption by authority. . . . The inflexible integrity of the moral code is to me the secret of the authority, the dignity, the utility of history.

Creighton's reply was impenitent. What he had meant was that

anyone engaged in great affairs occupied a representative position, which required special consideration. Selfishness, even wrong-doing, for an idea, an institution, the maintenance of an accepted view of the basis of society, does not cease to be wrong-doing; but it is not quite the same as personal wrong-doing: it is more difficult to prove, and it does not equally shock the moral sense of the doer. The acts of men in power are determined by the effective force behind them of which they are the exponents: their morality is almost always lower than the morality of the mass of men; but there is generally a point fixed below which they cannot sink with impunity.

There was something undeniably paradoxical about the man who had won an international reputation for his cool narrative of the Renaissance Papacy working as a vicar in Northumberland, and Creighton came to feel this himself. In 1884 he accepted an invitation to be the first Dixie Professor of Ecclesiastical History at Cambridge. Next year he was made a canon of Worcester and in that cathedral he contentedly spent his vacations. During term he showed Cambridge that there was little difference between the sacred and the profane. 'Theology has become historical, and does not demand that history should become theological', he declared. 'Ecclesiastical history must be pursued in exactly the same way, and with exactly the same spirit, as any other branch of history.'

3

After seven years, he was a bishop. As he wrote to a friend: 'A bishopric is to me personally after the flesh a terrible nuisance. But how is a man to refuse the responsibilities of his branch of the service?' As he listened to the regrets of his fellow-historians, he knew that his whole existence must be transformed. To another friend he now wrote that 'my position in life is changed. It is no longer to *teach*, but to *edify*. I have no longer to startle people out of self-complacency, but to be kindly, sympathetic, humble and helpful.' As a bishop he acted on the assumption that 'mankind want a religion: and it is as a religion that Christianity works in the world.' Although he had never used the Athanasian Creed at Embleton, he insisted on its regular use in his diocese. He lectured to the working men of Leicester or

Northampton, he smoked with the young men in the houses of the gentry, and he was (as his wife recalled) 'determined to like' Peterborough. After six years of it, he told a friend: 'I can truly say that I am happy, not through my public activities, or my social powers, but through growing sympathy in little matters with children, with the young, with the sorrowful, the tempted, the perplexed.' Perhaps so; anyway, Mrs. Creighton was happy. She quickly became the most formidable bishop's wife in England. In the biography of William Temple it is recorded that when Creighton was passed over for Canterbury in favour of William Temple's father, a schoolboy at Rugby commented: 'What a sell for Mrs. Peterborough!'

At this stage Creighton kept up some academic work. The fifth – and, as it turned out, last – volume of his *Papacy* appeared, together with books made up of Cambridge lectures on Elizabeth I and his Hulsean lectures of 1893–4 on *Persecution and Tolerance*. Creighton's Hulseans concluded that liberty is 'only secure under the guardianship of the Church; for the Church possesses the knowledge of man's eternal destiny – which alone can justify his claim to freedom.' A few months later he was delivering his Primary Charge to his diocese, again emphasizing liberty: 'the great question for the modern world to determine is how men are to be fitted to bear the heavy burden of liberty'. The message of the Church was indispensable to true progress: 'the service of men without the service of God becomes an intolerable burden.' Nothing is more striking than to see the confidence with which Creighton, ignored the growing secularization in English life. 'The truth of Christianity is apparent in the Christian life: and all the conceptions which support the non-Christian at the present day are of Christian origin, and owe their power to the vitality of the Christian faith. Current morality, philanthropy, high aims in politics, ideas of progress, of liberty, of brotherhood – what you will – owe their position to Christianity.' Equally striking was his failure to perceive, when he represented the Church of England at the coronation of the Tsar in Moscow in 1896, that Holy Russia was doomed as surely as the Renaissance Papacy.

His promotion to London in 1896 seemed natural, yet it was a mistake to give Creighton the busiest diocese. He felt that he had to talk as cleverly as possible on all the occasions when the Bishop of London was wanted and when his predecessor, Temple, had often been gruff or rude. He delivered 294 sermons and addresses during 1897. But his life as a student was now closed. Nor did he now enjoy many opportunities to influence individuals; he always had to rush on to another engagement or to write another administrative letter.

The mistake of imposing such duties on Creighton became murderous when he got involved in disputes with Anglo-Catholic ritualists. In London there were Anglican priests who put an almost Lutheran religious passion into the revival of the ceremonies which had been familiar to the Renaissance popes. Creighton could not understand such a reverence for historical precedent when it clashed with what had become the master-theme of his speaking and writing: the unity of the English Church with the English State under law. His predecessor, Temple, had in practice allowed such eccentrics to go their own way, while not troubling to conceal his contempt. Now Creighton set himself to bring the diocese to order, and this aim caught him in a dilemma because of his character. If he had cared less for good order, he would have put good will above it, as his successor Arthur Foley Winnington-Ingram was to do. If he had cared less for liberty, he would have prosecuted the rebels as Tait had done – or would at least have forbidden their practices firmly, as Davidson was then trying to do in the diocese of Winchester. What he did was to plead with them to accept order freely, for the sake of peace. And his health, poisoned by the overwork and anxiety, was certainly not improved by a foolish decision to which he adhered obstinately. He not only insisted that the officials throughout his diocese, including the suffragan bishops, should refer all substantial questions to him; he also declined to employ a single secretary. He would dictate some letters to his chaplain or to his daughters, but he wrote most of them with his own hand, often during meetings. His filing system was therefore mainly in his head.

The scholar who pretended to be a man of the world was tormented by the unimportance of the disputes which added to the burdens on his desk. 'It has been a permanent feature of the English people to show themselves incapable of theology', he lamented to his clergy. 'We have had contention enough, but we have contended not about ideas, but about external things. Englishmen cannot grasp an idea. . . .' But he allowed himself to be dragged down into these trivialities because he thought that he had incurred the obligation by agreeing to be an English bishop. He was the most patriotic of men, and called himself a 'fanatical' Anglican. 'I very much wish to have ecclesiastical matters raised above trivialities', he wrote, 'to a conception of the mind and intention of the English Church – the noblest exhibition of Christianity and therefore the most difficult to maintain'. In this context he would provocatively say, 'I am not ashamed to own that I am an Englishman first and a Churchman afterwards', before explaining the epigram: 'Church and State are the nation looked at from different points of view.' He hoped that when he had disposed of the trivialities he would live to see the nobility. In February 1899 he recorded what he had done in less than two years. He had worked through, and revised, all the services used in more than two hundred churches. 'All services that went beyond the Prayer Book have practically ceased.' He concluded:

Speaking generally, I have found a reasonable readiness to obey except on these points – (1) carrying the Communion to sick persons, (2) the ceremonial use of incense, (3) the introduction of lights at the Gospel. Of these I have remitted (2) and (3) to the Archbishop, who will soon hear the pleadings and pronounce decision.

The Archbishop was, however, the very man whose policy (or lack of it) while Bishop of London had brought such anxieties to his successor. In knowledge of, or interest in, ecclesiastical history Frederick Temple was no true successor to Benson, and his verdict, when it came, was based simply on the Act of Uniformity then 340 years old. That Act had prohibited any ceremony not ordered in the Prayer Book. The Anglo-Catholic incense and processional

...lished periodicals, is one of such unappreciative criticism as I
...uld not desire Your Majesty to see.'

...e Queen asked for a withdrawal and apology. The Dean
...used, and offered his resignation instead. A fortnight of
...nce followed. Then Victoria sent for him on another
...tter and nothing more was heard of the proposed book.
...a young man with Davidson's delight in the favour of
...great, such honesty was very brave indeed; and when
...returned to Lambeth as Archbishop, *The Times* justly
...mmented that he had kept his feet in slippery places.

...In addition to these duties in Windsor Castle, he was
...nsulted almost daily by Archbishop Benson. The Benson
...mily regarded Davidson as serpent-like in his wisdom, but
...e visionary archbishop frequently gained from the more
...orldly dean's advice about the personalities involved in
...urch politics. In these same years, Davidson's grasp of the
...story of the Church of England was further strengthened
...y his work (helped by William Benham) on the *Life of Tait*
...hich appeared in two volumes in 1891.

...Queen Victoria and Archbishop Benson made private
...mments about his ambition, but they knew that such a
...an should be himself a bishop. Various sees were discussed,
...mong them Durham and Winchester, but the Prime
...Iinister of the day, Lord Salisbury, offered him a humbler
...hoice, between Worcester and Rochester. Davidson chose
...he latter diocese, 'containing as it does all South London'.
...Vo historic palace was attached to the diocese of Rochester
...t that time, so he lived in the midst of his urban work, in
...Kennington Park Road. Bishop Ridding of Southwell wrote
...o him: 'Leaving your fatness, your sweetness, your good
...ruit and wine, to be promoted over such a forest – what a
...plunge from the comfortable to the un!'

...Davidson does not seem to have enjoyed the exchange.
...Later he recalled his visits to the parishes of South London.
...'Life in those parishes, and the almost insuperable obstacles
...to making it religiously bright and buoyant, weighed upon
...my thoughts by day and night.' To his despondent clergy
...he would quote Westcott's words: 'It is the office of the
...State to give effect to public opinion, it is the office of the
...Church to shape it.' But fair words were not enough. His

lights had not been so ordered; therefore, they should cease.
The next year Archbishop Temple delivered an equally
simple verdict on the practice of 'reserving' the consecrated
bread and wine for carrying to the sick (or, in some very
High churches, for adoration). The Prayer Book was
enough. 'The Church of England does not at present allow
Reservation in any form.'

Creighton defended his Primate and attempted to enforce
the decisions in the churches of London, remarking to one
indignant High Churchman that 'the Catholic Church
must go into the waste-paper basket'. However, his lack of
zest was disclosed in another widely reported remark: 'If
they want to make a smell, let them.' He vetoed two proposed prosecutions. In the feverish atmosphere he feared that
some Anglo-Catholics would leave and wreck the Church
of England, and thus ruin 'this ancient Christian land'; and
it sickened his heart. But even this fear brought out the
historian in him. He observed to his chaplain that the
nineteenth century had been one of the greatest ages in all
history, next to the thirteenth century and the Elizabethans.
It had been the great philanthropic age, when everybody
was eager to do good to others. But he added then that
most people had made the mistake of wishing only to do
good in their own particular way; and in a more flippant
mood on a previous occasion he had declared that 'no people
do so much harm as those who go about doing good'.

Amid such quips, a great weariness had settled on his
inner life. Although he was not more than fifty-seven years
of age, he told his wife that he had a horror of working on
like Archbishop Temple, and an equal horror of retiring
from work in exhaustion. When he suffered a severe
haemorrhage on 8 January 1901, he 'did not seem as if he
wished to live'. It was over within a week. He was buried in
the crypt of St. Paul's with Davidson representing the Queen
at the funeral. The Anglo-Catholic ritualists mourned their
bishop and carried on their practices. The next year Lord
Rosebery said of the man who had thus allowed himself to
be killed by trivialities: 'I think that the late Bishop of
London was perhaps the most alert and universal intelligence that existed in this island at the time of his death'.

## 4

Creighton's ancestors had been Scots. Randall Davidson was of pure Scottish blood, his father being a timber merchant in Edinburgh. He was born in 1848, and baptized in the Church of Scotland, but was sent to Harrow for his education. There he was confirmed as an Anglican and brought under the influence of Westcott, his housemaster for part of his schooldays. ('We had a very learned sermon from Westcott this morning', he wrote home, 'which might possibly have been intelligible had one been thoroughly well up in the Ecclesiastical histories of Rome, Greece and Syria for the first 5 centuries A.D.') In 1866 he was more or less crippled by being shot in the back by accident, and this accident accounted in large part for the disappointment of his time at Oxford. 'A poor, rather feckless, but aspirant invalid undergraduate' was how he remembered himself later. Creighton was one of this tutors in history, but took no particular interest in him.

After collecting his Third at Oxford, Davidson spent the next three years trying to recover his health and to read some theology. He had intended to be ordained for some time, and he made an earnest and aspirant curate for three years in Dartford in Kent. Any trace of fecklessness had already gone; his nickname was 'the Dean'. Then early in 1877 he had his chance. He had known Craufurd Tait intimately at Oxford, and it was Craufurd's suggestion that Archbishop Tait invited him to be his Resident Chaplain at Lambeth. 'I am now bound to see and do everything', he wrote to his father after a few weeks. 'I am certainly enjoying my life here hugely and making many friends.' Not many months later he proposed to Edith Tait, aged nineteen, and was accepted. 'Now all is smooth and utterly happy', he wrote to his own father. Randall and Edith Davidson had no children, but she was the perfect hostess in one ecclesiastical residence after another.

Such a son-in-law became indispensable when the weary old man was bereft of wife and son, but it was anyway Tait's practice to delegate as much as possible of his correspond-

ence. So while in his thirties this chaplain had th[e] of writing many letters which shaped Anglican of conducting confidential negotiations with He was recognized by honours such as a chapl Queen. When the Archbishop died in 1882, D the Queen an account of the deathbed wh touched' her. 'Would it suit you to come and Saturday?' she asked. He came; he saw; she was Soon Davidson was interviewing Mrs. Brow Queen's instructions, to discover whether Bish was fit enough to succeed Tait; was deciding that and was recommending to Victoria names bishops and deans. Next May he was Dean of the Queen's command.

In St. George's chapel in Windsor Castle, h smoothly over the four canons, half of whom appointed before he was born, but his chief dut the Royal Household. Here the young Scot, who a curate six years before, succeeded the great Dean as the Queen's intimate counsellor in all ecclesia spiritual matters. In 1883 Victoria had just lost Jo[h] the Highland servant who had to some exten substitute for Prince Albert, and many were between the old queen and the young dean a beyond the grave. 'She asked me', he wrote, there ever came over me (as over her) waves of doubtfulness whether, after all, it might be true.'

Davidson was a tactful courtier, but early in Queen proposed to publish another volume of he of her life in the Highlands. One volume of *Leave[s]* *Journal* had already appeared. Since all the other were afraid to anger her, it fell to Davidson to ex[p] view that the first volume was enough. He wrote:

Your Majesty will readily understand that such a spirit response to the gracious confidences so frankly given, is n[o] to be found, and I should be deceiving Your Majesty w[e] to admit that there are, especially among the humbler clas[s] (perhaps it would be true to say *many*) who do not show th worthy of these confidences, and whose spirit, judging

stomach ulcer brought on him three other grave illnesses, and, knowing how much evening work was essential in South London, he had no hesitation in accepting the invitation to move to Winchester in 1895.

Life in Farnham Castle, the historic seat of the Bishops of Winchester, was more congenial than life in Kennington Park Road, but the new diocese, if properly worked, was itself no light task, as Samuel Wilberforce had found; it still included the present dioceses of Guildford and Portsmouth. Such routine labours, after the failure of his time in South London, told on the sick man, who at Windsor had been so sure and so eager. Prominent laymen when they had been in conversation with him usually united to praise his good sense, but once Sir Edward Grey happened to share a silent railway carriage with Sir Michael Sadler and the Bishop of Winchester. When Davidson had got out, Sir Edward asked Sir Michael: 'Who was that bishop with such a puzzled face?'

Winchester diocese was (like Durham or Peterborough) largely exempt from London's liturgical extremes, but Davidson stirred up trouble for himself by issuing a detailed prohibition of Anglo-Catholic practices. Many of his clergy protested, and rather feebly he had to say that the notice which had been issued as *The Bishop of Winchester's Directions to Incumbents* was merely advice. In his first few months at Winchester his law-enforcing policy brought him into a dramatic collision with Father Dolling, an Anglo-Catholic priest (and Irishman) who was doing heroic and popular work as the Winchester College Missioner to the slums of Portsmouth. The immediate point at issue was Dolling's habit of praying for the dead, as emotionally as he preached to the living. An altar was to be specially dedicated for this practice at Requiem Masses. Confronted by this altar, Davidson acted to uphold the law which appeared to forbid Requiem Masses. He was as benevolent as possible, but he did not speak the same language as the slum priest, who resigned in a blaze of publicity.

Any puzzlement on Davidson's face was not eased by the embarrassment of his position when Archbishop Benson died. Lord Salisbury brutally pointed out to the Queen that her favourite 'was not distinguished at the university (he only took a third class); he has had no important pastoral cure; he has not published any work of note except the biography of his father-in-law; his speaking and preaching, though good, are not of unusual merit; he is the youngest of all the bishops on the English Bench.' But the Queen wanted him to return to Lambeth Palace at once, and Frederick Temple – the Grand Old Man who was appointed by Lord Salisbury to serve for a few years as Archbishop, despite the Queen's complaints about his manners – believed that immediate promotion had been Davidson's wish also. In the event Davidson, who had been prominent in the central decisions for nearly twenty years, and who was the heir-apparent, found himself cold-shouldered by Temple. 'Mind you keep me in touch so far as you can with what goes on', he wrote to the Archbishop's chaplain, 'for to me it is the strangest of all the changes in my life to find myself out in the cold. . . .' Only his friendship with royalty now enabled him to see behind the public stage. Thus he was prominent when Queen Victoria died at Osborne (in his diocese), and he planned the next Coronation as the intermediary between the invalid king and the aged archbishop; during the ceremony in the Abbey, he was Frederick Temple's prompter and guide.

Embarrassment increased with the funeral of Father Dolling in an Anglo-Catholic church in London in 1902. One of the greatest crowds in the history of the East end then heard the new Bishop of London, arrayed in black cope and mitre for the Solemn Requiem Mass, eulogising the faithful priest who had walked so closely after Jesus Christ. 'When everybody else had given a man up, it was always said, "Dolling will take him".' So Winnington-Ingram declared; and Davidson seems to have felt the stigma of being the bishop who had 'driven Father Dolling out'. Dolling was buried in Woking, next to the grave of Father Mackonochie who had featured as a rebel in the story of Tait.

At last, two days before Christmas 1902, Frederick Temple died. The casual Balfour was then Prime Minister. He simply wrote to Davidson: 'I mean to propose your name to H.M. for Canterbury. From conversations I have had with him, I have no doubt that he will agree. But, what next?' Davidson replied suitably to this 'momentous and most solemn intimation', and plunged with zest into the correspondence and discussions which Temple had neglected. He and his Edith were back where they belonged; and those near to him noted that it was not long before the weak health grew strong, and the puzzled face assumed a look of calm, wise dignity. Power suited Randall Davidson.

5

As Primate, he naturally reverted to Tait's habit of paying the closest possible attention to the politics and the politicians of the day. He had already made his mark on the House of Lords by arguing the case for curbs on the drink trade against a Conservative government which valued the support of the brewers; and when the Liberals, backed by open Nonconformist support, swept into power in 1906, he became very busy with all the negotiations which surrounded their vain attempts to pass an Act of Parliament curbing the church schools. His course was not easy. Because the Nonconformists urged temperance, many in the Church of England wished to defend the liberties of public houses. Even stronger was the Anglican defence of church schools; Edmund Knox, the staunchly Evangelical Bishop of Manchester, led a great demonstration in London, and the House of Lords threw the government's Bill out. Davidson suggested various compromises on education, only to be defeated by the ardour on both sides. Eventually the Conservatives' 1902 Act remained in force, although it proved less effective than had been hoped (or feared) in propping up the church schools. Most of these schools were nineteenth-century buildings, and many of them were in villages; but no public money could be spent on their material improvement. It was all too reminiscent of John Keble. Although when the century began there were almost two and a half million children in the 'voluntary' schools, by 1938 the number had almost halved.

Davidson was a force in such debates, but it is clear, if not edifying, that he gained much of his prestige with the statesmen by refusing to join most of the agitations which attempted to bring moral pressure on them. Thus when asked to join a protest against the British share in the opium trade in China, the Archbishop replied: 'I have no wish personally to promote the continuance of a trade which is undoubtedly productive of much evil, though apparently, in the opinion of many wise observers, it is also productive of a great deal that is wholesome and good.' When asked to receive a deputation of unemployed men who had marched to Lambeth from Leicester, he refused: 'I should master those facts better were I to study them in writing'. He also refused to act as host to a demonstration from Manchester in defence of church schools: 'we could not have a camp at Lambeth'.

The absence of drama was itself what he sought. England under Edward VII possessed many assets, but these did not include a sense of proportion. The Protestant bitterness over incense and candles in church, and the Romanizing romanticism which defied the law, were only parts of an overheated atmosphere in the nation. Davidson, doing the safe, sensible, and boring thing, moderated passions over denominational influence in the schools (at a time when almost half England's children left school at the age of fourteen); over the opposition by the House of Lords to the popularly elected government; over the prospect of civil war in Ireland as Ulster, egged on by some Conservative politicians, reacted to the Liberal policy of Home Rule. His shrewdness helped the Church of England to appear as one of the country's respectable and reliable institutions. It was no mean feat at a time when the victorious Liberals, inspired by the Nonconformist conscience and electoral support, pressed on with the disestablishment of that Church's four dioceses in Wales. Amid great excitement the Lords rejected Welsh disestablishment, and the Government had to force it through over their heads, under the Parliament Act of 1911. In England the dream of a union of Church and State survived remarkably well; and the supply of clergy was one barometer. True, it declined from 814 new deacons in 1886 to 587 in 1907, but the Lambeth Conference of 1908 had little doubt that the main cause of the decline was financial, and proposed remedies. The bishops certainly did not foresee the figure of 420 new deacons sixty years later. In 1913 they decided that in seven years' time all ordinands in the Church of England must normally be graduates. Only a few small back doors into the priesthood were to be permitted, such as the house at Kelham where the Society of the Sacred Mission had begun training poor boys. The Church was to be staffed by educated gentlemen.

Such stability in England had its consequences in the world-wide Anglican Communion, which was in those days the spiritual equivalent of the British Empire (with some citizens of the former American colonies). Tait and Benson had sustained much correspondence between Lambeth and the Anglican globe, but Tait was an old-fashioned defender of the ecclesiastical as well as the secular rights of the English Crown in the colonies, while Benson's romantic idea of the status of Canterbury aroused American and other suspicions of a new Papacy. Davidson did not fall into either trap; instead, he was the first successor of St. Augustine to visit Canada and the United States, in 1904. He went as the guest of the financier, J. Pierpont Morgan. In London in the summer of 1908, he had his reward, when a Pan-Anglican Congress included clergy and laity with the bishops attending the Lambeth conference. The congress resounded with oratory about the opportunities before Anglicanism, and impressed on the English mind the fact that the National Church had somehow become the mother of a multicoloured family. Nor was the Archbishop's blessing confined to the members of his own international denomination. He bravely agreed to address the World Missionary Conference at Edinburgh in 1910, the assembly which is usually reckoned the beginning of the modern ecumenical movement; and he did so in optimistic terms about the coming of the Kingdom of God.

Under Davidson, the teacups of the Church of England were still rattled by internal storms, but he made it his business to see that nothing much was split. A Royal Commission on Ecclesiastical Discipline was appointed in 1904 in order to study ways of breaking the deadlock

caused by the Anglo-Catholic clergy's defiance of Archbishop Temple's interpretation of the liturgical law.
Davidson submitted a masterly memorandum on the
tedious history of the question, and did as much as the
chairman, Lord St. Aldwyn, to secure the unanimous
recommendation of the two main conclusions. 'First, the
law of public worship in the Church of England is too
narrow for the religious life of the present generation. It
needlessly condemns much which a great section of Church
people, including many of her most devoted members,
value. . . . Secondly, the machinery for discipline has broken
down.' The report recommended that Letters of Business
should be issued by the Crown in order to enable the clergy
in their Convocations, taking counsel with laymen, to begin
the overdue revision of the Prayer Book; and that new
ecclesiastical courts should be set up. Other proposals
included the repeal of the Public Worship Regulation Act
of 1874 and the reservation to the bishops of the right to
decide appeals on doctrinal questions. And all the proposals
were accepted by Parliament. Although nothing much was
done in the Church (indeed, the 'anarchy' grew worse), this
report meant that there would never be another Mackonochie or Dolling case. Davidson had very few inflexible
policies of his own, perhaps only one: to keep the Church of
England together, despite the menace of an Anglo-Catholic
exodus which had so deeply worried Creighton. While
Davidson did not expect to see all the Anglo-Catholic
demands granted, he accepted some concessions as inevitable.

A second triumph in ecclesiastical politics – if 'triumph'
can mean the reduction of tension – now came to Davidson.
An Oxford clerical don, J. M. Thompson, published a book
denying the historicity of some of the miracles of the New
Testament, and drew on himself the censure of the Bishop
of Winchester (Edward Talbot, who was Visitor of Magdalen College where Thompson was Dean of Divinity) and
the Bishop of Oxford (Charles Gore, the Anglo-Catholic
leader). A doctrinal crisis broke out, for the Anglo-Catholics,
so recently under attack for their ceremonies, leapt to the
defence of the creeds against the Modernists; and one

evening at Lambeth in February 1914 Davidson had to cool Gore down by threatening to resign. As he noted at the time: 'I had some grave talk with Gore about Church affairs. I spoke of the possibility that I am myself growing to be out of touch with the strongest advances in the Church. . . . And I said that I should not remain at the helm if I found myself trying to steer a course clearly contrary to the best Church of England feeling and spirit.' Next morning Gore told Davidson: 'I am profoundly convinced, with a certainty that is unshakeable, that the very greatest disaster that could at this time befall the Church would be the loss of you from Lambeth.'

Davidson therefore got his way. The bishops had been asked by Gore to denounce disbelief in the virgin birth or physical resurrection of Jesus as being incompatible with a sincere acceptance of the obligations of a clergyman of the Church of England; but Davidson feared that such a declaration, if made without any qualification, would render the position of 'quite a large group of our best and most thoughtful clergy' untenable. He remembered what Frederick Temple had written to his own master Tait: 'If the conclusions are prescribed, the study is precluded.' Although he never confessed to any personal difficulty in accepting miracles, he did not wish to drive any Temple of the twentieth century out of the Church of England, any more than he wished to drive out Charles Gore. The resolutions as passed by the bishops in April 1914 therefore endorsed Gore's insistence that 'the denial of any of the historical facts stated in the Creeds goes beyond the limits of legitimate interpretation'; but they also stressed 'the need of considerateness in dealing with what is tentative and provisional in the thought and work of earnest and reverent students' – a very Davidsonian touch. The outcome satisfied the Archbishop. A secularized Thompson went on to become a history don, the author of standard works on the French Revolution; but almost all the other Modernists remained earnestly and reverently in the Church of England. And Davidson remained at the helm.

A third crisis in the small world of Anglicanism arose in 1913 when a conference of missionaries under the chairmanship of the mildly Evangelical John Willis, Bishop of Uganda, studied a proposal for a federation of the missionary churches in East Africa and together received Holy Communion from the bishop's hands. A neighbouring bishop, the Anglo-Catholic firebrand Frank Weston, promptly exploded and fired off the following indictment to Davidson: 'We, Frank, by Divine Permission Lord Bishop of Zanzibar and East Africa, do by these presents accuse and charge . . . the Right Reverend Father in God John Jameson, Lord Bishop of Uganda, with the grievous faults of propagating heresy and promoting schism.' Weston demanded that 'You and not less than twelve of Your Grace's comprovincial Bishops should act as judges. Both Weston and the accused Willis returned to England to see Davidson, who refused to get excited and referred the whole matter to other Anglican bishops overseas, including a Consultative Body which had been set up by the Lambeth Conference. Scholars were also set to work to establish the Anglican attitudes to episcopacy, thought by Weston to be seriously in danger although to him the bishop was the 'Christ-given centre of union.'

In the end, Davidson pronounced. He virtually declared that the proposal for a missionary federation had been admirable in its intentions but deficient in its theological care, and that the joint Communion had been admirable in its motives but should not be repeated. Neither side was now entirely happy, yet neither side was excessively angry. And since the date was now Easter 1915, most men found it difficult to remember why either side had been so excited.

6

Like most members of the English ruling class, Davidson had no idea that the world war was coming; but when it came, like them he behaved well. As a patriot he refused to get entangled in Archbishop Söderblom's efforts in Uppsala to use Sweden as a meeting-ground between the two camps. On the other hand, with an independence which aroused some surprise, he also refused to put his authority behind the war effort as many of the politicians and most of the public conceived it. His biographer – George Bell, who was to make a more public, and therefore even more unpopular, stand during the second world war – has recorded in detail how Davidson refused to encourage hate of the Hun; how he pleaded against lying propaganda, the use of poison gas, and reprisals against German civilians; and how he forbade the clergy to enlist as combatants. When in 1915 he was urged to lead a National Mission, he threw aside his caution and did give a lead to this ambitious enterprise, which was sub-titled 'of Repentance and Hope'. To some, the whole conception seemed too grandiose; to others, it was too sober a contribution to the glorious fight. Davidson was convinced that England must fight, but fight with clean hands. This gave him a great theme at a great hour. The Vicar of Ramsgate wrote to Mrs. Benson, describing the scene in Canterbury Cathedral when the Archbishop addressed his clergy. 'The first impression one got of *him* – and it remained strong to the end – was Power: he seemed to have regained completely mental and physical strength, and sureness of grip. He was quite certain of his message. . . . It was all very deliberate, very simple, very grave.'

Here, then, was Creighton's 'ancient Christian land' being tested as it had not been through the long peace of the nineteenth century. In the trenches the Church could not avoid meeting the consequences of its failure to baptize the English industrial revolution; nor could it escape acknowledging that the Victorian religious revival had insufficient strength to meet the shock of one of the great agonies in world history. The clergy who volunteered as chaplains to the Forces experienced, as they had not done amid the routine of their parishes, the alienation of Englishmen from the Church. They found that 'the padre' was an isolated, useless figure in that world of khaki, mud, the shadow of death, and pathetically endless talk about sex, unless they commended their Gospel by lives of exceptional appeal.

They had to do it in bitter places. In 1903 Mandell Creighton's son Oswin, then an undergraduate, had heard Bishop Gore preach in Oxford. He had then written home: 'He preached an admirable sermon on religious doubts and difficulties, but did not seem to make it very clear how to get over them. It is strange how nearly half the people I meet here have doubts, or say they have, and I am not conscious of ever having had any myself.' Now Oswin Creighton became a much loved padre and was killed in April 1918, but not before he had written:

The Church ... has degenerated either into emotional ritual, or hymn-singing, or secluded and entrenched piety. ... It neither understands the world nor touches it at any point.... The war reveals that the Englishman is the best hearted, most enduring, and most ignorant and least original man in the world. The work of the Church is to help him build up what he has not got on the basis of what he has.

Other priests such as 'Tubby' Clayton, whose hostel for troops at Poperinghe was the first base of the Toc H movement, had a vision of the Church as a brotherhood holding the secret of a world at peace. Within this brotherhood, class distinctions must go. The bishops must no longer lord it over the clergy; the clergy must no longer lord it over the laity. The priest was still someone special, but as a representative of the suffering Christ, as a spiritual leader. The new aspirations of social reform must be welcomed by the Church, because they could build a new age, the age of democracy. The best known of the chaplains, G. A. Studdert Kennedy ('Woodbine Willie'), would not hesitate to speak or write about God's suffering as 'the hardest part'. The new knowledge of science must be joined to the Church's belief, for it was God's new revelation. Almost incidentally, the padres added that the division of the Church of England into ecclesiastical parties must be ended. They virtually mutinied against control by a stoutly Evangelical ex-missionary bishop, Taylor-Smith, who was Chaplain-General from 1901 to 1925; and a much broader-minded Evangelical, Bishop Llewellyn Gwynne, had to be summoned from Khartoum to be their pastor as Deputy Chaplain-General in France.

Davidson did not know what to make of such new stirrings. 'The essence of kindness and sanity – without a glimmer of inspiration' was how William Temple described him to his mother in 1908. In all the basic questions which agitated sincere minds about the truth of Christianity, his policy was to preserve both the unity of the Church of England and the liberty of the 'earnest and reverent' scholars who might (he hoped) in due course, after their mysterious researches, reach conclusions which would support his own 'very simple, very grave' piety – and the piety of the English layman. He had himself little idea about how a constructive theology might emerge.

Eventually he agreed with the argument of Dr. Howard Burge, then Bishop of Oxford, and with Will Spens the lay theologian at Cambridge, that an Archbishops' Commission on Doctrine should be appointed with the following Reference: 'To consider the nature and grounds of Christian Doctrine with a view to demonstrating the extent of existing agreement within the Church of England and with a view to investigating how far it is possible to remove or diminish existing differences.' This was at the turn of 1922–3, and Davidson would probably not have consented to a policy which he believed to be fraught with the danger of further controversies, had not the Modern Churchmen's Union then seemed at the height of its promise (or threat).

The Union had sponsored a particularly controversial conference on 'Christ and the Creeds' at Girton College, Cambridge, in 1921. The conference had thrown Gore and others deep into renewed anxieties lest the fundamental Christian beliefs were being betrayed by Anglican clergymen; Henson had himself been shocked. Davidson had at last seen that the time had come for the 'earnest and reverent' to confer on a rational basis and under official auspices. Burge and Temple were to be the two bishops on it. The Archbishop did, however, take care to discourage the plan that this commission might issue an authoritative statement. He had no wish to bequeath to his successors new problems about the judicious interpretation of official documents after troublesome quarrels between intellectuals and fanatics. What he could not foresee was that by the time that this commission reported, in 1938, men would have lost interest in theological controversies, and even in an honestly truthful theological reconstruction, because the clouds of another world war held their frightened eyes.

Davidson also presided over the creation of the National

Assembly of the Church of England, which was not quite the thoroughly Christian rebirth of fellowship for which the enthusiastic prayed and campaigned, but which was something.

The advisory Houses of Laymen, starting in 1886, had been on a provincial (Canterbury and York) not national basis; and although the Representative Church Council, over whose birth Davidson had presided during the first year of his Primacy, had combined the clergy and laity of Canterbury and York, it had never been given legal powers. Davidson had shown little impatience to alter that situation; he was too much the heir of Tait and the *protégé* of Queen Victoria to be a democrat. But the campaign against the disestablishment of the Church of England's dioceses in Wales led to increased demands that the relationship of Church and State in England should be made more defensible by giving a clear legal status to the clergy and laity elected by the English dioceses, and by clearly assigning to them the chief responsibility for the Church's spiritual life. The Representative Church Council had resolved in 1913 'that there is in principle no inconsistency between a national recognition of religion and the spiritual independence of the Church'. An Archbishops' Committee on Church and State had been appointed under Lord Selborne, and had unanimously reported in 1916 that the Representative Church Council should be given legislative powers, subject to the possibility of a Parliamentary veto.

When the ardent young William Temple led the 'Life and Liberty' campaign for the enactment of this committee's recommendation, the Archbishop was as usual cautious. He had a special reason for caution: he regarded it as an unwise attempt to distract the attention of the Church from the graver questions of 1917. He was, however, gradually persuaded that the solid opinion of the Church which he loved was in favour of doing something about the matter, sooner rather than later; and that the Parliament which he also served was not against it. Eventually he got the proposal through with a characteristic argument. He did not appeal to a new vision of Christian brotherhood. Instead, he quietly explained that the pressure on the time of Parliament had become so great that it was difficult to secure attention for the legislation necessary to the smooth running of the Church. He made it sound a technical matter, on which all sensible experts were already agreed; and the Church Assembly was born with little opposition, except from a minority which feared the consequences of the lessening of Parliament's control over the National Church.

There were, in fact, only two major obstacles to be surmounted before Parliament passed an Enabling Act to recognize the powers of the Church Assembly (in the same summer of 1919 in which the final arrangements were made for the disestablishment of Anglicanism in Wales). The first dispute was the occasion of Gore's resignation as Bishop of Oxford. Gore insisted that the laity who sent representatives to the Diocesan Conferences (which were to elect the laymen sitting in the new Church Assembly) must be communicants. Davidson and the overwhelming majority insisted that it was enough for them to have been baptized, if they were resident in the parish or worshipped regularly in its church. This dispute over the composition of the parish churches' Electoral Rolls was an ominous indication that two ideals were still clashing in the Church of England: the ideal of the Church as the Body of Christ fed by Holy Communion, and the ideal of the Church as the Christian nation.

The other dispute concerned the nature of the Parliamentary veto over the 'Measures' to be passed by the new Church Assembly. It was at first proposed that the two Houses of Parliament should appoint an Ecclesiastical Committee which would advise the Crown to give its assent to a Church Assembly Measure 'unless within forty days either House of Parliament shall direct to the contrary'. In answer to an objection by the Lord Chancellor, the Archbishop quickly agreed that after advice by the Ecclesiastical Committee a definite 'Address' to the Crown from each House of Parliament should be necessary before a 'Measure' received the Royal Assent. This concession, which seemed harmless enough at the time to an archbishop confident that Parliament was on his side, made more likely the prospect which he had always striven to avert: the prospect of the House of Commons joining a controversy about legislative proposals which reflected the conflict of ideals in the Church of England.

### 7

Thus were sown the seeds of the Church of England's humiliation in 1927–8. Davidson would have been wiser had he resigned in 1923, the twentieth year of his Primacy and the seventy-fifth of his life. He was then at the peak of his prestige. He had appointed the Doctrine Commission to work towards a theological reconciliation. The Church Assembly, sitting regularly from 1920 onwards, had begun to tackle administrative problems such as the reform of patronage in the parishes. The Lambeth Conference of bishops in 1920 had issued an epoch-making 'appeal to all Christian people' for unity, and Lambeth Palace had been the scene of earnest, if abortive, conversations about re-union between Anglicans and Free Churchmen, in striking contrast with their bitter quarrels over education before the war. Other conversations were going on with Roman Catholics, at Malines in Belgium under the wartime hero Cardinal Mercier. The conversations had no official status. Davidson was too canny to be unaware of the continuing force of No Popery. Even if he had been slow at this point, Protestants full of suspicions had warned him loudly enough. On his side, Cardinal Bourne of Westminster had no intention of seeking any recognition of the Anglican heretics. But these Malines conversations looked forward to a day when some fellowship and even union might be renewed between separated Christians without any sacrifice of conscience, and Davidson had been wise not to impose a veto.

All over the world Anglicans and others now looked to Lambeth Palace for prudent counsel, and Cosmo Lang, Archbishop of York, was waiting to provide such counsel himself, as Davidson had waited during the Primacy of the aged Frederick Temple. But no Archbishop of Canterbury had ever resigned, not even George Abbot who accidentally killed a man while hunting in 1621; and Davidson in 1923 was flattered by all those whose voices he heard. He stayed on.

Disaster did not strike when it might have been expected. The Church of England was largely out of touch with the working class, and many anachronisms lingered in its own system. Davidson, for example, had only vague sympathies with Labour, and all that the man in the street knew about him was that his income was £15,000 a year. Another well-known 'fact' about the Church of England was that the Ecclesiastical Commissioners 'owned' brothels in Paddington. In reality the Archbishop of Canterbury had to meet almost all his official expenses out of his income, while the Commissioners had no control over the use of the houses leased from them in Paddington. But the man in the street was shrewd in his suspicions. Like their predecessors, the Davidsons kept a large domestic staff at Lambeth; and like other landlords, the Commissioners had taken inadequate precautions against the abuse of leases.

However, Archbishop Davidson was wise enough to see that the Church of England should not identify itself with the employers. During the General Strike of 1926, in agreement with other Christian leaders, he issued an appeal for reconciliation. Sir John Reith at the B.B.C. refused to broadcast it and Winston Churchill refused to print it in the Government newspaper, the *British Gazette*, because it included proposals that the Government should subsidize the depressed coal industry and that the mine owners should cancel the lowering of wages. Davidson surprised everyone, including it would seem himself, by this readiness to lend some support to the pro-Labour sentiments of colleagues such as William Temple; so much so that he found himself privately dreading a battle of 'the Church plus the Miners on the one side and the Government on the other side'. In such a battle, as he wrote to the Bishop of Lichfield, 'I should find it difficult to say where my allegiance lay'. From him, it was a warm tribute to Socialism.

So, in the 1920s the Church of England scraped through a social crisis rather more successfully than the Conservative Party with which it had often been identified in the 1900s.

Nor did disaster come immediately because of a lack of radical reform within the Church.

Opposition delayed into the 1930s obvious reforms such as the stopping of the sale of advowsons (the transfer of a parish from one patron to another for money) and the creation of a Diocesan Patronage Board. Three committees (in 1902, 1924, and 1933) reported that, as a first step towards financial rationalization, the Ecclesiastical Commissioners created in the 1830s should be merged with the body known as Queen Anne's Bounty, dating from 1704, for the work of the two offices for the parishes overlapped in the most confusing way; yet nothing was done. One problem was that there were too few bishops to give adequate leadership. A Church Assembly Commission in 1922 reported that fifteen dioceses needed dividing. In the end only four were split, with the creation of the new dioceses of Leicester, Blackburn, Derby, Portsmouth, and Guildford. If more bishops had been made, it would have been expensive: in 1921 bishops were averaging £4,000 a year plus palace, no less than ten times the average for the incomes of parochial incumbents. However, Davidson and most of the leadership of the Church were content to carry on as if no radical innovation was needed, and the price of this delay was not fully exacted until the 1940s.

Disaster came, instead, in the very sphere where Davidson like Tait, took pride in being expert: the handling of the Parliamentary business of the Church.

The process of liturgical revision led, after immense discussions, to the final draft of a Revised Prayer Book in 1927. This was supported by all but four of the forty-three diocesan bishops and by almost all the Diocesan Conferences; it was adopted by the Church Assembly; it was approved by the House of Lords. Then, on the night of 15 December, the 'Measure' from the Church Assembly was vetoed by the House of Commons, by 238 votes to 205, although a majority of English M.P.s voted in favour and all Roman Catholics abstained. In a sense, the defeat in the Commons was not the Archbishop's fault, for the House was swayed by the No Popery eloquence echoing a vanished age and by the feebleness of the M.P.s who tried to explain why the proposed Prayer Book, although it recognized many Anglo-Catholic practices, was not a capitulation to Rome. But Davidson by now possessed such a hold on the Church of England that the adoption of a policy which led to such a defeat did indicate a slackening of his grip on diplomacy and power; and the fatal mistakes which were made by the Church of England under him did show the gaps in the equipment which he had gained from Tait's Lambeth and Victoria's Windsor.

The first mistake was to concentrate on pleasing the Anglo-Catholic experts who wanted the liturgy enriched, instead of attempting to please the people by a radical simplification of worship, of the kind which the padres at the war had begun to desire. Placating liturgiologists was in itself a tricky business; two of the leading experts, the very learned Darwell Stone at Oxford and the very elegant Eric Milner-White at Cambridge, made no secret of their contempt for the half-baked proposals which emerged. And in the event, the liturgical fashions which seemed so desirable in the 1920s declined fairly rapidly, because the most pastorally minded of the Anglo-Catholics themselves saw the need to make make worship more corporate and more contemporary. As things turned out, it would have been wiser to heed those who wanted a collection of far simpler services, as an optional alternative to the 1662 book; such a modernization would have aroused controversy, but unlike the controversial proposals which were put forward in 1927–8 it might have caught the imagination of laymen. However, Randall Davidson was not really at home in these questions. He left the advanced liturgiology to the Bishop of Truro, Walter Frere of the Community of the Resurrection, the first monk to become an Anglican bishop; and he smiled at Frere's enthusiasm, as Tait had smiled when Benson came up from Truro. He also left the popular appeal to rather alarming progressives such as William Temple; for the 1662 book fed his devotional life satisfactorily. Davidson. who had no personal experience of responsibility for popular worship, believed that what was needed was the enrichment of 1662 in response to pressure, in order to get a new Prayer Book which could be enforced.

The second mistake was a failure to try out the proposals in an experimental period in the parishes. When the Church of England took up revision again in the 1960s this seemed the obvious way, but in the 1920s the Church burned its fingers because it proposed that the Revised Prayer Book should be enforced before it had been tested. Very few people in the 1920s suggested anything else, and the Archbishop was not among them. This mistake was part of the whole authoritarian approach of the period in which Davidson's mind had been formed. It was taken for granted that changes in the Church were discussed among bishops and scholars, among the weightier clergy, and even among the unusual laymen who sat in the Church Assembly. A compromise was hammered out in the course of these debates, and it was the function of the Diocesan Conferences to approve the outcome. Once the changes – or the refusal of any change – had been agreed among the people at the top, it would be imposed on the whole Church, if necessary by legal sanctions. No really creative role was allowed to the congregations, although the Parochial Church Councils had been set up at the same time as the Church Assembly; and the priest in the parish was usually the target of suspicion from his betters who feared that he might be 'eccentric' or 'extreme'. Worship could not spring out of the local situation; it must be regulated, if not by an Act of Parliament, then by a Measure of the Church Assembly. This account of the motives of the framers of the Prayer Book of 1927 is, of course, oversimplified; not one of them would have used exactly these words. But as a sketch of an attitude, it has the substance of the sad truth about the leadership of the Church of England under Davidson. When Protestant fanatics in the House of Commons claimed to speak for the silent laymen of the Church of England, the Archbishop could not argue that these laymen had already spoken for themselves.

The third mistake was a failure to acknowledge that there could be a clash between Church and State. So many crises had been averted by diplomacy since Tait had gone to Lambeth in 1868, and Davidson had been so conspicuously successful in smothering controversies, that the Church of

England in the 1920s walked into the trap. Hensley Henson, a bishop who owed much to Davidson's diplomacy, wrote in his journal after the crisis of 1927: 'It was one of those occasions on which his opportunism failed. The lifelong habit of "getting round" difficulties, instead of facing them, hardly prepares a man for the handling of a crisis. And the Church is now confronted by a crisis, the gravity of which can hardly be exaggerated.' Even when the trap had sprung on that December night in the House of Commons, the Church of England came back in 1928 for further punishment. Minor modifications were made in the Church Assembly's proposals, particularly in the regulations about 'Reservation'; and back they came for another defeat in the House of Commons in 1928. The modifications would probably have been effective had they appeased Protestant prejudices by leaving the Holy Communion service substantially unaltered, and by making no formal provision for the 'Reservation' of the consecrated bread and wine after the service. Archbishop Lang, who came from an Anglo-Catholic background, was in favour of such a concession to the Protestant M.P.s. But Davidson was convinced that the House of Commons did not really expect the Church to make a concession of this nature, which would have left the Church still confused over what was or was not its law about Holy Communion.

What was to be done now? The bishops agreed to a statement:

It is a fundamental principle that the Church—that is, the Bishops together with the Clergy and Laity—must in the last resort, when its mind has been fully ascertained, retain its inalienable right, in loyalty to our Lord and Saviour Jesus Christ, to formulate its Faith in Him and to arrange the expression of that Holy Faith in its forms of worship.

A mildly defiant act was undertaken: the 1928 Prayer Book was printed for use in churches, with a notice in each copy which reminded its users that it was not authorised for use. But Davidson still refused to agree that a divorce was desirable between Church and State. In his last speech to the Church Assembly, he pointed out that many of his M.P.s who had voted against the revision had 'believed, however mistakenly, that they were voicing the real underlying wish of a majority of Church folk in England'; and he declared his hope that the House of Commons would return to its reasonable spirit when it could be shown that the Church of England was united. He resigned the Archbishopric of Canterbury, becoming Lord Davidson of Lambeth, not because of this Parliamentary catastrophe, but because he wanted Lang to preside over the Lambeth Conference of 1930. His chief worry seems to have been a fear of boredom, now that his daily mail would be drastically reduced after so many years at Lambeth.

Henson in his journal sardonically noted the contrast between the tributes, verbal and financial, which now flowed to the aged Davidson and the lack of sentiment with which the House of Commons had thrown out the two Prayer Books. But Davidson himself seems to have felt nothing very strange in this, and did not intend his soul to be troubled because Anglo-Catholicism was not clearly legalized. The real issues for him did not lie in the sanctuary and the Church of England which he knew in his bones was not very much disturbed by the Prayer Book crisis. He had been ordained knowing little about such matters, and the fact that the completion of liturgical revision had been delayed for twenty years after the recommendation of it (by the St. Aldwyn Commission at the beginning of Davidson's Primacy) itself says something about his sense of priorities. A positive conviction, as well as his caution, determined his attitude; it was merely that he had grown used (as one critic said) to 'sitting on the fence with both ears to the ground'. Before, during, and after the horrors of 1914–18, he shared the belief of his fellow-Victorians that the preservation of the Christian character of the nation was what mattered. He also shared the belief of his master, Tait, and of the other Rugbeians in Thomas Arnold's tradition, that the legal establishment of the Church of England as the comprehensive 'Church of the English people' would do more for the Christian character than any enriched church services could do. Davidson was no intellectual, but we should remember that this was also Creighton's basic attitude. He was no mystic, but he could invoke the spiritually impressive name of Westcott.

He presented the Church which he knew, and for which he was prepared to fight, in his addresses to the diocese of Canterbury in 1912, printed as *The Character and Call of the Church of England*. He quoted from his old schoolmaster, Westcott, words which summed up his own belief that nothing vital was at stake in the controversies of the day:

The English Reformation corresponds with the English character, which is disinclined to seek the completeness of a theological system. It looks to finding truth through life rather than through logic, for truth is not of the intellect only. It is patient of hesitation, indefiniteness, even of superficial inconsistency, if only the root of the matter can be held firmly for the guidance of conduct; for spiritual subjects are too vast to furnish clear-cut premises from which exhaustive conclusions can be drawn.

# 8

# Gore and Henson

In the first year of the twentieth century, two prolific
authors and speakers with sharply contrasting interpretations of Anglicanism served together in Westminster Abbey
as canons: Charles Gore, later Bishop of Oxford, and Herbert Hensley Henson, later Bishop of Durham. Gore was
High, and Henson was Broad. It was the contrast between
Wilberforce and Tait forty years or so before, but with a
new tension.

Henson himself connected the tension with the contrasts
in their formation, socially and emotionally. Gore was a
Christian Socialist; 'the Socialist Party at Mass' was Henry
Major's summary of his influence. Henson, who was a
Protestant Conservative, wrote:

Gore's sympathy with the suffering and oppressed was deep and
generous, but he ever felt more keenly for classes and descriptions
of men than for individuals, and he seemed to me inadequately
sensitive to the personal rights of those from whom, whether on
religious or on economic grounds, he differed. His natural ardour
of temperament led him to express his opinions with an enthusiasm
and vigour which did undoubtedly commend them to public
acceptance, but were not always sufficiently regardful of public
law and private right. By birth and breeding Gore was an aristocrat, and took an aristocrat's view of legal obligations and personal
rights. I was from the middle class, in which these things have been
most highly esteemed, and by which they have been most valorously championed.

But here, for once, Henson was lacking in candour. He was
far from being a typical member of the comfortable middle
class. His own experience of humiliating poverty and
introspective despair had led him in the days of his success

to fight so 'valorously' for the right of the individual against Church or State.

Yet Gore never allowed his many controversies with Henson to lead him to think that Henson was dishonourable. 'I think he is a most lovable creature, though I own I am always a little nervous when I open *The Times* in case he should be writing something in it about me.' For his part Henson wrote that 'we were temperamentally opposed, but this opposition never affected the admiration which I felt for his remarkable courage and ability, nor the affection with which I regarded his person'. When Gore died, Henson gave this verdict: 'I judge him to have been the most considerable English Churchman of his time, not the most learned, nor the most eloquent, but so learned, so eloquent, so versatile, and so energetic that he touched the life of his generation at more points, and more effectively, than any of his contemporaries.'

2

Gore's birthplace in 1853 was in Wimbledon. The garden had forty acres, and the old Whig conventions were apparently permanent in the drawing room. His parents were descended from the Earls of Arran and Bessborough. But when he was eight or nine, Charles Gore came across a novel praising the conversion of a Roman Catholic priest to a sound Protestantism like the religion of Wimbledon. The boy felt instinctively attracted to the sights and sounds depicted in the earlier chapters, and about this time he began to preach to his sister in the nursery. He was sent to Harrow and emerged as a scholar in a school dedicated to athletics. In 1861 he heard Westcott preach in the Harrow chapel on *The Disciplined Life*. It was a mainly historical sermon, telling the boys about St. Anthony in the desert, St. Benedict and his monks, St. Francis and his friars, and St. Ignatius and the Jesuits, but concluding with a question whether the 'Saxon race' was not now summoned to accomplish the ideals of asceticism in a nineteenth century way. The schoolboy who heard that sermon founded the

Community (first the 'Society') of the Resurrection as an Anglican religious order for men twenty years later.

In Oxford he did so well in the Greats course of classics and philosophy as a Balliol undergraduate that his election to a fellowship at the college next door, Trinity, was natural. But it soon became evident that Gore would not spend his life as a classical tutor. He was not merely 'eloquent and well-connected', as a cynical colleague noted; he was also a pastor already. He was ordained, assisting as a curate first in Bootle and then in Liverpool church of Bell Cox, one of the priests who had been imprisoned under the Public Worship Regulation Act. In 1880 he went to teach the ordinands at Cuddesdon College; and he was the obvious man to appoint as the first Principal when on Pusey's death it was resolved to establish as a memorial an Anglo-Catholic centre in Oxford. Many of Pusey's disciples feared that the university was fast becoming secular, and resolved that Oxford should contain at least one citadel of the Faith: Pusey House. In order to allay some of the suspicions of the university, the Principal's assistants were termed Librarians. The term was not entirely inappropriate, for Pusey's vast collection formed the nucleus of a theological library. Newman wrote to Gore: 'I indulge the welcome thought that in promoting the interests of his School, you will eventually be advancing Catholic Truth as held and taught at Rome.'

In the 'Puseum' Gore continued to exercise a great influence on sympathetic young men. During the vacations he joined a group of theological dons who would discuss and pray together in a country rectory, the 'Holy Party'. Theirs was a Catholicism which, unlike Newman's, leaped with confidence into the questions of the hour. The needs of India held Gore's imagination and the Society of the Resurrection in Oxford was linked with the Brotherhood of the Epiphany in Calcutta; but he did not neglect the needs of England's workers, and began the Oxford branch of the Christian Social Union. And in order that the tradition expounded by Pusey should be brought into relationship with the English philosophy of the day, Gore edited in 1889 a volume called *Lux Mundi*.

This book, which seems so remote from later storms, was

controversial at the time because its occasional concessions seemed to some conservatives to open the floodgates of heresy. The Oxford University Press refused to publish it: it was printed in Oxford, but the publisher John Murray had to take the odium and the profit. When it appeared it broke the heart of Pusey's biographer, Henry Liddon, who died within a year (but still left Gore as his chief executor). While he was a bishop Gore was still followed by echoes of this controversy; the eccentric Anglican monk Father Ignatius would interrupt meetings with protests that the bishop was not sound on the Trinity. Even the mature Henson, who never sought the approval of the Anglo-Catholics, was to waver under similar attacks. Gore in his mid-thirties was badly shaken. He took every opportunity to show how orthodox his theology was; and, having survived the accusations of heresy, he developed what S. C. Carpenter called a 'Never Again Complex'.

*Lux Mundi* was a series of studies in 'the religion of the incarnation'. It included an essay on the Atonement by Arthur Lyttleton, and this held much of the Evangelical Gospel.

The cross was, on the one hand, the proclamation of God's ordinance against sin, on the other it was the response of man at length acknowledging the righteousness of the condemnation...He must pass through this last and most awful human experience ... because by the victorious endurance of it alone could the propitiation be accomplished ... If this is mysterious, irrational, transcendental, so is all morality; for at the root of all morality lies the power of self-sacrifice, which is nothing but the impulse of love to make a vicarious offering for its fellows, and the virtue of such an offering to restore and to quicken.

Yet Arthur Lyttleton rejected the Evangelical theory that the essential work of the cross was to substitute the *punishment* of Jesus for our punishment. Moreover the Mauricean connection between the cross and the common morality of men, brought out in that last sentence quoted, was a part of the book's main tendency. *Lux Mundi* went much nearer than the Evangelicals liked to concentration on the crib, and it seemed to expect the light shining in Bethlehem to be welcomed by the world. It was all very different from Henry

Liddon's description of religious work in the Oxford of his old age: 'combing the hair of a corpse'.

The tone was set by Henry Scott Holland's opening essay on faith. Faith is a whole-hearted surrender to Jesus Christ, an act of the deepest personal will showing that we recognize that we, too, are all sons of God. Surely this enthusiastic kind of faith will appeal despite 'the exciting transformation which has passed over the entire surface of our intellectual scenery'? Aubrey Moore proceeded to expound the doctrine of God: a 'severe' God (here he drew on Dean Church), but *not* an immoral one (like Lyttleton, Moore quoted with approval J. S. Mill's words: 'I will call no being good, who is not what I mean when I apply that epithet to my fellow-creatures'). The reality of this good God of Christian belief is, Moore claimed, attested both by the verdict of man's conscience and by the character of nature. God is revealed everywhere (or nowhere – as even Moore added). If philosophers can explain this away, they can also explain away the belief in the objective reality of nature, despite the 'consciousness of mankind'. Does the problem of pain finally count against belief in God? Not so, asserted the next essay, by J. R. Illingworth. Everywhere there is suffering, out of which comes progress. 'The sun is so much the cooler by the heat it daily gives to earth; the plant and tree the weaker by the force that has matured their fruit; the animal generations exhausted in continuing their kind.' Does history contain too many tragedies? Not so, announced Edward Talbot. All history, but specially the history of Israel and Greece as studied in Victorian Oxford, is a preparation for the coming of Christ.

Two essays now claimed that belief in the Incarnation is both the fulfilment of man's reason operating on nature and history, and the basis of all Christian dogma. The four last essays in the book drew out some of the consequences of this belief – in the Church as the continuing Body of Christ and therefore 'an organization for the spiritual life, for holiness'; in the sacraments as the means of grace which Christ appointed to feed this spiritual life; in the application of the Chu⠂⠂'s moral teaching to democratic politics (and here Westcott was quoted with the dictum that 'a national

Church alone can consecrate the whole life of a people'); and in the application of the moral law laid down in the Bible to the individual's problems in attaining holiness.

All these essays presented themes on which Gore himself was to write, and conclusions from which he moved little, although the war of 1914 was to challenge, if not confound, the cosmic optimism involved – and although Gore used to describe himself as a pessimist by temperament. These essays were generous and world-embracing in a way which was welcome after the negative tone of much orthodox theology, but they were not the essays which seemed most unusual at the end of the 1880s. In *Lux Mundi*, Gore handled the one theme which then appeared explosive: the challenge of biblical criticism. Westcott, Lightfoot, and Hort were commonly believed to have rescued the New Testament from the German professors, but knowledge about the Old Testament had been made available by German scholars who (conveniently summed up by Professor S. R. Driver of Oxford) were now beginning to be accepted in the English universities. Gore accepted this knowledge, and knew that it affected the New Testament, for it challenged the traditional idea that Jesus was infallible when he ascribed a particular law to Moses or a particular psalm to David, or when he repeated the story of Jonah and the whale.

Even before the publication of the essay in which he accepted this challenge, Gore was very nervous. Should he withdraw? Dean Church advised him to go ahead – but warned him that the disagreement on this matter between the older and younger Anglo-Catholics 'may mark the beginning of a severance which is like the little crack in the glacier, and may open out into a great crevasse'. The problem arose because Jesus Christ was believed to be both God and Man; the Second Person of the eternal Trinity had assumed human nature. Christians also believed that, while incarnate, he had retained divine attributes including omniscience or at least infallibility; exactly how, had been a question confusing even Athanasius. Yet a well-informed theologian such as Gore now had to recognize about Christ, on the crucial page 360:

He shows no signs at all of transcending the science of His age. Equally he shows no signs of transcending the history of His age. He does not reveal His eternity by statements as to what had happened in the past, or was to happen in the future, outside the ken of existing history. His true Godhead is shewn in His attitude towards men and things about Him, in His moral and spiritual claim, in His expressed relation to God, not in any miraculous exemptions of Himself from the conditions of natural knowledge in its own proper province.

These four sentences were intended to say 'how much may legitimately and without real loss be conceded', as the next page stated; but they seemed to many to deny the divinity of Christ, a noteworthy impression if left by the Principal of Pusey House. When *Lux Mundi* was reprinted in a fourth impression, Gore hastened to correct this impression by adding *Corrigenda* after the Contents. He announced that he had not intended to imply that Christ 'surrendered his human nature to fallibility'. Accordingly, Gore wished to substitute for the sentences just quoted: 'He willed to restrain the beams of Deity so as to observe the limits of the science and historical knowledge of His age. . . . He chose to reveal His true Godhead by His attitude. . . .' The 'willed' and 'chose' in this note of correction were Gore's concessions to the outcry raised by the orthodox. They implied that the divine omniscience was merely restrained, not abandoned, by the incarnate Son; and Gore himself later used this very phrase. The question for us is whether they were legitimate concessions, made without real loss to a theologian's integrity.

Gore gave the Bampton Lectures for 1891 on *The Incarnation of the Son of God*, and wrote a sequel. He attempted to defend himself by developing the 'Kenotic' (or 'self-emptying') theory of the Incarnation. He had already hinted at it in *Lux Mundi*, a footnote to that fatal page 360. 'This "self-emptying" of God in the Incarnation is, we must always remember, no failure of power, but a continuous act of Self-sacrifice; cf. 2 Cor. viii, 9 and Phil. ii, 7.' Such biblical texts were not enough to sustain the weight of philosophy which Gore attempted to place on them, and many of his fellow-theologians displayed both fervour and skill in demolishing his theory. Some of these critics, such as Liddon, protested because the theory was not in the Fathers. Others, however, including liberal theologians such as Hastings Rashdall and William Temple, attacked Gore because the theory seemed an implausible way of defending a Christology essentially patristic. These critics pointed out that Gore wished to maintain the Fathers' faith that the incarnate Lord was God the Son by conceding that his human nature was (to some extent and in some way) liable to ignorance and error; yet the concession which he made raised more problems than it solved. How could we know about the continuity between this fallible Christ and the omniscient, eternal Son? How could the Second Person of the Trinity, who had thus temporarily abandoned or restrained his divine power, at the same time continue to play his role in creating and upholding the universe? Was Gore really saying that Jesus 'had been God but now was a man', as Donald Baillie was to put it? Gore struggled to answer criticisms, although he could not get at one with Liddon: Liddon was dead. And eighty years after *Lux Mundi*, his answers had still not silenced critics, the general verdict being perhaps that Gore had set himself an impossible task by attempting to introduce *one* modern element, our knowledge of the intellectual limitations of anyone alive in the first century A.D., into the Christology of the Councils held in the fourth and fifth centuries.

This was Gore's most original contribution to theology, and it often seemed to have been a mistake. But the mistake showed his nature. He had surrendered his will to the Christ of the historic Church; he once confessed that he found it 'difficult to imagine how a good man really doubts our Lord's Godhead', although he liked to describe himself as a rationalist and a free thinker. He had made this surrender, because, as he used to say, it seemed the only alternative to believing that the ultimate was revealed in Nero. But the Christ to whom he had surrendered was not a Christ who had chosen to reveal his Godhead by displaying omniscience. Christ's claim was spiritual and moral.

3

Four years after the publication of *Lux Mundi*, its editor became a parish priest. To some extent Gore's withdrawal from Oxford recalled Newman's; and no priest since Newman had been given such a position among undergraduates. He wished to work in peace, surrounded by a religious community. But he went to the village of Radley, five miles away, where the Community of the Resurrection (as the 'Society' had become) shared the vicarage with him. In his care to get everything and everyone in his parish right, he wrote a long letter asking for the advice of his bishop, William Stubbs. He received this reply:

> My dear Gore,
> Don't be a bore

The truth was that, like Hort, Gore was made wretched by responsibility for average human life in a parish; and he was greatly relieved when at the end of 1894 Lord Salisbury the Prime Minister, summoned him to Westminster. As a canon of the Abbey he secured the institution of the daily Eucharist and the setting aside of St. Faith's Chapel for private prayer, preached the *Lux Mundi* vision, and presided over exciting discussions in his austere home. Henson maintained that Gore advocated the disestablishment of the Church of England in order to make a narrowed Church more definitely Catholic, and it was a shrewd remark up to a point – but it missed the vision. The sermon on the Mount was expounded as the law of Christ for his disciples. Keenly, publicly, and continuously, Gore embraced the threefold bulwark provided for the defence of Catholic doctrine by the creeds (Apostles' and Nicene), the canon (of Scripture), and the episcopate (in England, Anglican not Roman); but in *The Sermon on The Mount* he once again stressed as supreme the moral challenge of discipleship in the Church.

The Church of England [he said], in order to maintain the ideal of a national church, has in result allowed almost all the power of spiritual discipline, which she should have kept in her own hand, to be surrendered to a Parliament which is in the loosest possible relation to Christianity of any kind ... We must set to work to let men understand that, as the Church has a creed which she cannot let go, and a ministry and sacraments which are committed to her to exercise and to dispense, so she has moral standard, which if she is not to fall under the curse of barrenness, she must re-elect and be true to. Only when men have come to understand what the Christian moral standard is—in marriage and in the home, in commerce and in politics and to understand that it can no more be dispensed with than the creed or the sacraments, is there any prospect of a healthy revival of Church life.

In his book of 1901 on *The Body of Christ*, which also arose out of Westminster preaching, he advanced a doctrine of the Eucharist ahead of almost all Roman Catholic and of most Anglican teaching of the time. He saw Holy Communion as a sacrifice rather than a mere memorial; but there could be no possibility that a dead Christ in the bread was sacrificed afresh to the Father by the priest at the altar, although this was the implication of many devotionally 'Catholic' commentaries on the Mass. Gore believed in the Holy Communion as a 'living' and 'reasonable' sacrifice. The Christ who was really present in it was the living Lord who gave himself to feed his people. Responding and participating in faith, the congregation counted as well as the priest; through the sacrament, it became the Body of Christ entering the twentieth century. Here were the essential insights which were to be developed – often of course, without reference to Gore's book, despite its popularity among students of English theology – as the liturgical movement progressed during the century throughout the Christian world.

He was well aware that the Church of England was no model embodiment of such a conception of the nature of Christ's Church, and he edited a volume of *Essays in Aid of the Reform of the Church*. He pulled the book together by an essay pleading for a body of clergy and laity to represent the Church in each parish, diocese, and province and to be the constitutional instrument of reform. He was in many ways a radical when compared with conventional ecclesiastics, but there were significant differences between the Church Self-Government Association which tended to support the position outlined in this essay and the later Life and Liberty Movement of the enthusiasts under William Temple. The men gathering around Gore were theological at heart; and theirs was Catholic theology. Although interested in far more than administrative change in the Church, they were not interested in more freedom for the clergy to be 'modern' in their teaching. On the contrary, Gore hoped that more doctrinal discipline would be imposed on the clergy. And although interested in the national character of the mission of the Church of England, they were not interested in a 'broad' basis for the Church. On the contrary, Gore maintained that the right to elect the representative bodies of the Church should be confined to communicants.

Lord Salisbury had, however, kept his eye on him, and at the end of 1901 offered him the bishopric of Worcester. It meant promoting the most vocal of the younger generation of High Churchmen, and one with a sympathy, however guarded, with 'Ritualism' and 'Socialism'; Gore had just publicly protested against the Government's treatment of the Boers. On Gore's side, to become Bishop of Worcester would mean virtually leaving the Community of the Resurrection, which had just acquired its mother house at Mirfield in Yorkshire. It meant abandoning theological scholarship and a prophet's freedom. It meant accepting 'restraints' which (as Archbishop Lang commented on reading the biography) 'brought out all his testiness and petulance'.

In the end Gore accepted, but he immediately served notice on his brother bishops that he was not going to abandon his theological principles. He refused to be consecrated as a bishop until the objections of Protestant fanatics had been fully answered. He also refused to live in Hartlebury Castle, and hastened the creation of an independent diocese of Birmingham, to the endowment of which he gave the £10,000 which he had inherited from his mother. While Bishop of Worcester he denounced a vicar for disbelieving in the virgin birth of Christ (the vicar resigned), and threatened to prohibit the new *English Hymnal* because it contained hymns invoking the prayers of the saints (a separate edition of the *Hymnal* was issued for use by worried priests). He also attacked the 'new theology' of the Congregationalist heretic, R. J. Campbell (*The New Theology and the Old Religion*, 1907); Campbell joined the Church of England, was received into communion by Gore in 1915, and died a Canon of Chichester.

Gore became the first Bishop of Birmingham in 1905, and his radical zeal in politics combined with his prophetic moralism to win the respect of the (then largely Nonconformist) city. He was assiduous in teaching the clergy and people, in befriending those who needed his friendship in any problem, in confirming the young (his addresses to them were models), in speaking for civic and national causes (he supported the People's Budget and other Liberal radicalism), and in stirring up the social conscience of churchmen. His six years as Bishop of Birmingham were thus one of the glories of a period which men would view in retrospect as the golden age of the Anglican parish and diocese. His statue, erected by public subscription outside his cathedral, remains as a memorial to the time – like a great cathedral now begun in Liverpool or like the *English Hymnal* itself. It was inevitable that such a vigorous Church should burst the seams of a law which compelled men to argue endlessly about what had been the legal ornaments in English churches during the second year of the reign of Edward VI, 1548–9. But, aware that his ideals were contrary to the whole conservatism of the English ecclesiastical machine ('an ingeniously devised instrumentality for defeating the objects which it is supposed to promote'), Gore himself was restless. When the India Office asked him to suggest names for the vacant Bishopric of Bombay, he half-seriously suggested himself. In the end, he foolishly accepted a call to be the Bishop of Oxford.

He became almost as unhappy as he had been while Vicar of Radley. The slow ways of country folk again dismayed his ardent intelligence, and too often now his wit was used to express complaints. The diocese which Samuel Wilberforce had created was too large for a bishop without Wilberforce's obsessive energy or superficial rhetoric. It was Gore's conviction that no diocese ought to contain more than two hundred parishes or three hundred priests, and

Oxford contained three times as many. He never felt himself to be a master of all these parishes – although he did create the Diocesan Board of Finance, and (what mattered infinitely more to him) he did infuse a religious vigour into a diocese which had gone to sleep since Wilberforce's departure. If at Birmingham he had overworked, at Oxford (or rather, in Cuddesdon Palace) he overworried.

He was depressed because Henson, rather than he, represented the spirit of the best educated clergy and laity in his diocese. They tended to be conservative in secular and ecclesiastical politics, and they refused to untie their purse strings for a bishop with a passion for reform. They also tended to be liberal in theology, and rejoiced in the limitations on the legal powers of Gore as a disciplinarian. They had little of Gore's sense that the clauses of the creeds stood or fell together. William Sanday, the most respected among the Oxford theological professors, let it be known that as a result of his constant reading of new books from Germany he was losing belief in the miraculous elements in the old version of Christianity. B. H. Streeter, the editor of the Oxford volume *Foundations* (1912), wrote an essay which went far beyond any heresy approached by Gore in *Lux Mundi*, for Streeter seemed to think it probable that the resurrection of Christ had not taken place in a physical manner. Where Sanday and Streeter trod cautiously, some lesser men rushed in with public attacks on orthodoxy. And some of the Anglo-Catholic priests who were orthodox in doctrine were as undisciplined as the liberal theologians in practice, for they imitated Rome. Such rebels seemed to have created a crisis similar to that in the second century when the episcopate had emerged as the guardian of the scriptures and the creeds. Gore set himself to fight back. If modernizing or Romanizing priests would not do the right thing, which was to resign their Anglican Orders, he tried to make life in the Church of England uncomfortable for them. He poured out his wrath in a booklet of 1914, *The Basis of Anglican Fellowship in Faith and Organization: An Open Letter to the Clergy of the Diocese of Oxford*.

Such definite limitation of the theological basis of Anglican fellowship, excluding the 'disloyal' to the Left or the Right, showed Gore's masterfulness; but it was a futile masterfulness. The modernists answered back, the Romanizers carried on, and Davidson at Lambeth temporized. When Gore came down the front steps of Lambeth Palace, having been manoeuvred out of some demand for discipline, he would say to himself (he helplessly told friends) 'Now, Charles, you never meant to agree to that'. Once, walking back over Lambeth Bridge, he turned and impotently shook his fist towards the wily archbishop's study. He cared little about Davidson's struggle to preserve the legal basis of the Established Church; indeed, he brought fresh trouble on his head by agreeing with the Liberals that Anglicanism in Wales ought to be disestablished. Part of Gore's trouble was that inwardly he felt uneasy about this role as a disciplinarian in the company of bishops so spineless, against scholars whose intelligence he respected (and whose arguments he did not have the leisure to answer properly), and against ritualists whose rites – for example, devotions to the Reserved Sacrament – he personally enjoyed. As his biographer was to put it, he was utterly weary of fighting like a hired gladiator.

After preaching a mission to Oxford undergraduates in February 1914, and giving many of them Communion at the end, he broke down with uncontrollable sobs in the vestry of St. Mary's. The world tragedy which began six months later seemed a hideous enactment on a larger scale of the confusion which he saw in the mind of England. He confessed to a friend that he thought he had made a muddle of his life.

I suppose I shall never know in this world how far it is my fault. I do not *see* that it is, though I want to see. But I remain embracing with all my conviction an ideal of Liberal Catholicism which, it appears, no one is willing to listen to, neither 'Catholics' nor 'Liberals' nor the man in the street, nor anybody else except a very few old ladies and gentlemen. I suppose God has other purposes for the world and the Church. The only thing is to keep a good conscience and do one's best.

In March 1919, he finally told Davidson that he must resign. He refused a canonry back in Westminster and professorships at Oxford and London. He decided not to live with his own Community of the Resurrection; while he had been a bishop, it had developed at Mirfield under the direction of Walter Frere, who in addition to being a more advanced Anglo-Catholic was a Cambridge man. He refused to attend the Lambeth Conference of bishops. At the age of sixty-six he must be free.

4

He lived for thirteen years more, and they were his greatest period. Based on London, with part-time duties as a lecturer and preacher, and refreshing himself by travel, his sense of fun and his sensitivity to people returned. Occasionally he lost his temper, or would be found alone in despondent gloom; but such occasions mainly served to emphasize the victory over his demons. 'He seemed to me at the end rather a pathetic figure', wrote Henson in 1932, 'for his disciples had gone to the right, and to the left, and he was alone. . . . Probably this is the fate which overtakes every leader who has outlived his greatness, but in his case, it seemed to be emphasized by his tireless industry.' But what Henson was not to know in 1932 was that his own old age would be more bitter and lonely. Although Gore lectured the Anglo-Catholics about the folly of their un-English ways and about the moral grandeur of the Old Testament prophets, he abandoned none of his own 'Church principles', and weakened his hold on life by a trip to India in 1931 in order to investigate among many other things the scheme for the reunion of Anglicans with Protestants in a Church of South India. He still saw it as an essential function of the episcopate to uphold righteousness in society, and issued an indignant pamphlet about the bishops' concessions on contraceptives. And he wrote much more.

'The Christian creed, which I stand here to profess, is a purged or reconstructed creed, which in the truest sense can be called "catholic".' So Gore said in his Gifford Lectures delivered in the university of St. Andrews in the winter of 1929–30.

But I am not appealing to the authority of the Church, or of any church, on its behalf. That is an appeal which Lord Gifford barred. I am standing before you simply as one rational being speaking to other rational beings, and giving my reasons for holding that the Christian view of the world is the most rational view which men can entertain.

In these lectures, on *The Philosophy of the Good Life*, he gave his final version of the Plato on whose idealism he had admiringly lectured in nineteenth-century Oxford. He once again extolled the ordered beauty of nature, and once again quoted James Mozley's phrase: 'Nature . . . in the very act of labouring as a machine is also sleeping as a picture.' But the centre of Gore's 'natural' theology was the fact which to him was the centre of history, in preparation for Christ: the prophetic vision of an Absolute Goodness above nature. He paid tribute to the Persian prophet Zoroaster, but reserved his best eloquence for the uniqueness of the prophetic tradition in Israel.

Gore rated the religion of India low in comparison with Israel's. Hinduism seemed not to distinguish between good and evil; Buddhism seemed against all life. Although as a Gifford Lecturer he was expected to avoid appealing to any alleged revelation, the best chapter in *The Philosophy of the Good Life* was, of course, on Jesus Christ as 'the supreme teacher of the way of life for man'. This chapter included the inevitable remark that Christianity 'came into the world as a life to be lived by a community' which believed in the miracle of Christ's resurrection; and it concluded with a sentence which echoed Scott Holland in *Lux Mundi*. 'The primary adventure of faith is always the acceptance of the claim of the Life.'

He covered much of this ground in other writing also: in his book for the Home University Library on *Jesus of Nazareth*, in his lecturers on *Christ and Society*, in his contributions to a large *New Commentary on Holy Scripture* which he jointly edited, and in many sermons and lesser publications dating from this highly productive retirement. Most of the main ideas of a lifetime were gathered into his three volumes on *The Reconstruction of Belief* (1921–4), and into a militant answer to his critics (*Can We Then Believe?*, 1926); and his

*Reconstruction* was his greatest plea for a decision. He once said that it was better to decide wrongly than not to decide at all, and here he wrote: 'There are famous instances of protests by great thinkers that the search for truth was to be preferred to the finding of it, but I believe that, at bottom, this state of mind represents a disease of the intellect.' In over a thousand pages he did his best to give reasons in defence of the decisions which he had made during his first year in Oxford.

It is reason in me which demands goodness in God [he wrote]. If I am rationally sure of anything, it is that I find impressed upon my inmost conscious being the obligation of goodness—the sense that I exist in order to be good. And I am wholly unable to interpret this purpose of goodness, which I cannot doubt to be real, except in terms of the goodness of God.

Scientists or philosophers of the day were quoted against materialism, or against the natural selection of chance variations, as accounting for the organization of life. After 170 pages the reader was already in the midst of a discussion of 'The Historical Religion', and was being reassured about the historical worth of the New Testament: 'The only book of the New Testament which it seems to me the evidence shows to be pseudonymous is the Second Epistle of Peter.' Eye witnesses such as St. John had recorded the miracles and teachings of Jesus Christ. Christianity depended on belief in those miracles and on obedience to those teachings, for the miracles had shown that it was true as Jesus Christ taught – God is 'the transcendent Creator, under whose hands nature is plastic'. 'There can be no doubt', declared Gore, 'that one who holds the prophetic doctrine of God the Creator can find no *a priori* difficulty about the miracles of the Bible.' The Lord of nature could do anything, and it was clear enough what he had done. 'The fact of the empty tomb seems to me as indisputable as any fact of history.' Jesus Christ was neither (as Harnack assumed) a teacher of a simple Gospel about the Fatherhood of God and the brotherhood of man, not (as Schweitzer claimed) a deluded prophet sharing first century follies; he was the Christ who came from eternity to save us from sin, the

Christ who founded and legislated for the Church, the Christ who was rightly described in the Church's developed doctrine of the Trinity.

When the thesis of *The Reconstruction of Belief* is summed up in that manner, it is seen to rest on a series of dogmatic assertions. ('I could see his mind was an awfully jolly merry-go-round', a student said, 'but it never stopped where I was, so I could get on.') Yet these assertions were defended in a charitable and learned spirit, and Gore showed that he was abreast of modern literature even while he did not hesitate to reject its conclusions in favour of the faith which he had received. Far better than in the days when he had tried to wield episcopal authority, he thus vindicated by the quality of his teaching what he called 'the episcopal succession as the link of connexion and continuity in the Catholic body'; and far better than in the attacks which he made on his fellow-churchmen who differed from him, he illustrated in his own person what he wrote at the end of his *Reconstruction* about the Church of England.

I find that her history in many of its aspects and characteristics makes me feel ashamed and depressed. But if there is in history the stamp of a divine providence on any society, it is set on the Anglican Church. It was marked out in the sixteenth century to hold together the ancient Catholic tradition both in creed and order with the appeal of the Reformation to the open Bible as the final court of reference for Christians; and so to present a type of Catholicism which the world had forgotten, which should have priests but not be priest-ridden, and should accept the Catholic tradition but keep it purged by the free use of reason and an all-pervading scripturalness.

He caught pneumonia in January 1932. As he lay semi-conscious, Archbishop Lang heard him say 'transcendent glory'. William Temple assessed him after his death. 'Though I have had many tutors in Christ, he was perhaps above all others my father; and so far as I can picture Jesus Christ, I picture Him as not unlike the father whom I have lost.'

## 5

The life of Herbert Hensley Henson began in circumstances very different from Gore's. He was born to a Nonconformist ex-businessman in his fifties, who lived in a *bourgeois* retirement beyond his real means and who was obsessed with an Evangelical pietism; and his mother died when he was aged six. At odds with his home, the boy became a keen Anglican communicant and often slipped into churches. He was sent to an inefficient private school in Broadstairs on the Kent coast (where they lived), was miserable, and ran away. In 1881 he found his way to Oxford, where he was too poor to belong to any college; nevertheless he secured a First in history as an 'unattached student'.

Three years later life really began for him, when by examination he won a fellowship at All Souls College. Founded in 1436, All Souls had retained the original character of many medieval colleges or halls and had virtually no undergraduates. The fellows had been an aristocratic, idle lot in the years of the glory of Oriel and Balliol, and they still included those whose achievements were not academic, but when Henson was elected the aim was intellectual as well as worldly distinction. The college provided what his life had lacked: a stability and sense of ease, a warmth of friendship, an assured tolerance of the High Church extremes to which the young man was running, a conversation embracing the culture and politics of England. Throughout his life Henson – like his clerical colleague and rival, Cosmo Lang – loved All Souls as his second home.

His desire to be ordained, formed during lonely visits to churches in Kent as a boy, now wavered. He taught history in the university; he organized a Layman's League for the defence of the establishment of the National Church; he thought of becoming a barrister. When his vocation re-asserted itself, Gore at Pusey House was the first who heard the solemn news. But he was desperately immature, seeing himself as a kind of St. Francis among the poor. He was ordained as a deacon at Cuddesdon in 1887, and he made in his journal a boyish entry which shows how, despite his debt to Gore, he was now on the move.

I wrote a letter to Raleigh thanking him for the help he had given me by his example and counsel to shake off the chains of pseudo-Catholic theory ... Then I walked into the meadows beyond the Church and sat on a style to meditate. And as I thought the desire came over me to pledge myself to God, there and then; which I forthwith did, bareheaded under the open heaven, promising to be loyal to the Truth, wherever I found it, wheresoever it should call me to seek after it.

Twelve years later he copied out that entry for the benefit of another Fellow of All Souls who was being ordained, Cyril Alington, and he added:

The Church of England has little to offer in the present, and less to promise in the future, and the time may come to you, as it has come to me, when the pressure of a yoke which is irremovable is almost more than flesh can bear. It would not be true to say that I have ever regretted taking Orders; but it is true that I cannot imagine myself—seeing things as I now see them and realizing the bearing of all the issue of Ordination as I do now—having the courage to offer myself for the Ministry now.

The misery behind that heart's cry resulted from the two great mistakes on the part of the advisers of this self-tormenting intellectual. A month after becoming a deacon, he was appointed Head of Oxford House in Bethnal Green, a centre for social work in the East End of London. The young Henson hated the squalor around him, but disbelieved in Socialism as a cure. He also disbelieved in the High Church glamour of this mission which operated on a shoe-string, but he had no alternative to offer as a means of reaching the hearts of the poor. Understandably he accepted the first offer of alternative employment, but it was an appointment by All Souls as Vicar of Barking, a parish of over twelve thousand on the sordid outskirts of London.

At Barking he prayed, he preached, he led his curates, and he opened the garden of his over-large vicarage to his rough parishioners; but he was near to a nervous break-down. Craving affection, with his don's tongue he managed to insult many of the somewhat puzzled people around him. A born debater, he felt it his duty to try to be a pastor.

Wanting to be a scholar, he spent the years of *Lux Mundi* in dockland, immersed in local arguments and in parochial labours for which he had had no training and little inclination. But what he saved from the near-wreckage of his life was perhaps enough. It was an ineffaceable sense of the clergyman's duty. When as a bishop he looked back to his early years and addressed the young men whom he was about to ordain, memory did its usual trick of glamorizing the past; but there was enough in the truth about Barking to let this trick be played.

Nearly fifty years have passed since I was myself ordained [he said in 1936]. How little I guessed what lay before me! The immense failures which would overtake my too-ardent beginnings: the disappointments which would shadow my later course; the growing sense of inadequacy which would become a settled resident in my mind. The happiest years in my ministry were those in which, as the vicar of a great industrial parish, I was nearest to the people. Faces look out at me from the past—toil-worn faces, radiant with love and confidence. Nothing of what men foolishly call success is worth comparison with the experiences which those faces recall.

He was rescued from the strain of Barking by Lord Salisbury, who had been a Fellow of All Souls and who had been alarmed by the collapse of Henson's health. The peer was patron of a little almshouse, St. Mary's Hospital, Ilford, where the chaplain (or 'incumbent') had just accepted the Pope's verdict on Anglican Orders by resigning. Lord Salisbury appointed Henson to this post, thus enabling him to spend much more time at All Souls as a fellow with a small stipend. Henson's first book belongs to these years: *Apostolic Christianity*, a discussion of St. Paul's government of the Church in Corinth. But he could not secure any post in the university world, and he could not afford to marry. Then after seven more years, in 1900, Lord Salisbury came to the rescue again. He nominated Henson to the Westminster canonry to which was annexed the rectory of St. Margaret's, the parish church of the House of Commons.

The great Victorian Rector of St. Margaret's had been F. W. Farrar, a prince of the pulpit, and the delighted Henson at the age of thirty-seven set himself to revive that tradition by addressing his sermons there and in the Abbey to the basic questions of the time. As he now saw it, there were three foes to fight. The first was immorality in public life; here he was at one with Gore. The second was any attempt to stifle the freedom of the Christian theologians to be loyal 'to the truth', wherever they found it; here he made Gore very uneasy. The third was any attempt to fasten 'the chains of the pseudo-Catholic theory' on the Church of England. The Church ought, rather, to be enlarged on a definitely Protestant basis in order to be more clearly the 'Great National Church of the English people'; and here, he faced a collision with Gore. Amid these fights, there was one positive Gospel to proclaim, and he had kept his hold on this through the years of misery now closing.

I don't think any outsider can understand how much passion of soul is involved in the Ministry [he had written to Alington the year before]. There is suffering quite unique in nature and intensity wrapped up in this self-surrender to the Service of Souls. One's own faults come home to one with such cruel insistence, and, as the years pass, failures add their dead weight to the heart. One has dark hours, God knows, when the worth of the Ministry, the genuineness of that vast system of Religion, which the Ministry symbolises and interprets, are wrapped in doubt. Everything seems to go for a while, and one has a new anguish. It is not the common distress of mind which every thinking Christian must have experience of at some time or other, but a far more terrible trouble. You are the priest: you face your fellows on the basis of their confidence in your firm conviction: and you are not sure, you you do not know, you are not what you seem. I think these troubles will increase. ... Still, after twelve years of fault and failure and sorrow, I think of Ordination as having *essentially* little to do with subscriptions and formulae—being in reality the answer to Christ's personal vocation, an answer which one must make ...

In Ordination I see nothing less than that supreme acceptance of Christ's proposal. The poor little temporal and local incidents are just our secular uniform, which counts for little, and is always counting for less. Only that remains. 'Jesus Christ is the Same, yesterday, and to-day, yea for ever.' Everything else fails us: He alone remains. One is untrue to oneself: He is true to us always.

Henson had been in a wilderness unknown to most of his critics or defenders of the 'vast system of Religion'.

6

At Westminster, where he enjoyed a good income for the first time in his life, he married a Scotswoman, Isabella Caroline Dennistoun. In his own words, 'her presence mitigated the resentments which my personal idiosyncrasies and frequent controversies could not but provoke', but the marriage was childless. She was neither his intellectual equal nor very practical, and she grew increasingly deaf, so that writing up his journal (with references to 'the dear lady') gradually became his substitute for conversation with her. Despite his loyalty to her, Henson's solitariness was not really changed; and as he wrote, 'lonely men are apt to become horribly interested in themselves'. Nor did his combativeness grow less, and he argued so persistently with the Dean of Westminster, Armitage Robinson, that this was one of the factors persuading Robinson to exchange Westminster for the quieter Deanery of Wells.

As a preacher he found his vocation (despite his unattractively rasping voice), and in 1908 he refused the Prime Minister's offer to appoint him to the Professorship of Ecclesiastical History at Oxford. He did not hesitate to pronounce on public issues when morality seemed to be involved. For example, he pilloried a British company which was exploiting native labour in Peru. The company's directors threatened legal action, only to see the following reply to their solicitor's letter.

I differ so completely from your clients in their view of what is befitting a clergyman, a gentleman, and a man, that you will not be surprised to learn that I think nothing is required from me in any of those characters which would abate anything of the severity of the censure which I conceived myself called upon to pass on the directors of the Peruvian Amazon Company.

In other utterances which attracted publicity, he vigorously expressed his Protestant conception of the National Church. In 1909 Gore, now Bishop of Birmingham, issued a formal 'inhibition' against Henson's acceptance of an invitation to preach in the Institute attached to the historic Congregational Church in Birmingham, Carr's Lane. Henson hoped that, when he disobeyed this episcopal order, Gore would prosecute him in the courts and so give him an opportunity of demonstrating the illegality of the inhibition; but on reflection Gore allowed the incident to pass. In his Westminster pulpits Henson repeatedly urged inter-communion with eventual reunion between the Church of England and his wife's Church of Scotland, and between Anglicans and Nonconformists despite the bitter political quarrels of the time – quarrels on which he often commented in self-consciously independent journalism. He brought into the pulpit of St. Margaret's scholars such as J. M. Thompson who were in his view unjustly treated by the ecclesiastical authorities. What he himself said seemed to amount to a claim that belief in miracles was optional, and this caused a mild sensation at the time; but he preached the merits of the traditional devotion to the divine Redeemer within the traditional alliance of Church and State, and did so in beautiful prose.

When he was made Dean of Durham in 1912, 'the old ambition to be a student which I had laid aside when I left Oxford for Bethnal Green in 1887 . . . resumed something of its former authority in my mind.' But he was temper-amentally unable to give himself to the quietness of a learned dean.

He was speaking all over the diocese even before the war came with its summons to patriotic oratory. In pre-war Anglican controversies, near or far it was (in his own words) 'apparent from the first that I could not stand outside the conflict'. When the war produced the National Mission of Repentance and Hope, he stood outside what he regarded as a very mistaken enterprise – and he did so in a bellig-erently public manner. When the story was spread that at Mons the British troops had been assisted by angels, he scornfully preached his scepticism. When George V and Davidson appealed for total abstinence from alcohol during the war, he wrote to *The Times* that 'Total Abstinence is no part of morality'. When the Life and Liberty Movement was launched as an Anglican ginger group by what Henson called 'the casuistic facility and untiring eloquence of William Temple', he voted in a minority of one at the enthusiastic meeting in the Queen's Hall, London. He declared that he was voting against a resolution which claimed that 'the present conditions under which the Church lives and works constitute an intolerable hindrance to its spiritual activity.' But perhaps a deeper objection to Life and Liberty was revealed in a sentence of the witty report which he sent to Davidson (on his own initiative): 'The Bishop of Oxford's name was greeted with applause, but then the meeting was "Gore's crowd".'

When Lloyd George nominated him as Bishop of Hereford at the end of 1917, it was natural that Gore's crowd should explode in protest. Henson had lost few opportunities of taunting them and of befriending their enemies (apart from the Evangelicals). It was also natural that the more conservative Evangelicals, aroused by old Dean Wace from Canterbury, should counter-attack; and it was natural, too, that many ordinary churchpeople would be ready to believe the worst about a preacher who seemed so much in love with the sound of his own voice expressing his independence. Henson was, in a word, arrogant, and his attitude to those who now objected to his consecration was, in the mild Davidson's phrase, 'venomous'. Lang and Gore may have been right, from their points of view, to absent themselves from the consecration of such a man – although Henson, who was sensitive as many angry controversialists are, never really forgave him.

Nevertheless, Lloyd George may be seen to have been right to force the appointment through, and Davidson was right to make it possible. For Henson was humbled by being made a bishop, and saved for what he had called 'the Service of Souls'. He was humbled to realize the extent of the hostility he had aroused, and he was deeply hurt. Ten years later, he still thought of himself as isolated. He told Davidson:

It has been my misfortune in the course of my life to disappoint every person who has followed me, and every party that has allowed itself to build hopes on me ... A kind of Quixotic honesty, a fatal trick of lucid speech, and a temperamental indifference to the impressions I make, may perhaps explain the embodied paradox I seem to be.

If he really was indifferent to the hostility he had aroused, why did his journal contain so many passages of introspection and so many expressions of delight when men praised him?

With his half-hidden sensitivity, he was also humbled by the gravity of a bishop's work. It sobered him to be among the gamekeepers rather than the poachers. It was true, as he wrote in his journal: 'The real "H. H. Hereford" is a very different being from that which hatred and bigotry have imagined – a man full of fears as to himself, and mainly anxious to "do out the duty".' And although he never faced up to the fact with full 'candour' (a favourite word), he was also humbled by having to compromise his much-advertised conscience in order to persuade Davidson to consecrate him a bishop in the face of Gore's opposition.

For 'compromise' does seem to be the just word to use about the document which Davidson wrote for Henson's signature at Lambeth Palace on 17 January 1918. The document was in the form of a reply to a letter from the Archbishop. Davidson's letter to Henson ran:

I am receiving communications from many earnest men of different schools who are disquieted by what they have been led to suppose to be your disbelief in the Apostles' Creed, and especially in the clauses relating to Our Lord's Birth and Resurrection. I reply to them that they are misinformed, and I am persuaded that that when you repeat the words of the Creed you do so *ex animo* and without any desire to change them. I think I understand your reluctance to make at this moment a statement the motives of which might be misconstrued, and it is only because you would relieve many good people from real distress that I ask you to let me publish this letter with a word of reassurance from yourself.

Davidson also wrote, and made Henson sign, a two-sentence reply; it was the only way of silencing Gore. 'I do not like to leave any letters of yours unanswered. It is strange that it should be thought by anyone to be necessary that I should give such an assurance as you mention, but of course what you say is absolutely true.' To the end Henson blustered, and he got the Archbishop to take down a third sentence at his dictation. 'I am indeed astonished that any candid reader of my published books, or anyone acquainted with my public Ministry of thirty years, could entertain a suggestion so dishonourable to me as a man and as a clergyman.' As an echo of his rebuke to the directors of the Peruvian Amazon Company, this was out of place; for Henson, in order to go to Hereford, was willing to state that he accepted *ex animo* (sincerely), and had no desire to change, the credal statements that Jesus was conceived by the Holy Ghost and born of the Virgin Mary, and that on the third day he rose again. But in Westminster he had preached the view which he held to the end of his life: that belief in the virgin birth and physical resurrection was both optional and probably wrong.

It is evident that he retracted his heresies because he wanted to be a bishop, but it is not necessary to blame Henson for bowing to the Archbishop's insistence. His belief in Jesus Christ was what mattered supremely to him, and he accepted not a mere teacher but the Incarnate God and the Risen Lord – of 'yesterday' as well as 'today'. The Apostles' Creed was the only existing symbol of the faith of the community which thus worshipped Jesus Christ. If the question were put as it was in 1917, he had to answer that it would be false to 'disbelieve' in such a creed, and presumptuous to wish to change it. He had bared his heart to Alington in 1899 (and Alington now sent that letter to Gore). 'Everything else fails us: He alone remains. One is true to oneself: He is true to us always.'

7

Bishop Henson surprised his critics. He won the respect and even the affection of many of the laity, and even of most of the clergy, in two very different dioceses which he governed. He never allowed himself to be immersed in minor duties or pleasantries. He never admitted a telephone to the house (but would send out his chaplain with a pile of coins for use in the public kiosk), and normally spent his mornings reading and writing in his study unless he was in London. He ruled by sermon, article, or letter, writing out what he had to teach with a care for his prose which added to the distinctive and memorable quality of his mind. His wit could still hurt, and the love of controversy could still lead him into debates where he was in the minority because in the wrong, but as a pastoral bishop he was surprisingly tender. He had set great store by the unity of spirit and service among those who served Westminster Abbey or Durham Cathedral, and when he became the bishop of a diocese he built up a pride in it. Young men were attracted to work under such leadership. Many people already in the diocese gave him their hearts, and then his own inner nature responded. He took these duties in his own diocese far more seriously than his speeches in the provincial or national assemblies of the Church, although he enjoyed debates. When William Temple attended a meeting of bishops in York in 1921 he found that Henson 'spoke many times' but always refused to serve on committees. Archbishop Lang in the chair observed: 'My dear Bishop of Durham, if you think you can get out of doing the solid work of committees merely by making fantastic speeches, we shall have to prove that you are mistaken.'

When Lloyd George transferred him to Durham in 1920, the move was accompanied by many expressions of regret in Herefordshire and by many words of welcome back to the great Northern see ('The Bishoprick' as he liked to call it). When he resigned from Durham at the beginning of 1939, the tribute signed by all the clergy and lay officials in the diocese praised a 'great and generous episcopate'. His success was all the more striking because his historical and critical eye was quick to see how the conditions of his work were far different from those of the great divines whom he admired. The Victorian preachers had commanded attentive and intelligent congregations, and what they said had quite often got into the newspapers; but Henson came to think that he had spent too much time on the preparation of sermons. In the twentieth century, sermons seemed to count for little. The Victorian prelates had entertained the gentry and mediated in industrial disputes. Henson now consorted with 'the County' and warned the miners that Labour would ruin the country. Yet a bishop, even a

Bishop of Durham, was no longer a 'great national officer', despite Henson's nostalgic claim.

He constantly pictured himself as a man condemned to live in an age of decline. He inspected, without admiring, the age of democracy. He did not believe in conferences – and specially not in those which William Temple convened. 'I admire his industry and envy his various ability', Henson once confessed, 'but I distrust his judgment, dislike his company, and dissent from his reading of ecclesiastical duty.' He did not believe in movements, and specially not in Moral Rearmament, the American emotionalism under F. D. Buchman which many softer-centred church leaders wished to bless, but which Henson cursed eloquently. He did not believe in any simple panacea to cure the Church's alienation from the people. But he 'did out the duty', and he urged his clergy that if they were to be respected they, too, must work. He was never popular with the miners, but he was not mobbed by them as seemed likely. (They tried to throw a Dean of Durham into the river; some said that they thought that the Dean was the Bishop.) 'Now gentlemen', he ended on one occasion when his car had been surrounded by an angry crowd, 'I am not unemployed as unfortunately you are. I have much to do: and I must therefore bid you good-night.' These were not the words of another Westcott, but the unemployed broke into cheers.

The second surprise produced by Henson's twenty-two years as a bishop was this conversion from the eloquent defence of the Church of England 'by law established' to the eloquent recognition of disestablishment as inevitable if the Church's worship was not to be dictated by the secularized House of Commons. He hated to be called inconsistent, and there was indeed a basic consistency of conviction through his life, apart from the consistency of clarity, vigour, and acumen in all that he wrote or said. In his early twenties, when he had organized the Laymen's League in Oxford, he had been backing up Archbishop Benson's view of the nation's continuing history; in his forties, when he had preached the glorious comprehensiveness of the National Church, he had done so in a Westminster where Parliament, the Abbey, and St. Margaret's seemed good neighbours; and in his fifties, when he had owed his positions in the Church to two Liberal Prime Ministers, he had been convinced that statesmen and public alike wished the Church well under the right leadership. His ability to produce theological arguments or rhetoric in defence of the alliance of Church and State had always depended on a belief that it was a genuine alliance, with obligations acknowledged on both sides. When he became a bishop, the legal bent of his mind meant that it was like changing from being an advocate to being a judge. He regarded the episcopate as an institution for the government of the Church. The 'lawlessness' of the clergy distressed Henson as it distressed Gore – and he did not think it relevant that in the past he had often defied bishops himself, for the Anglo-Catholic lawlessness of the 1920s seemed to be directed against the Protestant nature of the National Church. The authority of the episcopate could not be restored, he believed, unless Parliament authorized a Prayer Book which the bishops could enforce 'inexorably' (his word to Davidson in 1923). When in 1927 – 8 the House of Commons refused to do this, Henson saw no honourable alternative to breaking up the Establishment. He had argued against Gore, for he had suspected that Gore favoured disestablishment in order to fasten a clerical and Anglo-Catholic control on the Church; but now he, too, would 'mend or end'.

In January 1928, between the Prayer Books, he discussed Church and State in a university sermon at Cambridge, taking as his text: 'Can two walk together, except they be agreed?' He announced his conversion to the view that the spiritual freedom of the Church was now paramount. In the summer he would like to have been offered York when Cosmo Lang went to Canterbury, but he knew that to the end he had been too controversial. William Temple was appointed, a man for whose confused sentimentality Henson nursed a suspicion exceeded only by his contempt for the glamour surrounding each 'sonorous platitude' from Archbishop Lang. 'The knowledge that I can have no other sphere of work than the diocese of Durham must have considerable effect on my performance of duty, and the effect ought to be wholesome', he wrote. But it was inevitable that he should continue to express independent opinions about Church and State, demanding a clarification in the relationship between Parliament and the Church Assembly; and it says much about where his heart lay that the Church's confusion following the insult from the House of Commons troubled him so deeply. We can compare Henson's lectures on *Anglicanism* at Uppsala in 1920 with his book on *The Church of England* in 1939, and note that the two volumes, while both being superb discussions of the Anglican system in the light of English history, reached opposite conclusions. In 1920 disestablishment would be like pulling down Westminster Abbey in order to improve the view of the surrounding buildings, but in 1939 the Establishment was morally indefensible. 'A faithful picture of an Effete Establishment' was how Henson himself described the latter book to Archbishop Lang, who had sent him a long and worried protest against its pessimism. On the other hand, the mind of the Church of England as a whole was neither so clear nor so legal as the mind of Hensley Henson, and in retrospect it may be seen that those who considered other things more important than Prayer Book revision understood the Church better than he did.

Moreover, the Englishman, whether in Church or out of it, is essentially practical (as Henson himself often stressed); and for all the astuteness of his analysis of the system and its crisis, Henson was seldom constructive or even realistic in his contributions to the debate about the immediate issues. To the creation of the Church Assembly, which on any showing held the key to Anglican independence and self-respect, he had contributed little except carping criticism, because he had thought the Church Assembly 'anti-national'; and when the Archbishops appointed a commission to examine the relations of the Church and State, he refused to send to it any comment except his certainty that it was wasting its time unless it advocated a complete revolution in the relationship.

In 1934 an episode showed how Henson regarded the spiritual crisis of the decade. A Unitarian minister was invited to preach in the new Anglican cathedral in Liverpool. It was Henson who led the protests against this apparent acceptance of the denial of the divinity of Christ. For some years now he had grown increasingly uneasy about a lack of reverence for the person of Christ in some of the utterances associated with the Modern Churchmen's Union. He had refused to join that body, and he seized the opportunity presented by the controversy about Unitarians in a cathedral pulpit to demonstrate clearly that he regarded the worship of the divine Christ as the heart of historical Christianity and as the essence of the teaching of the Church of England.

His Gifford Lectures, which Henson published under the title *Christian Morality: Natural, Developing, Final* (1936), were of no permanent importance, but they emphasized that the wide diffusion of a Christian spirit in the conduct of men and nations depended on the definite discipleship of the minority which fully submitted to the full claim of Christ. Over his large collection of history books he placed the figure of the One whom he regarded as the Judge of it all, on a crucifix. As he watched the societies of Stalin and Hitler, and the sensuality and 'puerile superstitions' of the secularized West, he saw the fulfilment of his warning in his Gifford Lectures that 'Christianity carries the fortunes of mankind, and that its failure would mean nothing less calamitous than the spiritual suicide of humanity.'

He retired at the age of seventy-six to Hintlesham, near Ipswich, just before the outbreak of the war; he sold off all the furniture he did not need, as if wanting to emphasize that the glory had departed from the empty rooms, cold floors, and peeling paint of Auckland Castle. In 1940 Winston Churchill dramatically reinstated him as a canon of Westminster, but cataract was now damaging his eyes and he had to resign. He lived on, fighting blindness and despair, until 1947.

# 9

# Frederick and William Temple

I

Anything more hostile to the New Testament than our modern English religion is difficult to conceive. Well, I believe that the only thing that can save us is a vigorous attack from within the Church on the existing conceptions of religion ... If I lived 700 years before Christ, I should call it the word of the Lord. I don't know whether Amos actually saw things: probably not: but his vision was mine—'I saw the Lord standing above the altar' (His own altar it was) 'and He said unto me, SMITE!'

It was a very undergraduate letter. Its author was William Temple, and he wrote it in 1901, in the palace at Canterbury which his father, Archbishop Frederick Temple, had recently caused to be built. Forty-one years after writing it, he became Archbishop of Canterbury, the first son to follow his father in the post. But he did not 'smite'. Instead, he followed his father 'within the Church'. When he died in 1944, he was eighteen years younger than his father had been at the time of his death in 1902. But although his life was cut short, at the time of William Temple's death there were many who voiced the conviction that he had proved himself among the noblest figures in the story of Christianity. Even his critic Hensley Henson agreed that he was 'the most variously distinguished of the 32 Archbishops of Canterbury since the Reformation.'

William Temple was very much his father's son; in Henson's words, 'he was magnificently endowed by Nature, and all the circumstances of his life favoured him'. The security of a youth spent in Victorian episcopal palaces, and in the school and college where his father had been headmaster and tutor, never left him. Both father and son

were self-confident and, while in theory they were demo-
crats, in practice they relied little on the views of colleagues
and cared even less about the attacks of critics. Both had the
rare endowment of a photographic memory. Over a
considerable period of time they could recall exactly what
they had read or whom they had met. Both shared wide and
keen interests in the history of thought and in current
problems, with an ability to pronounce on many matters
where less contemporaries would have pleaded ignorance
or modesty. William would recall that his father had been
reluctant to reveal his opinions, lest the son should agree
with them too readily. When he delivered his Gifford
Lectures he repeated the essential arguments of his father's
Bampton Lectures half a century before, and he described
a father's relations with his children:

He gave them being; to a great extent he shapes their circumstances; perhaps his influence over them is so great that they will
never knowingly act against his wishes; yet they are free to respect
his wishes or not; if they do so, it is because it appears to them good
to do so; when he controls them, he does not coerce them, because his control is effective through their wills and not either
apart from or against their wills.

Frederick Temple was always so formidable, and could
be so boorishly rude, that we might expect a clever and
sensitive son to rebel against him – as, say, Matthew
rebelled against Thomas Arnold. But the guidance of
Frederick always appeared good to William's will. This
temperamental affinity between father and son probably
owed much to the fact that the father was in his sixties, and
beginning to mellow, when he had two sons, of whom
William (the younger, born at Exeter in 1881) was the
brighter. An old man's delight that his name would be
carried on may account for the gentleness with which he
handled the boys; it was a delight which never came to the
childless William. A glimpse survives of Frederick Temple
coming out of daily prayers in the chapel of Fulham Palace,
his arms around his two sons' shoulders. But in Frederick
Temple's case, a special factor contributed to this normal
happiness, for his pride in William was not only the pride
of a father who had expected to be barren. It was also the

pride of one now immersed in ecclesiastical administration, who had been happiest when teaching boys. Frederick Temple was the greatest schoolmaster of his day, and on no pupil was his educational skill lavished more freely than on William. His many letters to William at Rugby and Balliol thus preserved the liberal Anglican intellectual tradition from the 1840s to the 1940s.

For all their closeness and love, however, the father and the son had minds which were bent differently. Frederick Temple had a high mathematical capacity, was really interested in science, and made a formidable administrator. He was fortunate that it was his lot to administer admiring schoolboys and subservient schoolmasters and clergymen, for in most walks of life his essential self-dependence, his brusque speech, and his frequent verbal brutalities would have crippled his work. 'To us, I think', Scott Holland remembered, 'he always appeared like a great ship, furrowing its way alone through the seas.'

William was in many ways the softer man. He would say that his ignorance of science was so immense as to be distinguished, and his critics added that his style in making appointments, in administering discipline, or in accepting engagements (for example, to write Prefaces to inferior books) revealed little shrewdness about ordinary human nature. He did not possess the physique of his father, hardened by a boyhood on a Devon farm; he was overweight from boyhood. He also suffered from gout from the age of two (although he never touched alcohol or tobacco). It cannot be said that he showed his father's toughness in adversity, for he had no opportunity to do so: although he supported reform in the Church and Socialism in the State, and made sacrifices in such causes, throughout his life he was surrounded by an admiring affection. His approach was always genial. He found it easy to reconcile apparently incompatible intellectual positions in a formula which dazzled men who already loved him for his friendliness and tranquillity. He was a great ecumenical figure among Christians, for although he embodied the highest Anglican assurance and defended the standard Anglican positions he did so without causing the slightest personal offence. In those human relations which are carried on at a deeper level than argument, he constantly communicated an unbreakable love for, and a basic agreement with, everyone. In a shrewd summary recalled by Henson in 1946, Randall Davidson observed that 'the worst fault of Willie is that he is so kind-hearted that he can say no to nobody'.

The whole contribution of Frederick and William Temple to Church and State sprang from the former's education on the Ionian islands of Santa Maura and Corfu at the hands of his mother. Mrs. Dorcas Temple was a straightforward Cornishwoman who understood very little of the Latin and arithmetic which, day by day, she made her son memorize. The family's bungalow was called Government House and its standards were strictly middle-class, but they were too poor to have butter on their bread. Frederick Temple looked after his mother with great devotion until she died in 1886, and did not marry until ten years later. His choice fell on the aristocratic Beatrice Lascelles, who lived until 1915, making her home with William. Frederick Temple used to say wonderingly that every peer now seemed to be a cousin, and William Temple shared his father's deep respect for this great lady; he would repeat his mother's remark that, while he knew more than she, she knew better. It was only after her death that William felt free to marry. He chose Frances Anson, who revealed her qualities by freeing him from all domestic cares while he lived, by accepting his self-sacrifice which brought problems to the first ten years of their married life, and by unobtrusive but deeply appreciated work as a prison visitor in Winchester during a long widowhood. The two archbishops owed much to these three exceptional and very different women.

2

Frederick Temple was born in 1821 on a small Mediterranean island because – as we saw in connexion with Gladstone – the Ionian Islands were virtually British colonies (after 1815). Major Octavius Temple was 'Resident' in Santa Maura, and then for a brief period held a post on

Corfu, before he found that he had saved enough to buy an inferior farm in Devon, at Axon near Culmstock. The family helped him to clear the land and to make a home out of the isolated house. But he became unpopular with his neighbours because of his criticisms of the conditions of British agriculture and of the Corn Laws which protected farmers. Never willing to control his tongue, he grew passionately angry with his children over trifles and got involved in some bitter quarrels. Neighbouring farmers denounced him as a radical. Worse, he could not make the farm pay – and he was overcome by the problem of educating the eight of his fifteen children who had survived infancy, specially the two sons then at home, Frederick and John (who became a colonel). There was a tradition of culture in the family, despite their present poverty; Octavius Temple's father had been a scholarly country clergyman. If the boys were to be sent to school, there seemed no alternative but their father's return to the colonial service. Octavius Temple, who had been too outspoken to be popular with his superiors, had to accept the Lieutenant-Governorship of the notoriously unhealthy Sierra Leone, leaving his family behind. Within ten months of his acceptance of the post he was dead.

The family struggled on under the severe guidance of the mother. Until the age of twelve, Frederick Temple had no education except two hours a day which she supervised. Most of the time he spent as a farm boy. When he became a schoolmaster he still loved to climb trees, and to recall his skill at ploughing and threshing; when he visited a Chartist meeting and all who entered had to show their hands to prove that they were working-class, his hands were horny enough. To the end of his days he retained the marks of his childhood: a rough accent, no small talk, clarity and directness of mind and speech, an unwearying strength of body which made light of the burden of incessant labour despite heart trouble and failing eyesight.

These basic endowments were supplemented by an education at Blundell's School, Tiverton. It was a small grammar school, but Frederick Temple's five years there raised his level in classics and mathematics sufficiently for him to be nominated by the trustees of the school to a scholarship confined to Blundell's boys at Balliol College. He was entirely shaped by his mother's insistence that he should win by working and conforming. Poor as he was, he was a strong Tory in his youth, and no revolutionary when he grew up. One of the trustees met him in a country lane after the meeting, and said: 'Temple, I cannot say what you are going to be, but this I am sure of, that if you live long enough, you will be one of the greatest men in England.' Frederick walked home on air.

And so he walked through Oxford, in clothes and shoes which had to be patched. He could not afford to drink any wine, or to light a fire, or to use his oil-lamp in the evenings. Night after night he would sit on the staircase in Balliol, at his books under the public light. But his mind stirred. He enjoyed the metaphysics of Kant and Coleridge, and the cleverness of his Balliol tutors, Tait and Ward. He was awakened to the new biblical criticism, explaining to his mother that the Bible which she accepted literally was the Word of God to her because it appealed to her conscience. He was thrilled by Newman's power to convey the reality of the unseen world in continuity with the apostles. But when he reported his excitements to his mother he received wise advice for a young man so poor, and obeyed it: 'Freddy, don't argue.' He secured the highest honours in classics and mathematics, with a fellowship at Balliol in 1842, and was ordained by Samuel Wilberforce. Although other Blundell's scholars had been despised, he had become a popular undergraduate in a college which respected his integrity, and which enjoyed his high spirits amid bleak poverty; and he now made a popular tutor also.

Tait invited him to join the Rugby staff, but Temple wanted to give his life to the education of boys in the 'workhouses', the rejects of Victorian society. He wanted to give them his practical sense, for he did not mind rolling up his sleeves or making sure that they were washed and combed; and he wanted to awaken their minds. From 1848 to 1857 he was, therefore, in the service of the newly formed Committee of the Privy Council on Education. For a year he worked as an examiner in the Education Office, but then the scheme which really interested him was launched. An estate near Twickenham, formerly owned by Sir Godfrey Kneller the painter, had been bought by the Government in order that a small college might be built for training schoolmasters to teach workhouse boys. In 1849 Kneller Hall Training College was opened. Frederick Temple was Principal, with the future compiler of the *Golden Treasury* of English poetry, Francis Palgrave, as Vice-Principal. He began with the highest enthusiasm.

But it soon became clear that the experiment would fail. Temple's fellow-clergymen worried about whether the new school was ecclesiastical enough. The pupils were few and mostly stupid, and the paternalist scheme for workhouse schools foundered. Temple made no secret of the problems as he saw them, and successive governments made no secret of their unwillingness to produce more money. The Principal tried browbeating the ministers; the ministers brushed him off, although they noted his abilities. At the end of 1855 Temple resigned from Kneller Hall, and employment was found for him as an Inspector of Training Colleges. He was a competent civil servant in the honourable work of the Education Office, and he had to his credit the fruitful suggestion that Oxford and Cambridge should sponsor examinations in the schools. But fifteen years after taking his degree, his outstanding energy and intelligence had not yet found adequate expression. He had hoped in vain to be elected Master of Balliol in 1854. Frustrated in his work, and unmarried while his mother lived, he was so miserable that he would read the obituaries in envy of the dead. What he had lost was his naive idealism (which William never lost); for after the failure at Kneller Hall his advice to the Education Office was chiefly aimed at strengthening middle class education by closer links between the grammar schools and the universities. The working class, he would suggest, needed only the rudiments. What he had gained was an experience of education at many levels and in many places – that, and a reputation for hard work.

Tait had wanted him as his successor at Rugby, but that had been when he had just begun at Kneller Hall, and he had not been willing to move. Dr. Goulburn, a stately and saintly Etonian, had been appointed. In 1857 Goulburn was leaving the school (which had declined) to be Dean of Norwich and a devotional writer; and Tait, now Bishop of London, again urged Temple on the trustees. This time Temple agreed to be a candidate. Matthew Arnold was not the only one to prophesy that the great days of Rugby would return, and the prophecy turned out right. When he had shocked people by walking from the station carrying his own bag, Temple reorganized a school which had been living too much on the Doctor's legend. Better arrangements were made for appointing and paying the masters, and more emphasis was placed on science and modern languages, which now had specialist teachers. With William Butterfield as architect, much more accommodation was built. The game of Rugby Football was made less barbarous. Temple forced these reforms through, and found that he had less of a battle than he had expected, for trustees and masters alike respected him, while the boys worshipped him. 'A beast, but a just beast' was the famous description given by a boy in a letter home. They hung on his every word, and told anecdotes about his crushing remarks. In their football clothes they crowded into the chapel on a Saturday afternoon to hear their headmaster prepare them for the next day's services. Parents responded almost as warmly as boys. Soon Temple had three times as many applications for places as he could accept.

Frederick Temple's share in *Essays and Reviews* was the only major mistake which he made as a headmaster. He admitted that he had underestimated the furore which the book would cause in the country, as the charge of heretical liberalism which had hung over Rugby since Arnold's time seemed to have been justified. Temple's own contribution was not heretical, or in any deep sense theological. It was simply an address to the boys which had been reworked to form a university sermon at Oxford. He had spent no more than ten hours on it. Its theme was 'The Education of the World', developing the stock comparison between the growth of an individual and the growth of mankind, and indulging in interpretations of biblical texts which did more credit to the author as a preacher than as a scholar. There were some carelessly written passages about the obedience of the law in the Old Testament being re-placed by the imitation of the example in the New, and about the imitation being replaced in its turn by an inner religion. These passages were not only echoes of Coleridge and Thomas Arnold; they were based on Frederick Temple's own experience of being liberated at Oxford from the over-simplicity of his mother's religion. William Temple was to restate the truth in them, when he delivered his Giff-ord Lecture on 'Authority and Experience.' But at the time they seemed sinister, because the orthodox placed them alongside some far more 'extreme' passages in other essays in the volume. The real worry, now as in the days of Thomas Arnold's indiscretions, was lest Rugby parents should be scared off.

When the book was attacked by the bishop who had ordained him, and apparently condemned by his patron Tait, all Temple's obstinacy was aroused. One seed of the idea of *Essays and Reviews* had been a conversation with Jowett at Kneller Hall when he had deplored the reticence of Christians in England over the intellectual challenges to the old orthodoxy; and he was not going to abandon the fight now. Another factor in his mind was that his chivalry forbade him to desert the other essayists by withdrawing his contribution in response to the clamour of the clergy or the cowardice of the bishops. He remained the friend of some of them (he often preached for Jowett at Balliol, and at the end it was he who buried Jowett). He sought to allay crit-icism by recanting his share in *Essays and Reviews* but by publishing another book, consisting of sermons exactly as he had preached them at Rugby. This did reassure parents and others. The boys needed little reassurance. 'Dear Mother', wrote a Sixth Former in response to an anxious inquiry from home, 'Temple's all right; but if he turns Mahometan, all the school will turn too.'

Although Temple generally admitted that it had been an indiscretion for a Headmaster of Rugby to get involved in a major religious controversy, he never went back on his conviction that it had been right for someone to break the conspiracy of silence; and when the storm blew over, others came to agree that Temple the churchman had not been wrecked by this solitary error on the part of Temple the schoolmaster. Partly because they had come to share a common belief in disestablishment in Ireland, Gladstone was ready to face opposition in order to promote a teacher so earnest in religion and so sensible in politics. When the Deanery of Durham fell vacant he pressed it on Temple, who refused. When the death of old Harry Phillpotts at last released the bishopric of Exeter, and Samuel Wilberforce's move to Winchester also freed Oxford, Gladstone bade Temple choose his bishopric.

Wisely he chose Devon, where he could constantly appeal to his status as a local boy who had risen by industry and self-help. The wrench of leaving Rugby was great, and a new storm broke, Soon after congratulating him on his appointment, Samuel Wilberforce joined those who urged him to withdraw his essay now. As Temple refused, Shaftesbury and Pusey joined forces to prevent the scandal to the Church. There was an attempt made to block his election by the Greater Chapter of Exeter, but the majority voted to obey the Crown. Another attempt was made to stop the legal ceremony of his 'Confirmation' as a bishop. A sister was summoned to testify whether or not he had been born in wedlock, since bastards could not then be bishops. When the day of the consecration, 21 December, arrived, Bishop Wordsworth of Lincoln entered a final protest, although Wordsworth's *protégé* Benson had defended Temple in *The Times*. Jackson of London, who presided in Tait's absence through illness, proceeded with the consecration, but in the crowded and dark Westminster Abbey Temple was white-faced. His anxiety partly excused his harshly arrogant conduct towards his successor at Rugby, a dim schoolmaster brought in by trustees who were exhausted by the Arnold tradition.

3

Three signs marked Frederick Temple's beginning as a bishop. In the middle of the Abbey service a crowd of working men entered. It was their dinner hour; they had come to pay tribute. Second, having frustrated his enemies, he at last withdrew his contribution to *Essays and Reviews*. Third, he preached at his enthronement in Exeter Cathedral a sermon which showed the worried orthodox what kind of a man had come among them. He had come, he said, to 'pour out before you all that is in my heart of devotion to you and to our common Master, our Lord God, the Son of God, Jesus Christ'.

His rule was all the more necessary because of the slackness in the diocese caused by the extreme Toryism and the long old age of Bishop Phillpotts, who had been reduced to muttering from his large palace on the outskirts of Torquay. In the event, Bishop Temple made his mark not as a liberal theologian (except through his shrewd advice to many young enquirers such as his own son William), but through the manliness of his addresses to working men on the evils of drink and through the vigour of his warnings to the clergy against neglect of duty.

Until his Rugby colleague and constant ally Benson was called to create the diocese of Truro, Temple had to travel over Cornwall as well as Devon. He enjoyed his journeys, particularly since they so often included confirmations of young people. As he watched the dull faces of the boys who knelt before him (he counted them easily, and thus discovered that some of them came to be confirmed twice), he formed a yet stronger resolve. Teachers must be trained; teachers must be sent into the parishes; and the clergy must themselves teach. He broke into the slumbers of Exeter Cathedral by insisting that its canons must work, and he established himself in a restored palace by the cathedral. He had no assistant bishop, the officials whom he appointed were his creatures, and the Diocesan Conference summoned amid talk of democracy in the Church listened to what he wanted.

In 1885, when the gentle Jackson died, the diocese of London needed the touch of an invigorating chief, and Temple was moved from Exeter. At this stage there was no theological outcry. It was not merely that the Church of England had grown somewhat more liberal under Tait. By the age of sixty-four, Temple had also changed. He had come to love more than anything else the response of simple people to his simple preaching. When in reply to Jowett's urging he had agreed to deliver Bampton Lectures at Oxford, the course had contained nothing on which heresy-hunters could fasten. What counted in these lectures – and what gradually filled St. Mary's, after a poor initial attendance – was the rugged honesty of the man. He was, indeed, rather sober and old-fashioned for Oxford. 'I am only working out to its logical conclusion what was said long ago by Bishop Butler in England and by Kant in Germany. . . . The fact is the doctrine of Evolution does not affect the substance of Paley's argument at all.' But the lectures showed that the Bishop of Exeter had continued to think about science, and to accept its teachings gladly in its proper sphere. The impact of the age of Darwin had of course made him stress that some truths were revealed only in the Bible, not in everyman's conscience or in science. But he clearly had no wish to contradict science; he speculated, for example, that the miracle of the resurrection of Christ would turn out to have been 'not a miracle, but the first instance of the working of a law till the day quite unknown, but on that last day operative on all that ever lived'. 'It is plain', he concluded, 'that the antagonism between Science and Religion arises much more from a difference of spirit and temper in the students of each than from any inherent opposition between the two.'

In London, as in Exeter, Temple concentrated on dio-cesan duties. The concentration was necessary if he was to deal with his ten thousand letters, five hundred meetings, and seventy confirmations a year, but his sense of duty made him proud of the drudgery involved. He once said:

The real student knows perfectly well, and it is the thing of great importance in practical life, that nine-tenths of all good work, whatever it maybe, is what we usually call drudgery, has a mech-anical character about it, requires nothing more than orderliness . . . Nine-tenths of all good work is labour in which those who are engaged cannot feel any conceit at all; . . . and the man of genius is distinguished from others mainly by this, that he sees, all through, what this mechanical drudgery is going to lead to . . .

Such a character repelled many of the sophisticated, and Benson noted this in his diary in 1891.

It is very, very painful to see the Lords always so unappreciative of the Bishop of London—the strongest man nearly in the House, the clearest, the highest toned, the most deeply sympathetic, the clearest in principle—yet because his voice is a little harsh, and his accent a little provincial (though of what province it is hard to say), and his figure square and his hair a little rough, and because all this sets off the idea of his independence, he is not listened to at all by these cold, kindly, worldly wise, gallant landowning powers. Some day his force and goodness *must* carry them.

The same qualities eventually carried the clergy. Their terribly earnest bishop, so overbearing and angular, could move them profoundly when he preached about the cross of Christ, or about righteousness in English life, or about the mission to the world. They knew all about his humble origins. (He had to borrow £5,000 in order to become Bishop of London, and could repay it only because his wife received a legacy.) But they revered him, and they welcomed him as Archbishop of Canterbury in 1896. Amid all the worldliness of imperial London as the Victorian age reached its sunset, Temple's integrity exerted an appeal. Here was a link with the early morning simplicity of an older England. So blind that extra large cards had to be printed showing him his words, Frederick Temple crowned Edward VII (but put the crown on back to front).

He had no general policy for the Church, for he had come to think it 'a young thing' to have a general policy; and 'Freddy, don't argue' was still his motto for particular problems, where he could either decide or keep silent. He had strong principles of morality and piety; these were what the drudgery of church life led to; and these he hammered home. He also had some liberal ideas, for example over divorce. 'The Church', he declared, 'always strongly dissuaded the innocent party from remarrying, but never forbad it.' But his liberalism was very far from being extreme. He told a disappointed General Gordon that even in order to convert Africa the Church could not allow three wives at a time. He told an equally disappointed Mr. Gladstone that Anglicanism in Wales, although a minority, was working hard and did not deserve to be disestablished. He was greeted often by working men, but he made little effort to be their champion. It was characteristic of him that during the great London Dock Strike, when he was on holiday, he returned in order to mediate between the strikers and the employers at the Mansion House alongside Cardinal Manning; but when he thought the strikers were being unreasonable (he said that they were going back on their word in the negotiations), he resumed his holiday, thus giving Manning the glory of ending the dispute. He was the constant adviser of Benson, but his was almost always practical advice; and when he went to Lambeth himself at the age of seventy-six, no one could be surprised that he took no advice.

As Primate he bothered little with affairs which he was too old to begin studying or remedying. When troublesome questions were submitted to him by the colonial bishops, the letters were left unanswered. When invited to Scotland, instead of a vision of the Churches' reunion he gave them sermons on the evils of alcohol. When invited to pronounce on ritual, he pointed to the Book of Common Prayer. The building and equipment of a palace close by the cathedral at Canterbury (as at Exeter) did interest him – and so did the renewal of the drainage and much stonework in Lambeth Palace, and the handing over the adjacent ten acres to the local authority as a playing field (a move which Randall Davidson did his best to stop). The money for the building came from the sale of Addington Park to a South African diamond merchant. As an excited undergraduate Frederick Temple had found calm, and as a depressed official in the Education Office he had found relief, in going to as many church services as he could; now as a half-blind archbishop, he delighted to attend worship in Canterbury Cathedral. He would kneel upright, explaining: 'I always do that. My mother taught me.' And there today he kneels upright in effigy, on a monument which recalls the best description of him in the prime of his manhood. He was 'granite on fire'.

4

The young William Temple once asked his father what he thought about Coleridge's speculations on the Trinity. Frederick Temple replied:

I cannot understand him; and I have never been able to feel sure that he understood himself. Nevertheless, I am obliged to confess that from seventeen to five-and-twenty I indulged largely in such speculations. But I felt all along like a swimmer who sees no shore before him after long swimming, and at last allows himself to be picked up by a ship that seems to be going his way. I do not want to check your imaginings. Go on as long as you feel that you get any good at all by doing so. But I rather fancy you will come to the same end as I came to long before you. My passing ship was S. John.

The theological story of William Temple is the story of the truth in his father's prophecy. The metaphysical speculations which he reported home were his chief interest from the time when he read the philosophers in his spare time as a schoolboy at Rugby to the day when he gave up teaching at Oxford in 1910. His later books reflected this interest. During the war he produced a book in the high metaphysical style, finishing it on the night before his wedding (*Mens Creatrix*, 1917), and while Bishop of Manchester he produced another, although this was more theological (*Christus Veritas*, 1924). As Archbishop of York he snatched intervals from his duties in order to conduct a general survey of his own philosophy and other people's in Gifford Lectures (*Nature, Man and God*, 1934).

What he did in this teaching, however, was to reduce the rhetorical conflicts of the metaphysicians to a clear order where every argument was crisply given its place and related to the Christianity of his father. The theologian Emil Brunner gently pointed out to William Temple on a post card that while he called his theology 'natural' it was in fact Christian; and the point was not unwelcome, for Temple stated his attitude quite frankly in the first of his Gifford Lectures. 'The plain and crude fact is that you can get out of philosophy just what you put into it – rearranged no doubt, set in order and rendered comprehensible; but while the machine may determine the size and shape of the emergent sausage, it cannot determine the ingredients.' In his Preface to that book, Temple acknowledged that his main conclusions were not the result of a conscious analysis of problems. 'All my decisive thinking goes on behind the scenes. . . . Often when teaching I·have found myself expressing rooted convictions which until that moment I had no notion that I held.' And the most deeply rooted of these convictions was that the truth of Christianity was beyond the reach of philosophy. 'The primary assurances of Religion are the ultimate questions of Philosophy', he noted in the second of these lectures. 'Religion finds its fullest expression in absolute surrender to the Object of its worship. But the very existence of that Object is a main theme of philosophical disputation.' It was a synthesis of worship and disputation which many of his contemporaries admired, even if (like some of those who grew up with him at Rugby and Oxford) they privately thought him a bumptious fat boy, or (like a tutor at Balliol) suspected that he sometimes thought 'that he had found a solution, when he had found a phrase'.

If Temple had done nothing more than to put the metaphysics of his Oxford into a Christian synthesis, his books might have rated a paragraph in a comprehensive history of English philosophy – but scarcely more, for the whole intellectual tradition of which he was a part and a climax collapsed during his lifetime, as he had the rare courage to acknowledge. While he was delivering his Gifford Lectures in Glasgow, Hitler came to power in Germany. The cosmic optimism of Oxford metaphysics was already under attack from a younger generation of sharper thinkers, and from Englishmen disillusioned by the 1914 war and its squalid aftermath. In the 1930s and 1940s it came to seem implausible and by 1970 it had been forgotten. The abiding impressiveness of Temple's life lay, however, in the application of an able mind, confident in its philosophical equipment, to the religious questions of the day.

He sensed this destiny when as a tutor of philosophy at Queen's College he confessed that he did not want to spend all his life lecturing in the morning and going to the Common Room in the evening. He was happy during his six years at Queen's – with ample leisure for reading; with duties which amounted to little more than expounding his views on Plato, or personality, or knowledge, or society, to young men who drank it all in; with music and friendship around him in the university; with his mother holding court in her Keble Road house. He used to say that he had to pray long for guidance when eventually a strong call came to leave Oxford. But he was an actor who wanted a larger stage: the Church of England, which he loved and was half-inclined to 'smite'. And more profoundly he was a churchman because, not content with a Platonic idealism, he wanted a word from eternity. His own masters were those who saw Christ standing as the answer. The poems of Browning moved him deeply, and he quoted them throughout his life. In sermons which he repeated on many occasions and finally revised to make his most enduring book, *Readings in St. John's Gospel* (first series 1939, second series 1940), St. John was presented as a Plato for whom the Word had become flesh.

His deliverance from a life of metaphysical swimming and cultured ease came through his inherited sense of duty towards the people's education. The Workers' Educational Association had come into being through the energy of Albert Mansbridge of the Co-operative Wholesale Society. Mansbridge visited Oxford looking for a leader for this movement, a leader who could stir the indifferent who were to be found equally among the university authorities and in the trade unions. He found this man in William Temple, who served as President of the Workers' Educational Association from 1908 to 1924. 'He invented *me*', Temple said later about Mansbridge, the explanation being that Mansbridge introduced him to the working class. He was never as familiar with everyday life as his own father had been, or as any parish priest has to be, and he often tended to believe that trade unionists would be interested in Plato or Browning; but the speaking that he did for the W.E.A., together with his visits to the Oxford Medical Mission in Bermondsey, broadened his horizons beyond the places of privilege where he lived, and were the making of the People's Archbishop of the second world war. Precisely because he was so privileged and secure in his own life, once he began to gain knowledge about the conditions of the people he felt free to conduct propaganda for the Labour movement – as his father had not felt free. (Between the father and the son was the same gap as between Henson and Gore.) Already at the Pan-Anglican Congress in 1908 the voice of William Temple was heard, urging that Christianity must be 'applied to the economic system' – the theme of the People's Archbishop in the 1940s.

The Student Christian Movement was another liberating force in William Temple's life, and also received the reward of a lifetime's loyalty as a spokesman and counsellor. The movement had grown out of the Evangelical revival and missionary enthusiasm of the 1870s, but when Temple was a young don at Oxford it was finding its way into a wider world. If the Gospel was to be received by students, and preached by them as their life's work, it must be related to intellectual questions. If it was to be spread through Asia and Africa, the social problems of Asia and Africa must be studied first. And if missionaries were to go out from Britain, there must be some study of Britain's own responsibilities as the world's leading colonial power – and of Britain's own problems as a capitalist state where there was gross inequality. With its summer conferences under canvas, its local missions, its magazine, and its eager Christian Unions in the universities, the movement then specialised in taking students and young dons from conventionally religious homes and making them think about Christianity's whole task in the modern world. William Temple was just such a man, and the General Secretary, Tissington Tatlow, soon spotted him. He became a fluent speaker on all the movement's concerns. His first book, *The Faith and Modern Thought* (1910), grew out of addresses to the London Intercollegiate Christian Union. In 1910 he attended the World Missionary Conference in Edinburgh as a steward appointed by the S.C.M., and from Edinburgh he went to Australia in order to conduct university missions.

Ever since the nursery (where he had kept a little mitre)

he had scarcely allowed any question that one day he would follow his father into the ministry of the Church of England. In 1906, however, he was brave enough to confess to Francis Paget, Bishop of Oxford: 'I am inclined, very tentatively, to accept the doctrine of the Virgin Birth, and with rather more confidence, that of the Bodily Resurrection of our Lord.' Paget, who shared the opinion of his successor Gore that confidence in both doctrines was essential as a priest, replied that he could not take the responsibility of ordaining him. Oxford theologians both Broad (Streeter and Rashdall) and High (Scott Holland and Gore) continued to advise Temple about his lingering doubts, and Randall Davidson refused to regard Paget's refusal as final. After a long talk with Temple in 1908, the Archbishop felt able to tell Bishop Paget that 'I myself regard him as being, *in all essential particulars*, an orthodox believer both in the Virgin Birth of Our Blessed Lord and in his Resurrection'; and he offered to ordain him. Davidson explained to Paget that Temple

has been definitely sharing in Christian and Evangelistic work (both in connection with the Student Christian Movement and otherwise) and he has shewn me, beyond question, that his whole attitude towards the Faith has undergone a change or a 'deepening', and that *credal* things possess now a reality for him which they did not, to anything like the same degree, possess before.

In 1909 William Temple was made a deacon, and in 1910 a priest, in Canterbury Cathedral. Some five years later, during a symphony concert in London, he experienced absolute certainty about the Virgin Birth. Already in *The Faith and Modern Thought* he had declared that reason and experience demanded belief; 'the whole creed is the only hypothesis that meets the facts'. Henceforth, his philosophy was tied securely within the framework of the Church's orthodoxy, and he never regretted his abandonment of individualist and intellectualist habits of mind. He had found the real world – indeed, he had found himself – by belonging to the society around him, and in particular to the Church; and with his whole heart he rejected the position of Descartes, 'I think, therefore I am'. 'If I were asked what was the most disastrous moment in the history of Europe', he declared as Gifford Lecturer, 'I should be strongly tempted to answer that it was the period of leisure when Rene Descartes, having no claims to meet, remained for a whole day "shut up alone in a stove".' That was the day of *je pense, donc je suis.* The basis of his own thought was shown in *Christus Veritas:* 'the self is capable of complete satisfaction in proportion as it is left outside the field of its own attention.' To this sentence on page 29, Temple added a footnote: 'In other words, joy is the fruit of humility.'

5

In a speech to the Oxford Union defending the Liberals' Education Bill of 1906, William Temple had stated his adherence to the tradition of Arnold Tait and his repudiation of the 'denominational ideal' championed by Gore; the National Church was 'the whole people of England in its religious capacity'. The first post that he accepted as a clergyman was accordingly a public school headmastership. Since Rugby was not vacant, he became headmaster of Repton, with ideas about reforming the public school system. But he found that he was not his father; he simply could not get interested enough in the problems of boys. He preached to them and he talked to them about the Greeks, but he soon knew that he would never make a good schoolmaster.

When he contributed to a volume of theological essays called *Foundations*, his Oxford friend Ronald Knox wrote about him:

> A man so broad, to some he seem'd to be
> Not one, but all Mankind in Effigy:
> Who, brisk in Term, a Whirlwind in the Long,
> Did everything by turns, and nothing wrong,
> Bill'd at each Lecture-hall from Thames to Tyne
> As Thinker, Usher, Statesman or Divine.

And when Ronald Knox wrote criticism which was intended to be more serious (a book called *Some Loose Stones*), accusing the contributors to *Foundations* of being obsessed with the question how much of orthodox Christianity a modern 'Jones' could be persuaded to swallow, William Temple gaily replied: 'I am Jones himself, asking what there is to eat.' However, he also made it plain to Knox that, like his father before him, he was more orthodox than those pages in the book which had given most offence, and like his father he kept criticism out of the school sermons which he published. Clearly the headmastership had been a false move, but what was he to do?

After two years at Repton he nearly accepted a post as a missionary in India, as Principal of St. John's College, Agra, only to find out that Davidson thought his contacts with the mysterious world of Labour in England too valuable for it to be right for him to leave the country. He did accept Henson's post at Westminster, only to find that the offer had to be withdrawn since he had not been ordained long enough to satisfy the Abbey's statutes. This negotiation about St. Margaret's, Westminster, was public knowledge, and in 1914 everyone was relieved when a London pulpit suited to his gifts was offered to him, as Rector of St. James's, Piccadilly.

It was in the pulpit of St. James's that he worked out his exposition of St. John. His educated congregation wanted deep preaching, not a superficial commentary on the war news as supplied by too many other clergy. Temple gave them a Christ who was the incarnation of the love of God in a world of selfishness and tragedy. He presented an attractive Jesus, not a mere symbol in a Catholic or Evangelical scheme, yet the presentation was never sentimental; when his mother died on Good Friday 1915, he kept the news secret until after he had finished preaching about the death of Jesus. He brushed aside critical questions to concentrate on this spiritual meaning of the text. And so he found, for himself and others, a centre which was affirmed when they sang in S. S. Wesley's anthem at his consecration as a bishop in York Minster, and when they inscribed on his grave in the cloister at Canterbury, the text: *Thou wilt keep him in perfect peace whose mind is stayed on Thee.*

When the war broke out so soon after Temple's move to Piccadilly in 1914, it created a crisis for England – and this was the beginning of the influence which he exercised over the mind of the nation during the next thirty years. He used his London church as a base for prolific consultation, speaking, and journalism. He became editor of the recently founded church newspaper, the *Challenge*, urging social and ecclesiastical reform. He became a secretary of the National Mission of Repentance and Hope, and supervised the production of its extensive literature. He was the youngest member of the Archbishop's Commission on Church and State; and when Dick Sheppard of St. Martin-in-the-Fields wanted a 'ginger group' to press for self-government and a radical renewal in the Church, he became chairman of the Life and Liberty Movement. It had the slogan: 'The rising tide of Life within the Church demands Liberty.' While in his mid-thirties he was thus a force of inspiration to the Church of England, and among church leaders he had by now a unique appeal to the intelligent young.

A few, such as Henson, resented this easy success, but during 1917 Temple disarmed jealousy by a brave act. Little more than a year after marrying Frances Anson, he resigned from St. James's. The church brought him a regular congregation which he had grown to love, the architecture of Sir Christopher Wren, a rectory in the heart of the capital, and an income over £2,000 a year. He exchanged all this for a salary of £700, in order to give his whole energy to itinerent propaganda work on behalf of the Life and Liberty Movement, despite the scepticism of Archbishop Davidson and the coolness of the Establishment generally. For William Temple and his young wife, the decision sacrificed comfort and won respect.

The Church Assembly which emerged from the propaganda disappointed idealists such as Temple and Sheppard. The new Parochial Church Councils listened not to the rushing wind of the Spirit but to comparatively minor matters, and no really effective steps were taken in Temple's lifetime to rationalize the deployment of the clergy, to equalize their payments, to reform canon law, or to revise the Prayer Book officially. But the Church of England did acquire an instrument of reform, however irresolute the hands might be which wielded it. And with the Church Assembly it gained one other asset: the knowledge that its best hopes were stored in the capacious figure of William Temple.

How was he to lead the advance? He was supplied with a home and pulpit at Westminster Abbey as a canon in 1919, and early in 1922 was consecrated Bishop of Manchester (with Dick Sheppard as preacher). Edmund Knox, the last bishop, had been an Evangelical martinet, and the leading laymen were stolidly Conservative. The diocese needed to be divided by the creation of a separate diocese of Blackburn (which was done in 1927) – and even after that, it was still the second largest in England. But such problems were conquered.

In April 1924 he presided over the conference at Birmingham where 1,500 delegates were harangued by Gore and others about the social teachings of Christianity. This 'Conference on Christian Politics, Economics and Citizenship' was the high-water mark of the wartime and post-war reforming tide. No conference in English history had been more thoroughly prepared. After a nation-wide discussion and a careful analysis of questionnaires, twelve volumes were produced in connexion with it, advocating many of the reforms which began to be put into effect twenty-one years later. There were those who regarded 'Copec' as a peak moment of English religion, before disillusionment in society brought a return to ecclesiastical obsessions and to doctrinal rigidity. And there were those who lamented that its oratory was never followed up in a long-term, large-scale organization which might have been a Life and Liberty Movement for the English nation, or at least an adult version of the Student Christian Movement. Instead, the formulation of a moral and social theology was left to the small Anglo-Catholic 'Christendom' group, which threw up some provocative ideas but suffered under the two handicaps of nostalgia for the Middle Ages and ignorance of economics.

Looking back, some have blamed William Temple for not leading the Anglican Establishment more boldly into Socialism, or for not working out more precisely what

Christian Socialism involved. Such a verdict, however, would not do justice to the historical situation in which Temple found himself. The Church was still for the most part deeply conservative in theology or in prejudice, in organization or in the lack of it, in politics or in the belief that religion should not get mixed up with the problems of society; and the fat and jolly William Temple owed his platforms to his basic conformity with this Establishment. (Even the leadership of Life and Liberty had not been an exodus into the desert.) Rejecting the intuition of Henson that the disasters of Prayer Book revision showed that a change in the relations of Church and State was essential to the Church's self-respect, Temple announced that the votes of the House of Commons had been the will of God.

On the other hand, while happily at work within the Anglican Establishment, Temple was by the standards of his time remarkably courageous and prophetic. It was a dismal time: the England of Ramsay MacDonald and Stanley Baldwin. Successive governments were unable to deal with economic slumps or with the dictators who had arisen in response to the even greater problems of unemployment in other countries. In the Church of England, Davidson and Lang drifted on. Temple was not able to arouse in the public, or perhaps in himself, any conviction that this stagnation could be cured quickly. The monthly magazine, *The Pilgrim: A Review of Christian Politics and Religion*, published by Longmans during seven years from 1920 as a vehicle for Temple and his friends, never paid its way and had to be abandoned, as the weekly *Challenge* had been. He did what he believed he could do; although he was ambitious in the sense of believing that a leader's role in great affairs was his natural lot, he spoke his mind with little thought about possible damage to his career, with the result that his life was unstained by worldliness or intrigue and even his critics who were irritated by his effortless superiority and tendency to omniscience, or by his personal popularity, admitted his integrity. From 1918 to 1925 he was a card-carrying member of the Labour Party – which was in the eyes of the Anglican Establishment an act of courage. (He resigned over Labour's foreign policy.) He constantly preached civic responsibility in industrial Lancashire where his pastoral duties lay, and although he was out of England, being treated for gout, at the time of the General Strike, with some other churchmen he attempted – rather amateurishly, he later admitted – to mediate between the owners, the miners, and the Government in the Coal Stoppage which followed. This activity in relation to working-class politics revived the tradition of Westcott and Gore, whom Temple always had in mind. Davidson suspected that it contributed to the unpopularity of the bishops' Prayer Book with the politicians; and the indignant Baldwin asked how the bishops would feel if the industrialists proposed to revise the Athanasian Creed. Such pleas to confine himself to ecclesiastical duties left Temple unmoved. When he was enthroned in Manchester Cathedral, he expressed the tone of his ministry in a sermon. It was an echo of another enthronement sermon: his father's in Exeter Cathedral in 1869.

I come as a learner, with no policy to advocate, no plan already formed to follow. But I come with one burning drive; it is that in all our activities, sacred and secular, ecclesiastical and social, we should help each other to fix our eyes on Jesus ... Pray for me chiefly that I may never let go of the unseen hand of the Lord Jesus and may live in daily fellowship with him.

6

'The Way of Renewal' was the title of a campaign for Bible study and prayer in groups, launched by the new leaders of the Church of England after Randall Davidson's resignation. Looking back, we can see that it would have been more renewing for the Church of England had William Temple been made Archbishop of Canterbury at the age of forty-seven. But it seemed impossible to promote anyone over the head of Cosmo Lang, who had been made Archbishop of York in the year when William Temple had been ordained a priest.

Lang, whose ambition came out of the England of Curzon and F. E. Smith, turned out to be the ecclesiastical equivalent of MacDonald or Baldwin. When he got ecclesiastical power, he did not know what to do with it. Part of the problem was that he felt seriously ill immediately after his move, but essentially his was the tragedy of the *arriviste* who arrived. As he signed on real letters the 'Cosmo Cantuar:' which he had practised while still a vicar, he sighed to his chaplain: 'What's the use, when it's all dust and ashes?' It was a characteristic piece of self-dramatisation by a man who took care to provide for his biographer both notes of guidance and also plenty of romantic material. He loved to act his part against the background of the palaces and gardens at Bishopthorpe and Lambeth, and in ecclesiastical pageants in York Minster or Canterbury Cathedral, while Temple was embarrassed by the splendour of the Bishopthorpe gardens and became the first Archbishop of Canterbury to open his own front door. When on holiday Lang would spend hours alone in prayer – and would grow introspective, recording his self-condemnation on paper. He had also put on paper while a schoolboy an imaginary *Who's Who* entry showing himself as Earl of Norham, Prime Minister, and the father of eight (all to his biographer's delight). In real life Lang the bachelor, the Scot who grew apart from his family, craved the affection of his chaplains and the company of England's grandees; Temple, although childless, was deeply happy as a son and husband, and does not seem to have needed the applause he so often received.

In 1924, the year of Temple's presidency over Copec, a number of friends arranged that a portrait of Lang by Sir William Orpen should be painted to hang at Bishopthorpe. 'They say in that portrait I look proud, prelatical and pompous', Lang remarked in Henson's hearing. Henson interjected: 'And may I ask Your Grace to which of those epithets Your Grace takes exception?' Yet Lang was, like Henson himself, more than a careerist. Archbishop Söderblom of Sweden, when shown the Orpen portrait, said: 'That is what the Devil meant him to be, but thanks be to God it is not so.' Orpen himself, when the Archbishop had been sitting for him, made the most profound of this series of remarks. 'I see seven archbishops. Which of them am I to paint?'

The meteoric rise of Cosmo Lang can be recounted briefly, since in the event it was less momentous for the Church of England than seemed likely at the time. He was the son and grandson of ministers of the Church of Scotland. Born in 1864, he was brought up in Glasgow. As a student at that university he was intoxicated by the metaphysics of Edward Caird, then a professor in Glasgow before becoming Master of Balliol. Walking in the park one day he shouted: 'The Universe is one and its Unity and Ultimate Reality is God!' (Could there be a better summary of the philosophy of William Temple?) In the year of Archbishop Tait's death, he entered Balliol. He flourished in the Balliol atmosphere of hard study and high debate, and after a period of uncertainty, when he struggled to be a barrister without leaving his heart in it, he became a Fellow of All Souls two years after Henson. Next year the thought came to him inescapably 'After all, why shouldn't *you* be ordained?'

Like Tait and Davidson, this young Scot chose the Church of England and was confirmed. Like Henson, he was ordained in the parish church at Cuddesdon and worked among the poor (as a curate in Leeds, having refused an invitation to be Henson's curate). After returning to Oxford for a short spell as Dean of Divinity at Magdalen and Vicar of St. Mary's, he became Vicar of Portsea at the age of thirty-one. He was at the head of fourteen or more curates, all living celibately in the vicarage and 'working' an artisan parish of about 40,000. He became an eloquent preacher, a tireless parish priest (when not away), a favourite of Queen Victoria at nearby Osborne – another young Samuel Wilberforce. In 1901 Winnington-Ingram, who had just become Bishop of London, arranged that Lang should follow him as Bishop of Stepney. He soon acquired a national reputation as the leader of the Church of England Men's Society. He was also a canon of St. Paul's; the aged Dean Gregory, when installing him, was under the impression that he was Charles Gore. His vision of the Church was indeed like Gore's but more than any of the great churchmen just mentioned he had a flair for the personal contact, for the common touch without losing dignity, for an appeal to the imagination. Much depended on his presence and voice, but something of his magnetism is preserved in his books. We have the novel about the Jacobite rebels in the heather, *The Young Clanroy*, based on stories told to the choristers at Magdalen; we have the published sermons about the miracles and parables of Jesus; we have the lectures at Cambridge on pastoral work. As he moved from scenes of historic beauty to scenes of modern poverty, he could urge the privileged to stoop with him and the poor to rise with him. For others as for himself, life could be the greatest romance.

He was made Archbishop of York at the age of forty-four. Asquith, the Prime Minister, believed that the Church of England deserved young and decisive leadership; and Davidson wanted a fellow-archbishop who would be more actively co-operative than Maclagan, who had just retired from York at the age of eighty-three. Lang was an ambassador of the High Anglican ethos into the coldly Low province in the North: the ethos of a warm humanity in service based on a dignified beauty in worship. In the diocese and the province alike, he made his mark as a pastor. But at the national level he was far less decisive, because there policy was shaped by the caution of Davidson. For nineteen years Lang played second fiddle to his fellow-Scot at Lambeth.

He played that instrument very gracefully; his was the command of English, and his was the skill as the chairman of the relevant committee, that made the Lambeth Appeal of 1920 so eloquent a plea for reunion. But the oratory did not present a thought-out policy of his own to seize the new opportunities in Church and State. In the conversation with the Free Churches after that Appeal, Lang caused excitement by acknowledging their nature as 'ministers of Christ's Word and Sacraments within the Universal Church of Christ which is His Body'. But, shrewdly, he had not said that they were ministries *of* the Universal Church – and, when the Free Churchmen pressed him, he showed no enthusiasm to march on to a reconciliation. He also did little to identify the Church of England with the poor, although his maiden speech in the House of Lords was a plea that the peers should pass the People's Budget of the Liberals.

Even in a body so conservative as the Church of England, Lang was beginning to seem like a figure out of the past which he could recount so well. The two most dramatic crises in his life as an archbishop brought him great unpopularity. In 1914, after this first experience of public abuse, most of his hair fell out and the remainder went white, so that he had to try wearing a wig until it got caught in a chandelier. The trouble arose out of a speech in York. Lang remembered how the Kaiser and Edward VII had knelt side by side at the bier of Queen Victoria, and he now declared that he resented 'coarse and vulgar' attacks on the Kaiser. 'A personal memory of the Emperor, very sacred to him,' made him feel that the Kaiser had got involved in the war 'not without great reluctance'. The British public responded to Lang with even coarser and more vulgar comments. Lang did not really learn his lesson, for when George V died in 1935 the Archbishop again came forward with an unctuous description of the deathbed.

In the abdication crisis of 1936, there was a similarly disastrous flight of eloquence. During the drama caused by the determination of Queen Victoria's eldest grandson to marry a lady with two husbands still living in the United States, Lang as Archbishop of Canterbury did little more than any man would have felt compelled to do if in the position of chief pastor of the Church of England in the 1930s; for Edward VIII was to be crowned and anointed in Westminster Abbey as King and Supreme Governor of the Church, at a time when that Church was doing its utmost to discourage remarriage after divorce. Lang made the Church's official attitude clear if it was ever in doubt, although he was never forced to declare what he would have done had the King insisted on Mrs. Simpson being crowned as Queen. However, the decisive voice raised against the King's marriage was not the Archbishop's; it was the British public's and Commonwealth's – or at least, it was public opinion as interpreted by Stanley Baldwin.

When Edward had abdicated and gone into exile, Lang

made a broadcast, lamenting this 'craving for private happiness'.

Strange and sad it must be that for such a motive, however strongly it pressed upon his heart, he should have disappointed hopes so high and abandoned a trust so great. Even more strange and sad it is that he should have sought his happiness in a manner inconsistent with the Christian principles of marriage, and within a social circle whose standards and ways of life are alien to all the best instincts and traditions of his people ... How can we forget the high hopes and promise of his youth; his most genuine care for the poor, the suffering, the unemployed; his years of eager service both at home and across the seas? It is the remembrance of these things that wrings from our hearts the cry—'The pity of it, O, the pity of it!' To the infinite mercy and the protecting care of God we commit him now, wherever he may be.

Baldwin congratulated Lang on this sermon: 'it was the voice of Christian England.' Its sentiments were those of many, including Edward's mother Queen Mary. Yet once again Lang's rhetoric had brought him to a fall. Many of those who believed that 'the King must go' believed also that the Archbishop should have exercised more restraint when the King had gone. Perhaps Lang should have confined himself to William Temple's robust comment: 'It has happened to many a man before now to find himself beginning to fall in love with another man's wife.'

Unlike William Temple, Cosmo Lang did not have the moral stature needed to carry off a prophetic rebuke. His whole style of life made it easy for the friends of Edward VIII to express an angry contempt for his snobbery and irrelevance to the times. Such men would, no doubt, have disliked any archbishop. But there were others, more sympathetic, who more sadly remembered the high hopes of his early years, his genuine care for the poor, his eager service, and who regretted that as an archbishop from 1909 to 1942 he found his happiness within an aristocratic circle increasingly alien from the life of the English people. And such people looked away from William Cosmo Gordon Lang (as he had been christened – but the William was too plebeian for use) to William Temple.

## 7

As a leader in the movement for Christian reunion, William Temple was in himself the most solid sequel to the 1920 Lambeth Conference's 'Appeal to All Christian People'. A united Church had then been glimpsed as essential to the service of the Kingdom of God, and glowing words had come from Lang's pen:

The vision which rises before us is that of a Church genuinely Catholic, loyal to all Truth, and gathering into its fellowship all 'who profess and call themselves Christians', within whose visible unity all the treasures of faith and order, bequeathed as a heritage by the past to the present shall be possessed in common, and made serviceable to the whole Body of Christ . . . The spiritual leadership of the Catholic Church in the days to come, for which the world is manifestly waiting, depends upon the readiness with which each group is prepared to make sacrifices for the sake of a common fellowship, a common ministry, and a common service to the world.

When the Lambeth Conference met again in 1930, it had to confess that no memorable advance had been made in the conversations with the Free Churches of England. At the conference itself William Temple, who was in charge of the committee on reunion, made one of his rare mistakes by leaving an impression of coldness on the Free Church visitors, but (as the Free Church leaders were the first to acknowledge when Temple later apologized) the lack of warmth in the Anglican atmosphere was far from being his fault. The early 1930s were a time when it was possible to hope that the Victorian Establishment, imperial or ecclesiastical, would last for a while longer; that decade saw the building of new Anglican cathedrals in Delhi and Cairo. And while most churchgoers probably shared the simple religion of the King-Emperor, George V, among the clergy these years were the heyday of Anglo-Catholicism. The influence of Keble, or Gore, and of many other spiritual teachers had won the hearts of many. The High Church party was confident during Lang's time at Lambeth; and when Temple feared in the 1940s that he was getting out of touch with the younger generation of theologians, it was to Anglo-Catholics that he turned.

Men who felt that a century after its beginning the Oxford Movement was triumphant were in no mood to make concessions to the Free Churches, which after their movement of political power in 1906 were now visibly in decline as religious forces in the nation. Conversations with the Eastern Orthodox churches, designed to develop the good will which Davidson had secured, seemed more important. Even more to the liking of the Anglo-Catholics was the 'Concordat of Bonn' negotiated in 1932 between Anglican representatives and the small Old Catholic body which had broken away from the Roman Catholic Church on the Continent. By this agreement, the Anglicans and Old Catholics established intercommunion without doctrinal or organizational uniformity. Not a single Anglican practice had to be sacrificed. It was otherwise in South India.

The prospect of reunion in South India – a scheme involving four Anglican dioceses, the Methodists, and an existing merger of Congregationalists and Presbyterians – was less congenial to Anglo-Catholic consciences, for it was the first attempt to bridge the gap between episcopal and non-episcopal churches and it did not include any act of reconciliation which might be interpreted as episcopal ordination. The places of the old creeds and of confirmation also seemed insecure. The United Church was, however, to have bishops in the apostolic succession, and gradually these were to ordain new presbyters in South India. (The question of episcopal ordination for incoming missionaries was left unresolved.) It was also relevant that South India was a long way abroad, and that the Anglicans there, although wishing to go forward to reunion with the blessing of the Lambeth Conference, did not insist that the United Church should be reckoned a part of the Anglican Communion. Thus Anglican concessions in the scheme did not seem to jeopardize any essential Anglican principle, or to be precedents for areas where Anglicanism formed a more enthusiastic denomination.

The South India story had gathered momentum at the Tranquebar conference of Indian Christians in 1919, under the saintly Bishop Azariah. 'We face together the titanic task of the winning of India for Christ – one fifth of the human race. Yet confronted by such an overwhelming responsibility, we find ourselves rendered weak by our un-happy divisions, divisions which we did not create and which we do not desire to perpetuate.' The spirit behind that manifesto had appealed to some High Anglicans, among them E. J. Palmer, an Oxford don who had become Bishop of Bombay in 1908 (when Gore had withdrawn). Palmer saw in the reunion movement an opportunity to renew the Church, to make it more truly Catholic, not by bargaining but by self-sacrifice and resurrection, not by making concessions but by uniting convictions, not by human diplomacy but by praying to be told a plan which already existed in the mind of God. It was a conception of Catholicity far more dynamic than the look backwards of a Newman or a Benson (or of C. H. Turner, the Oxford theologian who continued the appeal to Cyprian in the 1920s), yet it was plainly not individualism or congregation-alism. As the title of his book put it: *The Great Church Awakes*. 'Jimmy' Palmer greatly influenced the Lambeth Conference of 1920; and the Lambeth Conference of 1930 felt able to offer a guarded blessing to the 1929 scheme for a Church of South India. The bishops, however, then added notes of caution which were among the factors postponing the consummation of the reunion until 1947. Nor did they commit themselves to the precise terms of any future Anglican relationship with the United Church – a subject which caused much heart-burning at the next Lambeth Conference.

The crisis for Temple came in 1943, when the Anglicans in India had asked for further advice about the scheme. Would the Church of England break off communion with them if they allowed four of their dioceses to enter the Church of South India, thus condoning what the Anglo-Catholic organization in England, the Church Union, had roundly called 'an act of schism'? Temple led the English bishops in reassuring Anglican India on this point. Would the Church of England refuse to be in communion with the Church of South India because the latter would include some presbyters without episcopal ordination? Temple replied in terms which were not entirely clear; intercommunion would exist but would not be unrestricted. This was a departure from the normal Anglican line, to which Temple had usually adhered, that intercommunion should be regarded as the fruit of a unity established on a clearly episcopal basis. Temple had taken that line because he saw how intercommunion between the Free Churches had not led them to a fuller union; it seemed that the very pain of not being able to receive the Lord's Supper together might be needed as a spur to organic unity. Indeed, so sure was Temple about the place of episcopacy in reunion that he was pleased when the Anglicans in South India revived the idea of a service to reconcile the episcopal and non-episcopal ministries at the inauguration of the proposed Church. However, this idea had been abandoned in 1929 because High Churchmen such as Lang had objected to its ambiguity – and it was now abandoned again, this time because non-Anglicans suspected that it concealed a demand for episcopal ordination. So Temple and the Church of South India's other Anglican supporters had to envisage some intercommunion with a Church not wholly episcopalian.

Behind the confusion in this reply lay much pressure on Temple from Anglo-Catholic quarters, specially from the superiors of the religious orders. T. S. Eliot wrote a pamphlet, *Reunion by Destruction*, and there were many threats of an exodus from the Church of England – precisely what Davidson had feared. And Temple in the midst of the war was (like the Davidson whom he had goaded into Life and Liberty) preoccupied and tired. One thing he was determined to avoid: a full-dress debate by the English Convocations. When asked to arrange this by Anglo-Catholics who wished to probe the scheme in great theological detail, he replied that the discussion at the Lambeth Conference in 1930 had been enough to assist the English bishops in replying to the limited requests for practical advice which reached them from their brethren in South India. He was thus willing to face criticism in order to help the scheme through – but his tactics, by depriving the clergy of their

333

debate, stored up bitterness which exploded when the reunion had come in 1947, still without a full English investigation. When the Lambeth Conference met in 1948, 134 of the bishops of the Anglican Communion voted that the bishops, presbyters, and deacons of the Church of South India were bishops, priests, and deacons of the Church of God; but 94 voted against, including Garbett of York. About a hundred bishops abstained or were absent when the vote was taken. The same hesitation marked the resolutions of the Convocations of the clergy in England, and when some of the bishops sponsored an appeal for financial help to the Church of South India, nine of the diocesan bishops refused to sign it. By then Temple was dead, but he would probably have agreed with Bishop Sundkler, the historian of the protracted negotiations in South India, that the real tragedy was the delay. The delay robbed the United Church of the presence of most of those who had conceived the vision. It was inflicted largely by English, rather than by Indian, hesitations.

The South India scheme was by no means the only possible pattern of reunion. Another method, more congenial to many Anglo-Catholics, was to integrate the ministries of the uniting churches from the beginning by a service of reconciliation. Since this service would include the laying on of hands with prayer, it could be interpreted as episcopal ordination, and the hope was held that it would result in a church less untidy than South India. (This alternative was blessed by the Lambeth Conference in 1948, 1958, and 1968 for possible use in North India and Ceylon – and in England itself, for the projected reunion with the Methodist Church.) Gradually, as the hesitations which had surrounded and delayed the birth of the Church of South India were eclipsed by admiration for its worship and work, it was seen that, whether or not the South Indian method was suitable for imitation elsewhere, a similar courage in perseverance to the end was needed in all who accepted the spiritual authority of the ecumenical movement.

This movement, which became the most impressive aspect of twentieth-century Christianity, insisted that Christians must unite, and before that must meet. It was motivated by something very like Thomas Arnold's concern for change in the Church in order to fit the Church better to meet the reckless masses. But it did not make Arnold's mistake of underestimating theology; instead, it went along Newman's path into the whole history of Christendom, back to the apostolic unity, and along Maurice's road into the unifying confession of a faith in Christ as King. In the 1920s it attracted theologians such as Gore into its discussions of faith and order in the divided churches and by the 1930s it was ready to receive a focus by the formation of a World Council of Churches. It then owed much to William Temple who had shown his ability to master an international and interdenominational assembly at the Faith and Order Conference in Lausanne in 1927. To the prestige which the leaders of the Church of England then commanded in the Christian world, Temple added his own rare equipment, and he fell into place as the ecumenical movement's most prominent personality.

The institutional problems to be solved under Temple's guidance before a World Council of Churches could be built resulted from the history of the ecumenical movement's inspiration. The movement had attracted support mainly from students and many others interested in the 'Life and Work' angle and therefore inclined to rest content with co-operation. Temple's heart was in theology, and he chaired the Edinburgh 1937 World Conference on Faith and Order which reached an impressive degree of theological unity; at the 'World Conference on Church, Community, and State' held in Oxford immediately before the Edinburgh meeting, he had been almost silent. He was therefore trusted even by those who were worried by warnings, such as those issued by Bishop Headlam of Gloucester, to the effect that 'Faith and Order' was in danger of being swallowed up by a merely social Gospel. Yet Temple's days as Bishop of Manchester had made his social concern widely known, his political views were a great deal more acceptable than Headlam's, and during the discussions of the 1930s he was able to unite the two streams, theoretical and practical, in his flood of eloquence.

One problem Temple could not solve: the wish of the

missionaries to stay outside the churches' control, in the International Missionary Council. This hesitation was inevitable, for the Gospel of many of the missionaries was markedly simpler than the theology of, say, the Eastern Orthodox Churches. But the separation was never complete. For example, J. H. Oldham, Temple's close friend and collaborator, had been the brain behind the World Missionary Conference at Jerusalem in 1924 – and went on to run the Oxford Conference thirteen years later, when the main theme was the neopaganism of the European totalitarians. And although the stream which had started from the World Missionary Conference at Edinburgh in 1910 was not brought fully into the World Council of Churches until 1961, the world war, as interpreted by Temple, increased the spiritual unity in this ecumenical movement. When Temple was enthroned at Canterbury in 1942 the most quoted passage in his sermon referred to the ecumenical movement as 'the great new fact of our era'. He had two developments in mind: the missionary expansion which had made Christianity global, and the impetus to unity in the Christian mission which had remained in this world-wide fellowship through the war. The coming of the war frustrated the plan to constitute the World Council of Churches under Temple's chairmanship, but when the council was formed at Amsterdam in 1948 all who knew about its background agreed that he had played as large a role as any man in the expression and embodiment of its spirit – social, theological, and missionary.

Temple did live to see the creation of the British Council of Churches, in 1942. There had been many forms of co-operation between the Churches before this date, and in recent years many of them had been under Temple's inspiration, but the council now provided a single forum. As he declared at the council's inauguration in St. Paul's Cathedral: 'In days like these, when the basic principles of Christianity are widely challenged and in many quarters expressly repudiated, the primary need is for clear and united testimony to Christianity itself.'

8

As a leader of the Church of England, William Temple was at his best when testifying to his vision of God in Christ – as in his Mission to Oxford in 1931, when in Newman's old pulpit he repeated and excelled the spiritual triumph of his father's Bampton Lectures in the same place. 1931 was a year when St. Mary's church, full of fading memories, seemed a museum to many in Oxford. A historian in the college next door (E. L. Woodward) had just published these words about that church:

I know of few buildings where there is more of the bitterness which chills the heart ... The building is empty as a nursery when the children have left their home ... Now one who reads the Christian Fathers must climb some curious raised beach, dry it matters not how many years, and find only the fossils, the silt, the debris of old fangs: the dust of the beginnings of life ... Week in, week out, the flame grows fainter, the ashes of the fire are raked and re-raked.

But in 1931 a large and young congregation in St. Mary's, after listening to William Temple, whispered the old words (for Temple had pointed out that hearty singing might be insincere):

> Were the whole realm of nature mine,
>   That were an offering far too small;
> Love so amazing, so divine,
>   Demands my soul, my life, my all.

That was the spirit in which he took over the chairmanship of the Archbishops' Commission on Doctrine in 1925, and presided over its somewhat leisurely work; and what unity there was in the commission's report in 1938 derived in no small measure from his ability to set the disagreements of the theological parties in the context of that hymn. The report marked the failure of attempts such as Gore's to establish a wider uniformity of doctrine, but did so without too much worry that the Gospel itself was in peril. 'There are some among us who hold that a full belief in the historical Incarnation is more consistent with the supposition

337

that our Lord's birth took place under the normal conditions of human generation. . . . The majority of the Commission are agreed . . . that the tomb was empty because the Lord had risen.' So the great battles of Modernism had their echoes. But the positive agreements which had emerged about the nature of the scriptures and the sacraments, and the eirenic spirit of the whole report even when it failed to agree about miracles, were more important than these echoes. In his Introduction Temple stressed the agreements and their basis. He could fairly claim that 'it has always been our desire to set forth the truth of the Everlasting Gospel unchanged in substance'; and he could frankly confess that the years since Davidson's appointment of the commission had been years in which the gift of this Gospel of God to sinners had come to be prized more highly than the gift of diversity in Anglican theology. He wrote:

As I review in thought the result of our fourteen years of labour, I am conscious of a certain transition of interest in our minds, as in the minds of theologians all over the world. We were appointed at a time when theologians were engaged in taking up the prosecution of the the task which the war had compelled them to lay aside. Their problems were still predominantly set by the interests of 'pre-war' thought. In our country the influence of Westcott reinforced by that of the *Lux Mundi* school had led to the development of a theology of the Incarnation rather than a theology of Redemption . . . A theology of the Incarnation tends to be a Christocentric metaphysic. And in all ages there is need for the fresh elaboration of such a scheme of thought or map of life as seen in the light of the revelation of Christ. A theology of Redemption (though of course Redemption has its great place in the former) tends rather to sound the prophetic note; it is more ready to admit that much in this evil world is irrational and strictly unintelligible; and it looks to the coming of the Kingdom as a necessary preliminary to the full comprehension of much that now is. If the security of the nineteenth century, already shattered in Europe, finally crumbles away in our country, we shall be pressed more and more towards a theology of Redemption. In this we shall be coming closer to the New Testament.

'If we began our work again to-day', Temple wrote in this Introduction, 'its perspectives would be different. But it is not our function to pioneer.' It was no longer *his*

338

function; he felt that he had said what he had to say in philosophical theology, and that a new generation must take up the task in the new conditions. But it was a sign of the greatness of his spirit that at York and Canterbury he scarcely ever failed in sympathy with the struggles of younger theologians, however uncongenial their austerity might be. He backed the appointment as the first General Secretary of the emerging World Council of Churches of a young Dutch theologian whose master was the anti-liberal Karl Barth; and he enthusiastically commended (as supplying 'the principles of missionary policy for our generation') a book which was another Dutch and Barthian onslaught against the recognition of non-Christian religions advocated at the Jerusalem Conference of 1928.

He continued to read and to think theology because he enjoyed it. He was after all, a philosopher, or rather a philosophically minded preacher, and not a practical economist or politician. It was not that he was incapable of performing his duty to handle some secular details. On the contrary, his leadership of the study of unemployment which produced a large book on *Men without Work* (1938) was an outstanding example of ecclesiastical sponsorship for useful research and detailed recommendations in response to an urgent challenge in society. When the problem of unemployment was studied closely in six areas, he could use investigators who included many churchmen already interested and active in this concern, and when the development of 'occupational centres' for the instruction of the unemployed was encouraged by these findings, this work also involved many who were already associated with Temple either in church work or in the Worker's Educational Association. As the war approached and raged, J. H. Oldham, assisted by Eleanora Iredale, published the *Christian News-Letter* in order to spread the idea of experts taking counsel together about society's problems in the light of the Christian Gospel. Himself a layman, Oldham envisaged a network of small groups covering the country around the Christian Frontier Council in London. That plan never succeeded fully, partly owing to the failure of the Churches to release resources for the service of such groups;

but Temple as Archbishop of Canterbury set an example to other churchmen by his eagerness to listen to the well-informed discussions around the small, half-deaf, but always stimulating and fructifying, figure of Oldham. Yet all the time, even when dutifully attending to these investigations and debates in secular terms, Temple knew that the basic problems were spiritual.

His response to the spiritual crisis came out when in 1941 the Industrial Christian Fellowship organized a conference at Malvern which was to be the successor to Birmingham 1924. The aim was 'to consider from the Anglican point of view what are the fundamental facts which are directly relevant to the ordering of the new society that is quite evidently emerging, and how Christian thought can be shaped to play a leading part in the reconstruction after the war is over'. The continuity with 1924 lay in the broad sweep and the optimism, and in the rush and frustration of the conference itself. Above all, it lay in Temple's chairmanship, for he was able to astonish the conference by drafting its agreed conclusions after debates both brief and confused. But it was plainly not enough in 1941 to urge particular social reforms without a mastering vision of society. When Sir Richard Acland dominated the Malvern Conference by his demand that the Church should commit itself to the public ownership of the principal means of production, Temple was inclined to agree. However, the exhausted four hundred at Malvern were not willing to endorse Socialism so wholeheartedly in a hurry, and diplomats such as Bishop George Bell had to rescue the situation by a formula that 'private ownership of the main industrial resources may be a stumbling-block, making it harder for men to live Christian lives'.

That 'may be' about the Socialist panacea was not accidental. The speakers at Malvern were mostly concerned with somewhat philosophical attempts to work out 'the Anglican point of view', and came mainly from the Christendom group of Anglo-Catholics desiring a 'Christian sociology'. In his little book on *The Idea of a Christian Society* (1938), T. S. Eliot, who was very far from being a Socialist, had argued that Christianity was still a live option as the central dynamism in English life. With an eye on Hitler and Stalin, Eliot had urged that a society's basic necessity was to find a spiritual creed, and he believed that when the crisis came most Englishmen would wish to see Christianity as the creed of England – not compelling doctrinal uniformity but putting the social pressure behind, instead of against, Christian lives. Now, in 1941, the crisis had come; and the contribution of the Church must surely be weightier than any party politics. Churchmen thinking along these lines naturally relied on Temple more as a theologian than as an ex-member of the Labour Party.

However, neither the detailed discussions of the *Christian News-Letter* nor the theology of the Malvern conference could be enough. Some synthesis of the detailed with the general was needed. Temple supplied this synthesis for many thousands of Christian Englishmen during the second world war, when the social teaching which he had begun in the *Challenge* during the Kaiser's war came to its climax in the publication of his Penguin paperback on *Christianity and Social Order* in 1942. This was a small, highly compressed, and highly effective book: a book which was authoritative for more reasons than its author's high office. It attracted publicity by including some practical suggestions about the reform of the banking system and other controversial matters; and more publicity came as the Archbishop expanded these ideas in speeches. However, the central thrust of the book was theological. Its concern was to persuade readers that Christianity *was* relevant to social order, to the economic and political factors which so largely conditioned men's lives. There were, Temple claimed, some 'middle axioms' half-way between pure doctrine and detailed politics. Once these were stated – and Temple, after some thirty years of discussion, could state them magisterially – then surely men must go with a new vision into the politics of the emerging society, subordinating everything else to morality with its personal values.

Temple believed that a better order would include both state control and enterprise through competition, both public and private ownership, both a corporate spirit and civil liberties, and he stressed these different elements differently at different times of his life; but he did see some clear objectives for a Christian in social policy. He advocated the kind of housing which would provide for family life in privacy and the provision of universal education up to eighteen, as first charges on the economy. He wanted each worker to have a voice in the control of the enterprise for which he worked, a five-day week, and holidays with pay. As illustrations of how such principles might be worked out he was prepared to offer some controversial suggestions – but, as he stressed, as a citizen, not as an archbishop. Could each enterprise devote part of its profits to a fund to maintain wages and dividends in bad times, and part to the provision of amenities for the public? Could the public, rather than private bankers, gain the profit from the creation of credit? Could investors who had recovered in dividend more than the original sum invested be edged out of an enterprise by the withering away of the value of their capital, year by year? Could the land on which cities were built be nationalized, and could the taxation of rural landowners be adjusted in order to reward productivity? And could the costs of production be equalized internationally? Whatever the merits of such bright ideas – and few economists have acknowledged many merits in them – Temple's ingenuity was seldom at a loss before any challenge to be specific. Nor did his courage quail before the consequent indignation of bankers, shareholders, and landlords.

Temple's own major contribution to social progress was, appropriately enough, his share in the passage of the Education Act of 1944. He himself regarded the raising of the school leaving age to sixteen as the most important feature of R. A. Butler's plans for post-war development in the schools, but Butler and the other architects of the great Act relied on him for his leadership in securing church support for the religious provisions.

The Butler Act provided that every school day should begin with an act of worship. Every child, unless withdrawn by parents, should be instructed in the Christian religion according to a syllabus agreed between representatives of the churches and the Local Education Authority. And the Act provided both for the transfer to state control of those schools which the Church of England could no longer afford to maintain and for very large state subsidies to the running and capital costs of the smaller number of church schools and church colleges to train teachers – schools and colleges which the Church could still afford to control as its own distinctive contribution to the education of the people. In short, the Act of 1944 achieved a concordat between Church and State on questions which the Balfour Act of 1902 had been powerless to settle; and it witnessed a unanimity which would have seemed incredible to the contestants in the denominational disputes before 1914. Some idea of an agreement along the lines of the Butler Act had been in the minds of many men concerned with education. Many agreed syllabuses, for example, were already in operation. But the agreement in 1944 would have been far harder to achieve had Temple not been so enthusiastic over educational progress in general, had he not been so well equipped and entitled to answer secularist complaints, had he not enjoyed friendship of Free Church leaders such as the Methodist veteran Dr. Scott Lidgett, had he not outweighed Anglican leaders such as Bishops Headlam and Kirk who wanted the preservation of the Church's own schools given the first priority, and had he not been able to dismiss others such as Henson who wanted the Church's schools to be abandoned.

The Education Act had an immense effect on the life of the people after the second world war. It made provision for over three thousand church schools to be supported largely by the local authorities, and for the Church of England to retain some rights in a further two thousand schools; it also made possible the far more effective educational programme of the Roman Catholic Church. It provided the basic structure of education; and on the basis, it gradually became possible to move nearer to the ideal of the people's awakened mind – the ideal of the Workers' Educational Association. It provided also for the instruction of the people in the basic facts of Christianity. That did not usually lead to active church membership, but nor did it usually lead to an active hostility to religious education or to religion as a whole. The biblical stories and the Christian moral teaching which were imbibed in schooldays could be linked with religious broadcasts and television programmes; and since Christianity was in these ways still kept alive – imperfectly, but to the indignation of some secular humanists – a possibility remained. Here and there among the English people, a man or a woman might understand and enter the spirit of the Christian Church.

In his pastoral duties as Archbishop of Canterbury, Temple was both handicapped and helped by the war. Travel in over-crowded trains and the blackout became exhausting, yet his willingness to speak at large meetings in London and in other cities was essential to the two campaigns 'The Church Looks Forward' (1942) and 'Religion and Life' (1944). The campaigns recalled all the forward-looking vitality of 'Life and Liberty' days, with the added advantages of the prestige of his office and the expectancy of the wartime audiences now that at last an Archbishop of Canterbury had a constructive policy and the courage to advocate it. The work at Lambeth was more anxious than ever, for many correspondents wrote in with questions involving fundamental ethics; yet William Temple pronounced with all his father's decisiveness and with scarcely a trace of his father's gruff brevity. Should soldiers be issued with contraceptives for use in their off-duty hours? Temple protested that 'if men and women would abstain from fornication, the problem confronting the Minister of Health would be reduced to negligible proportions'. Must ladies wear hats in church? Temple decided not, to the relief of the authorities responsible for clothes rationing. May Christians fight? Temple argued against pacifism, but he argued at such a level that he retained the respect of the pacifists. May Britain retaliate against Germany by bombing cities? Temple was reluctant to criticize the British authorities publicly while they were waging war, and he died before the largest R.A.F. raids posed the ethical question in its sharpest form; but he did make some strong, if largely private, interventions against the growing tendency to hate and revenge – as did Davidson in 1914–18. Should Christians pray for victory? Lang, and also Cyril Garbett who succeeded Temple at York, encouraged this patriotism at prayer, but Temple went further than any other Anglican archbishop had ever done in saying that peace according to the will of God, not a national military victory, must be the chief aim.

The Archbishop of Canterbury who was harassed by so many problems, and left to cope without proper assistance at Lambeth, did not complain – in contrast with his predecessor, who went off to retirement in a self-pitying mood, 'from a somebody to a nobody'. The strain of those years wore down William Temple until a thrombosis following an infection from which he might have recovered in happier days killed him. Cosmo Lang was moved to find himself on his eightieth birthday, in his last great public ceremony, officiating at his successor's funeral.

These always anxious, and ultimately fatal, war years were William Temple's finest hour. As the American theologian Reinhold Niebuhr wrote: 'The man, the hour and the office stood in a creative relation to each other in a way we are not likely to see again in this generation.' Another American theologian, Joseph Fletcher, quoted in his study of Temple's thought the words of Richard Hooker about the cost of such work: 'Ministers of good things are like torches, a light to others, waste and destruction to themselves.' And this torch did flame; for Temple reached out to touch the imaginations of England and the free world. His politics got him quoted in the newspapers, but political controversy was not the secret of his serious influence. His voice could be heard through millions of wireless sets, continuing to teach about God in Christ. His thought, always clear, burned with its clarity now: with the clarity of his conviction that in the secular world Christians stood for the eternal Kingdom of God. It was not because he had views on politics, but because he saw God reigning over the everyday world, that he won the admiration of President Roosevelt and of many privates in the Army. To the emerging ecumenical movement which was finding the strength of its integrity in Christian Europe's resistance to Hitler he gave the comprehensive life of the Church of England – at a time when the ecumenical movement, later to be really world-wide, was small and

European enough to be impressed by the tradition of
English Church. To the emerging England, he gave the
best in Victorian religion – at a time when the democracy
was sufficiently conservative, or sufficiently frightened, to
welcome the reminder. He said privately that he intended
to resign in 1951, at the age of seventy, and to write a book
about the Holy Spirit; but when he died on 26 October
1944 (on the same morning as the last surviving child of
Queen Victoria, Princess Beatrice), he was still at the height
of his influence. 'I think he is *felix opportunitate mortis*', wrote
Hensley Henson to Cyril Alington, 'for he has passed away
while the streams of opinion in Church and State, of which
he became the outstanding symbol and exponent, were at
flood, and escaped the experience of their inevitable
ebb.'

9

As a philosophical theologian, William Temple regarded
the mind's apprehension of reality as both reliable and
supreme. He had no time for those who regarded man's
evolution as the product of blind chance in a universe
whose only laws were physical. 'That there should emerge
in the cosmic process a capacity to apprehend, even in a
measure to comprehend, that process', he wrote in *Nature,
Man and God*, 'is the most remarkable characteristic of the
process itself. . . . That the world should give rise to minds
which know the world involves a good deal concerning
the nature of the world.' And he did not hesitate to put first
the mind's spiritual rather than technical activity, just as he
did not hesitate to reject Marxist or Freudian explanations
of the economic or psychological causes of the mind's
decisions. He did not feel dwarfed by the universe. 'I know
the stars are there . . they do not know that I am here', he
told Oxford undergraduates in 1931. 'I beat the stars.' Nor
did he ever join Christians who received God's revelation
as a sheer miracle from a source wholly other than normal
existence. 'Unless all existence is a medium of Revelation,
no particular Revelation is possible', he asserted.

He frequently compared the mind's highest work with

the appreciation of a Beethoven symphony. Through music, or art, or religion, the mind of man reached out to apprehend and comprehend truthfully the beautiful goodness in the real world. And more: through relations with others men formed and deepened their ethical values, so that the supreme characteristic of life was its personal nature and the supreme activity of mind was its judgment of rightness. 'Your being is personal; live as a person in fellow-membership with all . . . your fellow-members in the community of persons.' Out of his own experience, out of his father's, out of all that had come to him through Rugby and Oxford, Temple drew the conclusion that all the life of the mind, all the life of fellowship, was a preparation for the revelation of God in Christ. For the mind cried out for an explanation of the universe, and 'if we ask for an explanation of the universe as a whole we are bound to formulate the answer in terms of Will'. And the mind cried out for the eternity of this beautiful goodness. 'Arising out of flux, and itself in origin an episode of the flux out of which it arises, mind declares its own nature by demanding permanence.' So the mind attained the conviction that the will of the eternal God was the origin of all that was valuable in the world; mind reached Mind. As Temple claimed:

The more we study the activity of God immanent, the more we become aware of God transcendent. The Truth that strikes awe in the scientist is awful because it is His thought; the Beauty that holds spell-bound the artist is potent because it is His glory; the Goodness that pilots us to the assured apprehension of Reality can do this because it is His character; and the freedom whereby man is lifted above all other nature, even to the possibility of defying it, is fellowship with Him.

Since 'the fullest revelation of truth is of persons to persons', personal worship of God was the heart of William Temple's religion. It was the only cure which he could see for the disease which he diagnosed in *Nature, Man and God:* 'It is the spirit which is evil; it is reason which is perverted; it is aspiration itself which is corrupt. . . . So long as the self retains initiative it can only fix itself upon itself as a centre. Its hope of deliverance is to be uprooted from that centre and drawn to find its centre in God, the Spirit of the

Whole.' When he came to comment on the woman of Samaria in his *St. John*, he wrote: 'Worship is the submission of all our nature to God. It is the quickening of conscience by His holiness; the nourishment of mind with His truth; the purifying of imagination by His beauty; the opening of the heart to His love; the surrender of the will to His purpose – and all this gathered up in adoration. . . .'

Worship thus understood was based by Temple on a foundation which did not involve the dogmatism of Newman (or the dogmatism of Shaftesbury); here he stood firmly in the tradition of Maurice. In *Foundations* he permitted himself to pronounce that the Council of Chalcedon's definition of orthodox Christology had declared the 'bankruptcy of Greek patristic theology', but in *Christus Veritas* he modified this phrase, claiming that the formula of Chalcedon 'did exactly what an authoratitive formula ought to do: it stated the fact'. However, he never believed that the acceptance of Jesus as 'God living a human life', as the Second Person of the Trinity adding this human life to his divine attributes, necessarily involved the acceptance of any philosophical formula of the past. 'It would be disastrous', he wrote, 'if there were an official Church explanation of the Incarnation.' He also moved, as we have seen, towards a more conservative use of the Bible. But he insisted that God's revelation of himself was chiefly through *events*, supremely the event of Jesus Christ – not through propositions. He taught that

there are truths of revelation, . . . propositions which express the results of correct thinking concerning revelation; but they are not themselves directly revealed. On the other hand, this does not involve the result that there need be anything vague or indefinite about revelation itself . . . What is offered to man's apprehension in any specific revelation is not truth concerning God but the living God Himself.

Religious experience was, he declared, 'the whole experience of religious persons'. He greatly valued the Church's sacraments, but in a sacramental universe; and he called Christianity 'the most avowedly materialistic of all the great religions'. He was clear that God did not depend on the world (he used the equation: 'God – world = God'), but he was also clear that God had chosen to create a world through which his love might be known; when he expounded the doctrine of God the divine love, shown in the divine humility of the cross, was always at the centre. His understanding of the Atonement was exemplarist, but with a profound difference from shallow theories about Christ the example. Here as everywhere else, Temple began his thinking with the vision of God. He wrote in *Christus Veritas:* 'We must first realize Him as exalted in unapproachable Holiness, so that our only fitting attitude before Him is one of abject self-abasement, if we are to feel the stupendous marvel of the Love which led Him, so high and lifted up, to take His place beside us in our insignificance and squalor that He might unite us with Himself.' The crucified Christ revealed to men the divine self-sacrifice. The cross showed what it cost God to enter all suffering, and to take away the self-centredness which was the cause of all sin. It cost a broken body, a broken heart. The love of God for the world, the purpose of God to spread his Kingdom of love in all the world: these were the basic lessons which William Temple learned from the teaching, death, and victory of Jesus.

# 10

# Leadership since 1945

I

A hundred and fifty years after Thomas Arnold's appointment to the Headmastership of Rugby School, the succession of leaders of the Church of England which began then seems to be a closed chapter of history.

What is striking now is not that these men differed from each other in temperament, or that they had dark moods of self-doubt, but that they were so assured in what they commonly took for granted. Thomas Arnold was confident about the central claims of Christianity, as was his son Matthew about Christian ethics. Newman and Keble agreed that the Catholic Church was to be loved and obeyed because it had the power to save and the authority to instruct; their disagreement was about whether the Church of England belonged to it. Wilberforce and Tait were both sure that the Church of England taught the truth and deserved hard work; exactly how the truth should be expressed, precisely and who should lead the work, were their only contentions. Shaftesbury and Maurice both worshipped Christ as the world's Saviour and King. Gladstone and Benson were both tirelessly devoted to Christ's Body, the Church. Lightfoot and Westcott were both prepared to teach Anglicanism to the miners of County Durham as to the students of Cambridge. Creighton and Davidson, although keeping an eye on each other, knelt side by side to become bishops. Gore and Henson, although at loggerheads, served as bishops in the same Church. As priests or archbishops, Frederick and William Temple preached the same message from the 1840s to the 1940s.

A whole complex of privileges combined to give them this

pride in belonging to their Church and civilization. However impoverished or unhappy some of them were as boys, they were all the sons of Christian homes, with their basic values clear from the beginning. Almost all of them were educated in strong Anglican schools. They almost all achieved distinction at Oxford or Cambridge, and the universities then honoured 'true religion' as well as 'sound learning' – in practice, the Church of England and the Greek and Latin classics. Apart from the natural celibates, they all had wives who suppressed, if they ever felt, any incipient rebellion against their lot in life. Their domestic circumstances were usually easy; they had servants even while they were parish priests or schoolmasters. When they talked or preached (and even laymen such as Matthew Arnold or Gladstone preached) they expected others to listen and learn. In their teaching they appealed to the authority of the Bible, reinforced by the authority of a Christian consensus which had shaped England for more than a thousand years. In discharging their administrative responsibilities in school or college, parish or diocese, nation or empire, they felt themselves to be members of a governing class, close to the Crown; and their fellow-rulers accepted them, inviting them to dinner, enquiring after their opinions, complimenting their ladies, mourning their deaths.

They were solid figures in the English Establishment, and the English Establishment was then dominant over national, and much of international, life. When an Archbishop of Canterbury had anointed a King or Queen he put into his monarch's hand an orb representing the world; and over this golden globe was a cross. Over the high altar of Westminster Abbey was written the text: *The kingdoms of this world are become the kingdom of our Lord and of his Christ.* The great dome of St. Paul's Cathedral rose serenely above the world's leading financial centre. Although the parish churches were less prominent in the life of the world's first industrial nation, clergy and churchgoers were numerous and active. The British Empire, under which a quarter of mankind lived (almost always quietly), was a scene where missionary courage went hand in hand with the imperialism of 'service'. The conviction that the Christian civilization of England had a lofty mission to the world was widespread and sincere. Many thousands of Englishmen volunteered to die for it in 1914. Those called to lead the Church of England were expected to maintain national self-respect and self-confidence, and if possible to elevate the moral tone yet further. Matthew Arnold viewed the Church of England as 'a great national society for the promotion of what is called commonly *goodness*'. That was partly why Dean Church wrote of the Church of England in the Victorian noonday as 'the most glorious Church in Christendom'; and partly why President Roosevelt cabled his grief when William Temple died.

In the 1970s it came to seem amazing that this England took so long to die. In 1945 it ought to have been possible to see clearly how sharp was the decline of the British Empire and of the Anglican pulpit at its centre. But in fact not many had this insight into current affairs, in England or elsewhere. The British Empire had just supported the United Kingdom in the second world war. For a time the Empire had stood alone. In the end it had, with its allies, defeated Hitler like Napoleon and the Kaiser – and had done so with idealistic patriotism. From the National Days of Prayer led by George VI to the coronation of Elizabeth II the spirit of this defiant nation and empire was consecrated publicly. It was clear that industry would have to be modernized, but the British had enough technical triumphs to their credit not to worry. In 1951 the Festival of Britain celebrated their confidence. It was also clear to most that Labour must be given its turn, but the construction of a Welfare State without a revolution was going to be one more British achievement. Some, even all, of the colonies would have to be granted independence; but the pace could be leisurely, and the independence of India in 1947 was widely regarded as an honourable transition from Empire to Commonwealth, with many continuing bands of loyalty. All agreed that England was placed more fortunately than its ruined enemies and could face the future with a reasonable pride in its tradition.

Meanwhile the Church of England still played a prominent role. It not only continued to appear as part of the royal and conservative Establishment; it also contributed to the moral power of a Labour Government in the persons of Attlee, Cripps, and others. It remained the Mother Church of the Anglican Communion and around the world many remained anxious to hear its views on matters such as Christian reunion. When the World Council of Churches was inaugurated at Amsterdam in 1948, an Archbishop of Canterbury was in the chair. In the Church as in the State it was possible to retain the illusion that nothing had really changed.

2

When William Temple died, two months passed before Winston Churchill made any definite move in the appointment of a successor. As Prime Minister at the height of the war Churchill had other matters on his mind, but at any time he would have had less time than Gladstone for the discussion of the rival claims of clergymen. It was said that, when rebuked for appointing a Socialist to Canterbury in 1942, he had briefly replied that William Temple had been 'the only sixpenny article in a penny bazaar'. When Temple died, the Conservative politician and gossip Sir Henry Channon recorded in his diary Churchill's complacency at outliving a younger contemporary who was a non-smoker and teetotaller; but then Channon himself reckoned Temple 'a fat fool of 63 with a fuddled, muddled brain who looked more like Queen Victoria than her daughter did'. What is certain is that Churchill, although a believer in God, had no appetite for theology or ecclesiastics. He once compared himself with a buttress, supporting a church from the outside.

When he broke off from the conduct of the war to study the Anglican scene, he could not seriously consider moving another archbishop from York to Canterbury. Cyril Garbett was an impressive figure who had followed Cosmo Lang as Vicar of Portsea and had done mighty work as Bishop of Southwark; among other toils he had overseen (as chairman of the advisory committee) the creation of religious broadcasting. After a comparatively quiet interlude at Winchester, he had succeeded Temple at York. Without any of Temple's originality he had acquired some of his popularity through hard work, common sense, a pastoral touch, and clear teaching (which he sensibly took care to make available in time to the newspapers: then an innovation). As he had grown older the strain obvious in his earlier Anglo-Catholic piety had somewhat relaxed, so that he had grown to be loved while never ceasing to have an instinctively aristocratic approach. He wrote some books which deserved their wide circulation as expositions of the position of the Church of England, and he travelled widely and enthusiastically. But he had been born in 1875, and now in his diary he summed up the valid arguments against his own further advancement. 'A third translation from York inexpedient; my age – I should be at least 73 by the next Lambeth Conference and ought to resign at 75; and I *know* I have not got the gifts for this post.'

George Bell, Bishop of Chichester, certainly seems to have had the gifts most needed for the Archbishopric. He had spent his first night in Lambeth Palace on the day when the first world war had been declared; Davidson had sent for him (he was then a young Oxford don) to be interviewed as a possible chaplain. He had remained at Lambeth until appointed Dean of Canterbury in 1924, and had become indispensable to the elderly archbishop, much as Davidson had been to Tait forty years before. In 1922 Davidson wrote to him: 'You and I have all these tempestuous years worked together, and it is our joint work, and not *my* work in any narrower sense, that has had such degree of effectiveness as belongs to it . . . The central work at Lambeth is so important, and your place in it so outstanding, that you ought to stay on here . . .' And since this time at Lambeth, twenty years had only increased Bell's capacity to handle this 'central work'.

In Canterbury he had brought the cathedral to life in many imaginatively bold details; for example, he had made it a home of religious drama (involving John Masefield and T. S. Eliot). As Bishop of Chichester from 1929, he had thrown himself into the encouragement of religious education and religious art. While Temple was often remote from the routine of parish life, Bell was a first-class pastor and administrator of the Church in the large county of Sussex, despite difficulties far greater than those facing any of the Victorians who had been praised as bishops. At a time when it was still thought that a bishop had a duty to fight Anglo-Catholic lawlessness, he had displayed more than a little of his master Davidson's liking for order and discipline. In a little joke in his diary in 1928 Dean Inge of St. Paul's had hoped that Bell might succeed Davidson immediately; 'everybody except Cosmo Lang would be delighted'.

In addition to his diocesan duties Bell had somehow found time to write two volumes on Davidson's life – a better book than Davidson's on Tait. Above all, he had kept up the involvement in international affairs, begun when he had attended the pioneering commercial 'Conference of Life and Work' at Stockholm in 1925. Then he had become a disciple of the far-sighted Archbishop Söderblom of Uppsala, and thus the man to make President of the international council carrying on the work of Stockholm and Söderblom. As such he stood more openly against the new Hitler regime than did any other Christian leader of the time; and not content with ceaseless study of, and pronouncement upon, the German church crisis or with the wider view set out in his *Christianity and World Order* (1940), he busied himself with befriending many refugees from Germany. The death of William Temple left him as the only figure of international stature among the bishops of the Church of England. This standing was to be recognized by the trust placed in him by colleagues in the early work of the World Council of Churches. He was made chairman of the Central Committee for six years, and then elected Honorary President.

Why, then, was he not appointed Archbishop of Canterbury? It was possible to point out defects in him (as in the men who actually became archbishops). He was a shy man and lacked small talk. At times he seemed too diffident; at times, too obstinate. All agreed that he was a dull speaker. The very care which as Davidson's ex-chaplain he took to assemble the history of a problem and to look at all its

sides meant that he almost always included too much
serious material in an address. Shrewder bishops made a
point, a joke, and an end. Because his scope was wider than
the parish and the diocese, there were complaints that he
did not give enough attention to the Church in Sussex;
while those who disliked his policies there complained that
he gave it too much. But his main fault in the eyes of
Winston Churchill at the end of 1944 was, no doubt, that he
had not been wholeheartedly in his support of the war
effort. Privately Bell expressed some sadness but no surprise
that no fresh place was offered to him before he retired
from Chichester in 1957. 'I have no illusions about Churchill's attitude to me', he wrote to a friend in 1944; 'he is the
last man to put me in any position of greater influence.'
Disappointment seems to have returned (irrationally in
view of his age) when after being told that he was being
considered he heard on the radio that another had been
appointed to succeed Garbett at York, and when his
retirement was not marked by any honour from the State.
He had paid the penalty.

Bell apparently committed serious sins in the eyes of the
small group of men – politicians, civil servants, and those
consulted by them – responsible for advising the Crown
about the Church of England's senior appointments and
about honours. The first sin was his activity in pressing for
a reform of the relationship of Church and State in England
in the 1930s. He wanted something to be done, when Lang,
Temple, and most others preferred things to drift on. During
the war he urged the government to relax its blockade of
German-occupied Europe in order to avert famine. He was
involved in the effort by anti-Nazi Germans to persuade
the Churchill government to indicate, however briefly, that
if the Nazis were removed from power the German people
would still have some dignified prospects. While he was
lecturing in Sweden in 1942, Bell found himself holding
discussions with anti-Nazi plotters from Germany (including the theologian Dietrich Bonhoeffer), and reported
them to Anthony Eden, then Foreign Secretary; but the
approach was not taken seriously in London. Churchill and
Roosevelt preferred to demand the German's uncond-

itional surrender. In the event, the attempt to assassinate
Hitler on 8 July 1944 was a failure. Thousands of
conspirators including Bonhoeffer were executed. Much of
the flower of the potential leadership of a democratic
Germany was thus removed before the post-war recon-
structions. The Germans fought on until half their country
was at the mercy of the invading Russians; and bitter years
followed until eventually the United States secured the
rearmament of West Germany against the Russians, and
France and Britain joined West Germany in the European
Economic Community.

But Bell's gravest indiscretions are on record in the
collection of his wartime address, *The Church and Humanity*
(1946). He refused to accept the doctrine that the war
must be waged ruthlessly to the end against the whole
German people, not merely against the Nazis and the
armed forces. In the House of Lords on 9 February 1944
he dared to criticize the policy by which the Royal Air
Force (at a grim cost in the lives of its own crews) attempted
the obliteration bombing of civilian areas such as the houses
in German industrial cities. As carried out, this policy
certainly added greatly to the material problems of a Germany already reeling under military defeats; but it also
seems to have increased the average German's hatred of the
British and Americans, and his willingness to work over-
time in the production of materials for war. Bell, however,
attacked the policy not by balancing military considerations
but by reiterating the Christian teaching, to which Britain
had previously been glad to appeal, that even during a war
civilians should be spared as much as possible. Finally, the
outspoken bishop protested against the American action in
dropping atomic bombs without warning on Hiroshima and
Nagasaki. In Chichester his own dean asked him not to
preach in his cathedral; but in the concentration camp at
Flossenburg Dietrich Bonhoeffer, shortly before his
execution, gave a British fellow-prisoner a message for the
Bishop of Chichester: 'Tell him that for me this is the end
but also the beginning. With him I believe in the principle
of our Universal Christian brotherhood which is above all
national interests, and that our victory is certain. Tell him

too that I have never forgotten his words at our last meeting.'

Bell's lack of luck in the gamble of promotion was not a major tragedy for him. Being the senior clergyman in Sussex cannot be martyrdom; nor does a failure to become a Companion of Honour necessarily mean disgrace. On the contrary, it has been to his lasting credit that this champion of justice and mercy spoke out after a training which had made him thoroughly aware of England's established conventions and rewards. In 1928 a gossip-writer who compiled a book called *The Looking-Glass of Lambeth* could thus describe him: 'He is bustling, eager, almost too obviously ambitious, and entirely self-assured. He is diplomatic, courteous, and the inheritor of the tradition of comprehensiveness and peace at any price.' The tragedy lay in the Church of England's inability to accept fully the vision which guided the man George Bell became.

3

Instead of George Bell, Geoffrey Fisher was enthroned in St. Augustine's chair at Canterbury as the armies and air forces of the allies fought the war to a finish; and he was a man possessed of gifts which Bell lacked.

Self-confidently at ease with people of all classes and with a knack of remembering names and personal details, he spread an eager friendliness and good humour. He thoroughly enjoyed guiding committees or assemblies so that they agreed to take what he thought was the sensible course; and he was very good at it. He was a master of the appropriate word, in a sermon for a village church or a speech after a businessmen's dinner. While himself a fully orthodox Christian, he had a great respect for men of the world such as Churchill and for the idealism which he found in them. While not slow to criticize politicians where he thought they deserved criticism, basically he accepted and enjoyed the English Establishment with a patriotism untroubled by concerns such as those which had driven Bell. While gifted with a mind indisputably in the first class, he had applied it to the practical problems of his various posts; he did not take the theologians or the poets or the artists as seriously as Bell did. He was sure where he stood.

He stood in the tradition of the rectory at Higham-on-the-Hill in Leicestershire. There his father was Rector for forty years, and his grandfather and great-grandfather had also been rectors for similar lengths of time. There he was born in 1887, and from there he went to accept, enjoy, and benefit from a public school and Oxford. At the age of twenty-seven, on the eve of the great war, he was appointed Headmaster of Repton in succession to William Temple. Since then he had always run things with the practical efficiency and the eye for human detail which the great Temple had lacked. For a short time at Repton there was trouble; Victor Gollancz, who while a publisher was to become famous for the Left Book Club, was on the staff and was running a suspicious-sounding Civics Class. But Gollancz went. Quietly and happily the school became a model of its type. So did the diocese of Chester, where Fisher was appointed Bishop in 1932 despite his lack of parochial experience.

He was still virtually unknown to the wider public, since he was not active in public life outside Cheshire. But the unobtrusive skill with which he got boys and men (were they very different?) to work together along the lines he wanted impressed many who knew that the diocese of London needed a firm hand. 1939 saw the end of the excessively charming and excessively long (since 1901) episcopate in London of Arthur Foley Winnington-Ingram, an Anglo-Catholic saint. The same year saw Fisher's appointment and the outbreak of a new war. During the war Geoffrey Fisher set an example to his six hundred parishes by doing his duty confidently; and when not coping with the blitz he dealt with the challenge of Anglo-Catholic ritualism with a determination that recalled the battles of Bishops Tait, Temple, and Creighton. At the same time he began to be busy in the central councils of the Church of England. His speciality was the administrative and financial work required to translate some of William Temple's ideas into reality. During his last summer holiday Temple, while talking with his wife about their retirement some day, re-marked: 'and I must give up in time to let Geoffrey have his whack.'

The whack which Fisher had as Archbishop of Canter-bury, 1945-61, is described in the autobiographical notes which William Purcell quoted extensively in *Fisher of Lambeth* (1969). Looking back, Fisher said: 'I've never tried to think out a considered plan of what I ought to do through the years; I've never tried to formulate a general policy that I ought to follow; I've just gone forward and taken up each task or group of tasks as they appear to demand attention, and no doubt there came to me some kind of pattern forming in my mind into which they all fitted . . .' But this self-assessment underestimated the strong character of his Primacy.

He described the revision of the canon law of the Church of England as 'the most absorbing and all-embracing topic of my archiepiscopate'. For years it had been acknowledged that these canons, last revised in 1603, needed to be clarified and modernized. Many of the conflicts which engaged the Victorian and post-Victorian bishops arose because the Church of England had ceased to have an accepted and enforceable code of regulations. Anglo-Catholics, Evan-gelicals, Broad Churchmen, or Modernists all took advan-tage of this situation. In reply the bishops argued that they were in their own persons the 'lawful authority' to be obeyed; and Archbishops of Canterbury tried to act as a court of appeal. But the situation was a nightmare to anyone with an orderly mind, and when a commission chaired by Garbett had reported to that effect in 1947, and had offered a draft of revised canons, action was seen to be neces-sary.

Fisher was certainly the man for this task. Year after year he guided the Convocations of the clergy and the House of Laity in the Church Assembly through their legislative labours, always doing his effective utmost to keep everyone in step. The rival ecclesiastical parties were made to acknowledge in the black and white of print how comprehensive the Church was, but also how limited must be the freedom which they claimed as members of the one fellowship. One by one the Victorian and post-Victorian controversies were tidied up in this manner. What a clergyman might wear was decided, and a variety was permitted. What a clergyman should teach was also decided; the Church of England was based on the Bible and the Creeds, with works of the Fathers and the Thirty-nine Articles enjoying a less clear authority. Fisher later recalled:

There were, inevitably, major clashes at certain stages ... There had to be a complete overhauling of the Ecclesiastical Courts, involving repeal or amendment of some two hundred Acts of Parliament ... There were, at times, dismay and discouragement over the time and the labour being absorbed by the seemingly endless task. More than once, to the bishops or in Church Assembly, I had to hold forth at length about the central place of canon law for the renewal of the Church. I knew that it was vital that the work should be carried through to completion; and of course, carried through it was.

Equally firm was Fisher's leadership (begun while Bishop of London) in the reorganization of the finances of the Church of England. In 1948 the Ecclesiastical Commissioners, the main trustees of the Church's endowments, were at last united with the smaller body, Queen Anne's Bounty; and the combined 'Church Commissioners' began investing their assets more boldly in industrial and commercial shares to supplement their traditional landowning and the holding of Government bonds. This reorganization, together with a clear appeal to the laity for new giving, came just in time to rescue the parish clergy from real financial hardship. Fisher, the son of a rector, had never grown out of touch with such facts of life. On the other hand, he was confident that the parochial system he had known as a boy could still be worked, and he took little interest in radical notions for reform.

He was also sure that subtler aspects of the unity of the Church deserved a cautious encouragement. He appointed two groups of Anglican theologians to present reports on *Catholicity* and (on the Evangelical wing) *The Fullness of Christ*; each of his two successors at Canterbury belonged to one of these groups. He spoke in his enthronement sermon of the vocation of Anglicanism as being 'to hold together in

LEADERS OF THE CHURCH OF ENGLAND 1828–1978

a due proportion truths which, though essential to the fullness of the Gospel of Christ, are through the frailty of man's spirit not easily combined – fidelity to the apostolic faith, and freedom in its apprehension and application; liberty of the spirit, and obedience to the disciplined life of the Church; the corporate unity of a divinely instituted people of God, and the free response of each in his own person to the grace and guidance of the Holy Spirit.' The re-ordering of the Church of England on the basis of 'a Christian faith which is not ashamed to be definite, explicit, and binding' was, Fisher laid down in that sermon, necessary because 'there is now a whole demon-ridden world to be re-ordered' and 'the Church has much to put in order if it is faithfully to serve the nation'.

While never aspiring to the sort of familiarity with the ecumenical movement that George Bell displayed when he edited four volumes of *Documents of Christian Unity*, Fisher did share something of the wider concern, in his own way. Finding the African or the Australian Anglicans dangerously exposed to the criticism of still being the Church of England in those parts, he made journeys there which had a double success: they loosened the constitutional, and strengthened the personal links. Max Warren, who watched him at this work, later wrote: 'In Geoffrey Fisher Africans saw a great church leader, and a European at that, actually abdicating authority, in Africa an event as yet without precedent in the State.' Finding the American bishops reluctant to contemplate another Lambeth Conference (memories persisted of Archbishop Lang's haughtiness in 1930), he went to the United States. By his friendliness he won his way to a harmonious and optimistic Lambeth Conference in 1948, followed three years later by a larger and even more successful Pan-Anglican Congress at Minneapolis, Minnesota. Finding that the inter-church discussions set alight in England by the Lambeth Appeal of 1920 had run out of steam, he got the engine moving again by a Cambridge University sermon in 1946, when he urged the Free Churchmen to consider taking episcopacy into their own system. The Free Church leaders already knew and liked Fisher through their share of work for the British

Council of Churches, and they responded warmly to this invitation to talks although in the subsequent thirty years they never actually took the step which the Archbishop had recommended.

Fisher was also a President of the World Council of Churches. Characteristically he recalled his leadership there. 'I enjoyed those great World Council Assemblies; but found the endless pressure of discussion and of trying to steer people clear of mis-statements or exaggerations in our resolutions very exhausting.' His most personal contribution to Christian reunion came, however, when in the autumn of 1960 he surprised everyone by visiting the holy places and the church leaders in Jerusalem, Istanbul, and Rome. His 'visit of courtesy' to Pope John XXIII was met with great suspicion among the Vatican officials. But when the Archbishop reached the Pope, these two Christian men of advanced years and a simple faith shared a delight in breaking through the barriers. Pope John read to him a passage from a recent address looking forward to 'the time when our separated brethren should return to the Mother Church'. Fisher at once said: 'Your Holiness, not *return*.' 'Not return?' asked the Pope. 'Why not?' Fisher replied: 'None of us can go backwards. We are each now running on parallel courses, we are looking forward until, in God's good time, our two approximate and meet.' Pope John commented: 'You are right.'

Before he knew definitely that the Archbishopric was to be offered to him at the end of 1944, Fisher told Garbett that he dreaded having to make frequent pronouncements on public affairs. There is no reason to doubt the sincerity of that hesitation; but the appetite grew by what it fed on. Fortunately for Fisher, his most public appearances were connected with the Royal Family, and supremely with the marriage and coronation of Elizabeth II. He got on well with the family; its values were his, and he gave them felicitous expression. What might have been an unpleasantness, as Princess Margaret seemed about to marry a man who had been divorced, passed when the Princess made up her own mind to adhere to the Church of England's teaching. In Fisher's time this teaching was clearer on divorce than on most matters, and he took care to expound it in public and private. When people who had been re-married by the State after divorce wished to receive Communion they were instructed to seek the permission of the bishop, who usually suggested a period of penitence. Only a few parish priests defied the Convocations of the clergy, which forbade the holding of the second marriage service in Church.

When Bishop Barnes of Birmingham published a Modern-ist treatment of *The Rise of Christianity* (1947), Fisher refused to sponsor a heresy trial but responded to many protests by declaring solemnly in the Convocation of Canterbury: 'If his views were mine, I should not feel that I could still hold episcopal office in the Church.' Barnes did not resign, but he was too old and confused to reply effectively. When a less famous clergyman, C. J. Wright, denied the virgin birth of Jesus, the Archbishop replied with a briefer reassurance that such a denial was contrary to the teaching of the Church. On the whole, the theological scene stayed quiet. New and radical ideas were being imported obscurely from Germany in scholarly books, but Fisher represented most members of the Church of England by ignoring them.

In political as in theological controversies, he was a brave defender of the old faith and the old virtues. He got into trouble when he invited Makarios of Cyprus – not only a fellow-archbishop but also the 'ethnarch' of the Greek population then in rebellion against British colonial rule – to attend the Lambeth Conference of bishops; and fresh difficulties, this time with the Eastern Orthodox, arose when on television he called Makarios 'a bad man'. He was never forgiven by the Conservative Chancellor of the Exchequer, Harold Macmillan, when he denounced the new Premium Bonds because of the element of gambling in them. 'The Government,' he told the House of Lords, 'knows as well as all the rest of us that we can only regain stability and strength by unremitting exercise, all through the nation, of the old-fashioned but essential virtues, integrity of character, strict honesty, the duty of honest work and honestly re-warded, saving and the like . . . The Government has chosen instead not a dazzling, but a rather second-rate, expedient, ...And when the Conservative government invaded the Suez Canal in 1956, the House of Lords heard the Archbishop of Canterbury cross-examining the Lord Chancellor who had claimed that the Egyptians were the 'attacking power' because they had resisted a 'peaceful intervention'.

His retirement in 1961 was a gracious act. He had been told by a chaplain that he was talking too much; he detected in himself some lessening of enthusiasm for conferences and committees; and he saw these as indications that he ought to go. In retirement he acted as a curate-in-charge in the Dorset village of Trent, and when he died in 1972, his eighty-fifth year, he was by his own wish buried there, not in Canterbury Cathedral. While staying with a son in Australia for three months in 1969 he found that he had nothing to do in the mornings, and so had set down his philosophy of life in disconnected chapters, later published under the modest title *Touching on Christian Truth* (1971). At the end he had said: 'It is in the course of doing simple things gracefully and with a care for others that the Kingdom of God comes among men.'

He could rightly say that he had taught the truth as he saw it and had defended the old-fashioned but essential virtues to the end; and many were grateful. His only fault was that he had survived into the wrong time. During the 1950s the rally of Christian confidence connected with patriotism during the second world war and with the personality of William Temple died away, and in the 1960s all the statistics of the Church of England showed the lower temperature like a battery of barometers. To respond to the crisis of religion, what was supremely necessary was a restatement of the Christian faith, accompanied by a revision of worship and a reorganization in the parishes and dioceses. Urgency in reuniting the Churches was one aspect of the radicalism of the courage needed. This Fisher did not see. Although with his head he knew that 'none of us can go backwards', he was at heart content with the Establishment he had entered on becoming a headmaster less than ninety years after Thomas Arnold, and he was confident that this old England could be brought alive by hard work – such as he himself gave without stint all his life. It was a misjudgment.

To reckon the revision of canon law 'the most absorbing and all-embracing topic of my archiepiscopate' showed that in the new age he was the eccentric. To make so much of global Anglicanism was to be blind to a revolution of which disappearance of the British Empire was only a part. To brush aside the unorthodoxy of a Bishop Barnes, or to denounce Premium Bonds when he had been so co-operative over the atomic bombs, showed that he had not really heard the questions which the new generation was asking. Dressed in the episcopal costume of apron and gaiters (and rebuking fellow-bishops who preferred trousers), he began to look, while holding office, a figure out of a dead world. And in his retirement he did not have the wisdom to stay silent.

He threw himself into the controversy about Anglican-Methodist reunion, contradicting and embarrassing his successor. In his 1946 Cambridge sermon he had said: 'My longing is not yet that we should be *united* with other churches in this country; but that we should grow to *full communion* with them.' In order that the Church of England might be able to grant full communion to the Free Churches (for there was no difficulty on the Free Church side), he had proposed that the Free Churches should have their own bishops, presumably consecrated by Anglicans. But in the course of the very protracted conversations which followed that initiative, it became clear that on the Anglican side there was a growing willingness to enter into full communion with the Free Churches without uniting with them; while on the Free Church side there was little interest in having bishops unless episcopacy was a part of a reunion with the Church of England. Fisher always thought talk of reunion premature. He thought the Churches did not really want it, and was not shaken even when the Methodist Conference voted overwhelmingly in its favour. He feared that a union with the Free Churches must mean the end of the Church of England as the Established Church in its own country and as the centre of a world-wide Anglican network. He therefore dismayed many of his former admirers by urging in pamphlets and letters the rejection of the Anglican-Methodist reunion scheme. He lent the authority of his name to a collection of opponents who without that aid might not have been able to deny the official scheme the majority of three-quarters needed for its acceptance in the General Synod of the Church of England.

William Temple died at the height of his prestige. That was not the good fortune of Geoffrey Fisher. He, who while in authority had always insisted on obedience, lived to become a destructive rebel, defending an outmoded idea of the Church of England.

4

Since the retirement of Geoffrey Fisher it has become clear that the Church of England is to be led, if it is to be led at all, by people influencing other people in groups – not by individualists. The Church's General Synod met for the first time on 4 November 1970. It was the old Church Assembly transformed. The new Synod had a smaller membership, with fewer *ex officio* members; and combining clergy and laity, it had power over doctrine and worship as well as over more worldly matters. Four years later Parliament agreed that its own consent would no longer be required for changes in doctrine and worship. Similar synods, on smaller scales, were formed in every diocese and deanery throughout the Church of England, while in parishes there was increasing emphasis on the rights and responsibilities of the laity whose elected representatives met (it was hoped, regularly and amicably) in the Parochial Church Councils. This new system of synodical government did not hold the key to expansion, and was not thought to hold it; practically no one in the 1970s retained the enthusiasm which William Temple had spread in the 'Life and Liberty' movement. Had disillusionment been needed, the statistics would have supplied it. In 1924, when the first rolls of electors were compiled in the parish churches, about 3,500,000 people put their names down. Half a century later the number had shrunk to two million. But the new system of government was inescapable if the Church was to keep up with the times.

The new system was profoundly different from the atmosphere of hierarchy and paternalism in which the Victorian Church had reflected the structures of the surrounding society. But it could not properly be called democratic.

The bishops, the clergy, and the laity could be separated into 'Houses' in these synods. The agreement of all three Houses was necessary for the most important proposals, which also had to be referred by the General Synod to dioceses and even then not finally passed except with a majority of three-quarters. These elaborate precautions against over-riding substantial elements in the Church contrasted with the decision-making by a simple majority normal in democratic politics. Such arrangements preserved something of the idea that Christians ought to agree about the guidance of the Holy Spirit. They also preserved something of the idea that the Church of England was governed by bishops. By the 1970s bishops were less often called 'My Lord' and less often regarded as indispensable apostles; but as hard workers who coped with many problems, they were still entitled to respect.

Further checks on the power of the General Synod, and of the staff and councils appointed by it, were provided by other arrangements. The Synod's budget had to be financed by the laity in the dioceses and any tendency to develop a large bureaucracy in London met with suspicion and a financial veto. In practice, therefore, the General Synod's central machinery depended on the co-operation of the Church's forty-three dioceses for its effective working. Even when the General Synod could be brought to agree on a matter, it could not impose its decision on dioceses. Moreover, the General Synod did not have control over the main endowments of the Church; these remained in the hands of Church Commissioners, who merely reported to the Synod. The Commissioners remained the trustees of investments used almost entirely to pay the clergy.

The whole financial structure of the Church embodied the same principle that power should be spread and agreement secured. In the age of inflation more and more money was needed from the living laity, whose goodwill therefore became essential. But it was also necessary to invest endowments shrewdly, which meant centrally; so that almost all the inherited resources were placed under the care of the Church Commissioners and their expert staff. It became the practice for the Commissioners to give grants to the dioceses, which were then allocated to the clergy. In practice not much flexibility was possible when making these allocations since from the mid-1970s the Commissioners put their weight behind plans agreed by the bishops nationally to distribute to the clergy. The Commissioners also suggested the minimum stipends of the clergy and effectively discouraged any idea that the formerly privileged few should receive any more favours. As the real value of the old 'plums' declined, the pay of parish priests was virtually equalised. The rectory or vicarage now became the responsibility of the diocese and even the annual Easter Offerings given by the parish to encourage the rector or vicar over many centuries were now deducted from the sum given from outside the parish in order to bring the stipend up to the minimum. These arrangements were accompanied by many suggestions that the clergy should be treated as employees of the Church as a whole, or of the dioceses, instead of as individuals enjoying all the independence traditionally associated with a 'freehold 'position. Significantly they ceased to be 'self-employed' persons for insurance purposes, although in 1978 they were still protected legally from most forms of regimentation apart from their stipends. In accordance with the levelling spirit of the age, the bishops' stipends were also standardized, although exceptions were maintained for the dioceses of Canterbury, York, London, Durham, and Winchester. It became something more than rhetoric to speak of the laity as being the Church, and to speak of the clergy, including the bishops, as being a band of brothers.

The main task of leadership in this new situation often seemed to be securing agreement. On all the major decisions it had become necessary to persuade the General Synod. Its proceedings were often inconclusive and usually verbose.

The bishops spoke alongside everyone else and often against each other; and the Archbishop of Canterbury shared the presidency over the debates with a panel of chairmen. In 1969 the Convocations of the clergy, and in 1972 the General Synod, refused to provide an adequate majority for Anglican-Methodist reunion, despite the passionate pleas of the Archbishop of Canterbury – who after the 1969 vote said 'there will be bitterness, anger and cynicism', and who in 1972 spoke of 'darkness'. Anything like the style of leadership which Fisher had exercised was now plainly out of the question. In their own dioceses, the bishops found it vital to co-operate with the elected representatives of the clergy and laity in the Diocesan Synod, in the Bishop's Council, and on every occasion of diocesan business. In the parishes the clergy found themselves frustrated and lonely unless the regular churchgoers (often a small company) gave the support and affection that could only come out of a shared responsibility and a common mission. The most successful post-war enterprise in the Church of England, the modernization of its worship leading up to the Alternative Services Book of 1980, depended on the new services being tried out and generally approved in the parishes; the proposals were also subject to detailed amendment in the General Synod, after long preparatory work by the Liturgical Commission. In one new order for the Eucharist, the priest was described as 'the President'. The designation perhaps implied the back-ground of this change: the patient chairmanship of a discussion before an agreement.

The hundred diocesan or suffragan bishops now at work in the Church of England, together with their assistants such as archdeacons and the diocesan secretaries, faced many problems in maintaining the Church's structure as this had been bequeathed from its Victorian heyday, but they had no hope of dealing with their problems if they tried to be autocrats. In 1975 there were about 12,000 clergy in parish work, about 11,500 fewer than in 1900 although the largely urban population was larger by fifteen millions; and a typical problem was how to persuade villages which had been separate parishes since the Middle Ages that the time had come when no more than one parish priest could be afforded. The instinctive reaction in each village was to refuse to attend services except in its own parish church, preferably with its own vicar (not that the villagers were usually eager to go to church at all, or to welcome a resident priest's spiritual ministry). Overcoming this territorial instinct needed both determination and tact in the diocesan officials, who had to listen and to be seen listening before they stood a chance of being heard. It was not a scene where an imperious bishop could be happy; and it was only realistic that in 1977 a committee of churchmen, partly national and partly diocesan, was elected to put names of possible bishops to the Prime Minister.

In the 1970s the bishops' sayings and doings were still quite often reported as news. The thirty-one senior bishops could still speak in the House of Lords and outstanding personalities among them could stand out in a new way on television. In his chronicle of a hundred Archbishops of Canterbury (*Cantuar*, 1971), Edward Carpenter, Dean of Westminster, referred to this invention. 'The effect of radio and television', wrote the Dean, 'has been to make the Archbishop known to the rank and file of the population in a way quite impossible before the coming of this mass medium.' Yet the Dean also observed that 'the established status of the Church of England is being increasingly eroded and its built-in educational outreach diminishing'. As a matter of fact very few bishops made an impact through the House of Lords or television. Although television gave unprecedented publicity to any Archbishop of Canterbury (not of York), on the whole the effect of the medium was to increase the anti-authoritarian trend of the period. Most of the output of TV, including the religious programmes, was journalism or entertainment; and inevitably so. Anyone who attempted to use TV to teach on was properly balanced with opposing voices, and properly reminded that he appeared as a guest in the viewer's home.

And who was to teach, apart from the occasionally brilliant TV journalist such as Malcolm Muggeridge (a Christian who made a point of being anti-Establishment)? While the preoccupations of the bishops and their staffs were pastoral or managerial, it was not easy for them to study intellectual problems or attend to the demands of a serious conversation with a largely secular world. In any case, the background from which most (not all) bishops had traditionally been chosen was not one very likely to encourage a pioneering creativity in the new society arising; it was a background of privilege, as critics complained. In a stern study of 'The Bishops 1860-1960: An Elite in Decline' contributed to the *Sociological Yearbook of Religion* (1972), James Bentley wrote very sternly:

The Church of England ensured that the quality of her bishops declined in the twentieth century. Her leaders had failed to cope with the challenge of science, leaving the Church intellectually discredited. The number of bishops had been increased to provide for the new urban population, but no serious attempt was made either to recruit or promote members of the new class. Instead the Church preferred to draw on the public schools which at a time when boys of increasingly inferior calibre were offering themselves for the ministry. The system of preferment, with its overtones of nepotism and connexion, often made next to no assessment of the ability of these men. Finally, the tradition of preferring clerical schoolmasters was not abandoned, even though the supply of these was drying up.

Something could certainly be done by the deans and canons of the cathedrals and of the royal churches at Westminster and Windsor. St. George's Chapel, Windsor, for example, sponsored a conference house which among other activities ran courses to train men for senior positions in the Church – a contribution long overdue. The cathedrals and great churches were, however, no longer leisured. They, too, had financial difficulties. Tourists poured through most of them and most of them were busy with services and meetings specially designed for the laity not accustomed to churchgoing. Monasteries, convents, retreat houses, centres of evangelism, and other communities, together with missionary societies and charities, were active in living and spreading the Gospel and to some extent paperbacks made up for the pulpit's decline; but the weakness lay in basic theology.

In that field the public had to rely on the growing numbers of teachers of theology or 'religious studies' in the universities and colleges. Such scholars were seldom church-men in the style of Lightfoot and Westcott in Victorian Cambridge and Durham. Most of them felt little interest in the problems of the parishes and little zeal for church reform; some of the ablest of them turned down proferred diocesan bishoprics. Many of them were deeply impatient with the conservatism, introspection, and anti-intellectual-ism which they observed in church life. They were convin-ced that the truth in religion needed a radical review and restatement which would leave few of the ancient land-marks of Christendom untouched. In 1962 a group of Cambridge theologians put together a volume of essays designed to take account of some of the new challenges to doctrine, and the first essay was entitled 'Beginning All Over Again'. The editor of the book, Alec Vidler, recalled *Essays and Reviews* which had opened up a doctrinal debate a century before, and commented that he and his colleagues believed like the pioneers of 1860 that 'there are very important questions which Christians are now being called to face, and which are not yet being faced with the necessary seriousness and determination'. In 1963 another, and longer, storm broke with the publication of *Honest to God* by John Robinson, a Cambridge scholar who was at that time Bishop of Woolwich. Robinson questioned some of the foundations of traditional Christianity such as the image of a personal God. In the 1970s the debate did not die down but moved to a basic reconsideration of orthodox beliefs about Christ. In 1977 another volume of radical essays included among its contributions the Regius Professor of Divinity at Oxford (Maurice Wiles, formerly Chairman of the Church of England's Doctrine Commission) and the Warden of Keble College, Oxford (Dennis Nineham, formerly Regius Professor at Cambridge). The book bore the title: *The Myth of God Incarnate*.

Not surprisingly there was, at the same time, a revival of Evangelical simplicity. This found its form in two congresses of clergy and laity in modern universities, at Keele in 1967 and at Nottingham ten years later. It had no dominant leader apart from John Stott, a preacher, writer, and evangelist whose ministry was based on the London

church of All Souls, Langham Place. Its fundamental
theology made few concessions to the new radicalism; yet
Victorians such as Lord Shaftesbury would have felt uneasy
in its atmosphere of informal enthusiasm which included
for many an insistence on contemporary idioms in evangelism and an excitement in 'charismatic' or ecstatic joys.
It was an eager movement in which youth was well represented; its backbone was in the students' Christian Unions;
and it was reckoned to supply about a third of the diminished
numbers of recruits to the Church of England's parochial
ministry. Men trained by this school of thought became
bishops, but as a whole the movement depended on bishops
no more than it did on theological professors. Its spirit was
shown in the title of the three volumes prepared for the
1977 congress: *Obeying Christ in a Changing World*.

Such movements were more vigorous than the Church
as a whole. The 'loss of nerve' in the Church of England in
the 1960s was often described – as by a bishop, F. R. Barry,
in his autobiography, *Period of My Life* (1970), or by a parish
priest, Trevor Beeson, in his astringent survey of *The Church
of England in Crisis* (1973). One of the ablest of the younger
generation of parish priests, Nicholas Stacey, wrote
ominously about the 'failure' of his ministry in South
London (in a 1971 book called *Who Cares*) and chose to
become Director of the Social Services in Kent. Many young
men turned away from an ecclesiastical machine which
seemed worn out and exercised their Christian idealism
in the (better-paid) professions such as the social services,
teaching or the B.B.C. The public also voted with its feet;
the number of Easter communicants in the parish churches,
related to the total population, halved in the period 1900-
70. In many ways the Church of England now gave an
appearance like the Church in the 1820s, when the young
Gladstone overheard a conversation between two privates
of the Guards on top of the London-Eton coach. 'Come
now, what is the Church of England?' 'It is a damned large
building with an organ in it.' In the midst of a post-war
society absorbed in making money (or in keeping it against
the ravages of inflation), the Church found its organization
in disarray and its message uncertain. There was talk of the

'death of God'. Perhaps Newman's prophecy in 1877 had come true: 'a time of widespread infidelity, when only the tops of the mountains will be seen like islands in the waste of waters.'

There were, however, some signs of hope. Regular churchgoers were fewer in the 1970s, but they were taking part more often in the Holy Communion, which in most parish churches had become or was becoming the main act of worship each Sunday; and they were keen both to meet each other outside services and to give generously to the Church's needs. As churchgoing had ceased to be a part of middle-class respectability – indeed, as churchgoers found themselves laughed at for superstition or at least for unfashionableness – this lay commitment was impressive. So was the self-sacrificing dedication of the clergy, facing the hardhips of their own poverty and the general indifference to their message. The stirrings in the universities and among youth, whether aggressively radical or conservately Evangelical, at least bore witness to the continued fascination which religion held for some of the most alert and sensitive.

Many surveys suggested that public opinion as a whole, although it was unable to accept the old Christian certainties in belief or behaviour, was not anti-religious or explicitly atheistic. People might still pray when in need. Parents still wanted their children to be introduced to religion in the schools and viewers still wanted religion on television. If the old forms of organized religion were now abandoned, a superficial materialism was equally condemned as being unable to satisfy a permanent spiritual hunger.

Sensing its plight but also perhaps the beginning of a new era, the Church of England in the 1970s was humbler than it had been in its Victorian prosperity. It was less insistent on the old formularies. The Athanasian Creed was almost never heard; the clergy's adherence to the Thirty-nine Articles was relaxed to the point where extreme radicalism went undisciplined; and with the authorization of 'alternative' services, the use of the Prayer Book was being made optional. The Church of England was more convinced that the love of living people was true religion.

It was more ready to accept other Churches as fully Christian and to work with them. It was more ready to listen to contemporary critics who might convey the voice of God, and to support 'secular' causes which might be the work of God. It was more interested in spiritual meditation. In the 1970s as in the 1820s, it needed courage to wait for the revival of the tradition: for Arnold's 'heavenly spark' or Newman's 'kindly light'. But it was possible to wait.

5

It was also possible to recognize leaders who combined some of the Victorian greatness with a modern reluctance to be, or to seem, dogmatic. This is not the place to write about the living or the recently dead. But it would not be right to end a study of the chief leaders of the modern Church of England without mentioning the names of Michael Ramsey, Archbishop of York 1956-61, the hundredth Archbishop of Canterbury 1961-74; Ian Ramsey, the ninetieth Bishop of Durham 1966-72; and Donald Coggan, Archbishop of York 1961-74 and then of Canterbury.

Michael Ramsey is a product of Cambridge theology and of Anglo-Catholic spirituality. Although he had been a boy at Repton under Fisher, he brought to Canterbury a character unlike his ex-headmaster's. Essentially he remained the professor he had been. A layman who worked with him in the Church Assembly and General Synod (not Ramsey's favourite scenes) has depicted his personality in words which at this stage cannot be bettered. Sir Kenneth Grubb wrote in his *Crypts of Power* (1971): 'His appearance, with a marked impression of the venerability of age which his years denied, was both engrossing and puzzling, until one appreciated his homely humour as well as deep spirituality, two qualities which ride well in tandem, each enriching the other. Dr. Ramsey does not easily amass popularity, and the somewhat artificial cadence which accompanies his public speaking puts off many who do not appreciate his depth. He has a rare spiritual touch, a combination of simplicity, humility, and Christian love, which is very moving, but which requires time to explore for it is not devoid of much shrewdness.'

The story of his leadership is mainly spiritual. Although for the Church it was a time of numerical decline and of administrative reorganization, neither that problem nor that solution touched the scholarly archbishop's heart. When he was enthroned in 1961 he was expected to advance the cause of Catholic reunion. He did visit Pope Paul VI very happily, and with him sponsored a series of theological conversations between Roman Catholic and Anglican theologians. But his enthusiasm was put without much result into the cause of Anglican-Methodist reunion. He was also expected to maintain the Anglo-Catholic insistence on personal and corporate holiness in a style detached from the conflicts of the time. In fact, without weakening his personal loyalty to that tradition he made his main mark as one who understood the new radical stirrings in theology and who sympathized with the impatient demands of hungry nations overseas for justice or revolution. As he wrote in a pamphlet commenting on *Honest to God*:

As a Church we need to be grappling with the questions and trials of belief in the modern world. Since the war our Church has been too inclined to be concerned with the organizing of its own life, perhaps assuming too easily that the faith may be taken for granted and needs only to be stated and commended. But we state and commend the faith only in so far as we go out and put ourselves with loving sympathy inside the doubts of the doubting, the questions of the questioners, and the loneliness of those who have lost their way.

Michael Ramsey's namesake (but no relation) Ian Ramsey was for a time expected to follow him at Canterbury, maintaining the same emphasis. Before becoming Bishop of Durham, Ian Ramsey had been Professor of the Philosophy of the Christian Religion at Oxford, and he was well aware of the pressures making for a reconsideration of traditional doctrine. When a Doctrine Commission was appointed in 1967, he was put in the chair. He was also an active supporter of causes such as the struggle against racism in Africa. While Michael Ramsey incurred unpopularity by saying that the use of force against the white settlers' regime in Rhodesia would be moral, Ian Ramsey led protests against any British identification with the white government in South Africa. Ian Ramsey's interests were, however, wider and more up-to-date than Michael Ramsey's. He was eager to discuss (in an accent recalling humble origins in Lancashire) education, medicine, science, industrial relations, or any other topic of the day; and he made a practice of never saying 'no' to an invitation he could accept. Somehow he crowded into an overfull life eager visits to the parishes of County Durham, everywhere spreading interest and liveliness. He spoke at the annual miners' gala and was loved for it. But before he had the chance to show whether or not this breathless willingness to be involved could survive the responsibilities of the Archbishopric of Canterbury, he died of a heart-attack at the age of fifty-seven.

A Labour Prime Minister (Harold Wilson) appointed to Canterbury in 1974 a man who has little of the Ramseys' interest in radical theology or Left-wing politics but who has his own definite convictions and a calm, straightforward simplicity in stating them. Characteristically Donald Coggan did not hesitate when asked what was his purpose for the diocese of York in 1970. He replied that his vision would involve 'such a training of the people of God in the diocese in worship and in the knowledge of the faith as would enable them to reach out with an infectious faith to wholly untouched or only nominally Christian people within the diocese and to have a world-vision of the purpose of God, with a strong conviction that they are implicated in making it a reality'.

Dr. Coggan is an Evangelical. Born in 1909, he spent twenty-one years of his life teaching in Evangelical theological colleges in Toronto and London. His appointment, matched by the move of another Evangelical (Stuart Blanch) from Liverpool to York, paid tribute to the present strength of that movement in the Church of England, and the two archbishops lost little time in issuing, mainly through television and radio, a 'call' to the nation. For Dr. Coggan it was a sequel to the vigorous challenges he had issued while Bishop of Bradford, his 'Opportunity Unlimited' campaign in York Diocese, 1968-9, and his later and wider 'Call to the North'. The 1975 call was made when an economic recession had put the nation in a mood for self-examination. The archbishops did not offer any detailed plan to Church or State but challenged their hearers to think out for themselves what sort of society they wanted, and what sort of people they had to be in order to build that society. The response was mixed. The nation as a whole was untouched by anything any clergyman might say. The sophisticated laughed at the archbishops' naïvety. But there was a warm response from those who detected in the archbishops' questions a defence of what Geoffrey Fisher had called the 'old fashioned but essential virtues'; and it seemed possible that this welcome had brought to the surface an undercurrent which was widespread in inarticulate public opinion. As it entered the last quarter of the twentieth century England perhaps knew that it could not return to the Victorian age, but that the Victorians had achieved a Church and a civilization on which future generations would look with interest and respect.

# For Further Reading

The best history of *The Victorian Church* is by Owen Chadwick in two volumes (Black, 1966-70). Documents are collected in *Religious Controversies of the Nineteenth Century*, ed. A.O.J. Cockshut (Methuen, 1966), and *Church and State in Britain since 1820*, ed. David Nicholls (Routledge, 1967). English religious thought is surveyed in B.M.G. Rearden, *From Coleridge to Gore* (Longman, 1971), and A.M. Ramsey, From *Gore to Temple* (Longman, 1960). Surveys by distinguished historians include G. Kitson Clark, *Churchmen and the Condition of England, 1832-85* (Methuen, 1973), and E.R. Norman, *Church and Society in England, 1770-1970* (Oxford, 1976). A sketch was provided by Roger Lloyd, *The Church of England, 1900-65* (SCM Press, 1966). See also Kenneth Thompson, *Bureaucracy and Church Reform, 1800-1965* (Oxford, 1970).

A.P. Stanley, *Thomas Arnold* (Fellowes, 1842), is supplemented by T.W. Bamford, *Thomas Arnold* (Cresset Press, 1960) and *Thomas Arnold on Education* (Cambridge, 1970). See also E.L. Williamson, *The Liberalism of Thomas Arnold* (University of Alabama, 1964). The Arnold circle has been studied in J.P. Gell, *The Doctor's Disciples* (Oxford, 1954) and Meriol Trevor, *The Arnolds* (Bodley Head, 1973). *The Poetical Works of Matthew Arnold* were edited by C.B. Tinker and H.F. Lowry, who also wrote a commentary on *The Poetry of Matthew Arnold* (Oxford, 1950). Matthew Arnold's *Letters* have been edited by G.W.E. Russell (Macmillan, 1895) and his *Complete Prose Works* by R.H. Super (University of Michigan, 1961 onwards).

Wilfrid Ward, *The Life of John Henry Cardinal Newman* (Longmans, 1912) is supplemented by Maisie Ward, *Young Mr. Newman* (Sheed and Ward, 1948). *The Letters and Diaries of John Henry Newman* (Nelson, 1961 onwards) were edited by C.S. Dessain, who wrote a short study of *John Henry Newman* with a bibliography (Nelson, 1966). See also Meriol Trevor, *Newman's Journey* (Collins, 1974). Sir John Coleridge's *Memoir of the Rev. John Keble* (Parker, 1869) is supplemented by Georgina Battiscombe, *John Keble*:

*A Study in Limitations* (Constable, 1963). See also Owen Chadwick, *The Mind of the Oxford Movement* (Black, 1960).

*The Life of the Right Rev. Samuel Wilberforce, D.D.*, in three volumes ed. A.R. Ashwell and R. Wilberforce (John Murray, 1880-3) is supplemented by Standish Meacham, *Lord Bishop* (Harvard, 1970). The more discreet *Life of Archibald Campbell Tait* in two volumes by R. Davidson and W. Benham (Macmillan, 1891) is supplemented by P.T. Marsh, *The Victorian Church in Decline* (Routledge, 1968). and M.A. Crowther, *Church Embattled* (David and Charles, 1970).

*The Life and Work of the Seventh Earl of Shaftesbury* in three volumes by Edwin Hodder (Cassell, 1886) is supplemented by G.F.A. Best, *Shaftesbury* (Batsford, 1964), and Georgina Battiscombe, *Shaftesbury* (John Murray, 1974). See also Kathleen Heasman, *Evangelicals in Action* (Bles, 1962), and Ian Bradley, *The Call to Seriousness* (Cape, 1976). *The Life of Frederick Denison Maurice* in two volumes by Frederick Maurice (Macmillan, 1884) is supplemented by A.M. Ramsey, *F.D. Maurice and the Conflicts of Modern Theology* (Cambridge, 1951) and Frank McClain, *Maurice the Man and the Moralist* (SPCK, 1972). See also Torben Christiansen, *Origin and History of Christian Socialism, 1848-54* (Aarhus, 1962).

*The Life of William Ewart Gladstone* in three volumes by John Morley (Macmillan, 1903), and *Correspondence on Church and Religion of William Ewart Gladstone* in two volumes ed. D.C. Lathbury (John Murray, 1910), are supplemented by A.R. Vidler, *The Orb and the Cross* (SPCK, 1945); Philip Magnus, *Gladstone* (1954); S.E. Checkland, *The Gladstones* (Cambridge, 1971); *The Gladstone Diaries*, ed. M.R.D. Foot (Oxford, 1968 onwards). *The Life of Edward White Benson* in two volumes ed. A.C. Benson (Macmillan, 1899) is supplemented by A.C. Benson, *The Trefoil* (John Murray, 1923), and Betty Askwith, *Two Victorian Families* (Chatto and Windus, 1971).

*Lightfoot of Durham*, ed. G.R. Eden and F.C. Macdonald (Cambridge, 1932), is less full than *Life and Letters of Brooke Foss Westcott* in two volumes ed. A. Westcott (Macmillan, 1903). See also A.C. Benson, *Leaves of the Tree* (Smith, Elder, 1911), and P.d'A. Jones, *The Christian Socialist Revival, 1877-1914* (Princeton, 1968).

*Life and Letters of Mandell Creighton* in two volumes edited by his widow Louise (Longman, 1904) is supplemented by W.G. Fallowes, *Mandell Creighton and the English Church* (Oxford, 1964). *Randall Davidson* in two volumes by G.K.A. Bell (Oxford, 1935) was reprinted with a new Preface in 1952. Wider surveys include John Oliver, *The Church and Social Order, 1918-39* (Mowbrays, 1968), and Alan Wilkinson, *The Church of England and the First World War* (SPCK, 1978).

G. L. Prestige, *The Life of Charles Gore* (Heinemann, 1935), is supplemented by James Carpenter, *Gore: A Study in Liberal Catholic Thought* (Faith Press, 1960). *Retrospect of an Unimportant Life* in three volumes by H. H. Henson is supplemented by his *Letters* and *More Letters*, ed. E. F. Braley (SPCK, 1951-54). Owen Chadwick is writing a biography of Henson.

*Memoirs of Archbishop Temple by Seven Friends* were collected in two volumes by E. G. Sandford (Macmillan, 1906). F. A. Ironmonger, *William Temple* (Oxford, 1948), is supplemented by O. C. Thomas, *William Temple: Philosophy of Religion* (SPCK, 1961); Joseph Fletcher, *William Temple* (Seabury Press, 1963); Robert Craig, *Social Concern in the Thought of William Temple* (Gollancz, 1963); J. D. Carmichael and H. S. Goodwin, *William Temple's Political Legacy* (Mowbrays, 1963). See also J. G. Lockhart, *Cosmo Gordon Lang* (Hodder and Stoughton, 1949).

There is much material in Charles Smyth, *Cyril Foster Garbett* (Hodder and Stoughton, 1959), and in the biographies of *George Bell* by R. C. D. Jasper (Oxford, 1967) and Kenneth Slack (SCM Press, 1971). Edward Carpenter, who is writing the official life of Geoffrey Fisher, edited *The Archbishop Speaks* (Evans, 1958). A 'portrait from life' was provided by William Purcell, *Fisher of Lambeth* (Hodder and Stoughton, 1969). Essays in honour of Michael Ramsey (including a long one by D.L.E.) were edited by Christopher Martin under the title *The Great Christian Centuries to Come* (Mowbrays, 1974) and specimens of his own teaching were collected as *Durham Essays and Addresses*, *Canterbury Essays and Addresses*, and *Canterbury Pilgrim* (SPCK, 1956-74). See also David L. Edwards, *Ian Ramsey* (Oxford, 1973); Donald Coggan, *Convictions* (Hodder and Stoughton, 1975); Anne Arnott, *Wife to the Archbishop: the Life Story of Jean Coggan* (Mowbrays, 1976). Recent surveys of the Church of England include Leslie Paul, *A Church by Daylight* (Geoffrey Chapman, 1973), and John Adair, *The Becoming Church* (SPCK, 1977).